A GENEALOGY OF TERROR IN
EIGHTEENTH-CENTURY FRANCE

A GENEALOGY OF TERROR IN
EIGHTEENTH-CENTURY FRANCE

RONALD SCHECHTER

THE UNIVERSITY OF CHICAGO PRESS
CHICAGO AND LONDON

The University of Chicago Press, Chicago 60637
The University of Chicago Press, Ltd., London
© 2018 by The University of Chicago
Published 2018
Printed in the United States of America

27 26 25 24 23 22 21 20 19 18   1 2 3 4 5

ISBN-13: 978-0-226-49957-4 (cloth)
ISBN-13: 978-0-226-49960-4 (e-book)
DOI: 10.7208/chicago/9780226499604.001.0001

Library of Congress Cataloging-in-Publication Data

Names: Schechter, Ronald, author.
Title: A genealogy of terror in eighteenth-century France / Ronald Schechter.
Other titles: Genealogy of terror in 18th-century France
Description: Chicago ; London : The University of Chicago Press, 2018. |
    Includes bibliographical references and index.
Identifiers: LCCN 2017049044 | ISBN 9780226499574 (cloth : alk. paper) |
    ISBN 9780226499604 (e-book)
Subjects: LCSH: France—Civilization—18th century. | Terror—France—
    History—18th century. | Terror—Social aspects—France.
Classification: LCC DC33.4 .S37 2018 | DDC 303.6/25094409033—dc23
LC record available at https://lccn.loc.gov/2017049044

♾ This paper meets the requirements of ANSI/NISO Z39.48–1992
(Permanence of Paper).

To J-P

CONTENTS

The French Revolution gave terror a bad name. This is not a facetious statement. For many centuries prior to the Revolution the word "terror" had largely positive connotations. In the Bible God is "terrible," and this is a good thing. Terror (or terribleness) is one of God's most important attributes, a sign of his power, justice, and majesty, and terror is the appropriate emotion for human beings to feel in the face of their Creator. Accordingly, theologians from Saint Augustine to the priests of eighteenth-century France described it as "salutary," and even the stripped-down theology of the deists made room for a God who inspired terror. As a consequence of their divine right to rule, kings under absolutism acquired godlike features, including the rightful capacity to instill terror in their enemies, and a reliable way of flattering a monarch was to call him "the terror of his enemies." By the end of the eighteenth century sovereign nations could be praised in similar language. Meanwhile, judicial commentators invoked the "terror of the laws" when explaining the need for severe punishments, and they adapted from theology the notion that such terror was "salutary." Even opponents of the death penalty based their argument on the claim that executions failed to inspire the requisite terror in malefactors. Theater critics praised tragedies that fulfilled Aristotle's requirement of imparting terror and pity, though by the end of the eighteenth century they focused increasingly on terror. Aesthetic writers, drawing on Edmund Burke (whose work was translated into French), made terror a precondition of "the sublime." Even medical writers, learned and popular, propagated the idea that terror was literally salutary—in the sense of healthful—and reported cases of the strong emotion curing ills as varied as malaria, gout, rabies, and epilepsy. Overall, terror had a positive "feel." The word was reminiscent of power, legitimacy and glory, and it had something sacred about it.

All that changed very quickly. Within days of Robespierre's execution on

July 28, 1794, terror came to mean something very much like what it means today. Instead of conveying a sense of legitimate sovereignty, it epitomized illegiti-
mate force. Rather than signifying justice, it indicated gratuitous violence. Far
from evoking majesty, it now smacked of degradation. Its connection to the sacred was lost: few things could match terror in profanity. From a rational force of
law and government it came to stand for profound irrationality, even madness.

What had happened to provoke this stunning cultural transformation? The
short answer is: the Terror. Revolutionaries had chosen "terror" as a rallying
cry, from September 1793 demanding repeatedly, "Make terror the order of the
day." They had made it into an abbreviation for a set of laws and institutions
designed to rid France of its enemies. They therefore associated it with surveillance committees, revolutionary tribunals, and above all the guillotine. Following the fall of Robespierre on July 27, 1794 (9 Thermidor) his adversaries used
the term to discredit him and his allies, and quickly the word came to indicate a
period of tyranny. Within weeks the words *terrorisme* and *terroriste* were coined.

We are still living with the consequences of that transformation. Even
today we choose to call the acts of killers "terror," provided that there is
some political motivation to them. We are repeatedly told that the West hates
terror, that we are engaged in a war against it; but how deep is this hatred? In
the long-term history of the West, condemnation of terror is relatively recent.
Given this fact, and given the ubiquity of "terror" in contemporary political
discourse, it is perhaps salutary (if I may use that word) to recall a lengthy
period, in the heart of the Western world, in which people praised "terror"
and used the word to speak or write of God, justice, magnificence, and health.
This book examines a neglected but crucial chapter of what might be called
the Western romance with terror.

A Genealogy of Terror in Eighteenth-Century France simultaneously in-
tervenes in a classic historiographical debate. How could a movement that
began with the Declaration of the Rights of Man and Citizen end with thousands of "suspects" guillotined? The present book argues that the appeal of
the Terror stemmed in large measure from the appeal of "terror." The positive emotional connotations of *terreur* facilitated adherence to a program that
adopted this term. From our perspective today, it appears odd that otherwise
rational, liberal-minded people would embrace terror when naming their
movement, but in the context of the word's historical semantics, the decision was understandable. Put in marketing terms, it was successful branding.

I do not expect this book to end the debate on the origins of the Terror, a complex phenomenon with many causes, but I hope to reinvigorate
it. Above all, I hope to show that enthusiasm for terror is not an import to
Western civilization but rather a domestic product with a long tradition.

On September 5, 1793, in the midst of a massive insurrection against the French National Convention, a group of insurgents approached the bar of the revolutionary legislature. The deputation comprised members of the Society of Friends of Liberty and Equality—otherwise known as the Jacobin Club—and forty-eight urban militants or sansculottes, one for each of the wards or sections of Paris. The orator, a Jacobin named Claude Royer, addressed the republican lawmakers:

> Mandatories of the people, the dangers to the *patrie* are extreme; the remedies must be equally [extreme]. You have decreed that the French shall rise en masse to repulse far from our borders the hordes of brigands who are ravaging them; but the henchmen of the despots of Vienna and Berlin, those tigers of the North who carry devastation everywhere, are less cruel, are less for us to fear than the traitors who agitate us from within, who divide us, who arm Frenchman against Frenchman; the impunity of the guiltiest ones emboldens them; the people are murmuring, are discouraged to see the most insolent conspirators ceaselessly escape the national ax; all the friends of liberty, of equality are astonished, indignant at seeing that the abettors of federalism have not yet been brought to judgment; in the public squares, in groups, all the republicans speak of the many crimes of Brissot; from one end of the Republic to the other his name is uttered only with horror; we remember that this monster was vomited by England to disturb our Revolution from the beginning and to impede its progress.
>
> We shall not list all his crimes when all of France accuses him; we ask you that he be immediately judged, together with his accomplices. The people can hardly conceive that there are still privileges under the

reign of constitutional equality; that the Vergniauds, the Gensonnés, and all the scoundrels degraded by their treasons from the dignity of representatives of the people should have palaces for prisons while the brave sansculottes languish in dungeons and expire every day under the federalists' daggers. It is finally time for all the French to enjoy that holy equality that the Constitution guarantees; it is time to overawe the traitors and conspirators with striking acts of justice.

Make terror the order of the day.

Let us look closely at Royer's words. The orator calls the representatives "mandatories" (*mandataires*) to emphasize their submission to the people who voted for them in France's first election based on universal male suffrage. He congratulates the legislators for having decreed mass conscription (*levée en masse*) to fight the Austrian and Prussian enemies. But his focus is on other foes: the Girondins. These were the deputies (led by Brissot and including Vergniaud and Gensonné) who proclaimed allegiance to the Republic but had been proscribed ("degraded from the dignity of representatives of the people") in an earlier insurrection (May 31–June 2). In the eyes of the insurgents these men were traitors, allied to the "federalists," who, during the summer of 1793, had risen up against the National Convention in a series of municipal revolts—in Lyon, Marseille, Bordeaux, and elsewhere—and imprisoned or killed "brave sansculottes." Yet the Girondins had not yet been punished for their treasonous activities, hence the need "to overawe the traitors and conspirators with striking acts of justice."

It was in this context that Royer uttered the famous words, "Make terror the order of the day" (*Placez la terreur à l'ordre du jour*). What he meant by "terror" he specified in the following sentences:

Representatives of the people, may the sword hover indiscriminately over all heads. Promptly organize a truly revolutionary army: let this army be divided into sections; let each of them be followed by a frightful [*redoutable*] tribunal and by the horrible [*l'épouvantable*] instrument of the vengeance of the laws until the entire surface of the Republic is purged of all traitors and until the death of the last of the conspirators.

The "truly revolutionary army," not to be confused with the regular national army, was to be composed of sansculottes who would have the authority to arrest suspects and bring them before revolutionary tribunals.[1] These "frightful" courts would in turn quickly mete out justice in the form of the guillotine, the "horrible instrument of the vengeance of the laws."

Royer concluded his speech with a peroration targeting the class of enemies that he and his fellow insurgents believed to be at the heart of France's
troubles:

> Before doing anything else, banish from all the armies that insolent caste
> that has always been the enemy of liberty and equality. The nobles were
> always the scourge of humanity: may they be excluded from all civil
> and military positions; and to remove from them all means of harming
> [us] and augmenting the number of our enemies, may they be placed
> under arrest and imprisoned until the peace. Innumerable misfortunes,
> acts of treachery, treasons of all sorts attest to the danger of leaving that
> degraded and bloodthirsty race at the head of our armies for long. The
> souls of our eviscerated brothers ask you for vengeance, and the voice of
> the people commands you.[2]

In this brief oration Royer sketched out a set of policies that would indeed characterize the phase of the French Revolution customarily known as
the Terror. He simultaneously outlined much of what would be thought of
as "terror" in the modern political sense: the empowerment of paramilitary
vigilantes to arrest political suspects; the use of special tribunals to deliver
summary justice (i.e., execution); and the proscription and preemptive incarceration of a suspicious class (in this case the nobility). He thus appears
to have spontaneously defined a modern political concept. On closer inspec-
tion, we shall see that a great deal of cultural work had to be done before
Royer's words could be understood and (perhaps more to the point) have an
emotional impact on those who heard or read them.

The rallying cry took off quickly. Later that day Deputy Bertrand Barère,
speaking on behalf of the Committee of Public Safety, declared that the
proposed "revolutionary army" "will finally execute this great expression
that we owe to the commune of Paris: '*Plaçons la terreur à l'ordre ju jour.*'"[3]
The Commune was the municipal government, which was largely under
the control of the sansculottes. Perhaps it was there that revolutionaries invented the slogan.

Whoever originated the expression, soon revolutionaries throughout
France were repeating it. On September 20 the Popular Society of Langres
in the Haute-Marne department sent a letter to the Convention urging it
to "'make *terror* the order of the day,' as our brothers in Paris have said."[4]
On October 2 the Convention received a letter from sixty-seven citizens
who called themselves "the free Montagnards of the commune of Moyen-
vic" (Moselle) and who urged the lawmakers, "Leave terror as the order of

the day."[5] On October 6 Deputy Jacques Boilleau of the Yonne department affirmed "that it was right to make terror the order of the day, for liberty must be terrible when it is in the presence of despotism."[6]

In the coming months many more revolutionaries spoke or wrote similarly. The *Archives parlementaires*, a multivolume compendium of documents relating to the revolutionary legislatures, records 139 instances of people calling for or praising terror as "the order of the day" from September 5, 1793, to the fall of Robespierre on July 27, 1794 (9 Thermidor).[7] Among the lawmakers who used the expression were Danton, Barère, Billaud-Varenne, Hérault de Séchelles, and Prieur de la Marne, all of whom served on the Committee of Public Safety and were active in implementing the Terror, and more than a dozen other deputies are recorded as having supported terror as the order of the day.[8] Representatives of the Parisian sections came repeatedly to the Convention to make the same demand,[9] as did members of the Jacobin Club of Paris.[10] More than fifty provincial Jacobin clubs wrote to the Convention, sometimes appending hundreds of signatures, to call for terror as the order of the day or praise the legislature for having accomplished that goal. At least twenty municipal governments sent in similarly worded communications, as did officials in charge of districts and departments, members of local "revolutionary committees," soldiers at the front, National Guardsmen, gendarmes, and ordinary citizens.

In addition to these 139 instances, the *Archives parlementaires* records nearly six hundred occurrences of revolutionaries advocating or praising *terreur* between the beginning of September 1793 and the end of July 1794. What they meant by the word varied. In some cases "terror" simply referred to the emotion, the extreme fear that enemies of the Republic, foreign or domestic, supposedly felt or ought to feel. In other cases it referred to the legal apparatus of the Terror: the laws that facilitated bringing suspects up on political charges, the Revolutionary Tribunals, and the guillotine.

It is impossible to know just how influential Royer's oration was in the proliferation of statements promoting terror during the following ten months. But my aim is not to determine the Jacobin's personal impact on revolutionary discourse. I am more interested in why Royer and other revolutionaries spoke or wrote of *terreur* when describing their goals and values. To twenty-first-century sensibilities the word is jarring. It is so saturated with implications of injustice, irrationality, fanaticism, and cruelty that it requires a great deal of historical imagination—to say nothing of research—to comprehend the thinking of those who conceived of terror as a good thing. It may be surprising to many nonspecialists, as it was to me when I first began to study the French Revolution, that this was not a term of abuse invented by counterrevolutionaries to discredit the Revolution, but rather a rallying cry designed by revolutionaries themselves to *legitimize* their measures.

Yet Royer's language is not only startling in light of present-day associations. It also clashes with certain elements of eighteenth-century thought, in particular with aspects of the Enlightenment. Historians have long linked the Enlightenment to the Revolution, either by positing a direct influence or by noting the esteem in which revolutionaries held Enlightenment thinkers.[11] Yet the Enlightenment is known for having militated against all forms of fear. Even Max Horkheimer and Theodor Adorno, the movement's greatest critics, claimed that Enlightenment "pursued the goal of taking fear away from human beings and establishing them as masters."[12] Where could a positive conception of terror have fit into such a worldview? Moreover, eighteenth-century sources would appear to support the position of Horkheimer and Adorno. For example, Montesquieu famously identified fear (*la crainte*) as the "principle" of despotism.[13]

Why, then, did revolutionaries who otherwise aligned themselves with Enlightenment principles—liberty, equality, and human rights—extoll terror as a legitimizing principle and a priority ("the order of the day")?

Of course, this question is not new; contemporaries posed it as soon as the Terror began, and apologists and critics of the Revolution have argued over it for more than two centuries. The debate was particularly heated in the years leading up to the bicentennial in 1989: "Jacobins" claimed that the Revolution had faced real enemies and needed to take emergency action, while "revisionists" saw the Terror as the product of a political culture in which compromise was unthinkable. I will discuss at least some of the voluminous historiography of the Terror in the conclusion to this book. For now I am mainly interested in addressing a set of related questions that historians have not posed up to now. Why did the Jacobins and sansculottes conceive of their goals for the French Republic in terms of terror? And to return to Royer's speech, why did it call for *la terreur à l'ordre du jour*? What was the appeal of the word "terror"? What did it mean to Royer and others who embraced it? And finally (and more speculatively), how did the word *feel*? What emotions did it evoke in those who uttered, heard, wrote, or read it?

These questions are relevant to an understanding of why the revolutionaries adopted the policies conventionally understood as the Terror. The name a political group adopts for its program is no doubt relevant to its success. Appealing slogans help to solidify loyalties, and it seems likely to me that by using the language of terror, revolutionaries stimulated enthusiasm for the Terror. But it would be naive to assume that this language was the only cause, or even the principal cause, of the Terror.

At one level, then, my goal in this book—explaining the appeal of the word "terror"—is more modest than that of historians who have sought an overarching or comprehensive explanation of the Terror. Yet at another level my goal is more ambitious. To explain why requires a clear statement of my thesis: the appeal to terror in the French Revolution was conceivable and popular because it drew on a long tradition of writing and thinking in which terror was a good thing. According to this tradition, God instilled terror in his creatures—and rightly so. Kings derived their power from God and were consequently praised for the terror they inspired in enemies. (They were often flattered precisely as "the terror" of their enemies.) Society depended on the "terror of the laws." Terror had positive aesthetic value, providing a precondition for both high-quality theater and "the sublime." It even had medicinal value and was widely believed capable of treating or curing numerous illnesses. To support these claims, it is necessary to delve into the much-neglected history of attitudes toward terror prior to the Revolution.[14] I have chosen approximately one century of this history because a longer sweep would have been beyond my capacities, but I also believe that a century is sufficient to make my case. The result of this investigation— and here is the book's more ambitious goal—will be a contribution to the history of Western attitudes toward terror. So much of our contemporary political discourse takes an orientalist approach to terror and characterizes it as an invention of the inveterate foes of Western civilization. It is important, I believe, to disrupt this narrative by recounting a significant chapter in what might be called the Western romance with terror.

But what exactly is the subject of this book? Is "terror" an idea? A concept? A discourse? A word? And what methods will be employed in its study?

On one level, this book is a traditional contribution to intellectual history, with significant attention paid to *ideas*. I do not believe that the word "terror" corresponds precisely to a discrete idea, but certain recurrent ideas appear in conjunction with the word. To give just one example, there is the idea of *salutary terror*, according to which the experience of terror is productive of health, safety, or even salvation. I would even go so far as to argue that salutary terror is a "unit-idea," as defined by Arthur Lovejoy, insofar as it appears in different periods in history (from the Bible to Augustine to the Enlightenment and finally the French Revolution), in different "provinces of history" (e.g., theology, jurisprudence, aesthetics, and medicine) and in both canonical and noncanonical sources.[15]

Yet the history of terror before the Terror is more than the history of an idea. The word "terror" had (and no doubt still has) too many meanings to be contained by a single idea. Conceivably, then, it is more of a concept than an idea. Reinhart Koselleck characterized concepts (*Begriffe*) as inherently *mehrdeutig*, a term that can mean "ambiguous" but is more literally translated as "polysemous" or "multivalent." According to Koselleck, a concept, unlike a mere word, contained a "plenitude" (*Fülle*) of meanings. Koselleck gave as an example the concept of the state (*Staat*), which included within it such diverse things as "dominion, territory, citizenship, legislation, jurisdiction, administration," and so on.[16] Could terror also be an example of such a "plenitude" or concentrate? Certainly it was multivalent. It could indicate an emotion, a form of fear (specifically, an extreme, gripping fear), a style of rule, or a military tactic; or, metonymically, it could stand for the source of terror, as when rulers, commanders, or nations were the "terror" of their enemies. During the Revolution it often meant the policies adopted between September 1793 and July 1794, and subsequently the word served as the name of a period that had ended with the fall of Robespierre.

There is an argument to be made for terror having become a concept precisely during the Year II, when a disparate field of the word's earlier meanings came together in the Terror. Indeed, the capitalization of the word, a practice as early as December 1793, suggested a kind of congealing or concentration of prior meanings.[17] That terror became a concept at this point is suggested by the "Terror, Terrorismus" entry in the monument to conceptual history (*Begriffsgeschichte*), the multivolume lexicon that Koselleck coedited: *Geschichtliche Grundbegriffe* (Basic concepts in history). Actually, to call it an entry does it a disservice: it is more of a monograph, comprising 122 pages, 622 footnotes, and roughly 60,000 words. But nearly one hundred of these pages are devoted to the postrevolutionary period, and only eleven pages are allocated to the meanings of "terror" under the Old Regime. This is because the author, Rudolf Walther, sees references to terror in the prerevolutionary period as constituting the "prehistory" (*Vorgeschichte*) of the concept. The section on the Revolution also comprises eleven pages. But for Walther, terror becomes a concept only in 1793–94, when for him its actual history begins; and the remainder of the article, approximately one hundred pages, deals with *Terrorismus* as understood throughout Europe from the fall of Robespierre to the 1970s.[18] A similar pattern can be seen in Gerd van den Heuvel's article "Terreur, Terroriste, Terrorisme," in the *Handbuch politisch-sozialer Grundbegriffe in Frankreich, 1680–1820* (Handbook of basic political and social concepts in France, 1680–1820), edited by Rolf Reichardt and Eberhard Schmitt. In this eighteen-thousand-word entry fewer than three thousand words are allocated to the Old Regime.[19]

My objection to treating the meanings of terror in the Old Regime as a "prehistory" is that the term is teleological and suggests an inevitable unfolding of "history." Of course, one could object that the term "Old Regime" is equally teleological, as is the adjective "prerevolutionary." But some of Koselleck's other remarks about *Begriffe* and especially *Grundbegriffe* (fundamental concepts) indicate a belief in a metanarrative about the course of history that I do not share. Specifically, Koselleck believes that the proliferation of *Grundbegriffe* between 1750 and 1850 reveals "the dissolution of the old world and the emergence of the modern world."[20] My emphasis is much more on continuities than on "the emergence of the modern world." Indeed, the value placed on terror (and "the Terror") in the Revolution depended heavily on traditions that might otherwise be dismissed as "prehistory." Moreover, Koselleck wrote of words' being "promoted" to the status of "modern concepts," which similarly hints at a predetermined telos.[21] As a heuristic device, the distinction between words and concepts has some value. Specifically, it could be used to argue that the long-standing valorization of the word *terreur* facilitated a similar valorization of the concept of *la Terreur*. I shall return to this question in the conclusion, but for now it is important to observe that even if terror (or the Terror) can be understood as a concept, this takes place only at the end of my story. Ultimately, the unit of analysis in this book is a word (or, to be linguistically precise, a lexeme), not a concept.[22]

To use a distinction adopted from semantics, the emphasis is on semasiology (the study of what particular words or phrases mean) rather than onomasiology (the study of the words or phrases that are used to indicate a particular concept or idea). In other words, rather than asking the onomasiological question, "What words or phrases were used to express the concept or idea of terror?" I will be asking the semasiological question, "What did the word 'terror' and phrases including it (such as 'salutary terror' or 'the terror of his enemies') mean to those who wrote, uttered, heard or read them?"[23] And I will be adding the question, "How did it feel to say, hear, write, or read it?"

The subject of this book, then, is what I am choosing to call "terror speech." This terminology deserves explanation lest it be misunderstood. The word "speech" often refers to the act of talking and could potentially be reminiscent of the expression "rights talk," which the conservative American legal scholar Mary Ann Glendon simultaneously popularized and disparaged.[24] Although Dan Edelstein has more recently used the expression evenhandedly, Glendon's imperious attitude toward "talk," which looks very much like "chatter," might remain in some readers' minds.[25] In the present book, however, the word "speech" is strictly descriptive. Rather than implying the laziness of "talk," it describes both oral and written expression and includes both systematic statements and casual remarks. In this respect it borrows from the linguist Ferdinand de Saussure's idea that speech (la parole) is simply language as it is used in everyday life, as opposed to language (la langue), which is conceived as a formal system of rules.[26]

My research questions and methodology are informed by the kind of historical semantics practiced by Nietzsche and embraced by Foucault. Trained in the nineteenth-century philological tradition, Nietzsche was sensitive to the changing meanings of words, and he applied this awareness most famously in his book On the Genealogy of Morals, where he argued that the word "good" had originally referred to amoral personal attributes such as strength, health, and power but with the advent of Christianity came to have moral meanings (e.g., meekness, selflessness), while what the pagans had valued as "good" came to be seen as "evil."[27] As Foucault observed, Nietzsche's notion of "genealogy" is a corrective to the tendency of historians to search for origins. Whereas "origins" imply inevitable outcomes, genealogy "must record the singularity of events outside of any monotonous finality."[28] A Genealogy of Terror likewise eschews a teleological search for origins and recognizes that the history that occurred is not the history that had to occur. It does not argue that a tradition of valorizing terror made it inevitable that revolutionaries would embrace the language of terror, still less that the Terror as we know it was the unavoidable consequence of a culture in which terror was praised. In other respects the revolutionaries departed from past practice; they were not doomed to embrace this particular tradition. Moreover, other European countries similarly had traditions of valorizing terror in multiple contexts, whereas the Terror took place only in France.[29] Nietzsche is also helpful—and not only filtered through Foucault's interpretation—because his genealogy provided a classic example of what he called "transvaluation" (Umwertung).[30] Just as Christianity turned "good" characteristics into "evil" ones, in Nietzsche's view, beginning in late 1794 France saw a revolution in common understandings of terror. Long an indicator of glory, majesty, legitimacy, and other positive qualities, "terror" came to stand almost exclusively for cruel and pointless violence. Although my study focuses on the "before" side of this revolution, a Nietzschean conception of Umwertung enables us to appreciate the historical changes that have occurred in attitudes toward terror since 1794.

A further advantage of the genealogical approach is that it highlights emotions. Foucault writes of genealogy, "It must seek [events] in the most unpromising places, in what we tend to feel is without history—in sentiments, love, conscience, instincts."[31] This proposition is particularly appropriate for the study of the word "terror," which among other things refers to an emotion. Any attempt to trace the history of an emotion word must reckon with the "emotional turn" in the humanities and social sciences. Particularly relevant to this study is William Reddy's *Navigation of Feeling: A Framework for the History of Emotions*. In that groundbreaking work Reddy introduces the concept of the "emotive." Drawing on J. L. Austin's distinction between "constative" or purely descriptive statements and "performative" statements (such as "I hereby pronounce you man and wife") that *do* things, Reddy adds a third kind of statement that he calls an "emotive."[32] One example of an emotive is "I am angry." Drawing on studies of cognitive psychology, Reddy notes that people change their emotional state in the process of uttering statements about what they perceive that state to be. Thus a person who says "I am angry" might become even angrier in the process and immediate aftermath of making the statement; on the other hand, she might also notice that she is not as angry as she thought and as a result become calmer. In either case, the act of making an emotional claim changes the emotional condition of the person who makes it.[33]

Emotives allow Reddy to make a larger argument about the importance of assessing the "liberty" or oppressiveness of "emotional regimes" by gauging the range of emotions they allow. My aim in this book is not to assess the emotional liberty of the Old Regime or the Revolution, but Reddy's concept of the emotive is helpful because it provides a model for interpreting statements about emotional conditions. Strictly speaking, most of the statements in this book that include the word "terror" do not meet Reddy's standard for emotives, since Reddy restricts this designation for first-person, present-tense statements, and most of the statements analyzed here are in the second or third person.[34] But I would like to suggest that even second- and third-person statements regarding terror can be understood as emotives insofar as they changed the emotional condition of the person who uttered or wrote them. Take, for example, the words of Bishop Jean-Baptiste Massillon in a speech he made in the 1720s or 1730s (later published in a book) to priests about "the need for ministers to renew the spirit of their vocation." Massillon claimed that whereas priests typically grew "insensitive" to the environment of the Mass, infrequent churchgoers responded much more emotionally. He claimed, "The believer who rarely approaches the altar is struck with holy terror [*d'une sainte terreur*] when he has to participate in such a frightful [*redoutable*] action: the approach of a solemn ceremony [i.e., the Eucharist] . . . reminds him of himself; he feels all of his indignity; he throws himself at our feet, filled with fear [*crainte*] and compunction." Priests, on the other hand, are used to "this terrible [*terrible*] ceremony," and therefore it loses its effect. The Mass "does not awaken anything in us, neither fervor nor terror [*terreur*] of holy things, nor pain at our faults, nor resolutions of a more priestly and faithful life."[35] It is reasonable to assume that Massillon felt something as he employed the word *terreur* (to say nothing of the related words *terrible*, *redoutable*, and *crainte*), though he did so in third-person statements. Without speculating in depth on how Massillon felt, we are justified in believing that it felt *good* to use this word, which was so closely linked to the holiness and majesty of God and the prospect of personal salvation. Indeed, the word *terreur* was linked with its opposite— hope or confidence—and was only truly fearful when Massillon considered its absence in the hearts of jaded priests.[36] It is perfectly plausible that the word had similar emotional connotations for those who heard or read Massillon's speech.

Or consider the letter that General Jean-Baptiste Jourdan wrote to the National Convention on October 16, 1793. It described a "bloody battle against the vile slaves of despots" in which 6000 enemy troops were killed and 200 republican soldiers were lost but which resulted in the restoration of the city of Maubeuge to French control. The letter ended with the claim, "Terror has taken hold of our enemies and I believe it will be impossible for these slaves to withstand the courageous efforts of our brave republicans."[37] Jourdan's statement about the emotional condition of the enemy was a third-person claim and therefore (according to Reddy) a constative. But was it not pleasurable for Jourdan to describe the terror he imputed to the enemy? The accompanying claim about the "courageous" condition of the "brave" republicans suggested that it was precisely the prospect of a terrified enemy that emboldened or encouraged Jourdan and his soldiers. Presumably the general also expected the lawmakers and the French public (who read his letter in newspapers) to feel similarly encouraged.

Of course, in the former example terror was a good thing for a good person to feel, and in the latter it was good for the enemy to feel. Paradoxically, Massillon expected feelings of terror to be reassuring, but Jourdan's reasoning was more straightforward, suggesting that it was salutary for the French when the enemy experienced terror. But in both cases a claim of terror made in the third person appears to have felt good to the person making the claim and may also have felt good to the claimants' readers or auditors. Thus in both cases the word *terreur* had a positive emotional valence.

It might be objected that any speculation on the emotional condition of people in the past is, well, speculation. But historians are normally confident that they can apprehend the cognitive state of people in the past or, to use Keith Michael Baker's expression, to describe their process of "intellection."[38] How different are emotions and cognition? Again *The Navigation of Feeling* can be helpful. In that book and elsewhere Reddy relays the findings of many cognitive psychologists who have failed to distinguish between the two mental processes.[39] I am therefore less skeptical than historians such as Peter and Carol Stearns, who have contented themselves with "emotionology," or the examination of which emotions a particular society deemed appropriate, though a considerable part of the present study will be to determine who was expected to feel terror and under what circumstances.[40] Nor do I think it necessary to stop at the "emotional communities" that Barbara Rosenwein argues will "help us understand how people articulated, understood, and represented how they felt," and I disagree that this is "about all we can know about anyone's feelings apart from our own."[41] Absolute certainty in such matters is unlikely, but a reasonable approximation on the basis of evidence is possible.

What were the emotional connotations of *terreur* before and during the French Revolution? In order to provide at least a partial answer, this book examines six distinct subjects or genres—or, to use Lovejoy's expression, "provinces of history"—in which "terror" played a prominent role.[42] The first of these genres consists of theological expressions, specifically in the Judeo-Christian tradition. Chapter 1 examines both the Latin and French editions of the Bible available to Old Regime readers as well as a diverse array of theological writings by ultramontane Catholics, heterodox Jansenists, and even some anticlerical *philosophes* to show that "terror" (Lat. *terror*, Fr. *terreur*) was widely described as the proper condition of human beings before their Creator. (We have already seen this in the example of Massillon.) One of God's principal attributes was accordingly his terror (or terribleness),[43] a trait that corresponded to his power, glory, and righteousness. In short, referring to God as the being who most appropriately instills terror was another way of highlighting his majesty. Chapter 2 examines another form of majesty: that which was attributed to kings and expressed in what might be called the speech of sovereign terror. Here the principal sources are political writings, some more philosophical, others more strictly acclamatory, in which kings are described as rightfully instilling terror in their enemies or even as *being* the terror of those enemies. Insofar as kings reputedly derived their power from God, their terribleness was every bit as holy and therefore legitimate as God's. Chapter 3 explores legal writings, especially those works of jurisprudence that commented on the kinds of punishments most effective in instilling terror in criminals and potential malefactors. Here one encounters such expressions as "the terror of the laws" and "the terror of punishments." We retain these concepts in the word "deter," which literally means "to terrify from [committing an act]," though when using the word "terror" Old Regime legal commentators simultaneously evoked the majesty of the law and of the earthly and heavenly sovereigns who created it. Chapters 4 and 5 examine aesthetic writings. In chapter 4 the emphasis is on theater criticism, and in particular commentary on the perceived necessity of terror as a component of tragedy. The argument is that while many commentators recalled Aristotle's maxim that a tragedy must evoke terror and pity in spectators, increasingly in the course of the eighteenth century theater critics ignored the "pity" side of the dyad and stressed the need for terror. The effect of terror on audiences was thought to be morally improving, whether spectators then "purged" the emotion (as Aristotle prescribed) or maintained it. In similar fashion, chapter 5 shows the link in aesthetic philosophy between terror and "the sublime." Focusing on Edmund Burke's key contribution to the discussion—his *Philosophical Enquiry into the Origin of Our Ideas of the Sublime and the Beautiful* (1757) was translated into French in 1765 and clearly influenced Diderot, among other French writers—it traces the notion that in order for a work of art or experience of nature to be "sublime" it had to impart terror. A crucial component of Burke's plea on behalf of terror was the conviction that the emotion was healthful. (Burke maintained that terror impacted the mind in the same way that physical exercise affected the body.) In chapter 6 we shall see that many medical writers concurred on the "salutary" effect of terror on the human organism, and that both learned treatises and popular digests of medical knowledge made extraordinary claims on behalf of the emotion. Thus terror (though recognized to be typically dangerous) was capable on occasion of curing a variety of illnesses. Notably, a doctor named Jean-Paul Marat shared the widespread belief that terror could imbue the human organism with extraordinary strength.[44] This chapter raises the question of whether revolutionary beliefs about the salutary effects of terror on the "body politic" might have been informed by Old Regime medical thinking. Taken together, the first six chapters of the book point to a tradition of valorizing "terror" and suggest that the word often had positive emotional connotations.

The last two chapters trace terror speech, both spoken and written, in the Revolution. The principal source for this section is the *Archives parlementaires*, particularly volumes 9 through 93. Chapter 7 analyses "terror before the Terror," or terror speech from June 1789 through August 1793. It argues that the revolutionaries of this phase inherited from the Old Regime both the language of judicial terror, which was used to legitimize new laws (including the Constitution), and the idea of terror as a weapon to be wielded against the nation's enemies. It also shows that "terror" was an ecumenical term, used not only by radical Jacobins or Montagnards but by their "moderate" enemies the Girondins, and even the conservative Feuillants, who sought to preserve the power of the monarchy. This universality helped to make it an attractive rallying cry during Year II of the Republic.

Chapter 8 examines terror speech during the Terror itself (September 5, 1793–July 27, 1794). Here we find a decline in utilitarian or "exemplary" terror, in which the prospect of punishment deters adversaries, and an increase in the sense of terror as a principle of vengeance and extermination. Moreover, terror paradoxically became holy in much the way it had been for Bishop Massillon. This can be seen in the language surrounding "the Mountain," a term that originally meant simply the radical members of the National Convention who sat on the highest benches of the assembly hall but came to be described as a "holy Mountain," capable of casting thunderbolts and spewing lava at France's enemies. The atmospheric effects of this figurative geographical feature also resembled prerevolutionary statements about the terrible sublime, and those revolutionaries who praised the Mountain for conjuring fresh air and drying up the miasmas of the counterrevolutionary "swamp" (marais) recalled medical ideas about salutary terror. In addition, chapter 8 argues that terror speech was therapeutic to the revolutionaries of the Year II. Specifically, those who used it contrasted the terror supposedly felt by enemies with their own feelings of "consolation," "hope," "confidence," and "courage."

From the very beginning of the Revolution to the fall of Robespierre, as both chapters 7 and 8 will show, "terror" retained its prerevolutionary emotional connotations. It still felt good to utter, write, hear, or read the word. The source of this feeling was a set of ideas—and here again ideas and feelings are closely linked—including security, safety, and salvation. Terror was salutary not only in the sense of saving the person experiencing it by deterring dangerous behavior, but also in the sense of preserving society from the danger posed by its enemies. Moreover, it recalled the salvation that according to prerevolutionary generations had come from a terrible, glorious God. In this context the revolutionary word salut, often translated as "safety," also alluded to salvation.

Finally, a conclusion will place this book's findings in the context of the historiographical literature on the Terror, navigating between ideological and circumstantial explanations and addressing more recent scholarship that takes an "emotional turn." The conclusion will also highlight the sudden shifts in the meaning of "terror" that took place in the days and weeks following the fall of Robespierre. It identifies the Thermidorian period as the moment when the word lost its connotations of justice, legitimacy, majesty, and salvation and came instead to indicate unjust and pointless violence.

The following excursion through six provinces of history—not counting revolutionary France—might at times feel like a frenetic dash, the first casualty of which will be contextualization. I will rarely linger in my descriptions of the historical actors behind the statements that constitute the core of this story, and—until my account of the Revolution—I will say little about the social and intellectual contexts in which they were uttered or written. Contextualists in the tradition of Quentin Skinner might be disappointed by this approach, but part of the reason for this contextual sparseness is simply practical. I am not a specialist in biblical studies or the history of French Catholicism. I am not an expert in Old Regime political theology, jurisprudence, theater criticism, aesthetics or medicine. A fully contextualized study of each prerevolutionary chapter would also add considerably to the book's length. Nor do I believe it would substantially change the argument. For example, in the chapter on medical understandings of terror, I could linger over the eighteenth-century transition from Galenic to neurological models or discuss how a new generation of vitalists opposed their Cartesian/mechanist forebears, but none of this would change my main point in that chapter, which is the fact that physicians— whatever their intellectual or social affiliations—often credited terror with the power to cure illnesses or impart strength to the body. Peter Gordon has recently argued that contextualism has limited explanatory power in works of intellectual history.[45] I believe this book to be an example of a study that calls for only limited contextualization.

Did "terror" always have positive emotional connotations during the prerevolutionary period? Certainly not. For Old Regime and revolutionary commentators alike, the word could be a term of abuse denoting despotism, and though Montesquieu typically used the word *crainte* (fear) to describe the "principle" of despotism, others substituted the term *terreur*.[46] Similarly, for numerous *philosophes* "terror" (or, more frequently, "terrors") denoted the "superstitious" fear of hell promoted by the church and allegedly designed to control credulous people.[47] My argument is not that terror was always a good thing in the utterances, oral or written, of Old Regime and revolutionary commentators, but that there was a strong enough tradition of positive terror speech to make the term an attractive option for a rallying cry in September 1793. I am not suggesting that "terror" as the "order of the day" was an inevitable slogan; rather, I am providing reasons for its having been a thinkable one.[48]

The difference between terror speech for most of the eighteenth century and terror speech after the Terror is not that "terror" was initially considered a good thing and subsequently a bad thing. Rather, the word went from having both positive and negative meanings to having almost exclusively negative ones. "Terror" most certainly has a postrevolutionary history as well, with the conflation of terror and (a specific form of) terrorism after 9/11 defining the most recent chapter. But it was the Revolution—or more specifically a set of narratives about the Revolution produced after the fall of Robespierre—that largely bequeathed to us the set of emotional connotations attached to the word today.

Robert Darnton has advised students of history, "When we cannot get a proverb, or a joke, or a poem, we know we are on to something. By picking at the document where it is most opaque, we may be able to unravel an alien system of meaning."[49] A more old-fashioned way of putting this comes from Herder, who believed that one of the primary goals of historical study was "to feel oneself into" (*sich hineinfühlen*) a different age.[50] Few things are harder to "get" today than the expression *Placez la terreur à l'ordre du jour*, and few things are harder to "feel oneself into" than a culture in which *la terreur* could sound and feel good. But the stakes are high. Even partial success will provide a better understanding of both the French Revolution and the history of Western attitudes toward terror. Let us therefore look more closely into the genealogy of terror in eighteenth-century France.

CHAPTER ONE

Holy Terror and Divine Majesty

INTRODUCTION

Our quest to understand what terror meant to the French revolutionaries begins with the Bible. The ultimate source of terror in the Judeo-Christian tradition is God, who throughout the biblical narrative instills terror via threats, judgments, and punishments. If this seems a long way back to search for sources of terror speech in eighteenth-century France, it is worth recalling that the Bible was a best-selling book in prerevolutionary France.[1] From the Bible we shall proceed to writings of eighteenth-century theologians, then to the texts of sermons from the same period, and finally to the writings of *philosophes* who diverged from Christianity on theological matters but agreed that God was a legitimate source of terror for his human creatures. Taken together, these sources reveal a tradition of regarding terror as a suitable emotion in the face of the Almighty. To use a word frequently paired with "terror," it was "salutary," which suggests that it both promoted health and assured salvation. Paradoxically, terror of God could reduce the terror of his wrath. Those who blithely ignored the prospect of divine punishment were that much more likely to suffer it. In addition to being an emotion, terror was the source or object of that emotion. It was a chief attribute of God to be "terrible," and this descriptor also had positive emotional connotations, as God's capacity to terrify was closely linked to other divine attributes, namely glory, majesty, and justice. In the context of theological discussions, the words "terror" and "terrible" sounded good, and it felt good to write, speak, read, or hear them.

TERROR IN THE VULGATE

Bible reading was widespread in eighteenth-century France, and not in opposition to any church policy.[2] Nor was it restricted to Jansenists, though
they were known to be particularly staunch advocates of studying the holy
scriptures.[3] As orthodox a Catholic as the Jesuit Père Guillaume-Hyacinthe
Bougeant wrote in a catechism of 1741 that literate Christians who failed
to read the Bible "would have to reproach themselves for having dispensed
with one of the most useful means they had of nourishing their piety and
for neglecting from among all readings that which is most capable of inspiring Christian sentiments in them."[4] The official version of the Bible
for French Catholics was the Vulgate of Saint Jerome, who had translated
the scriptures into Latin. Though not all literate French people would have
been able to read the Vulgate, it was central to the education of priests, who
in turn interpreted the Bible for their flocks and instructed the faithful on
their proper relationship with God.

The word *terror* (including its inflected forms) occurs forty-seven times
in the Vulgate.[5] All but one of these instances appear in the Old Testament.
The word is first used in Genesis 9:2, where God endows the sons of Noah
with dominion over animals, decreeing, "And may the terror of you [*terror
vester*] and the trembling [*ac tremor*] be over all the animals of the earth
and over all the birds of the sky." Thus the right to instill terror in creatures epitomized the power to rule over them, and the image of power*less*
creatures trembling with terror dramatically symbolized the idea of divine
power.

The Old Testament repeatedly depicts God striking terror into people
and in the process signifying his sovereignty over them. The most famous
example is in the liberation of the Israelites from Egyptian bondage. The
prophet Jeremiah offers a thanksgiving prayer to God for having "led your
people Israel out of the land of Egypt with signs and portents and with a
strong hand and an outstretched arm, and with great terror."[6] King David
expresses his gratitude in similar language in the book of Chronicles, where
he thanks God for liberating his people with "greatness and with terrors."[7]
God had plans to terrorize Egypt once again, according to Ezekiel, who put
these words into his mouth: "I shall destroy the likenesses and I shall make
the idols of Memphis cease and the ruler of the land of Egypt shall be no
more and I shall spread terror in the land of Egypt."[8] Interestingly, the pro-
phetic sequence of divine events did not begin with terror as a means of
ridding Egypt of its idols and its ruler, but concluded with it, presumably

when the main work of purging the country had already been done. In this case terror was not utilitarian. It was instead a sign of God's power.

What Ezekiel predicted for Egypt, Isaiah prognosticated for Assyria. In a passage that concisely links terror with glory, the prophet declares, "And the Lord shall make the glory of his voice heard and shall show the terror of his arm with the threat of fury, and the flame of devouring fire shall crash down with a swirl and with hailstones."[9] Further, Isaiah refers to "the Assyrian," whose "courage will give way to terror" when God punishes his wicked nation.[10] In a more generalized threat, the same prophet warns, "Behold, the Dominator, the Lord of Hosts shall shatter the flasks [of the arrogant] with terror, and the height of the lofty one shall be cut down, and the exalted ones shall be humbled."[11] Nor was Israel exempt from terror. Among the many punishments God threatens for disobedience, in Deuteronomy he tells the Israelites that they will be driven "mad with terror."[12] Similarly, Jeremiah reveals what God will say on the day of his vengeance: "I have multiplied [Jerusalem's] widows to more than the grains of sand in the sea . . . I have suddenly cast terror over the city."[13] Again, as in Ezekiel, the invocation of terror succeeds the actual violence and serves to legitimize it.

While the Israelites were in God's favor, however, they enjoyed the privilege not only of immunity to his terror, but of participation in the terror that God inflicted on his (and their) enemies. Just as they had the right to terrify the animal kingdom, they possessed a deputized power to terrify—and kill—proscribed nations. In the book of Exodus, after enumerating the Ten Commandments and other precepts, God promises, in exchange for fidelity, "I shall send my terror ahead of you, and I shall kill every people to whom you come, and I shall turn the backs of all your enemies from you."[14] Likewise, in Deuteronomy God assures his people that if they keep his commandments, "no one shall stand against you; the Lord your God will spread the terror and fear of you [terrorem vestrum et formidinem] over all the land that you tread on."[15]

Elsewhere in Deuteronomy Moses tells the Israelites that God will make them terrifying. He relays this promise: "Today I shall begin to put the terror and the fear of you into all the peoples who live under heaven, that they may be terrified and, in the manner of one about to give birth, tremble, and remain in pain."[16] In the book of Joshua the prostitute Rahab turns against her compatriots in Jericho and assists in the Israelite conquest of her city, explaining, "I knew that the Lord had given you the land [of Jericho] because the terror of you rushed over us and all the inhabitants of the land slackened."[17] In both cases gendered imagery reinforces the power dynamic of a terrible

God (or his people) rightfully triumphing over a trembling parturient or "slackened" adversary. Moreover, it is significant that in Rahab's reasoning the land must belong to Israel *because* the people of Jericho are terrified. Again, terror itself stands for legitimate power. Finally, if terror borrowed from God could facilitate the conquest of land, it could also lead to conversion. After Esther foiled Haman's plot against the Jews of Persia and the wicked minister was executed along with his ten sons, "many other people were joined both to the sect of [the Jews'] religion and to their ceremonies, for a great terror of the name Jew had taken possession of everyone."[18]

If the Chosen People were authorized to serve as God's proxies and spread terror in his name, other nations clearly did not possess that privilege. Indeed, Ezekiel prophesies nemesis for those who arrogate the power to terrorize. He enumerates various peoples that have ended up "in the midst of hell" for having committed this sin.[19] "Elam is there," he reports, referring to the civilization east of Mesopotamia, whose inhabitants "had placed their own terror in the land of the living."[20] The use of the possessive adjective *suum*, in this case meaning "their," is significant. God's terror was of course allowed, either directly or through authorized intermediaries, but the Elamites had spread *terrorem suum*, their own terror, and the penalty for this transgression was damnation. Ezekiel also describes the perdition of the Phrygian kingdoms "Meshech" and "Tubal," which "had descended into hell" because "terror of the bold [i.e., arrogant] ones had been spread in the land of the living."[21] The pharaoh comes at the end of Ezekiel's list of damned souls, and here it becomes explicit that terror belongs only to God, whom the prophet quotes as saying, "For I spread my terror [*terrorem meum*] in the land of the living."[22]

Just as the noun *terror* indicated God's power, so did the adjective "terrible" (*terribilis, terribile*, etc.), which appears sixty-one times in the Vulgate and almost always refers to God or his deeds. The descriptor first occurs in Genesis. Following his famous dream, Jacob exclaims, "How terrifying [*pavens*] and terrible [*terribilis*] is this place. This is none other than the house of God and the gate of heaven."[23] For Jacob, as for many other biblical characters, "terrible" means awesome, glorious, and mighty and is therefore an obvious attribute of the Divinity. In the Song of the Sea, where Moses celebrates God's drowning of the Egyptian army in the Red Sea, the Almighty is simultaneously "terrible" and "praiseworthy."[24] In Deuteronomy God assures his people that they need not fear their enemies, as they have on their side a "great and terrible God."[25] Later in the same book he describes himself as "a great and powerful and terrible God" who has done "great and terrible things" for his people.[26] The Psalms use the word "terrible" twenty-eight times, typically to glorify God. The faithful are enjoined to shout with joy, "for the Lord most high is a terrible, great king."[27] The psalmist is elated because God's "works" are "most terrible" and urges the faithful to "come and see the works of the terrible God."[28]

The word "terror" is rare in the New Testament, occurring only once, in the Gospel of Luke, where Jesus describes Judgment Day: "There shall be earthquakes in different places, and pestilences, and famines, and there shall also be terrors from heaven, and great signs."[29] "Terrible" appears only twice, both times in Paul's Epistle to the Hebrews. The apostle warns the Jews that if they continue to sin after learning "of the truth," they should feel "a terrible expectation of judgment and fire" that will "consume" them.[30] Still, overall the Bible provided many examples of terror and repeatedly linked the word with notions of God's power, majesty, and righteousness.

French readers who could not understand Latin or simply preferred their scripture in their native language had many options, the most popular of which was a French translation by the Jansenist Isaac Louis Le Maistre de Sacy (1613–1684), which appeared in thirty-four editions between 1701 and 1790.[31] Sacy used the word *terreur* fifty times when translating the Bible.[32] In twenty-five of the instances in which Jerome wrote the word *terror*, Sacy substituted the cognate *terreur*.[33] For example, this is how Sacy translated God's promise to Noah in Genesis 9:2:

> Que tous les animaux de la terre, & tous les oiseaux du ciel soient frappés de terreur & tremblent devant vous, avec tout ce qui se meut sur la terre. [May all the animals of the earth, and all the birds of the sky be struck with terror and tremble before you, with all that moves around the earth.][34]

Similarly, where the Vulgate has God promise, "I shall send my terror ahead of you," Sacy has him say, "I shall have the terror of my name march before you."[35] Where Saint Jerome has God assure the Israelites, "Today I shall begin to put terror and fear of you into the peoples who live under all the skies," Sacy has him declare, "I shall begin today to cast the terror and fright of your arms into all the peoples who live under heaven."[36] Jeremiah's prayer of thanks to God for having delivered the Israelites from Egypt "in great terror" appears thus in Sacy: "It is you who drew your people Israel out of Egypt with miracles and wonders, with a strong hand and an outstretched arm, and in the terror of your judgments."[37]

In other cases Sacy chose synonyms for *terreur* where Jerome selected *terror*. For example, whereas Jerome has Moses report that God is going to test his people "that his terror may be in you and you will not sin," Sacy's Moses conveys the message that God's purpose is "to imprint the fear of him in you, that you not sin."[38] Elsewhere the Vulgate has God threaten that his people will become "mad with terror" should they disobey him; Sacy translates God's words as "beside yourselves with fright" (*hors de vous par la frayeur*).[39] Jerome's psalmist laments that "terrors of death fell upon me," whereas Sacy translates the complaint as "I was seized with fright and trembling" (*J'ai été saisi de frayeur & de tremblement*).[40] In several other places Sacy writes *frayeur* where Jerome wrote *terror*.[41] Alternatively, he uses *l'épouvante*, a word that could be translated into English as "terror" or "horror," instead of *terreur*.[42]

Yet as often as Sacy employed a synonym for *terreur* to translate a passage in which Jerome chose *terror*, he used *terreur* to render a passage which Jerome had not translated with *terror*.[43] For example, the Second Book of Chronicles (Vulgate version) records that *pavor Domini* prevented the kingdoms surrounding Judah from waging war against King Josaphat. *Pavor* is synonymous with terror, and *pavor Domini* can be translated as "terror of the Lord." Thus Sacy was translating in the same spirit when he attributed the inaction of Judah's enemies to "terror of the name of God."[44] Elsewhere in the same biblical book Sacy chose *terreur* where Jerome had chosen *pavor*. Jerome wrote that "the terror [*pavor*] of the Lord came over all the kingdoms of the earth when they heard that the Lord fought against Israel's enemies." Sacy's version of that passage was: "And the terror [*la terreur*] of the Lord spread over all the neighboring kingdoms when they learned that the Lord himself had fought against Israel's enemies."[45]

In some cases Sacy used *terreur* where Jerome had used *timor* or *formido*, words that are typically translated into English as "fear." Thus Ecclesiasticus 36:2 (in Jerome's version) urges God, "Send fear of you [*timorem tuum*] onto the nations" who worship other gods, while Sacy's rendition reads, "Spread your terror [*votre terreur*] over the nations."[46] The First Book of Maccabees, in the Vulgate, reveals that "the enemies [of Judah the Maccabee] were repulsed by fear of him [*prae timore eius*]," whereas Sacy wrote, "The terror [*terreur*] of his name made his enemies flee before him."[47] Elsewhere the reader of the Vulgate learns that "the fear and dread [*timor . . . et formido*] of Judah and his brothers fell over all the nations in their vicinity," which Sacy rendered, "Then the terror [*terreur*] of Judah and his brothers spread from all sides among the neighboring nations."[48]

Whether eighteenth-century French readers encountered the Latin *terror* or the French *terreur* when examining their Bibles, the message they received was similar. In addition to indicating emotions that might otherwise be indicated by words such as fear, fright, or dread, the terms *terror* and *terreur* suggested the power to instill these feelings. In most cases the source of these emotions was God, whose power to provoke them was an index of his might, his majesty, and his glory. He could delegate this power to his Chosen People, but their terribleness was contingent upon their obedience to him. Even when terror was attributed to nations God held in execration and was therefore a justification for their punishment, the word still had sacred connotations. Israel's enemies were being punished for wielding a sacred weapon to which they had no right, but that only enhanced the weapon's sense of sacrality.

TERROR IN THE WRITINGS OF FRENCH THEOLOGIANS

In the century prior to the Revolution, a wide variety of French Catholic writers drew on the biblical tradition of depicting terror as an instrument of God and a sign of his glory. Jacques-Bénigne Bossuet epitomized the Catholic position on piety-induced terror (and terror-induced piety). A bishop, court preacher, and tutor to the dauphin, Bossuet defined orthodoxy in the age of Louis XIV. In one work he told the story of Ananias and Saphira, a husband and wife who, according to the Acts of the Apostles (5: 1–11), sold land to donate the proceeds to the apostles but lied about the amount they had received from the sale and kept the difference. Peter discerned the deceit and confronted the couple, asking them why they had lied to the Holy Spirit, upon which Ananias and Saphira died. This event led to "great fear" among the people and, in Bossuet's view, solidified Peter's power as head of the apostolic church. Bossuet wrote that in killing Ananias and Saphira with his probing question, "Peter achieved the first miracle to appear in confirmation of the resurrection of Jesus Christ; it was he who made an example of Ananias and Saphira: this first thunderbolt which inspired salutary terror in the faithful and affirmed the authority of the apostolic government proceeded from his lips."[49]

It is possible that Bossuet derived the idea of "salutary terror" from Augustine, who had insisted to his followers, *ubi terror, ibi salus*, an aphorism that could be translated as "Where there is terror, there is health," or "Where there is terror, there is salvation."[50] After all, Augustine, whom Bossuet cited hundreds of times in his works, has been described as "Bossuet's teacher."[51] Whatever the source of his wording, for Bossuet the idea of terror as salutary suggested both salvation and health. In both respects, terror was good for the person who felt it. Of course, Ananias and Saphira had to die for this effect to be felt, but the ensuing terror assured the power of the church, which in turn assured the salvation of souls.

Bossuet accordingly lauded prophets and preachers who instilled terror in their flocks. Lamenting the shortage of effective ministers in his day, he yearned for a new Elijah. He asked, "Who will give us an Elijah to convert us to the Savior?" and apostrophized, "Come, Elijah; come, preachers of the gospel with a heavenly fervor; move, unsettle our hearts, excite the spirit of penitence, fill us with terror at the sight of the judge who is to come. May we fear him in order that we may love him."[52]

The linkage between terror and love may also have been inspired by Bossuet's reading of Augustine, who in his *Confessions* wrote with great affection of "all the exhortations and terrors" as well as the "guidance and consolation" he received from God as inducement to convert.[53] Elsewhere Augustine used the word *caritas*, which can mean either charity or love, when he maintained that this "is to be built by God's very severity, by which route the hearts of mortals shake with a most salubrious terror [*saluber-rimo terrore*], so that one rejoices to see oneself loved by him whom one fears and dares to love him back."[54] But even if Bossuet was not directly influenced by Augustine in this point, he shared that Christian father's paradoxical view that divine terror and divine love are two sides of the same coin.

A contemporary of Bossuet who similarly praised the religious effects of terror was Madame Guyon (1648–1717). A proponent of Quietism, a variety of mysticism that encouraged passivity in relation to God, Madame Guyon briefly enjoyed favor at the court of Louis XIV. She found a disciple in Archbishop Fénelon, tutor to the king's grandson and eventual rival to Bossuet. Guyon's skepticism regarding the efficacy of Catholic clergy and institutions gave Bossuet the opportunity to have her and Fénelon condemned as heretics; Fénelon was exiled and Guyon was sentenced to prison followed by exile. Though she died in 1717, her works were republished frequently throughout the eighteenth century.

Despite her differences with Bossuet, Guyon shared the bishop's belief in the salutary nature of religious terror. In her *Lettres chrétiennes et spirituelles*, first published just after her death, Guyon advised an unnamed lady undergoing a psychological crisis. Among other disorders, the anonymous correspondent suffered from "terrors" or "panic terrors." Guyon reasoned that the devil was terrifying her friend, but that God was complicit in his attempts to terrify. "You know that for some time you have often been subject to these panic terrors [*ces terreurs paniques*]," she wrote to her troubled friend. "The demon is only trying to agitate you in this way, and God permits him so that you will abandon yourself to him [i.e., God]."[55] Elsewhere Guyon linked terror and abandon as steps towards salvation: "Do not be surprised, Madame, about your terrors and your sufferings. These will only be destroyed when you yourself are entirely destroyed. Let yourself be crucified and destroyed by all the providential things that happen to you."[56] Indeed, Guyon counted "the terrors of demons" among the "extraordinary" means by which God brought his creatures to proper worship.[57] "Fears [*des éfrois*], terrors, and even an infinity of irregular feelings and movements" could actually be the sign of "a good cross," that is, a beneficial burden.[58] Guyon reassured her friend that "we hardly ever see dissolute people think they are damned," since the devil "removes from them all thoughts of the future, for fear that salutary terror might convert them."[59]

Opposing Madame Guyon did not entail an aversion to religious terror. Just as Bossuet espoused terror while condemning Quietism, Esprit Fléchier, the bishop of Nîmes, wrote a poem that discredited Madame Guyon yet emphasized the salutary nature of divine terror. The "Poëme chrétien sur la béatitude, contre les illusions du Quiétisme," first written between 1696 and 1699 but republished as late as the 1780s, praises this emotion, which Quietism (in his view) suppressed through its emphasis on abandon. Thus Fléchier affirmed the emotional condition of the devoted Christian who lives "in holy terror of seeing himself reproved."[60] Fléchier may have overestimated Madame Guyon's indifference to the fate of her soul, as she certainly shared his belief in the terror of hell as a powerful conversionary impulse. Nevertheless, the value he placed on salutary or holy terror was not in doubt, and indeed he was praised for his ability to induce terror in his audiences. Writing nearly a century later, the literary critic and grammarian Bridel Arleville cited Fléchier's oratory in particular for its ability to "impress on the soul a certain salutary terror mixed with astonishment and respect."[61]

In the generation following Madame Guyon's death, one of the most ardent and prolific French Catholic advocates of religious terror was Jean-Baptiste Massillon. A protégé of Bossuet who preached at the courts of Louis XIV, the Regent Philippe d'Orléans, and Louis XV, Massillon became bishop of Clermont in 1717. His thoughts on the proper emotional condition of priests can be gleaned from his sermons to fellow ecclesiastics at a series of synods in the 1720s and 1730s, though compilations of these discourses appeared throughout the eighteenth century.[62] At one such address, Massillon counseled priests on the danger of losing their zeal in the course of repeated religious ceremonies. In particular, he warned against a diminution of sacred terror. At the beginning of their careers, when priests "began to approach the holy altar, the majesty of the terrible mysteries, . . . the silence and the terror of the angels themselves who surrounded the sanctuary, all this struck our hearts with a holy seizure [*d'un saint saisissement*]; we trembled under the weight of the sacred vestments." Paradoxically, Massillon greatly feared a disappearance of that sacred terror.[63]

In 1724 Massillon reiterated this concern. Railing against indifferent pastors, he urged his fellow priests, "Make piety respectable by making yourselves respectable; inspire fear [*la crainte*] and terror of the holy mysteries through the profound reverence with which you treat them."[64] In 1727 he urged ministers, "Inspire in the people respect for holy things by treating them yourselves as holy: appear at the feet of the altars . . . struck by the majesty of God . . . and let the modesty, the terror, the profound religious feeling with which you will accompany your fearsome [*redoutables*] functions teach the faithful the holy conduct they must have when participating" in services.[65]

Six years later Massillon implored his brethren to feel "holy terror" in order to convey the same emotions to their congregants.[66] He warned priests who performed their functions without feeling that their "obduracy" was actually a punishment for their sin: it made them feel too secure, which itself led to damnation. Massillon therefore urged his fellows, "Let us enter, my brothers, into these feelings of terror and religion."[67]

In 1736 Massillon returned to the theme of "insensitivity," which for him was "the most widespread . . . curse attached to the holy functions of the ministry." He proclaimed, "The believer who rarely approaches the altar is struck with a holy terror when he has to participate in such a fearsome [*redoutable*] action: the approach of a solemn ceremony [i.e., the Eucharist] . . . reminds him of himself; he feels all of his indignity; he throws himself at our feet, filled with fear [*crainte*] and compunction." Priests, on the other hand, are used to "this terrible ceremony" and it therefore loses its effect. The Mass "does not awaken anything in us, neither fervor nor terror of holy things." Similarly, whereas the common people are "struck with terror at the Judgments of God" when hearing the Gospel read to them, priests are too familiar with the text and lack the requisite emotional reaction, and the "serious pomp of religious services" impresses ordinary believers but "loses in us all its terror and majesty." The only solution for priests was to pray for God to "rekindle the divine fire" in their hearts so that they could experience the salutary terror that paradoxically reduced the danger of perdition.[68]

In 1738 Massillon wrote again of the problem of waning terror before God. He compared the situation of the desensitized pastor to that of the ancient Israelites who grew used to miracles. The priests and Levites who had carried the Ark of the Covenant through the desert after miraculously crossing the Red Sea relied on another miracle: a column of light that was present night and day. Massillon recalled that this "apparition . . . struck [the Israelites] for some time with holy terror" and "a renewed respect for the orders of Moses and the duties to their state," but he added that when they saw "this miraculous light every day," it eventually became nothing to them but "an ordinary sight, which no longer made an impression." The spiritual rulers of Israel were "soon confounded with the murmurers and adorers of the Golden Calf." Likewise, too many of Massillon's fellow priests had experienced a "cooling" in their zeal.[69]

Other theologians added to the chorus of writings in praise of religious terror. Jansenists were among the most prolific. Despite the peculiarities of Jansenism—above all its focus on predestination—its view of salutary terror was in line with that of mainstream Catholicism. Thus Antoine Arnauld, whose 1643 book *De la fréquente communion* remained popular among Jansenists throughout the eighteenth century, faulted priests who were too quick to console sinners and proclaim their absolution. He wrote, "Fear of death, terror of the horrible [*épouvantables*] judgments of God must prevent us from falling into sin and bring us to do penance if we are unfortunate enough to have fallen into it." Security about one's salvation provided by "precipitous absolution," by contrast, was evidence of demonic intervention. "Here . . . the demon erases all these apprehensions in order to precipitate us into crime."[70] Arnauld advocated public penance in which sinners would be required to wear hair shirts, prostrate themselves, and beg for forgiveness before being allowed to take the Eucharist. In the meantime they should be "cut off publicly from Holy Communion," the author proposed, asking rhetorically, "Who could doubt that this curtailment would be very useful . . . in giving sinners salutary terror?"[71]

Eighteenth-century Jansenists echoed Arnauld's views. In his *Instruction pastorale* (1776), Archbishop of Lyon Antoine de Malvin de Montazet saw religious terror as particularly important in the struggle against the Enlightenment. In a diatribe against the *philosophes*, he argued against the position that morality is possible without religion. He did not deny that "some men, without the aid of religion, have appeared temperate, fair, faithful to certain duties of society," and that "pride succeeded in imposing silence on their other passions," though in his view such instances were rare.

Yet if one believed in the possibility of "restraining in the same boundaries a vulgar and frenzied multitude," and if, after "having broken the sacred barrier of religion and its salutary terrors," one insisted that "abstract ideas of justice and honesty" would stop the effect of "so many passions," Montazet claimed that this was "to misunderstand the nature of man."[72] Elsewhere, in a discussion of suicide, Montazet argued that the pagans of antiquity were susceptible to this sin because they considered themselves "above the salutary terror of eternity."[73]

The sacralization of terror was evident in other writings by eighteenth-century Jansenists. Both Jean Antoine Gazaignes and Bonaventure Racine, in separate books appearing in 1767, cited a 1708 work in Latin by Nicolas Petitpied, who (in their French translation) recalled "the holy terror" that had reigned in the Jansenist convent of Port-Royal before Louis XIV destroyed it in 1707. In 1786 a Jansenist woman named Poulain de Nogent, also citing Petitpied, referred to the "holy terror" that pervaded Port-Royal.[74] These sources suggest that in the collective Jansenist memory of Port-Royal one of the most appealing aspects of the persecuted institution had been the terror one felt in its midst.

Poulain's remarks appeared just three years before the outbreak of the French Revolution. Some historians, most notably Dale Van Kley, have seen in Jansenism the roots of the Revolution. Members of the *parlements*, the royal law courts that challenged absolutism and advocated separation of powers, were often Jansenists themselves, or at least sympathetic to the movement.[75] One might cite Jansenist views of terror as additional evidence of the linkage between the religious movement and the French Revolution, especially the phase of the Terror, yet Jansenist praise of holy or salutary terror looked very much like similar assertions in a wide range of Judeo-Christian writings from antiquity to the eighteenth century.

TERROR IN CATHOLIC SERMONS

A brief look at eighteenth-century sermons suggests that the audience for such expressions glorifying divine terror was large. There are thousands of volumes of published sermons from the century prior to the Revolution. It is impossible here to conduct a thorough examination of them, but even a cursory glance suggests that from their pulpits throughout France priests spoke of God's terror in the same breath with which they spoke of his majesty, that they saw terror in the face of divine wrath and punishment as salutary, and that they considered terrifying their congregations to be an integral part of their job.

Priests repeatedly linked divine terror with God's majesty. The Jesuit preacher Timoléon Cheminais de Montaigu urged his congregation to picture "this God . . . casting terror everywhere, carried on a cloud in the midst of lightning bolts, his visage full of august majesty . . . more brilliant than the sun . . . more thunderous than he appeared to Moses on the mountain, more terrible than the Exterminating Angel."[76] Though Père Cheminais died in 1689, his sermons were reprinted twenty-five times over the following century, and in addition to the many Christians who absorbed his message through the medium of print, it is easy to imagine many churchgoers whose parish priests imitated the style and message of the famous preacher.[77] Closer to the time of the Revolution, Jean François Copel, otherwise known as Père Élisée (1726–1785), presented God's majesty as a source of terror. In his sermon "On Prayer" he intoned, "What condemns . . . our half-heartedness in prayer, what leaves us without an excuse, what must strike us with terror is the majesty of God before which we appear, and which rejects all faint homage."[78] In his sermon "On Communion" he described sinners who converted as "struck by the majesty of the God whom they have offended, and penetrated with the terror of his judgments," and he took pleasure in picturing a worshipper who "glimpsed . . . all the glory of the supreme majesty [of God] and the terror that it inspires."[79]

Sermons also repeatedly characterized divine terror as "salutary." The Oratorian bishop of Senez Jean Soanen (1647–1740), whose sermons were published in at least three posthumous editions in the eighteenth century and who likely provided a model for other priests, preached before the young King Louis XV and courtiers at Versailles. He recalled Saint Bernard's dictum that (in Soanen's words) "death . . . is the terror of the sons of Adam," adding that "one cannot envisage it without its horrors, without experiencing a seizure that chills all the senses." But he urged his auditors to envisage death, since it was "fitting . . . to inspire salutary terrors in you, and to tear you away from the madness and vanities of the century!"[80]

Soanen was a Jansenist,[81] as was the Oratorian priest Pierre Pacaud, who told his flock that "if the love of God is the true character of the Christian, man needs to sustain himself by the terror of his judgments; and it is in truth ill-conceived delicacy to be unable to occupy oneself with the thought of death and Hell."[82] But churchmen who were quite vehemently opposed to Jansenism also used their sermons to characterize the terror of God as salutary. Thus on Tuesday of the fifth week of Lent (probably in the 1730s) the Provençal Oratorian and anti-Jansenist Père Jean-Baptiste Surian asked his congregation to picture their fate should they fail to repent: "See those enraged demons, those blazing fires, those devouring flames, . . . if you do not become just, that is the fate that awaits you." He anticipated that his parishioners would "complain that I am horrifying you" (que je vous épouvante), to which he replied that "the terror that I am inspiring in you today . . . is just . . . is reasonable . . . is Christian," and he asked rhetorically, "So what if it troubles you, if it seizes you, as long as it excites in you the sentiments, desires and the works of salvation?"[83]

In his sermon before the king during Lent in 1764, Pierre-Anastase Torné similarly emphasized the salutary nature of divine terror. He asked the congregation, "Have you been plunged into disorder? [God] wants to recall you from deep lethargy, from the sleep of death . . . to strike you with the terror of his judgments; to make you tremble at the [prospect of the] afterlife by punishing you now in this life; to force you . . . to search for nothing but the glory of his name."[84] As a member of the Doctrinaire order, Torné had dedicated himself to the task of catechizing the people of the countryside, and one can easily imagine him delivering the same sermon to the peasants of the Pyrenees near his native city of Tarbes. Torné would go on to become a revolutionary, serving as constitutional bishop of the Cher department and supporting the radical Montagnards in the Convention, and it is conceivable that his apprenticeship in religious terror helped to make the political Terror of 1793–94 attractive to him.[85] In any event, Torné was only one of many preachers who helped to make the word terreur sound good by associating it with the salvation of the soul.

That priests regularly sought to terrify their flocks, whether in Versailles or in their provincial parishes, is strongly suggested by their repeated claims, in the sermons themselves, that they were bound by their calling to instill terror. It was part of their job, and in this sense it was also part of their identity. Thus Father Soanen summoned all the terror he could when beginning his sermon "On the Last Judgment": "Should my tongue, like a torrent of fire, come to set your souls ablaze and fill them with the greatest fright [du plus grand effroi]; should my words, like molten lead, penetrate into all your bones to imprint in you the most vivid terror, if my eloquence, in a word, resembled that of the prophets, I would not be able to give you the right idea of this great day that threatens us and which, recalling the original chaos, will seize us with fear and horror [nous saisira de crainte & d'horreur]."[86]

Modesty prevented Soanen from equating himself with the prophets, but clearly they were his model, and specifically in their ability to instill terror; and though Soanen conceded that no degree of eloquence could capture the terror of the Last Judgment, he avowed to do the best he could to terrify his congregation. He made this goal more explicit still in his sermon "On Death." Personifying death and treating her as a muse, he enjoined, "Oh Death! Lend me those somber and lugubrious colors that you spread wherever you go, that I may paint you in the eyes of my auditors; give to my words that frightful tone [ce ton effrayant] that you give to those whose friends and relatives you remove, that I may imprint salutary terror."[87] In both passages Soanen highlighted his own presence, using first-person pronouns, and underscored the goal of instilling terror as part of his larger effort to secure the salvation of his congregation.

The expectation that preachers would attempt to terrify their audiences was such that when Abbé Denis-Xavier Clément spoke at the consecration of the church of Notre Dame des Victoires in Paris in 1740, he felt the need to insist that his sermon was not merely a performance. He addressed the spectators: "When the Ministers of the living God warn you to return to him, when they thunder his anathemas at you to bring you to penitence; admit, Messieurs, that you are stunned; sometimes regarding these threats as pure declamations, as jeux d'esprit; sometimes treating as panic fears [en frayeurs paniques] the salutary terror that we wish to inspire in you." But he contended that this was precisely how the Israelites had reacted to the prophets, and they suffered God's wrath. Clément went on to interpret the bad harvest of that year as an indication of God's displeasure and a form of chastisement that only foretold greater punishments.[88]

Other priests concurred that their job was to emulate the prophets and terrify their flocks into repentance. In his sermon "On the Last Judgment" Abbé Paul César de Ciceri explained to his congregants their responsibilities to the priests who preached to them: "All you have to do is listen to the threats and reproaches that they issue, to feel for a moment the terror with which they try to fill you."[89] The Jesuit Martin Pallu, who died in 1742 but whose sermons were republished in the 1750s, acknowledged to his congregation that the point of his preaching was "to inspire salutary terror instead of deceitful assurance [of salvation] that [would] seduce you."[90] In 1777 Abbé François-Valentin Mulot, a future revolutionary, began a sermon at the Hôtel-Dieu of Paris with the supplication, "Holy Spirit, deign to protect me at this time, spread your light upon me, and . . . give to my words the power of terror."[91] Like so many of his fellow ministers of the gospel, Mulot eagerly took up the challenge that Bossuet, in search of a new Elijah, had posed to preachers: "fill us with terror."[92]

It would be easy to extend this survey of terror as employed in eighteenth-century French sermons.[93] But at this point it should be clear that terror in prerevolutionary Catholic discourse was linked to divine majesty and justice, and that it was salutary—that is, conducive to the salvation of souls. It is impossible to know the precise effect of the sermons cited in this chapter on the people who heard them. But the fact that some priests had the reputation for particularly effective preaching and that published collections of their sermons proliferated in the eighteenth century suggests that many priests believed in the power to reach their auditors through rhetorical techniques that both provoked and celebrated terror. It would be simplistic, however, to assume that the only feeling congregants experienced upon hearing their preachers' jeremiads was terror. After all, terror itself was *salutary*, meaning that believers could simultaneously experience the terror of God's wrath and the reassurance that their very condition of terror would protect them from punishment. It is also possible that believers felt schadenfreude at the thought of malefactors and infidels enduring the torments of divine justice. And feelings of awe and respect at the majesty of a terrible Creator were likely present as well. As to the priests themselves, they clearly cultivated a terrified disposition in the face of their Creator, and the terrible words they spoke functioned much like the "emotives" that William Reddy has argued are capable of changing the emotional state of those who utter them.[94] To put it more simply, they whipped *themselves* up into a state of terror, the better to benefit from this pious attitude. All the while they participated in divine majesty by preaching the gospel and must have experienced great joy at this delegated power. Whatever the precise feelings of preachers and their congregants, though, Catholic terror speech undoubtedly lent positive characteristics to the word *terreur*.

SACRED TERROR AND THE ENLIGHTENMENT

One would expect the Enlightenment, famous in its opposition to the Catholic Church, to have eschewed calls for sacred, holy, or "salutary" terror in the face of the divine. And indeed this was usually the case, with *philosophes* criticizing the church for allegedly using terror to manipulate people and augment its power.[95] But there were also currents of Enlightenment thinking that showed respect for the idea of divine terror. Montesquieu, for example, saw religious terror as productive of morality. This might seem surprising coming from the *philosophe* who famously wrote in *De l'esprit des loix* that fear was the principle of despotism.[96] Still, in that very same work he described the positive effect of terror in Greek religion on public morality. "The first Greeks," he wrote, were "pirates on the sea, unjust on land, without regulation and without laws. The fine deeds of Hercules and Theseus," he added sarcastically, "show us the state in which this nascent people found itself." But "religion" emerged and gave the Greeks "horror of murder." It instilled the belief that the ghost of a murdered person "inspired in [the murderer] trouble and terror" and banished him from the community.[97]

The chevalier de Jaucourt, the most prolific of all contributors to the *Encyclopédie*, similarly believed in the social utility of religious terror, and like Montesquieu he cited history. In an article titled "Enfer" (Hell) he suggested that the idea of a place of postmortem punishment had been socially useful to the Romans. Citing Polybius, Jaucourt wrote: "'The greatest advantage,' this judicious historian says, 'that the Roman government had over all other states, is something that is normally decried: idolatry and superstition.'" In a society of wise people this would not have been necessary, "'but since the multitude is always agitated with illicit desires and violent passions, there was no surer way of suppressing them than this secret of fictions and of terrors.'" It was therefore "'prudently and wisely that the Romans inculcated in minds the cult of their gods and the fear of the punishments of Tartarus.'"[98] Jaucourt reproduced this paraphrase without comment, but it constituted the very end of the article and therefore gave Polybius the last word.

The republican political theorist Abbé de Mably similarly conveyed the message that religious terror could be socially useful. He presented the argument in an imagined conversation between a Swedish *philosophe* and an English milord in which the Swede, observing that many criminals escape human punishment, asked rhetorically, "How will citizens who experience the narrow limits of human wisdom be persuaded that the guilty do not escape punishment if they do not know that they are under the eyes of a Supreme Being who governs the world and whose justice rewards virtue and punishes crime?" The Swede added that "this doctrine . . . inspires salutary terror in the wicked."[99] His position was consistent with the deist affirmation of a just God who rewards virtue and punishes vice.[100]

In some cases Enlightenment writers affirmed the positive effect of religious terror on specific rulers. For example, when discussing the Merovingian Franks of the sixth century, Montesquieu wrote, "These princes were murderous, unjust and cruel. If Christianity seemed to soften them at times, this was only through the terrors that Christianity inspires in the guilty."[101] Of course, Montesquieu's claims are very qualified: Christianity only *seemed* to make sanguinary rulers milder, and only *at times*; thus, the author cast doubt on the very notion that it effectively restrained the Merovingians. But Montesquieu's assertion that Christianity strikes terror into "the guilty" is made without qualification and suggests that at least under certain circumstances, religious terror restrains princes. Similarly, in a eulogy to Bossuet delivered before the Académie Française in 1772, the encyclopedist Jean Le Rond d'Alembert recalled the utility of the bishop's *Discours sur l'Histoire Universelle* (1682). Written for the edification of Louis, the Grand Dauphin, Bossuet's book relied heavily on the Old Testament to prepare the young prince for his future as successor to the throne of Louis XIV. D'Alembert remarked that in this frightening book, designed to restrain the Bourbon scion from committing abuses later in life, "the threats of the afterlife, so terrible to tyrants, came to the assistance of the wise instructor to frighten his pupil usefully [*pour effrayer utilement son élève*]."[102]

At a much lower level of the Enlightenment, the Grub Street journalist Mathieu François Pidanzat de Mairobert made a similar point. He wrote in his best-selling *chronique scandaleuse* of Louis XV's mistress Madame du Barry, "The principal occupation of the favorite during this Lent [of 1773] and afterward must have been to destroy the impressions of terror that the preacher [Abbé de Beauvais] was spreading in the mind of the king. To this effect she had to have recourse to strange seductions, spectacles, *fêtes*."[103] Mairobert was hardly a defender of the clergy, but here he suggested that at least the terrors of hell had the potential to prevent the king from straying from his duties, and that one of the harmful effects of Madame du Barry had been precisely to disperse those terrors.

While utilitarian concerns were often behind Enlightenment endorsements of religious terror, in some cases "philosophical" writers embraced the sensation of sacred terror as a sign of the virtue of the person experiencing it or as an indication of the greatness of the divinity that provoked it. For example, in Jean Pechméja's 1784 novel *Télephe*, loosely based on Greek mythology, the eponymous hero confesses to a wise old priest of Jupiter (Sophosène) that he has accidentally killed an innocent man in the confusion of a battle and asks whether the gods will ever pardon him. Sophosène explains that remorse is a gift from the gods because it makes people do the right thing. Wicked people do not feel it, but Télephe should not envy them, since they do not experience happiness. "In speaking thus Sophosène was animated with all the fire of youth. His noble mien, his exalted and touching voice inspired in Télephe respect mixed with terror. He felt himself to be in the presence of a divinity."[104] Here the emotion of terror is not utilitarian. Télephe already regrets his crime, and Sophosène is comforting rather than threatening him. The protagonist's experience of terror is an augmentation of his respect for the holy man and, by extension, for the gods. Later in the novel Télephe is about to marry a woman he believes to be Caridée, the daughter of the man he accidentally killed, thus fulfilling a promise he made to his dying victim, but at the last minute his would-be bride reveals her true identity as Iphinoë, a queen who needs a strong husband to help her rule (and who also loves Télephe). "These words, pronounced in a low voice and from behind a veil, filled Télephe with terror. He was going to appear in the presence of the gods and deceive them after having been deceived himself."[105] Here terror is a sign of piety and hence virtue. When Télephe refuses to marry Iphinoë, she goes to the temple of Venus to pray for a change in his feelings. Though she had been deceitful, she was now pious, as Pechméja's description indicates: "She hardly dared to utter her wishes, to cast her eyes on the image of the divinity who filled her with terror."[106] Finally, after a series of plot twists that allows the marriage to take place after all, Télephe wants to solicit the help of the gods in governing, and a priest of Eleusis instructs him, "Yes, it is only here that men, prostrate before the Gods, are equal by the awareness of their insignificance. Before this plenitude of grandeur and power all those frivolous distinctions granted to the importunate demands of vanity and pride disappear. Here the unfortunate one is consoled because he is before the eyes of his protectors, and the powerful man becomes modest because he finds his masters here." The priest adds, "Pride needs terrible images to bring it to justice; and these images renew themselves ceaselessly in the temples."[107] The images in question are the sight of animal sacrifices, but the priest's point is that religiously induced terror promotes equality. Though this is arguably a utilitarian point insofar as equality leads to greater happiness, the claim suggests a more immediate belief in the value of humility in the face of divine terror.

Pechméja was an abolitionist who has also been described as a utopian socialist.[108] He was certainly an heir to radical Enlightenment ideology.[109] *Télephe* concludes with the new king taking office following an election, as the new legislator (Télephe himself) abolishes the practice of hereditary rule. Yet Pechméja did not dispense with the religious terror that had long supplied the reputed bulwark of social stability and public morality. To be sure, he located these ideas in the depiction of an ancient religion that he neither practiced nor expected his readers to practice. But his novel suggested that even a radically reformed society required feelings of terror for some higher power. Indeed, this feeling was positively constitutive of equality.

If Pechméja deployed the distant past to display a kind of unorthodox piety that was compatible with the Enlightenment, Louis-Sébastien Mercier endorsed religious terror in a tale about the distant future. In his futuristic/utopian novel *The Year 2440*—which Robert Darnton ranks as the number 1 "forbidden best-seller" of prerevolutionary France—Mercier writes from the perspective of an eighteenth-century Frenchman who has fallen into a centuries-long sleep and awakes in a society that has solved its problems.[110] Among these is religious dogmatism. The narrator describes his visit to a deist temple, a magnificent building with a dome of "transparent windows" through which one could see thunderstorms revealing "how fearsome [*redoutable*] this God is when offended." He describes his reaction to seeing the worshippers at prayers:

> Everyone was struck with a religious and profound respect; many were prostrate, their faces against the floor. In the midst of this silence, of this universal respect, I was seized with sacred terror: it seemed as if the divinity had descended into the temple and filled it with his invisible presence . . . in these moments of adoration silence was so religiously observed that the sanctity of the place, combined with the idea of the supreme being, brought to everyone's heart a profound and salutary impression.[111]

The proximity of the words "terror" and "salutary" here is telling. Even in a utopian writer who criticized virtually every aspect of his own society, including its religious beliefs and practices, the notion of a terrible God was self-evident and the Augustinian idea of salutary terror persisted.

CONCLUSIONS

The appeal of the word "terror" for the revolutionaries derived in part from the theological meanings it had accrued over centuries. As an emotion, terror was the proper condition of humanity in the face of the divine, and it was salutary in the literal sense of promoting salvation. As the source or cause of that emotion, terror (or terribleness) was an attribute of God and a sign of his sovereign power, glory, righteousness, and majesty. To be sure, there were significant tensions, even contradictions, between the conceptions of terror outlined in this chapter and the stated goals of revolutionaries. In particular, the revolutionaries who called for terror "as the order of the day" claimed that only traitors, enemies of the nation, and "the wicked" need experience this emotion and that patriots had nothing to fear, whereas in the Judeo-Christian tradition terror in the face of judgment and punishment was typically required of all people, and indeed all the more expected in the virtuous (who were known as "God-fearing") than in the wicked. Moreover, if religious terror was traditionally salutary in the sense that it assured the salvation of those who felt it, for the revolutionaries the connection between *terreur* and *salut* was looser. Though revolutionaries sometimes envisaged terror as a means of converting lukewarm citizens to the right cause, they often had neither the intention nor the desire to save their adversaries. Rather, they sought the *salut* of the nation, which meant that of those who were already good citizens. Still, I am not arguing for continuities of or consistency in doctrines, or for a coherent religious idea of terror that served as a template during the Revolution. I am arguing for mental associations that made the word *terreur* look, sound, and feel a certain way.

To what degree were revolutionaries familiar with the kinds of texts examined in this chapter? Timothy Tackett has shown that "at least two-thirds" of the Third Estate deputies in the National Assembly "had probably received training in the law," which meant that they had "completed the full cycle of secondary education."[112] In other words, they were among the roughly seventy thousand graduates of the 570 *collèges* that had been run and staffed by Oratorians, Doctrinaires, or (prior to 1761) Jesuits. At these *collèges*, the historian of education Maurice Gontard has observed, "sacred history always occupied a special place" in the curriculum.[113] If the pupils had paid attention in class, they would even have understood the Vulgate, as several years of instruction were devoted to Latin.[114] Many more revolutionaries, deputies or otherwise, would have attended church in their childhood and youth, where they would have heard references to the Bible and the fulminations of priests seeking to instill in them the salutary terror of God. Even those revolutionaries who were or became religious skeptics would have been tempted to appropriate theologically tinged language as they assumed the position of God and sought to remake humanity in their own image. And as for Claude Royer himself, it is worth noting that he was also known as Abbé Royer.[115] When he thundered, "Make terror the order of the day," this priest-turned-revolutionary could not have been immune to the emotional connotations furnished by centuries of religious terror speech.

CHAPTER TWO

The Terror of Their Enemies:
Kings and Nations

INTRODUCTION

Just as descriptions of divine power and majesty made liberal use of the word *terreur*, those who wrote of worldly power also drew on the term. This should not be surprising, as monarchs of the early modern period modeled themselves on God as a means of securing legitimacy. Bishop Bossuet, whom we saw in the previous chapter calling for a new Elijah to imprint human beings with a salutary terror of God, described princes as "gods" whose absolute authority to rule was derived from God's ultimate authority. In a posthumously published book of advice to his pupil the dauphin, he paraphrased the advice that Gregory of Nazianzus, archbishop of Constantinople, gave to emperors in the fourth century: "Therefore be gods to your subjects. That is to say, govern them as God governs, in a manner that is noble, disinterested, benevolent, in a word, divine."[1] Of course, as we saw in chapter 1, a key component of God's governance was terror.

Supporters of absolutism *à la Bossuet* accordingly lauded their rulers for striking terror in their common enemies and frequently called them "the terror" of their enemies, or of their neighbors, or of the whole world. This was a particularly effective way of likening the monarch to the divine source of monarchical power, and it served as a kind of shorthand for praising the ruler's military might, decisiveness, courage, and effectiveness. It could also apply to commanders, military forces (armies and navies), and social classes, who were also acclaimed for instilling terror in, or for being the terror of, their enemies. Finally, insofar as sovereignty came to be seen as an attribute of nations rather than princes, those nations too could be the terror of enemy nations. In this way they also acquired the charisma previously reserved for monarchs.

French dictionaries of the Old Regime reveal the habit of pairing "terror" with rulers who instilled the emotion in others or embodied the quality of terribleness. In 1690 Antoine Furetière, author of the *Dictionnaire universel*, began his definition of *terreur* as "Great fright [*effroy*], passion of the soul caused by the presence of a frightful [*affreux*], horrible [*épouvantable*] object." Yet he immediately gave as an example the sentence, "The great conquerors gained provinces by the simple *terror* of their name, of their arms."[2] The Académie Française, Furetière's competitor and the institution that expelled him for publishing a French dictionary on his own, provided a similar definition of *terreur*. Its entry in the 1694 dictionary begins, "Horror [*Espouvante*], great fear [*crainte*], violent agitation of the soul caused by the image of a present ill or a coming danger." This definition is immediately followed by examples revealing the relationship between the emotion and the great leaders who instilled it: "*Cast terror among one's enemies; spread terror wherever one passes. Fill with terror. He carried terror everywhere.* It is said of a great prince, or of a conqueror, that *he fills everyone with the terror of his name*, to say that his name inspires terror everywhere."[3] The fourth edition of the dictionary, published in 1762, added new examples testifying to the word's meaning as an attribute of rulership: "When speaking of a great captain, one says that *he is the terror of his enemies*. And of a severe judge, that *he is the terror of scoundrels*."[4] As we shall see in chapters 7 and 8, the proximity between the captain and the judge in the academicians' thinking is strikingly similar to the associations revolutionaries would make between military terror and the terror of punishment. Moreover, this pairing of the brave commander and the just magistrate reinforces the sense of terror as a legitimizing attribute. Whoever could instill terror appeared to be rightfully powerful.

Other dictionaries similarly linked terror and rulership. The *Grand vocabulaire françois* (1767–74), published by the celebrated printer Charles-Joseph Panckoucke, defined terror as an "emotion caused in the soul by the image of an imminent evil or peril, horror, great fear," and then gave as its first example, "He spread terror among them." The entry went on to explain, "When speaking of a conqueror, one says that *he fills everyone with the terror of his name*, to say that his name imprints terror everywhere." The *Grand vocabulaire* then plagiarized the Academy dictionary of 1762, writing, "When speaking of a great captain, one says that *he is the terror of his enemies*. And of a severe judge, that *he is the terror of scoundrels*."[5] Finally, shortly before the Revolution Jean-François Féraud's *Dictionaire critique de la langue française* (1787–88) included in the definition for *terreur* these examples of usage: "He filled everyone with the terror of his name: His name alone imprinted *terror*." Though Féraud did not say that a ruler or commander who instilled terror was necessarily right to do so, it is significant that the examples cited above came immediately after this quotation from the poet Jean-Baptiste Rousseau: "To punish the wicked your faithful anger / Has death and terror / March before it."[6] Rousseau's lines came from a poem based on Psalm 75 and recalled God's punishment of the wicked. In this context the subsequent reference to rulers instilling terror was not merely descriptive but morally charged. The implication was that rulers who spread terror were imitating God.

KINGS AND COMMANDERS
AS THE TERROR OF THEIR ENEMIES

Of course, dictionary definitions alone are not sufficient.[7] It is necessary to examine many additional sources to determine how any given word was used. A close look at other documents confirms that the dictionaries were accurately reporting habits of usage. In particular, writers repeatedly praised French kings by describing them as the terror of their enemies. This was not merely flattery. Kings were expected to be terrible. It was part of their job description. The coronation ceremony in France itself included a prayer that the king's sword might "be . . . the terror and dread of foreigners and plotters."[8] Jean Bodin, the sixteenth-century jurist and theorist of absolutism, confirmed this obligation when writing that "a great king" must be "terrible to his enemies, courteous to honest people, frightful [*effroyable*] to the wicked, and just towards all."[9] Thus terror and justice went together.

In the century prior to the Revolution, a wide variety of texts likewise linked the terribleness of French kings, from Clovis to Louis XVI, to their effectiveness and justice. Thus the poet Le Jeune characterized Clovis as the "terror of crime."[10] The encyclopedist Louis de Cahusac likewise referred to "Clovis, who filled Europe with the sound of his conquests and the terror of his name."[11] Pierre Laureau wrote glowingly of him, "This prince, born to overthrow empires and to destroy the most formidable powers, who, like the thunderbolt, struck down everything he encountered, was the terror of his century, the fright [*l'effroi*] of the nations and the conqueror of his kingdom."[12]

The Carolingians followed suit, according to numerous eighteenth-century writers. Henri de Boulainvilliers noted that kings and ambassadors from "the most distant nations" observed Charlemagne's annual convocation of his nobles, and he wrote that from these "spectacles" they "brought back an idea of terror and veneration . . . which today is preserved in the

Orient."[13] Another historian, Gabriel Daniel, praised Charlemagne for having "carried the terror of his arms beyond the Alps" and wrote that in the year 788 "the terror of his name spread beyond the farthest reaches of Germany."[14] Both Boulainvilliers and Gabriel wrote early in the eighteenth century, but Charlemagne's reputation was the same in the 1780s, when the historian Gabriel-Henri Gaillard wrote, "Charlemagne was preceded everywhere by the terror of his name."[15]

Louis IX, or Saint Louis, received similar plaudits. For the festival of Saint Louis on August 25, 1681, the celebrated preacher Esprit Fléchier delivered a panegyric in honor of the saintly monarch in which he recalled the battle of Taillebourg between the king and his rebellious brother, the count of Poitiers, in 1242: "It was then that, assisted by the help of heaven and more concerned with the justice of his cause than with his own interests, carrying terror into the foreign lands and troops, he showed that true piety is not in contradiction with true valor." This sermon was reprinted numerous times during the eighteenth century.[16] Likewise, at the beginning of the eighteenth century Archbishop Fénelon instructed the duc de Bourgogne (the heir to the French throne) to imitate the crusading king, "the delight of the good, and the terror of the bad."[17] A hymnal issued by the archbishop of Paris in 1745 included a hymn, to be sung on August 25, in which the faithful recalled the "severe zealot of justice" who was "the delight of his peoples and the terror of his enemies."[18] In a pastoral letter on the occasion of the death of the dauphin in 1766, the archbishop thought it fitting to remind the faithful that the blood of Saint Louis stilled flowed in the dauphin's children, and he prayed, "May his name be always the delight of the nation and *the terror of its enemies*."[19] As late as 1786 the court preacher Abbé Joubert recalled how the Crusader king "brought terror into the camp of the Saracens."[20]

Early modern French kings were also acclaimed as the terror of their enemies. Charles VIII was "this great prince, who had been the terror of Italy and the admiration of all of Europe at the age of seventeen," according to Dreux du Radier, a historian who was more critical of his own king, Louis XV, and ended up in exile for seditious comments about him.[21] The chevalier d'Eon wrote of the same king's progress in the Italian wars, "Terror marched before him."[22] The priest and historian Augustin Simon Irailh concurred: "Charles VIII crossed the Alps, cast terror into all of Italy, was crowned emperor of the Orient at Rome, just as Charlemagne had been [crowned emperor] of the Occident, flew rapidly to Naples, entered equally as the conqueror of that city, and made Bajazet II tremble on the sultan's throne."[23]

The beloved Henri IV received enthusiastic praise for his alleged ability to inspire terror. On the occasion of the birth of the duc de Bourgogne in 1682, a poet (an anonymous "lady") held out high hopes for the Bourbon scion, whom she expected to prove "Worthy of the scepter of the French: / Numerous Louis, a Charlemagne, / A Henry terror of Spain."[24] In 1750 the lawyer and publicist of causes célèbres Gayot de Pitaval recalled the "horrible assassination that removed from his kingdom Henry IV, who was its delight, and the terror of his enemies."[25] The memory of Henri IV as terrible even found its way into the libelous books that sullied the reputation of Louis XV. In one such *libelle*, a fictitious spy overhears the royal mistress Madame de Pompadour berate the king by comparing him unfavorably with his ancestors. Beginning with Henri IV, the first of the Bourbons, she says, "Like you, he loved women to excess, he was their dupe, as you are, but he compensated for his faults with so many brilliant qualities that they [his faults] were all forgotten." She adds, "He was frank, humane, affable, popular, he was the terror of his enemies and the father of his people."[26] The figure of Madame de Pompadour is not sympathetic in this depiction, but her assessment of Henri IV was expected to be shared by readers.

The king most frequently associated with the word *terreur* was Louis XIV. Both in his own day and after his death he was praised for the terror he instilled in his (and France's) enemies. This is a testament to the success of what Peter Burke has called the "department of glory," or those productive flatterers hired by the Sun King to sing his praises, but it is significant for our purposes that he was flattered precisely by being called a terror.[27] Madame de Montpensier, who had fought against Louis XIV (or, rather, against the Regency of his mother) during the Fronde, came back to his side and in 1658 praised him as "the love of his peoples, the veneration of all the court, and the terror of his enemies."[28] On his visit to Orléans following his marriage to Marie-Thérèse in 1660, the king was addressed as "the delight of the human race, the admiration of all the peoples, the love of your subjects, the terror of your enemies, and the savior of France."[29] In 1665 the French clergy remonstrated with the king, urging him to impose and enforce "very vigorous penalties" on those Catholics who converted to Protestantism in order to marry Protestants, and as part of their effort to flatter him they called him "the love of your people, the terror of your enemies, the glory of sovereigns and the happiness of your century."[30] Georges d'Aubusson de La Feuillade, the archbishop of Metz, harangued Louis XIV upon the king's visit to that city in 1673, calling him "the love and delight of your subjects, the hope of your allies, the terror of your enemies, and the admiration of all the world."[31]

Other subjects, famous and obscure, took advantage of a variety of occasions to glorify their king as terrible to his enemies. In a eulogy for the Sun King's wife in 1682, Bishop Bossuet used the occasion to observe that "French bravery carries terror everywhere with the name of Louis."[32] Following the king's recuperation from illness in 1687, Jean-Barbier d'Aucour, a member of the Académie Française, made a speech in which he recalled the recent revocation of the Edict of Nantes, by which the king became "the victor over the heresy" of Protestantism. D'Aucour added that "the very idea of this victory casts terror into the souls of his enemies."[33] In an ode written to Louis XIV in 1687 on the subject of his support of nobles' education, Antoinette Deshoulières did not fail to laud the monarch for "spreading terror from the Ganges to the ice floes."[34] In the dedication to a 1693 compendium of peace treaties that France had concluded over the previous three centuries, Frédéric Léonard, First Printer to the king, praised his sovereign as "the terror of your enemies, and the delight of your people."[35] One finds such acclamation in the most unlikely places, as in the 1694 book by the obstetrician François Mauriceau, who, after reporting on the remarkable fecundity of a woman who had been infertile for fifteen years, observed that it had also taken Anne of Austria many years to have her child: Louis XIV, "the love of his peoples, and the terror of his enemies."[36]

Following his death Louis XIV continued to enjoy the reputation of having been a terror to his enemies. In a eulogy on December 6, 1715, Abbé Lafargue listed the deceased king's qualities: "the admiration of his century, the honor of the world, and the terror of his enemies." He went on to call Louis "the support of justice, the scourge of heresy, the protector of religion," placing the quality of "terror" in good company according to the standards of the day.[37] A poem recited at the dedication of the equestrian statue at the Place Vendôme in Paris the following year interpreted the mounted king thus:

From the height of his horse, this monarch, so just,
Dazzling with majesty shows his brow august.
He seems still to burn with that noble ardor
That he showed when the Rhine was seized with terror.[38]

At his inaugural discourse upon entry into the Académie Française in 1728, Abbé de Rothlin recalled the Sun King, who had been "born to be the love of his people and the terror of his enemies."[39] When Voltaire wrote his *Siècle de Louis XIV* (1751), he celebrated the most victorious years of the reign (in the 1670s) as a time when the king was "the terror of Europe" and France was a "happy nation."[40] When a merchant guild opposed a reduction in the production of certain goods during the Seven Years' War, its spokesmen pointedly argued to Louis XV that "there were no fewer manufactures . . . when your august predecessor, Sire, supported those corps of formidable troops that made him the terror of his enemies."[41] In his overview of French history "from Clovis to Louis XV," published in 1770 and republished in 1773, Abbé Claude François Xavier Millot contrasted Louis XIV's treatment of foreigners to that meted out to his own people, writing, "If Louis inspired terror in foreigners, he worked without respite to make the [French] kingdom more flourishing."[42]

The Bourbon successors to Louis XIV also bore the title of "terror." Even the regent, the duc d'Orléans, who ruled after the death of Louis XIV and during the minority of Louis XV, was flattered by a petitioner who wished to abolish the salt tax: "During the peace, this famous hero will end with humanity what he began with valor during the war [of the Spanish Succession], and in him alone will be seen in one person the terror and the delight of the human race."[43] Louis XV, despite the bad press he received from the *libelles* that Robert Darnton has shown to have been damaging to his reputation, nevertheless was called "the terror of his enemies" by those who approved of him or at least wished to flatter him. He was so honored while still a little boy. At Louis XIV's funeral Abbé Edmé Mongin predicted for the five-year-old heir to the throne: "LOUIS, royal child, your reign will be long and glorious: you are destined to be the defender of the religion of your fathers; the protector of kings, the terror of your enemies."[44]

As a reigning king Louis XV frequently enjoyed similar acclamation. In a "dialogue between the century of Louis XIV and the century of Louis XV," published in 1751, the latter century praises its king, asking rhetorically, "Who in effect was more deserving of the honors of Parnassus than LOUIS LE BIEN-AIMÉ[?] Is he not the terror of his enemies, the love of his subjects, the soul and the ornament of his century?"[45] In 1754 Abbé Pierre Barral, a political theorist who supported the *parlements* in their struggles with the monarchy, nevertheless wrote of Louis XV, "He is the admiration of his enemies, as he is their terror."[46]

The *parlementaires* themselves deployed the language of monarchical terror, as a compliment, when arguing for the augmentation of their own power. On August 4, 1756, shortly after the outbreak of the Seven Years' War, the Parlement of Paris wrote to the king: "already the terror of your name is causing the most impregnable fortresses to tremble; soon the proud usurpers of the sea [the British], succumbing under the efforts of your victorious troops, will humble themselves before you." This flattery took place in the context of the Parlement's protest against a series of Orders in Council that had tried to rein in the magistrates' recalcitrance in the face of new taxes. But it reveals that one rhetorical strategy for sweetening bitter words was to refer to the terror of the interlocutor's name. Elsewhere in the same remonstrance the Parlement compared its own duty to the defense of the kingdom, writing: "The magistrates are no less necessary than those other supports of the throne, those other faithful subjects who shed their blood for the defense of the state and for the glory of the monarch. While these intrepid warriors are carrying abroad the terror of his arms . . . the interior of the kingdom would be delivered over to disorder and confusion if the magistrates did not maintain everywhere . . . the empire of the laws."[47]

There were other testaments to the king's terribleness during and after his lifetime. For example, Abbé de l'Attaignant wrote a poem that included this acclamation: "*Vive le Bien-Aimé* LOUIS! / The terror of his enemies, / The father of his subjects."[48] Similarly, the comte Du Buat, the French ambassador to Saxony, reported after the king's death that "the terror of his name filled all [foreign] councils."[49]

Louis XVI began his reign amid hopes and prayers that he, like his Bourbon predecessors, would instill terror in France's enemies. He received a traditional coronation at the Cathedral of Reims on June 11, 1775. At this ceremony the Archbishop blessed the sword of Charlemagne, which the king inherited. Although the benediction was in Latin, a bilingual pamphlet was printed for the occasion, thus making the meaning of the blessing available to those who did not read Latin as well as to those who were not present at Reims. In the Latin formula the archbishop prayed for the king's sword to be "the terror and dread [*terror & formido*] of foreigners and plotters," and in a printed French translation the archbishop asked God to make the sword "inspire fear and terror in anyone who will dare set traps for our king."[50] The ceremony continued with the king receiving the sword while the archbishop prayed that he be "*inimicis . . . terribilis*," or "terrible to his enemies." According to the French translation, he prayed, "May the force of his royal power make him the terror of his enemies."[51] Later in the ceremony the archbishop prayed, "May he bring terror to the infidels with his power," which the French version rendered, "May his power inspire terror in the infidels."[52] At Châlons-sur-Marne a curé named Dortu celebrated the coronation by assuring his congregation that Louis XVI would be "the shield of your subjects, the terror of your enemies, the admiration of all your neighbors."[53] Elsewhere an adoring subject named Henri Boniface marked the occasion with a poem in which he wrote of the new king:

He has two arrows: one that he darts at us,
Which burns love into our heart;
The other that he keeps for his enemies
And which fills them with terror.[54]

I have no post-coronation references to Louis XVI as a terror. In this respect the last eighteenth-century Bourbon monarch stands in stark contrast
to Louis XIV and even to Louis XV. The brevity of his reign could account in
part for this difference, though it does not fully explain it. It is also possible
that the shortage of affirmations of the king's terribleness is itself a gauge of
the declining respect that subjects felt for Louis XVI, for, as we have seen,
terror and respect were closely related.

It was not only French rulers who received praise from French writers
for being terrible. In his *Histoire de Dannemarc*, Paul Henri Mallet praised
Charles X of Sweden for "his passion, his talent for war, his activity . . . the
respect and the terror that he had inspired within and without his states."[55]
Referring to the same king's campaign in Poland in 1655, Abbé Mably wrote,
"Never had progress been so rapid; everything bent under the initial blows
of Charles; terror went before him, his enemies fled, their arms fell into his
hands."[56] Charles XII of Sweden enjoyed similar acclaim. Voltaire wrote of
that king's battle against the forces of the Russian tsar and the Danish and
Polish kings in 1700: "King Charles [XII], at the age of sixteen, vanquished
all three. He was the terror of the north and was already esteemed a great
man at an age when others have not even finished their education."[57] In his
Histoire de Charles XII Voltaire referred eight times to the terror of the Swedish king's arms or name, all with positive connotations.[58] Mably followed suit,
calling Charles a "hero" and writing of the aftermath of the battle of Nerva
(1700): "Terror preceded Charles in Poland; it chased Augustus [king of Po-
land] and gave the crown to Stanislas," the Swedish-supported candidate.[59]

Frederick the Great also had the reputation of being the terror of his enemies. Voltaire wrote to the Prussian king in 1742, in the midst of the War
of the Austrian Succession (in which Prussia and France were allies), "I
worry about humanity, Sire, before I worry about you; yet after having wept
with the [pacifist] abbé de Saint-Pierre for the human race, of which you
have become the terror, I give myself over to all the joy that your glory gives
me."[60] In his subsequent history of the War of the Austrian Succession, Voltaire described Frederick as a "useful" ally for France because he "was the
terror of the Austrians."[61] Shortly after Frederick's death, the French historian Pierre Laureau wrote a "panegyric" containing these words of praise:
"He braved death on the battlefield and at the approach of citadels, and

was in his armies a model of bravery and firmness. Presenting a menacing brow, ready to charge at the first sound of the trumpet, he let his subjects rest in the protection of his arms, and his enemies were restrained by their terror."[62]

Just as monarchs held the title of terror of their enemies or neighbors, their generals and admirals enjoyed the same distinction in deputized form. Eighteenth-century writers judged military leaders past and present in large measure on their ability to inspire terror. One particularly striking example of this tendency comes from a sixty-seven-volume work of French history—the *Collection universelle* (1785–90)—edited by Alexandre-Claude Bellier-Duchesnay. Two volumes deal specifically with the fourteenth-century French soldier Bertrand du Guesclin, "the terror of the English and the Spaniards, and the preserver of the crown of France."[63] "His name alone," the reader learns, was "the terror of the English and the Navarrese."[64] Bertrand was a man "who had made himself the terror of all Europe through the memorable expeditions he had launched, and whose name alone was so redoubtable that it cast fright [*frayeur*] and fear [*crainte*] into the minds of his enemies."[65] In Spain people could not even pronounce his name without trembling.[66] After one battle that Bertrand won, "the whole countryside was frightful to see, being covered with heads, arms, overturned helmets, all bloodied, and broken swords. This pitiable scene gave such terror to the English that they hardly fought anymore."[67]

Eighteenth-century French writers also praised contemporary commanders for instilling terror in the enemy. The 1747 edition of the memoirs of the fifteenth-century French diplomat Philippe de Commynes is dedicated to the maréchal de Saxe, "the hero of our day . . . the terror of the Austrian."[68] Another marshal, de Richelieu, was praised in verse in 1784 for being the "terror of the Englishman."[69] The marquis de Bussy, the commander in charge of the land forces east of the Cape of Good Hope, was known for "the terror that his name inspired in enemies" during the campaign against the British in India in 1783.[70] Likewise, a pro-American abbé celebrated the arrival of the comte de Rochambeau in Rhode Island in 1781 for the terror that he inspired in British forces and loyalist colonists.[71]

EXCURSUS ON MILITARY TERROR

The association of sovereign powers and their commanders with terror stemmed in large measure from their role in the prosecution of war, and as writers in the seventeenth and eighteenth centuries attempted to describe (and prescribe) the conduct of war, whether based on their own experiences or in light of general principles, they typically endorsed military terror as a legitimate aim. The German legal theorist Samuel Pufendorf wrote in 1682, "Although force and terror [*vis et terror*] are the most proper way of acting in war, nonetheless it is permitted to employ trickery and sleight of hand, as long as honor is not impugned."[72] What precisely he meant by maintaining honor while setting traps for the enemy need not concern us. The important point is that for Pufendorf it was subterfuge that needed justifying; terror went without saying. Significantly, the author began his sentence with the word "although" (*etsi*), indicating that he expected his readers to take terror, like force itself, for granted. A French translation of 1740 likewise made it clear that for Pufendorf "terror and overt force are the proper character of war."[73] A generation later Leibniz was even more explicit in his endorsement of terror, going so far as to justify the custom of "destroying entire cities and running the inhabitants through with swords in order to excite terror in others," as this practice could "shorten a great war or rebellion," thus "sparing blood by spilling it."[74]

Experienced practitioners of war confirmed the theoretical pronouncements of Pufendorf and Leibniz. The marquis de Feuquière, a veteran of Louis XIV's wars, encouraged commanders to camp in places that were amenable to quickly sending "large detachments to reduce by the terror of arms the extremities of the country."[75] Gathering troops in large, visible musters was another means of "inspiring terror in the enemy."[76] Once terrified, Feuquière wrote, entire garrison towns could be taken and their inhabitants held as prisoners. Thus Louis XIV "made use of the terror of the people" and took twenty thousand prisoners during the Dutch campaign of 1672.[77] Feuquière was instrumental in the notoriously brutal subjugation of the Palatinate in 1688, where he claimed to have seized an infantry captain who was "stupid enough" to approach him without first asking for his word of honor—as in Pufendorf's maxim, a ruse is permitted when it does not damage one's honor—and when news spread of the capture, "terror" similarly spread among the people of the region.[78] When quartering for the winter in a subject town or city in which the population was reluctant to provide sufficient contributions, commanders were advised to spread terror by "kidnapping some important persons in the area or burning a large residence."[79] Finally, nothing spread terror like surprising an army at night and "tormenting" it with artillery.[80] In the preface to a later edition of the marquis's memoirs, his brother could think of no greater tribute than to write that for thirty-five years "he spread terror everywhere."[81]

The comte de Guibert, though he penned his thoughts on tactics after Feuquière, is better known to students of European military history. His proposed reforms in the French army in the wake of its defeat by Prussia during the Seven Years' War (1756–63) ushered in a more modern, rationalized force, which in turn made possible the revolutionary and Napoleonic armies.[82] Yet Guibert did not shy away from advocating the very traditional goal of inspiring terror in the enemy. He praised the motley Austrian army, the product of many provincial militias, because it "recalls to the imagination those proud soldiers of Dacia and Panonia, their ancestors, who were long the terror . . . of the Roman Empire."[83] He admired Gustavus Adolphus, who together with his army at the time of the Thirty Years' War (1618–48) constituted "the terror of the Empire."[84] And he recalled with patriotic pride the maréchal de Catinat, who had won Strasbourg for France by using a devastating combination of "bribery and terror."[85]

THE NATION AS THE TERROR OF ITS ENEMIES

Terror or terribleness was not only an attribute of monarchs and their commanders. It also characterized nations. It should not be surprising that insofar as the "nation" came to be seen as sovereign, it took on the traditional characteristics of princely sovereigns, including that of being terrible to enemies. Yet even in texts that were far from being republican, nations (including the French) are described as carrying terror to their enemies.

One readily available model for the terrible nation was Rome. In discussing the Romans, Abbé Mably wrote that with their "civic virtues, political virtues, love of glory, love of the fatherland, austere and wise discipline" they "could inspire terror in their enemies."[86] Yet other ancient nations received praise for their ability to incite terror. For example, the French translation of Girolamo Belloni's Latin treatise De commercio (On commerce) reported that through trade the Carthaginians "became the terror of the Romans."[87] The Gauls, seen as ancestors to the French, presented a model of terror through different means. Pierre Laureau wrote, "This victorious people inspired such terror, despite the small number of its army which did not exceed twenty-five thousand men, that it made almost all the nations between Mount Taurus and the sea into tributaries." Elsewhere Laureau called the Celts "the terror of [their] enemies" and "the terror of our hemisphere."[88]

More modern polities, whether conceived of as states, nations, or peoples, were also regarded as terrible. Many authors attributed such terror-inducing power to commercial and naval might. The French bishop and academician Pierre-Daniel Huet wrote that the English navy during the reign of Queen Elizabeth had been "the terror of the ocean," and in this

way he alerted his readers to the importance of the French navy.[89] Jacques
Savary des Brûlons, whose *Dictionnaire universel de commerce* appeared in
1723, also saw British sea power as decisive to the terror the nation could
incite in others, though he stressed commerce as a means of buttressing this
power. He wrote that "it is by foreign commerce that England has become
the support of her friends and the terror of her enemies."[90] In 1756 (the year
in which the Seven Years' War broke out) Abbé Coyer, an economist who
encouraged the nobility to become involved in commerce, made a similar argument about the role of maritime trade for the acquisition of naval
power: "Let us never forget that it is commerce that forms the navy; that we
would not have any armed fleets if we had not begun with merchant fleets;
and that the Romans conquered in fifty years since they had vessels what
they had not conquered in three hundred. Land armies only carry terror to
a single place. The sea unites power with speed, it surrounds the land and
forces it to submit."[91] Of course, Coyer's observations were not strictly academic. The *abbé* wished for France to be the terror of its enemies and was
providing a plan for that goal.

By contrast, for the chevalier d'Arcq the means of acquiring this status
was to keep the nobles in the military, where he believed they belonged.
D'Arcq opposed Coyer's scheme of enlisting the nobility in commerce because he worried that putting nobles in proximity with vulgar sailors would
degrade their sense of honor, but he justified his concern by pointing out
that the nobles were "a people constantly bellicose since its origin, . . . a
people whose armies were almost always followed by victory and preceded
by terror."[92] In another work, d'Arcq expressed his desire that the nobles
"become the model for other nations and that France be the terror and the
support of her neighbors."[93] Both Coyer and d'Arcq wanted the same thing:
terrible nobles in the service of their state. They simply disagreed on the
best way of assuring the requisite terror.

Other writers similarly used the word "terror" when reflecting on the
most effective means of strengthening the nation. For example, in 1766
Abbé Pierre Jaubert published a book in praise of *la roture*, or the commoners. Whereas the chevalier d'Arcq had sniffed at the prospect of nobles associating with common sailors, Jaubert turned this received wisdom on its
head: "What great men the class of commoners has furnished in the navy!
Avengers, or defenders of their fatherland, how many times have they been
seen carrying terror into the midst of the proudest and bravest enemies?"[94]
Another publication appearing in the same year linked terror and the French
nation more directly, without the intermediary of a specific social class. In
a remarkable poem published by Alexis Piron six months after the death

of the dauphin, the prince addresses the French from beyond the grave. He tells them that he has spoken with God, who assures him that the French are his "chosen people" and that their country will be "a second paradise on earth." God warns that "the demon of envy, trembling with rage"—a clear allusion to Britain—"will vomit his dark legions onto your coasts." But God goes on to promise:

> Their courage will dissipate in smoke:
> You will fight under me, the God of armies,
> Immediately I shall bring down terror
> And have the exterminating angel march before you.[95]

The sacralization of the French nation could not have been any clearer. France was now Israel, chosen by God from among the nations, and its enemies were as justifiably the objects of terror as the enemies of the biblical Israelites had been.

One common expression that linked conceptions of terror with an understanding of Frenchness was *la terreur du nom François*, or "the terror of the name Frenchman." (I have chosen not to translate this as "the terror of the French name" because "François" was usually capitalized.) The phrase was particularly popular in works of history. For example, in 1772 the historian Claude-Louis-Michel de Sacy wrote that during the reign of Charlemagne "the name Frenchman [had] become the terror of Europe and Africa."[96] Similarly, in their thirty-volume history of France, published between 1755 and 1786, Paul François Velly, Claude Villaret, and Jean-Jacques Garnier wrote that the armies of Charles V "brought to diverse places the terror of the name Frenchman."[97] In one historical dictionary the editors described the conquests of Charles VIII in Italy in 1494 and 1495: "The terror of the name Frenchman opened the gates of Capua and Naples to him."[98] When trying to explain the failure of the Neapolitan king to repulse the French in 1495, the historian Charles Jean François Hénault also had recourse to that figure of speech, explaining that "the terror of the name Frenchman was too great" for Ferdinand to be able to mount a successful defense."[99] Describing an episode from the year 1504, during the reign of Louis XII, Sacy wrote of the French king's support of Pope Julius II in the latter's fight against the rulers of Perugia and Bologna: "as soon as these lords . . . saw the French flags, they threw down their arms at the feet of the Holy Father, who entered into these cities with all the pomp of a conqueror. The terror of the name Frenchman did more than the army of Julius and his warriors."[100]

The expression *la terreur du nom François*, or some variant thereof, appears in other sources as well. In a multivolume history of the church, Abbé Antoine-Henri de Bérault-Bercastel attributed "the terror of the name Frenchman" to the Moors who fought the Gauls in Spain during the eighth century.[101] In a book called *Le militaire chrétien* (1779) Abbé de Maugré asked, "How many of our annals remind us of the illustrious heroes, the glory of the name Frenchman, the terror of our enemies, the soul of our armies, whose Christian virtues illustrated [their] military talents?"[102] Even a letter from a French Jesuit missionary in Libya to his superior revealed the popularity of the expression *la terreur du nom François*. The missionary was describing a caravan voyage in an area infested with bandits. He wrote, "These brigands greatly fear firearms, and [they fear] even more the French without arms than they do the Turks with arms," adding, "This is very glorious to our nation, and from it one can judge the extent to which the terror of the name Frenchman has spread."[103]

TERROR IN NARRATIVES OF DECLINE

The tendency to view terror as a sign of valor, virtue, or legitimacy was so strong that statements about the decadence or decline of powers often contrasted their current state of weakness with a prior age when they inspired terror. In some cases an individual suffered from such a loss in prestige. Thus the disgruntled courtier and memorialist, the duc de Saint-Simon, writing toward the middle of the eighteenth century but reporting events that had taken place during the reign of Louis XIV, described "the Grand Condé," the aristocrat who had led the Fronde rebellion during the Sun King's minority, as *autrefois la terreur de ce règne*. The word *autrefois*, meaning "once" but conveying the sense of "once upon a time," emphasized the fact that this condition no longer obtained. Saint-Simon completed his description by noting that this former terror had been "trembling before his ministers [of state], since his return" following the Peace of the Pyrenees in 1659.[104]

In other cases, writers signaled the decline of states or nations by underscoring the terror they had once exhibited. For example, Abbé Raynal contrasted Spanish naval power in the age of Philip II with the situation at the end of the eighteenth century. Of "this armada which was so formidable" he wrote, "But what spread terror and admiration two centuries ago would serve as a joke today."[105] The pairing of "terror" and "admiration" speaks volumes about the meaning of terror in political writing. Raynal cast claims of British decline in similar terms of lost terror. In 1748 he reported that at the beginning of Queen Anne's reign—and before "the terror and the glory of English arms" were "brought all the way to the banks of the Danube"—the country was in a bad way. "This crown, which for more than half a century had sealed the destiny of nations, found itself in a state of humiliation that seemed to announce its ruin. Its armies, which had always been keen, always triumphant, always invincible, were nothing more than monstrous corps without discipline, without intelligence. Its generals, whose name alone had inspired terror and admiration, saw themselves the toy of their enemies and their soldiers."[106] For Raynal, national decline was reversible, and terror that once affected one's enemies could return under the right circumstances.

Descriptions of other states or peoples past their prime used the expression *autrefois la terreur* to underscore their decline. An anonymous writer described Sweden in 1758 as "once the terror of the house of Austria and of Germany, as [it was] of the Danes and the Muscovites."[107] Voltaire also called Sweden "once the terror of the house of Austria," noting that by the end of the Great Northern War (1700–1721) it "could no longer defend itself against the Russians."[108] Commentators had similar things to say about Poland. Simon-Nicolas-Henri Linguet (better known for his *Mémoires de la Bastille*) dramatized this country's decline when he wrote, "The Poles were once the terror of the Germans, the Muscovites, the Swedes, and the Tartars."[109] An *Histoire universelle*, also reporting on the decline of Poland in the second half of the eighteenth century, called it "this republic so proud, once the terror of Russia."[110]

Many other former powers were described with precisely the same phrase. The Parthians were "once the terror of the Romans."[111] The Tartars were "once the terror of the Orient."[112] The Albanians were "once the terror of the Turks."[113] The Portuguese were "once the terror of India and the admiration of Europe."[114] Even the Inquisition, the bane of *philosophes* and Protestants, could be described in the eighteenth century as a *former* terror if the need to diminish its prestige exceeded the need to publicize its misdeeds. Thus Antoine Jacques Roustan, a Swiss Protestant and disciple of Rousseau, wrote, "The frightful [*affreux*] tribunal of the Inquisition is feeling slip from its bloody hands this murderous sword with which it struck so many victims on the banks of the Tagus [i.e., in Lisbon]." Roustan claimed that even the popes were reluctant to make use of the Inquisition, which was "once the terror, now the source of contempt of peoples."[115]

When lamenting their own supposed decline, the French could also imagine a prior state in which their ancestors had instilled terror in their enemies. In 1775 Nicolas Bricaire de La Dixmerie wrote in the guise of a "Gallic Sybil" who intoned, "The Gaul has stopped being formidable to the nations? He used to bring war to all inhabited climes; his name alone used to spread terror among a hundred bellicose peoples."[116] There was an implicit antiaristocratic tone in this call for Gallic regeneration, as the nobles habitually justified their privileges by claiming descendance from the Franks who had conquered the Gauls. In retrospect it appears to have been a short, though not inevitable, step from such valorization of ancient terror to support of revolutionary terror.

CRITIQUES OF SOVEREIGN TERROR

Despite the ingrained habits of speech and thinking that linked legitimate sovereignty with terror, there were writings in eighteenth-century France against the belief that terribleness was a laudable attribute. The abbé de Saint-Pierre, the utopian advocate of "perpetual peace," complained in 1729 of the tendency of history writers to glorify conquerors by dwelling on the obstacles they had to overcome. He wrote, "When Attila, when Tamerlane surmount great difficulties to make great conquests, these successes make a great impression on the world due to the terror that they cast in people's minds." Morally, however, they have no value, Saint-Pierre argued. Conquerors surmount difficulties "only for their own aggrandizement, and to satisfy their avarice or their other unjust passions," and are therefore "not at all virtuous or by consequence glorious."[117] Although Attila and Tamerlane were historical figures who engaged in specific attacks, Saint-Pierre made them stand for raw aggression at all times and in all places. Moreover, the author's decision to cite non-Europeans as examples of terror underscored the barbarity of European rulers who fancied themselves superior.

In addition, three books that appeared in 1756, just as France was entering the Seven Years' War, cautioned against the kind of expansionist terror that most other writers praised. In L'ami des hommes, the marquis de Mirabeau, pioneer of physiocracy and father of the revolutionary count, counseled against foreign conquests and the acquisition of colonies: "The spirit of conquest rules only by terror, and terror cannot have too few neighbors."[118] That same year the Milanese philosopher Giovanni Castiglione, who had lived at the court of Frederick the Great and seen close up a king known as the terror of his enemies, nevertheless questioned the wisdom of expansionism in monarchs. In his Discours sur l'origine de l'inegalité parmi les hommes, written in response to Rousseau's famous book on the same subject, Castiglione (who published in French under the name Jean Castillon) wrote, "Kings are made only for the happiness of the people, yet they care about nothing but expansion. Expansion, this alarms neighbors of whom one becomes the terror.[119] Even the chevalier d'Arcq, whom we have seen praising French nobles for the terror they spread in enemies, was not always so sanguine about terror. He wrote in 1756, "Shouldn't one say to a young prince: you can achieve immortality in two ways, the one by shedding blood, the other by spreading benefits? The former, by making you the terror of the human race, makes you the object of its hatred; the latter makes you the object of its love."[120]

Other writers expressed similar concerns. The encyclopedist Jean Le Rond d'Alembert critiqued the desire of sovereigns to terrorize their neighbors. He wrote of the sixteenth-century Holy Roman Emperor Charles V that he refused the honor of being praised by savants, preferring the "less real and more destructive [honor] of being the terror of Europe."[121] Comparable sentiments characterized the reasoning of an anonymous book of 1788 criticizing rulers who use terror to conquer nations: "The conqueror who forces a people into submission by terror and force" does not thereby acquire a right to rule. "The injury is the same, the crime is equal, whether it is the work of a private citizen or that of a sovereign. The rank of the malefactor neither adds to nor diminishes the crime."[122]

One of the most vociferous critiques of the supposition that kings should be the terrors of their enemies was, ironically, Abbé Mably, a writer whom we have seen elsewhere praising the Swedish king Charles XII as both a terror to his enemies and a hero. In an essay titled *Le destin de la France* and published in 1790, five years after his death, Mably wrote, "A king covets the title of conqueror: 'Victory,' he says, 'calls me to the end of the earth; I shall fight, I shall win, I shall crush the pride of my enemies, I shall burden their hands with irons, and the terror of my name, like an impenetrable rampart, will prevent entry into my empire.'" This desire to be terrible is insane and ruinous, Mably charges: "Drunk with this spirit [of conquest], [the king] forgets that fortune is inconstant, that the burden of misery is almost equally supported by the conqueror and the conquered."[123] In an essay he wrote for the prince of Parma in 1778, Mably imagined going back in time and haranguing the Russian tsar Peter the Great: "Why [do you engage in] conquests while you have deserted provinces that you could populate? . . . I see everywhere the captain and the conqueror who wants to inspire terror; but I would like to see the profound legislator who casts the foundations for eternal happiness."[124] Mably had similar complaints about his own country's former leaders, especially Louis XIV. In an essay "on the history of France" published in 1765, just one year after Mably's praise of the terror that Charles XII had spread, Mably linked the Sun King's policy of terror against foreign enemies with his oppression of subjects at home.

He accused the king of "taking advantage of the terror that his arms spread abroad to govern more imperiously at home" by forcing the registration of laws by the sovereign courts without remonstrance or amendment.[125]

Yet critiques of sovereigns who sought to be terrors of their enemies were rare, and one wonders how noticeable they were amid so many other statements (sometimes by the very same authors) that linked terribleness with strength, valor, virtue, and legitimacy.

CONCLUSIONS

In *Gulliver's Travels* the diminutive ruler of Lilliput describes himself as the "most mighty Emperor of Lilliput, delight and terror of the universe." The French enjoyed Swift's entertaining tale, which was quickly translated as *Voyages du capitaine Lemuel Gulliver* and went through at least a dozen editions between 1727 and 1789. In the French version the Lilliputian leader styled himself *Très-Puissant Empereur de Lilliput, les Delices [sic] & la Terreur de l'Univers*.[126] This was funny because the ruler was a miniature monarch (no taller than six inches) of a tiny realm ("about twelve miles in circumference") using the kind of language that supporters of European sovereigns employed to praise them, not because there was anything funny about a real, powerful monarch being both a terror and a delight. Indeed, this was what real, powerful rulers were supposed to be. The French got the joke, which worked equally well in both languages, since both the British and the French had kings who (along with other European sovereigns) were called "terror" and "delight" by their admirers.[127]

This chapter has explored a broad range of works, from high philosophy to *libelles*. It has drawn on treatises of law, political philosophy, economics, military science, medicine, social philosophy, and metaphysics. It has made use of dictionaries, petitions, remonstrances, academic speeches, prayers, sermons, pastoral orders, novels, newspapers, memoirs, and personal correspondence. The authors of these works came from a wide array of class, philosophical, and political orientations. This diversity of subject matter, form of expression, and ideological inclination is itself significant, as it reveals that habits of speech and thinking about terror were ecumenical. The words "terror of his enemies" slipped off the tongues, and flowed from the pens, of many different kinds of people and in many different contexts. This ecumenism made such expressions universally recognizable, legible, and durable.

Is it possible to glean from such diverse sources any coherent idea or doctrine of sovereign terror? Perhaps it would be more accurate to say that several related ideas revolved around the expressions that cast rulers, commanders, classes, or nations as terrors of their enemies, of their neighbors, or of the world. Specifically, in order to be a good sovereign one had to instill terror in one's enemies. There were practical, utilitarian reasons for this imperative. Intimidated enemies were less likely to attack and more likely to yield to invasion or diplomatic demands. But terribleness was not only a matter of practicality. It had moral meanings as well. A ruler who was the terror of his enemies—and in France the sovereign from the time of Louis XIV's majority was always a "he"   was virtuous. Not only was he brave, he was also dependable. He was his subjects' protector. It is in this context that we can understand the frequent but otherwise puzzling proximity of "terror" with words such as "love," "delight," and "father."

Terribleness as the attribute of a nation was a different matter conceptually, since a nation was not its own father—or its own love or delight, for that matter—but the model of sovereign terror was nevertheless transferable from monarchs to nations or peoples by virtue of its dignity and majesty. To be the terror of one's enemies was an attractive identity, one associated with might, virtue, and justice, and it is easy to see why those who came to view the nation as a sovereign power would have been drawn to it.

Ultimately, however, what mattered most was not any conceptual consistency or systematic rigor in the application of expressions such as "the terror of his enemies" or "the terror of their enemies." What mattered was that these expressions felt a certain way. They hinted at power, majesty, dignity, and virtue. Like the terror that God instilled, the worldly terror so often invoked in the age of absolutism helped to invest the very word *terreur* with an appeal that would last into the revolutionary period.

CHAPTER THREE

The Terror of the Laws: Crime and Punishment

INTRODUCTION

The most famous act of judicial terror in eighteenth-century France was in all likelihood the gruesome execution of the failed regicide Damiens on March 28, 1757. As Michel Foucault memorably recalled, Damiens was publicly lacerated " 'with red-hot pincers,' " burned with " 'molten lead, boiling oil, burning resin, wax and sulphur,' " and drawn and quartered, and his ashes were " 'thrown to the winds.' "[1] To call this punishment an act of terror is not an anachronistic judgment or the imposition of terminology from a later era. Rather, it conforms to the language used at the time by those who wrote or spoke of the punishment of criminals. The anonymous author of the "History of Robert François Damiens, containing the particularities of his parricide and his torments" asked rhetorically, "What . . . would be the security of princes, if terror were not a brake [un frein] capable of stopping the blow of some maniac's dagger raised toward thousands of subjects in the person of the monarch who maintains their lives and their goods?" Since a "parricide" was actually "the homicide of an entire nation," he was "worthy of the most terrible punishment." Indeed, the author believed that Damiens deserved even greater punishment than he received.[2] As we shall see in the course of this chapter, the language the author used to describe and justify punishment was typical. Though writers disagreed about what precisely instilled the greatest terror in criminals or potential criminals, they almost all agreed that such terror was a good thing, that it served as a *frein* or brake on the otherwise natural and inevitable force of crime and that the security of society was therefore dependent upon the terror of the laws. These beliefs in turn contributed to the appeal of terror as both an instrument and a sign of justice.

THE TERROR OF THE LAWS IN OLD
REGIME JURISPRUDENCE

The principle of terror is prominent in the writings of legal theorists in the age of Louis XIV, many of which were republished numerous times in the eighteenth century. For example, in a work of jurisprudence that would go through at least twelve editions between 1660 and the Revolution, a barrister and jurist from Montpellier named Antoine d'Espeisses justified leaving the corpse of a condemned criminal attached to the gallows. He gave two reasons. The first was "to give terror to the wicked." The second was to provide "consolation to the relatives of the murdered person."[3] (As we shall see in chapter 8, revolutionaries often invoked "consolation" when writing or speaking of policies that induced "terror" in counterrevolutionaries.) Writing more generally about the reasons for punishment, the jurisconsult Philippe Bornier also provided two justifications. In a book that appeared first in 1678 but would go through at least twenty-two editions over the next century, Bornier explained the punishments contained in Louis XIV's criminal code (the *Ordonnance* of 1670). He maintained that penalties were "introduced by the law . . . for the punishment and correction of the one who committed the infraction, and for the example, that others be diverted from it by the fear of the penalty, and by the terror of the torment."[4]

Similar reasoning is evident in the work of Jean Domat, one of the most widely read jurists of the century prior to the Revolution. His *Lois civiles dans leur ordre naturel* was first published in 1689 and came out in at least twenty-eight editions between then and 1777. In this work Domat explicitly and repeatedly affirmed the link between justice and terror, especially in matters of punishment. He posited two "ministries" instituted by God: that of religion and that of "the police," by which he meant government more generally. Whereas "the spirit of religion, which regulates the interior," or the conscience, "must insinuate itself into the hearts of men through the love of justice," the ministers of "the temporal powers" were "armed with the terror of penalties and torments to maintain the exterior order."[5] As the previous chapter has shown, many churchmen would have argued that religion also depended upon terror, and that the "love of justice" was insufficient to keep sinners on the straight and narrow path. And indeed Domat himself did not always abide by the distinction. In later editions of *Les loix civiles* he included a speech he had delivered in 1666 to the annual assizes, in which he justified the terribleness of temporal authority in terms of God's desire to terrify the wicked: "We learn from . . . Saint Paul that the temporal powers are established to imprint not tenderness and mildness, but fear and terror in unjust and wicked minds, against which God has made [the temporal powers] ministers of his anger and his vengeance."[6] Elsewhere in his writings Domat reinforced the position that temporal powers must instill terror in the wicked. In a treatise called *Le droit public*, first published in 1697 and then appearing in subsequent editions of *Les loix civiles*, he wrote that it was the duty of those in positions of temporal authority "to give confidence and the protection of justice to the good, and to inspire the terror of penalties in the wicked."[7] (We shall see similar pairings of "confidence" [for the good] and "terror" [for the wicked], particularly during the Revolution.) Domat also wrote in *Le droit public* that "the police of human Laws . . . has established penalties proportionate to different crimes, and that [penalty] of death itself against some who would not be sufficiently repressed by lesser penalties; and it has even added torments that imprint more terror than simple death."[8] Clearly what he had in mind were such elaborate and protracted means of execution as breaking on the wheel.

Other jurisprudential writings could be cited to support the claim that terror was central to penal theory in the late seventeenth century.[9] But let us examine eighteenth-century judicial commentators who reinforced the idea that the law had to instill terror in order to maintain civil peace and security. The most famous of such jurists was Henri-François d'Aguesseau, who served as chancellor to Louis XV and whom Voltaire called "the most learned magistrate France has ever had."[10] In an essay on the "study of history," first printed in 1716 but republished as late as 1787, he declared that "the terror of penalties and punishments" had always been one of the principal "aids of government," along with a powerful military, "abundance," and "consistent revenues." He described this terror as a means "by which the prince conducts a sort of domestic and continual war on the enemies of peace and the interior security of the state."[11] In his "Essay on the Institution of Public Law," also written in 1716 and republished in 1787, d'Aguesseau envisaged a skeptic asking: "Do I need an exterior power to come and frighten me by the terror of the penalties with which it threatens me, to force me to love everything I ought to love?" The imagined interlocutor expressed a preference for laws that appeal to the human desire for happiness and that rewarded rather than punished. D'Aguesseau replied that "the fear of evil acts much more powerfully on the majority of men than does the hope of good," and that it "is by the power of this fear that the law is respected." He therefore inferred that "the absolute legislator, the most powerful monarch has no other way to have his laws executed than to spread terror by the threat of the penalties which he has at his disposition." Otherwise the law is "no more than simple advice, or an almost always ineffective precept."[12] In his "Metaphysical Meditations on True or False Ideas of Justice," written between 1722 and 1726 but only published in 1759 (and again in 1779 and 1780), d'Aguesseau reaffirmed the necessity of legal terror, writing that "society" prevents crime "by the security that it procures for us, and by that terror of the laws that it establishes as a kind of safeguard around each individual."[13] D'Aguesseau did not simply advocate the terror of the laws—he instilled it. In 1760 Barnabé de Morlhon, first president of the presidial court of Toulouse, gave a speech to his fellow judges in which he recalled the late chancellor's tenure as Procureur Général for the Parlement of Paris: "This new career cleared for him a new route to glory. Armed with the sword of Justice, he only used it to imprint terror on crime [i.e., criminals], to defend innocence, to confound the usurper, to avenge the rights of the poor, and to protect the widow and the orphan."[14]

Claude-Joseph de Ferrière reinforced the notion that the law must be terrible. Son of a Parisian *parlementaire* who himself had written on the necessity of terror in punishments,[15] Ferrière inherited both his father's seat in the Parlement and his ideas about terror. He propagated this doctrine in several of the entries in his *Dictionnaire de droit et de pratique*, which was first published in 1740 and appeared in at least a dozen editions prior to the Revolution.[16] For example, in his entry for "penalty" Ferrière wrote that penalties were instituted "so that those whom the love of virtue could not divert from doing evil would be diverted by the fear of torments, and that the punishment exercised against criminals would imprint terror on others and hold them to their duty."[17] He made a similar case in his entry "Bodies of Criminals Executed and Put to Death," where he observed that in France executed criminals were typically exposed in public places near the scene of the crime. Ferrière explained that this practice "is founded on the example that one owes to the people; for nothing is better at maintaining [the people] in its duty than the terror that such horrible spectacles inspire naturally in all men."[18] In his entry for "Leze-Majesté," the crime (often spelled *lèse-majesté*) of "injuring" the majesty of the monarch, Ferrière justified depriving the guilty person's children of their inheritance. Though these children were "innocent" and their inheritance "belong[ed] to them by the right of nature," the efficacy of terror trumped considerations of natural law. Disinheriting the children of the guilty was necessary "in order to give more terror to those who would have conceived such a detestable design, in the apprehension of having the penalty brought to their children."[19]

Other eighteenth-century jurists concurred on the need for the law in general and punishments in particular to instill terror. In a 1732 treatise on criminal law, Guy Du Rousseaud de La Combe, barrister to the Parlement of

Paris, wrote that the execution of a poisoner and confiscation of his or her property were necessary "for the sake of the example and to give terror to the wicked."[20] Pierre François Muyart de Vouglans, barrister at the Parlement of Besançon, wrote in 1767 that "the judge must take care that the punishments he pronounces are such that they fulfill at once the three objects that the Law proposed for itself when being established[,] namely: (1) to correct the guilty, and to prevent him from falling back into the same crime or others; (2) to avenge the offended person of the disadvantage that he suffered through the crime; (3) and, finally, to assure the public order by turning others away through the terror of punishments from committing similar crimes."[21] François Serpillon, the chief law enforcement officer in Autun, asserted in 1767 (in a book that would be republished in 1784 and 1788), "The example is the principal object of justice, which has the intention of inspiring terror in the wicked in the same place where the crime was committed."[22]

Genevan jurists of the 1770s reinforced the conviction that punishments must be terrible. Jean-Pierre Sartoris wrote in 1773 that penalties were "for the reparation due to the public and to the individuals injured by the crime; but above all, that the terror of the example divert the wicked from violating public order, security, and tranquility."[23] In 1777 Joseph Nicolas Guyot wrote that "one punishes a crime as much to prevent the guilty one from committing it again as to contain [*pour contenir*] by the terror of punishments those who would be disposed to make themselves criminals like him."[24] The following year he wrote that "the temporal magistrate, in the punishments that he pronounces against criminals, limits himself to procuring public reparation of the crime . . . and inspiring terror with the prospect of the punishment."[25]

Legal theorists offered different justifications for punishment, including "correction" of the criminal and reparations (or "consolation") for the victims, but they were united in their conviction that the "example" of punishment would serve as a "brake" against criminal actions by instilling terror in malefactors. Repeated calls for judicial terror by such luminaries as Chancellor d'Aguesseau contributed to the appeal of the word *terreur*, and the positive emotional connotations attaching to the term would continue into the Revolution.

PRACTICAL APPLICATIONS: TERROR SPEECH IN LAWS, EDICTS, RULINGS, AND REMONSTRANCES

In addition to the writings of jurists, many texts by state authorities used the word *terreur* to indicate the goal of laws, punishment, and justice, and the provenance of these state-generated texts lent further majesty to the word.

Kings themselves declared the necessity of terror in matters of justice. Thus in an ordinance making the criminal tribunal known as La Tournelle permanent, Francis I explained that his intent was "to have the good and swift expedition of justice, crimes and misdemeanors punished, corrected, and repressed promptly to the terror of the wicked, the honor of God, and relief of all our people."[26] When this same king introduced the practice of breaking burglars on the wheel in 1534, he justified the law by affirming that the punishment was meant "to give fear, terror, and example to all other people."[27]

Louis XIII issued repeated edicts in which *la terreur* served as a justification. When he abolished dueling in 1609 he declared that anyone contravening the law would be guilty of *lèse-majesté* and susceptible to the same penalty (i.e., death), "hoping by the gravity and terror of said penalty to repress the . . . detestable custom of these combats."[28] The following year he issued a declaration prohibiting militias, armed assemblies, and the keeping of unauthorized arsenals. He asserted that all contraventions would be treated as *lèse-majesté* and that violators would be immediately tried by the criminal courts, "in order for an exemplary punishment to be made, which could give terror to all others, and retain each one in his duty."[29] In 1639 he responded to a wave of kidnappings by declaring, "We have resolved to oppose to the frequency of these evils the severity of the laws, and to restrain by the terror of new penalties those whom neither the fear nor the reverence of divine and human laws can stop." These penalties consisted of death and confiscation of the kidnapper's property.[30]

The last three kings prior to the Revolution also used the language of terror in their declarations and edicts. In 1712 Louis XIV declared that corpses could be subject to trial if the persons in question had committed *lèse-majesté*, committed suicide, or used violence against law enforcement agents. His reasoning was that "cadavers are tried in order to imprint terror onto the living; *Malè tractando mortuos terremus viventes* [By treating the dead badly we terrify the living]."[31] In a royal declaration on fraudulent promissory notes in 1733, Louis XV affirmed, "The protection that We owe to our subjects, to assure their commerce and to prevent false engagements from taking the place of true ones, obliges Us . . . to repress [the crimes] by the terror of penalties."[32] When announcing his decision in 1788 to reverse the provision in Louis XIV's *Ordonnance* that required the condemned to be executed on the day of conviction, Louis XVI nevertheless acknowledged that "this promptness could be useful in those particular cases where it is important to reestablish good order, by the terror of an example that does not allow delay."[33]

The Parlements also used the language of terror in their official statements. As self-proclaimed guardians of the law, they naturally drew on words that elevated their calling, and as we have seen, terror speech often contributed dignity to the law and its practitioners. Without a doubt the most notorious case in which a Parlement used both the language and the reality of terror was that of Jean Calas, who was executed on March 10, 1762. The previous day the Parlement of Toulouse (falsely) found the sixty-eight-year-old Protestant merchant guilty of murdering his twenty-eight-year-old son Marc-Antoine, presumably because the son was planning to convert to Catholicism. In their sentence the magistrates ordered the executioner to "break and crush" the condemned man's legs and hips, then break his back on the infamous *roue* or wheel. With his face "turned toward heaven," Calas would remain "in pain and repentance of his crimes and misdeeds . . . for as long as it shall please God to keep him alive." Finally his corpse would be "thrown onto a roaring bonfire" and "consumed by the flames" and his ashes "cast to the wind." The judges justified this treatment on the grounds that the execution would "serve as an example" and "give terror to the wicked."[34]

The very next year the Parlement of Paris employed the language of terror in a case involving religious orthodoxy. It was charging the author of a pro-Jesuit publication with attacking the Gallican church and questioning its independence. The church itself was seeking the authority to try the controversial author, but the Parlement insisted that "the laws made against heretics . . . charge the royal judges with punishing them," and that "far from encroaching on the ecclesiastical jurisdiction, the prince on the contrary defends and protects it by frightening with the terror of acute penalties the rash persons who would rise up against the doctrine of the church."[35]

The most complete defense of judicial terror on the part of a Parlement appeared in 1786, when the Parlement of Paris issued a 324-page *arrêt* or ruling condemning a book titled *Mémoire justificatif, pour trois hommes condamnés à la roue* (Supporting Memoire for Three Men Condemned to the Wheel) to be lacerated and burned by the public executioner. Jean-Baptiste Simare, Charles Bradier, and Nicolas Lardoise had been convicted by a bailiwick court of robbery and grave assault and sentenced to galley slavery for life, but the Parlement of Paris increased the sentence to death on the wheel. Jean-Baptiste Mercier Dupaty, himself a *parlementaire* (from the court in Bordeaux), wrote the *Mémoire justificatif* not only to defend the three men but to denounce inhumane punishments such as execution by the wheel. Eventually the sentence was overturned (by the Parlement of Rouen), but in the meantime the Paris Parlement had responded to Dupaty's work as though the very principle of judicial terror were at stake and, by implication, the efficacy and majesty of the law.

The *arrêt* asserted that "the law, in ordering the punishment of the guilty one, seeks less to remove the criminal from society than to frighten, by example, those who would imitate him." The Parlement added, citing the thirteenth-century Italian jurist Accorso di Bagnolo's gloss on the Julian Laws, that "everywhere the torment of a single person is the terror of the others," and quoting Accorso's maxim *Ubique poena unius est metus multorum* (and the punishment of one is the fear of the many).[36] The *arrêt* affirmed, "Reason has taught you that the laws were introduced only to prevent trouble in society; that they were necessary only to punish the guilty, and to frighten by the terror of torment."[37] This language is clearly defensive, suggesting that the *parlementaires* are not seeking punishment for its own sake. In this respect the principle of terror serves to defend the magistrates' humanity, a strategy that reappears when the authors complain about "indulgent reformers" who "have appealed the decisions of the law to the tribunal of humanity, as if . . . the gravity of penalties and the horror of the scaffold had not been introduced as much for preventing crime by the terror of the example as to punish it."[38]

Elsewhere the *arrêt* drew again on the discourse of humanitarianism, likewise adding appeals to *sensibilité* and equality, but it joined them all with the imperative of terror:

> The law is just, whatever its decision, because it is the law. It is the same for everyone, it is the safeguard of the citizen who sleeps peacefully in his home; he rests on the law, and the law watches over his security. But it is also the terror of the guilty one ready to commit the crime that he is planning, it horrifies him by the horror of the torment [*elle l'épouvante par l'horreur du supplice*] even before it can condemn him. True humanity is not that which cries over the fate of a scoundrel; it is that which stops being sensitive, that which appears cruel, for the peace, repose and preservation of the human race.[39]

Thus the appeal to terror by a Parlement could be consonant with Enlightenment ideals. If the Parlement of Paris used these ideals to justify a conservative agenda, the Parlement of Grenoble appealed to terror when calling for a significant legal reform. Specifically, on February 13, 1788, it remonstrated against the use of the *lettre de cachet*, that infamous abuse that allowed for arrest without trial and simply on the authority of royal orders. Among other things, the Parlement objected to the secrecy of the process, arguing that the *lettres* "have the disadvantage of substituting a mute punishment that is revolting for a public punishment which would imprint salutary terror."[40]

VOLTAIRE, BECCARIA, AND THE TERROR OF HARD LABOR

It was not only jurists and government officials who legitimized practices of punishment by referring to the terror that they inspired. *Philosophes* reinforced the connection between punishment and terror. Voltaire is a case in point. At first glance this might be surprising. After all, it was Voltaire who made the Calas affair into a cause célèbre, exposing the fanaticism of the Parlement of Toulouse and prompting the judges to rehabilitate the wrongfully convicted man.[41] Yet Voltaire never challenged the principle of exemplary terror in penal law; indeed he explicitly promoted the notion that the law should instill terror in those who were inclined to commit crimes. He simply believed that killing the culprit was not the best way to accomplish this goal. Thus in the second volume of his *Histoire de l'empire de Russie*, published in 1763, he praised Tsarina Elizabeth for abolishing the death penalty for all crimes except treason.[42] He wrote, "Malefactors have been condemned to the mines, to public works: their punishments have become useful to the state." This development was "no less wise than humane." "Everywhere else," Voltaire claimed, no doubt thinking of the Calas case of the previous year, "we only know how to kill a criminal with pomp, without ever having prevented crime." And further: "The terror of death makes less of an impression perhaps on wicked people who for the most part are lazy than the fear of painful work that is reborn every day."[43] Crucially, Voltaire endorsed the terror of the laws; he simply believed that "wicked" people would be more frightened by the prospect of continuous and painful work than by death.

Comparable reasoning informed what is doubtless the most famous eighteenth-century book against capital punishment, Cesare Beccaria's *Of Crimes and Punishments*, first published in Milan and Leghorn in 1764 and republished repeatedly and in many languages (including French) over the following decades. Like Voltaire, Beccaria invoked terror (*terrore*) to justify the abolition of the death penalty except in times of civil upheaval. In the French versions, consequently, the word *terreur* occurs repeatedly and at key points in the text. For example, in the Italian original Beccaria asks, "What is the political goal of punishments?" and he answers his own question, "The terror of other men."[44] In the 1766 French translation by André Morellet, which was reprinted seven times that year and reached seven thousand readers, according to the translator, the question and answer are replaced by a simple declarative sentence: "The political goal of the establishment of penalties is to inspire terror in other men by the force of example."[45]

Elsewhere Beccaria denounced the "spectacle" of public executions. Morellet's version, which closely follows the original, reads, "The death penalty inflicted on a criminal is nothing for the majority of men but a spectacle, or an object of compassion or of indignation. These two sentiments occupy the souls of the spectators much more than the salutary terror that the law claims to inspire."[46] For Beccaria, a more effective "brake" on crime was to make the convict into an "example" by turning him into a "beast of burden" for the public to see, and Morellet preserved this terminology in his French translation.[47]

Even the simple detention of a criminal was sufficient to incite terror in others, according to Beccaria, so greatly did people value their liberty. Arguing against the practice of torturing suspects to obtain the names of accomplices, he observed that torture was always ineffective (as weak people would confess to anything and strong people would remain silent) but particularly useless in this case because the accomplices would have fled, "while the penalty of the criminal who is in custody obtains its goal, namely to remove the other men with terror from [committing] a similar crime."[48] Morellet's translation preserved this meaning, rendering the clause "while the punishment of the guilty one that [society] has in its hands serves to remove the other men from crime by the terror of the example," and reinforcing the exemplary nature of the punishment by adding the key word "example."[49]

In 1773 a second translator, Étienne Chaillou de Lisy, made Beccaria's work available to French readers, and in 1782 the future revolutionary Jacques-Pierre Brissot reprinted Lisy's translation. This version also relayed the key idea that "the political goal of torments" was (in Lisy's formulation) "the terror that they imprint in men," and it similarly warned that "compassion" by observers of public executions would offset the "salutary terror" that the punishment intended to instill.[50]

Both Morellet and Lisy clearly conveyed Beccaria's conviction that the visible imposition of hard labor on criminals was the most effective means of instilling "salutary terror." As we have seen, Voltaire preceded the Italian jurist in this observation. Yet he was not the first to have written enthusiastically about the terror of hard labor. In his 1759 *Essais sur les ponts et chaussées, la voirie et les corvées* (Essays on bridges and roads, highway maintenance and compulsory labor), Charles Duclos wrote that there were three advantages to the use of criminals in chain gangs. The first was that "these men would no longer be, as they are now, absolutely lost to the state." (Voltaire would echo this point four years later.) The second was that "they would no longer be able to corrupt society, as they do today." And the third "would be to inspire by this imprescriptible penalty more terror in scoundrels, and to cause the germ of crime more surely to wither."[51]

INVOKING TERROR IN THE
DEBATE ON THE DEATH PENALTY

The arguments of Voltaire and Beccaria provoked a strong response from advocates of the death penalty, who insisted that executions would indeed impart the requisite salutary terror to prevent crime. For example, Jean-Nicolas Démeunier, writing in 1776, insisted that watching an execution was a truly terrifying experience: "The terror that the sight of death inspires often stops villains, no matter what is said to the contrary, and perpetual slavery, hard and painful labor, even public infamy do not suppress as strongly" the impulse to commit murder.[52] The Anglican clergyman William Coxe similarly doubted the deterrent value of confinement and hard labor. In a 1784 account of his travels in Russia, translated into French in 1786, Coxe commented on Voltaire's enthusiasm for Elizabeth's penal reforms: "According to Voltaire the fear of a punishment and of painful work that is renewed everyday makes a greater impression on the multitude than does the terror of death"; but, he replied, "the terror of death has always been regarded as the greatest of the fears that can operate on the mind of men."[53]

The most widely read intervention on capital punishment was most likely a chapter-length scene in *L'an deux mille quatre cent quarante* (The year twenty-four forty) (1770), a novel by Louis-Sébastien Mercier, who would later become a revolutionary. The number 1 "forbidden best-seller" of prerevolutionary France, according to Robert Darnton,[54] the novel includes a depiction of an execution along with the reflections of a fictional narrator, a Parisian who has awakened in his native city after a sleep of 670 years. Though social problems have largely been solved in this futuristic utopia, crime still exists, as does capital punishment. What is utopian about the death penalty in Mercier's novel is that it is dignified, effective, and, crucially, terrible. The chapter begins with the sound of drums. The civic guard was "slowly making the rounds, sounding the alarm; and this sinister march, which was echoed in everyone's mind, brought profound terror." To this sound were added funeral bells. The narrator learned from a resident that a man had killed his rival in a love triangle. This was the first murder in Paris in thirty years, suggesting the relative stability of this society (and perhaps the particular effectiveness of a death penalty that was used sparingly).

The Parisian urged his visitor, "Come, run with me to the voice of justice, which calls all the people to be witnesses to its fearsome [*formidables*] decrees." The execution took place in a large square adjacent to the courthouse, "under the eyes of the people," and Mercier had the judges "give to this judgment all the pomp, all the importance that it merited." On one side the lawyers' association stood by, "prepared to speak for the innocent, to remain silent for the guilty." On the other side the bishop and the pastors, their heads uncovered, "silently invoked the God of mercy and edified the people." Unlike the revolting judicial killings of the eighteenth century, however, this execution conformed to the enlightened year 2440. Mercier included a footnote denouncing the criminal justice system of his own day: "Our justice does not horrify, it disgusts" (*Notre justice n'épouvante point, elle dégoute*). He specified, "If there ever was an odious, revolting spectacle, it is seeing a man remove his lined hat, deposit his sword on the scaffold, climb a ladder in a silk or brocade suit, and dance indecently around the unfortunate whom he strangles." He asked rhetorically, "Why not give the executioner the fearsome [*formidable*] aspect he should have? What does this cold atrocity mean?" He added revealingly: "The laws lose their dignity, and the punishment its terror."

The ceremony continued with the condemned man kneeling before his judges and kissing "the sacred book of the law." The criminal read the statute forbidding homicide and admitted to his crime. The bishop then delivered a "vehement and touching speech on the danger of passion," on which the narrator commented, "It was so beautiful, so true, so touching, that all hearts were seized with admiration and terror." The bells of the city rang, the drummers started their "lugubrious march" again, and the criminal was executed by a firing squad. The narrator was so moved by the execution ceremony that he exclaimed to his informant, "Oh! How humanity is respected among you! The death of a citizen is a universal bereavement for the fatherland!" To which the Parisian of the future replied, "It is just that our laws are wise and humane: they tend toward reformation rather than punishment; and the means of making crime horrible [*d'épouvanter le crime*] is not to make punishment common, but fearsome [*formidable*]."[55]

One of the most extraordinary endorsements of capital punishment for its efficacy in instilling terror comes from Abbé Raynal. Famous for his bestselling denunciation of slavery and the slave trade, *Histoire philosophique et politique, des établissemens & du commerce des Européens dans les deux Indes* (Philosophical and political history of the settlements and commerce of Europeans in the two Indies) (1770), the philosophical *abbé* was nevertheless in favor of public executions.[56] The effect of such exemplary killings was so salutary, in his view, that the guilt or innocence of the executed person was secondary. In his discussion of one of the century's most famous executions—that of Admiral Bing for failure to defeat the French at the Battle of Minorca in 1757—Raynal focused on the positive social impact that he saw in the killing. The author congratulated William Pitt for his "inviolable attachment to the public interest" in having the admiral executed and noted that "neither [Bing's] rank, nor his talents, nor his family, nor his friends could save him from the severity of the law." Raynal depicted the spectacle for his readers. "The mast of his vessel served as his scaffold," he wrote, recalling the maxim that the malefactor should be punished at the scene of the crime.[57] He added, "At this tragic event all of Europe was struck by astonishment mixed with admiration and fright," thus linking the feelings of fear and respect. Moreover, by casting the execution as "tragic," Raynal invoked its theatricality, its spectacular character, as well as the irrelevance of the main character's guilt. He continued in this vein with an allusion to the Roman practice of decimation, or killing a tenth of an army unit that had fought unsuccessfully: "One seemed to be transported to the time of the ancient republics." As in the case of decimation, the actual guilt of the executed persons mattered less than the impact on observers of the exemplary killing. Similarly, Raynal wrote, "The death of Bing, *whether or not he was guilty*, announced in a terrible way to those who served the nation what fate would await them if they betrayed the trust that was placed in them." Republican nationalism was therefore connected in Raynal's thinking with *terrible* spectacles. Raynal further imagined the thought process of witnesses to Bing's death: "There would not have been one person who did not say to himself, in the depths of his heart, at the moment of combat, 'It is here that I must die rather than in the infamy of execution.'" "Thus," Raynal wrote, "the blood of a man accused of cowardice became the germ of heroism."[58]

Raynal's readers would have been familiar with an even more famous account of Bing's execution, namely Voltaire's description in *Candide*, in which the protagonist is told that in Britain "it is good to kill an admiral from time to time to encourage the others." For Voltaire the expression *pour encourager les autres* was ironic, and it has entered the modern lexicon as a sign of the twisted reasoning of despots, but for Raynal there was nothing at all ironic about executing a military officer as a means of literally encouraging, or instilling courage in, others. He referred to the execution as "this spring of fear instilled to conquer fear" (*ce ressort de crainte fait pour vaincre la peur*], and also called it, perhaps with Voltaire in mind, "an encouragement."[59] Still, as with the other instances of exemplary terror discussed in this chapter, the point was to frighten people into doing their duty, which in the case of combatants was to overcome their fear.

Other commentators were persuaded by the arguments of Voltaire and Beccaria against the death penalty, and they accordingly used the language of terror to make their points. For example, in his *Discours sur la nécessité et les moyens de supprimer les peines capitales* (Discourse on the necessity and means of suppressing capital punishments) (1770), the dramatist and lexicographer Louis Philipon de La Madelaine asserted that "there is nothing more apt to cast terror into the midst of a soul than the image of dishonor and opprobrium." Consequently he urged his readers, "Well then! Let us form a horror [*un épouvantail*] for crime by using the most revolting kinds of work and shame." He recommended permanently shackling the criminal's legs and writing on his cheeks, "in indelible strokes, the distinctive characters of his misdeed." In this way the convict "would ceaselessly sow before him the horror of crimes [*l'horreur des forfaits*] and respect for the laws.[60]

A similar case for the abolition of the death penalty came from the economist and social philosopher Jacques Accarias de Sérionne. Echoing Voltaire's psychology of the "scoundrel," Accarias criticized those who "believe the terror of death to be the most efficacious brake to prevent crime," for they were applying "their own sensitivity" to the case of insensitive people.[61] He wrote, "The brigands who give themselves over to theft in houses and on the highways regard death on the scaffold with the same eye as they regard a natural death. . . . They say to themselves that they will have to die someday, a little earlier or a little later . . . and in the meantime they want to procure for themselves well-being, pleasures, and above all protection from work, which they detest." Therefore "the spectacle of public work, compulsory and in chains, [and] the horror they have for work, which is infinitely stronger with them than the idea of death," would induce such scoundrels to refrain from crime.[62]

Similar reasoning characterizes the argument of Antoine-Nicolas Servin, a lawyer from Rouen who wrote *De la législation criminelle* in 1782, and who proposed a lifetime of "slavery" as a more effective punishment than death. Like Sérionne and other commentators on penal law, he tried to view things from the criminal's point of view. He even gave the criminal an inner monologue: "What is this death . . . that makes it appear so fearsome [*si redoutable*]? Is it not the end of all [my] sufferings, a cruel instant, without a doubt, but the last of all those that I have endured? Besides, mustn't it

come sooner or later . . . ? I will suffer . . . burning pains . . . but how many
illnesses cause a thousand times more suffering to innocent people?" But
what if, Servin asked, "instead of death, the law threatened slavery such
as I have announced?" This would be more frightening, since the criminal would already have had experiences similar to slavery. Therefore slavery would be "best suited to produce the impression of terror that the law
wishes to effect."[63]

In the same year that Servin published his book on criminal legislation,
the editors of the *Journal politique, ou Gazette des gazettes* published an
article that reinforced the Voltairean and Beccarian position. It began with
the claim that "the various treatises on criminal legislation . . . have almost
all missed their goal, which must be less to punish the crime committed
than to give terror to scoundrels," and added that "the death penalty above
all is very far from producing this effect." The author asserted that "defying
death is too often but a game for those atrocious souls accustomed to crime;
but slavery, work, and prolonged infamy are a brake much more feared [*red-
outé*]." The article continued with an account of the Holy Roman Emperor
"Joseph II, whose ideas on all the points of administration are so just and
great," and who "has just given to this subject an example far superior to all
that the criminologists [*criminalistes*] have imagined." It relayed the story
of a coachman who had murdered a woman and was condemned to be broken on the wheel. Just prior to the scheduled execution the emperor "com-
muted the sentence into the following punishment, namely: that the criminal would be driven in an elevated carriage up to the place of execution; that
there, after having heard his sentence, he would be marked on both cheeks
with a stamp reddened by fire, and imprinted with a wheel." Following that
painful and humiliating ordeal the prisoner would be "relegated to a dun-
geon, loaded with chains, and fed on bread and water four days a week." The
prisoner would also be "employed in the most painful public works, and
separated by infamy from the other prisoners." Finally, on every anniversary of the crime, the criminal would be beaten fifty times with a stick. The
author concluded, "This torment, much more terrible than death, is capable
of frightening [*d'effrayer*] the wretches whose passions can lead them to
crime."[64] Whether this story was true is less important than what it tells us
about the role of terror in arguments against capital punishment.

One work conveniently summarized the two sides of the capital-
punishment debate and revealed the importance of terror in both positions.
De la législation, ou Principes des loix (On legislation, or Principles of laws)
(1776), by the abbé de Mably, contained an imagined debate over capital
punishment between a Swedish *philosophe* and an English milord.[65] The

Swede argues in favor of the death penalty. He shows his familiarity with the reasoning of Voltaire and Beccaria: "I know, milord, the reasons of certain philosophers such as you for wishing to proscribe capital punishment. According to them, there are deprivations, prisons, irons, works that can make life more terrible than death." But the Swede is skeptical. He believes that death is the most effective deterrent to crime, since life "will always be considered the greatest good among men." He is certain that "not one of those scoundrels who are brought to the gibbet would not see as a favor the harshest prison and the most arduous labor." As to the supposedly terrible sight of prisoners in chains, the Swedish *philosophe* claims to have witnessed a gang of convicts who had just been sent to the galleys: "Never was a spectacle less appropriate for serving as an instructive example; they were singing with all their might; if they had not been begging, if I had not seen their chains, I believe I would have envied their fate."[66] He acknowledges that the death penalty does not always have the desired effect on spectators, but he speculates that "it is perhaps because the death penalty is too common in some countries that it inspires less salutary terror."[67]

The "milord" responds with an alternative view of what strikes terror into the minds of potential criminals. He agrees that legislators should "place before our eyes striking examples of the misfortunes into which vice drags us." He simply does not believe "that the death penalty is necessary to produce this effect." His argument rests on his understanding of the psychology of "scoundrels." In his view they are inured to the thought of death. They expect to be apprehended one day and put to death, and "they get used to this idea." The "ignominy" of execution does not affect them because "their lives are full of ignominy." How can such persons be made fearful? "What would strike them with greater force," the milord assures his friend, "is the fear of a future in which they will see nothing but dungeons, irons, and continual labors."[68] Recalling Beccaria, he continues, "The execution of a criminal condemned to death is for the majority of men nothing more than a spectacle that does not leave very deep traces in their minds."[69] He adds, drawing on now-familiar language, "One sees nothing but an object of compassion or indignation. One does not feel at all that salutary terror that is impressed by the long punishment of a man condemned to the harshest servitude." Moreover, whereas the sight of criminals condemned to hard labor "continually instructs citizens," the death penalty "only gives passing instruction."[70]

Mably's own position on the death penalty is difficult to discern. The author accorded the pro–death penalty Swede a longer speech than he gave the anti–death penalty Englishman, as well as the final word in the dialogue.

But more important than Mably's own opinion is the fact that both of the positions he relayed rested on the assumption that the goal of punishment was exemplary and "salutary" terror.

The debate on capital punishment carried over into the French Revolution, as we shall see in chapter 7, and the revolutionaries inherited the practice of justifying their positions, whether for or against capital punishment, by invoking the terror that their preferred method of punishment supposedly induced. This contentious debate therefore masked an important consensus on the role of terror in punishment. The consensus, in turn, reinforced the positive emotional connotations of the word *terreur*.

DISSENT AND AMBIVALENCE

Eighteenth-century French commentary on the terror of the laws or of punishments was not always unequivocally positive. In his 1747 book, *Théorie des sentimens agréables* (Theory of pleasant sentiments), Louis-Jean Lévesque de Pouilly faulted "philosophers and the majority of legislators" for assuming that ordinary people were incapable of moral reflection and for having "had almost no other brake to contain them than the terror of torments."[71] Of course, he did not say that the torments should not be used at all, only that they should not be the only brake on crime. Jean Castilhon, a barrister at the Parlement of Toulouse, won his city's famous essay contest, the Jeux Floraux, in 1756 with a *discours* in which he wrote that "fear of the executioners" and "the terror of torments" are the "shameful motivations" of a "slave" in a despotic state. Drawing on Montesquieu, the writer contrasted this emotional climate with that of a republic in which "virtue" motivates the citizen "to march to the defense of his fatherland," and he added that in a monarchy "the tenderness of the prince and the affection of [his] subjects are the most powerful supports" of the government.[72] The *philosophe* Pierre-Jacques Changeux, writing in 1767, agreed that terror of punishment was a base motivator: "True authority only acts on the mind and on the heart; it is truth and love that are its most powerful arms." This authority "makes virtuous and happy men." By contrast, "force, which acts on the body, only knows the terror of punishments, and only produces cowards and miserable people."[73] Baron d'Holbach was also doubtful about the efficacy of judicial terror. In his *Système de la nature* (1770) he argued that criminals broke the law because they saw the state as unfairly distributing its resources, allowing some subjects to become rich while others were destitute, and that under these conditions "the terror of torments in this world is itself too weak against necessity, against criminal habits, against a dangerous organization [of society]."[74]

Doubts about reliance on the terror of the laws also appeared in the *Encyclopédie*. The article titled "Vertu," by Jean-Edmé Romilly, acknowledged that "the laws . . . will be able to remove some guilty people, prevent some crimes by the terror of punishments," but a government only able to wield this weapon will have "a precarious existence." The laws will only have force "through the *virtue* of those who are subject to them." Romilly apostrophized the "shades" of the Roman republicans Camillus and Fabricius: "Tell us by what happy art you made Rome the mistress of the world, and flourishing for so many centuries: was it solely by the terror of the laws or by the *virtue* of your fellow citizens?" Romilly clearly thought that terror alone was not enough, since he went on to write that "if you remove the brake of conscience and of religion to establish a mere right of force . . . you give free entry to all the disorders, you favor . . . all the means to elude the laws and to be wicked," and he asserted that "a state is very near its ruin when the people who compose it fear only the rigor of the laws."[75]

Even Rousseau, despite his famous claim that violators of the social contract must be executed as public enemies, did not praise punishment for being "terrible." Indeed, he observed that "the countries in which punishments are the most terrible are also those in which they are the most frequent," suggesting that the terror of punishments was actually counterproductive.[76] Enemies needed to be removed from society, but not because doing so imposed terror, rather simply because they were a threat. The comte de Mirabeau went one step further, and in 1783 he wrote, "The rigor of punishments is but a vain and culpable recourse imagined by narrow minds and bad hearts to substitute terror for the respect that they cannot obtain." He added, perhaps inspired by Rousseau, that "it is a universal observation and confirmed by the most vast experience that torments are nowhere more frequent than in the countries where they are terrible." Terrible punishments had other bad consequences, according to Mirabeau: "The cruelty of penalties infallibly creates a multitude of criminals, and . . . in punishing all with the same severity, one forces those who are most often only guilty of foibles to commit crimes to escape the punishment of their faults."[77]

As late as 1787 Abbé Gabriel Brizard, speaking of laws, claimed, "It is necessary that they be mild and humane; it is necessary, if I dare say, to plant the root of the laws into the hearts of citizens." Unfortunately, in Brizard's view, "the majority of legislators have only known how to imprint terror; they have forgotten that the laws are not only avengers of crimes, but conservators of innocence and of virtue."[78] As with Castilhon, Changeux, and Romilly, the *abbé* was displaying a republican conviction that laws must instill civic virtue, but he did not dispense with the need for terror in the laws. After all, he faulted "legislators" for *only* knowing "how to imprint terror," suggesting that it was one of the tools legitimately available to them.

CONCLUSIONS

Even qualified criticism of judicial terror, however, was rare in the century leading up to the Revolution. By far the majority position was the belief that without the terror of the laws, society would fall victim to "scoundrels." Frederick the Great spoke for many others, including other francophone exponents of the Enlightenment, when he wrote to Voltaire in 1760, "The majority of our species is stupid and wicked. . . . Every man has a ferocious beast within himself; few know how to enchain it, [and] most give it free rein when the terror of the laws does not restrain them."[79] He put things a bit more diplomatically in a published work in 1751, when he wrote, "As the laws are dikes that stop the overflow of vices, they must make themselves respected by the terror of penalties."[80] Yet both statements reveal the same dim view of human nature.

Frederick's stance, and that of most of his contemporaries, might be termed an absolutist view of human nature, which sees people as prone to selfishness, excess, and crime. It looks very much like the Christian belief of human beings as fallen creatures who cannot be relied on to handle their own affairs, a belief that sustained monarchs who sought to rule with absolute power. Only some powerful, external force, such as "the law," can bring them into line. The mechanical, even hydraulic language of "brakes" or "dikes" "restraining" or "containing" the passions only reinforced the notion of human beings as in need of terror to rein in their dangerous proclivities. This view of human nature explains why the suffering of the criminal had to be visible, whether in the form of a public execution or (as Voltaire, Beccaria, and other reformers would have preferred) a work gang.

This absolutist view of human nature was not incompatible with a humanitarian outlook. The commentators on crime and punishment whom we have examined in this chapter offered proposals that claimed to lead to the happiness and security of humanity. It is not an accident, in this context, that Beccaria not only grappled with the most effective application of terror but also conceived of the utilitarian formula, later adopted by Jeremy Bentham, of the "greatest happiness shared by the greater number."[81] Beccaria and other writers on crime and punishment saw terror as a means of reducing human suffering. By being exemplary it served a pedagogical function, and in this respect it was salutary.

In retrospect, the discourse of judicial terror appears to have been a poor fit for the revolutionaries. The absolutist view of human nature that it often revealed was the opposite of the more optimistic, republican conviction that human beings could freely handle their own affairs through the application of will tempered by virtue. And yet the revolutionaries, as we shall soon see, did not share Rousseau's suspicion of judicial terror and instead adopted the language, and the practice, of terror wholeheartedly. It is easier to understand why they did, however, if we see the accretion of texts on the terror of the laws as a language that induced certain feelings rather than a doctrine that dictated specific propositions. The word *terreur*, when employed together with nouns such as "security," "order," and "justice," or when modified by the salvific-sounding adjective *salutaire*, paradoxically helped to reduce terror, namely the terror of danger, disorder, and injustice. Likewise, by conjuring images of the threats to security, order, and justice— the "wicked," the "bad," and the "scoundrels" who were assumed to be ready to attack at any moment—and by imagining them as susceptible to the terror of punishment, commentators on crime and punishment created a reassuring emotional climate, one in which respectable, law-abiding, virtuous citizens were both safe and powerful. In a revolutionary situation, in which one did not have to be paranoid to picture dangerous enemies, the language of terror, even if tainted by absolutist traditions and attitudes, was bound to be reassuring.

CHAPTER FOUR

Terror and Pity: The Springs of Tragedy

INTRODUCTION

By now we have seen how writings on religion, government, and law lent positive emotional connotations to the word "terror." Writings on aesthetics also added to its appeal. In particular, eighteenth-century theater critics used the standard of terror when judging tragedies. Drawing (often loosely) on Aristotle, writers praised tragedies for instilling terror and pity in spectators and discounted tragedies that failed to stimulate these feelings. Often, however, and particularly in the later decades of the century, theater critics neglected to mention pity in their assessments of tragedy and focused exclusively on terror. There were ethical implications to such judgments, because critics believed that viewing a terror-inspiring tragedy was morally improving. As a term used to praise exemplary works of drama, "terror" had a dignified, elevating feel to it, and it was a compliment, perhaps the highest, to call a playwright "terrible."

TRANSLATING ARISTOTLE ON TRAGEDY

Critics writing on tragedy seldom failed to refer to Aristotle, either directly or indirectly, and in particular to his definition of tragedy as laid out in Book VI of the *Poetics*. Aristotle wrote: "Tragedy . . . is an imitation of an action that is serious, complete, and of a certain magnitude; in language embellished with each kind of artistic ornament, the several kinds being found in separate parts of the play; in the form of action, not of narrative; through pity and fear effecting the proper purgation of these emotions."[1] Yet whereas this translation rendered the Greek *phobos* as "fear," the vast majority of French commentators translated it as *terreur* (as opposed to *crainte*). Writers referred typically to *la terreur et la pitié*—though less often they translated the Greek *eleos* as *compassion*—and this pairing also helped to give "terror" positive emotional connotations, since pity was also generally regarded as a praiseworthy emotion. The fact that Aristotle advocated a purging or *katharsis* of both passions mattered little, since most French commentators either argued that Aristotle did not truly call for a purging of terror and pity or simply remained silent on the subject.

The canonical French translation of Aristotle's *Poetics* was the work of André Dacier, who in 1692 rendered the famous definition of tragedy as "an imitation of a serious, complete action and which has an appropriate grandeur: whose style is pleasantly seasoned, but differently in all its parts, and which, without the help of narration, by the means of compassion and terror succeeds in purging in us these kinds of passions and all similar ones."[2] Yet Dacier quickly reassured the reader that "to purge the passions" did not mean "to chase them, to uproot them from the soul." Rather, he aligned himself with the Peripatetics, who were "persuaded that it is only the excess of passions that is harmful, and that regulated passions are useful and even necessary," and who believed that purging the passions amounted to "reducing them to a just moderation."[3] Dacier explained the utility of viewing a tragedy: "It excites [terror and compassion] in us by placing before our eyes the misfortunes that our fellows have drawn onto themselves by involuntary errors, and it purges them by making these same misfortunes familiar." Dacier wrote that there was an additional positive effect of tragedy, namely that "while purging terror and compassion, it purges at the same time all those other passions that could precipitate us into the same misery, for by displaying the faults that have attracted to these unfortunates the penalties that they suffer, it teaches us to be on our guard not to fall into them, and to purge and moderate the passion that was the only cause of their fall." He offered as an example the case of Sophocles' *Oedipus*, assuring his reader that "there is no one who when watching [the play] does not learn to correct in himself the temerity and the blind curiosity that are the sole causes of his misfortunes, if not his crimes."[4] Dacier concluded, "Tragedy is therefore a true medicine, which purges the passions," thus recalling the idea of salutary terror, but he added that "it is a pleasant medicine, which only achieves its effect through pleasure."[5] Thus Dacier made Aristotle conform to Christian morality, according to which terror and pity were both "salutary" emotions.

Other critics had divergent interpretations but nonetheless sought to reconcile Aristotle with their own ethical ideals. For example, Jean Terrasson wrote in 1715 that Aristotle never intended terror and compassion to be purged. Rather, "the moral goal of tragedy" was "to purge all those unregulated passions by those two [i.e., terror and compassion] which tragedy must excite appropriately and in salutary fashion [*salutairement*]." By "unregulated passions" Terrasson seems to have meant lust, greed, ambition, and rage—in other words, the stuff of Greek tragedy—and the use of the term *salutairement* highlighted the moral aim of tragedy, which in a Christian context was to save the viewer from falling into sinful behavior. Accordingly, when translating the famous passage from Aristotle's *Poetics*, Terrasson left out the morally problematic notion of purgation altogether, treating tragedy as a "heroic poem" that, among other things, "excites compassion and terror, and teaches men to repress their passions and correct their vices."[6]

Abbé Charles Batteux also adjusted Aristotle to make him morally acceptable. In his *Cours de belles lettres distribué par exercises* (Literature course arranged with exercises) (1750) he referred repeatedly to the emotions that a well-written tragedy was supposed to instill. "Tragedy . . . attracts us by the sentiment of *compassion*," he wrote, "and retains us by that of *terror*."[7] Elsewhere in his *Cours* Batteux wrote an abbreviated version of Aristotle's definition, proclaiming that "tragedy is the representation of a heroic action designed to excite terror and pity" but leaving out any mention of the catharsis.[8] He distinguished between epic and tragic poetry by observing that both involve heroic action but that the hero in tragic poetry must "excite terror and pity," and again he failed to refer to the subject of purging.[9]

Twenty-one years later Batteux finally addressed the thorny issue of the catharsis, but in a way that made it acceptable to contemporary morality. In a book comparing four theories of poetics he translated Aristotle's definition, writing, "Tragedy is the imitation of a serious, complete action that is extended up to a certain point; by speech clothed in various charms, each of which, in the different parts in which they are employed, contributes to the effect of the poem; to operate not by narration, but by terror and by pity, the purgation of these same passions."[10] He highlighted the moral difficulty of this definition by asking, "To whom . . . could this inhumane thought have occurred to wish to cure men of pity, which is the refuge of the unfortunate; of terror, which is the safeguard of virtue[?]"[11] Batteux's solution, like that of Dacier, was to make *purger* mean something other than to eliminate. The *abbé* recalled that Aristotle also wrote of purgation in his *Politics*, in Book VIII, chapter 7, where he recommended music to children because it purged the passions, including terror and pity; but Batteux clarified that (for Aristotle), "as medicine purges the body by correcting the excess or the vice of the humors, music likewise purges the soul by correcting, by removing, either the excess, or the vice of the affects."[12] He continued, "The purgation of terror and pity consists therefore in tragedy in removing from these two passions what they have in excess or what is harmful in them."[13] Batteux did not clarify where or how the passions might have been vicious or virtuous, but the important point is that he believed terror (like pity) should not be eliminated in the spectator to a tragedy.

In 1752 Louis Racine, the son of the great playwright, offered his interpretation of Aristotle's troubling definition. He began by objecting to the use of the term *terreur* as a translation of Aristotle's *phobos*, arguing that Latin translators typically used the word *metus* (fear) rather than *terror*.[14] He did not explicitly say how he thought fear (*la crainte*) differed from terror, though he did acknowledge that plays that incite terror were better than those that only incited fear.[15] In other words, no play that failed to incite fear could properly be called a tragedy, but plays that incited terror were superior tragedies. This reasoning might indicate that Racine *fils* viewed terror as an intensified form of fear. In any event, the fact that he felt it necessary to correct the French for using *terreur* as a translation of *phobos* reveals how widespread its usage was.

On the question of the catharsis, Louis Racine simply could not believe that Aristotle ever conceived of the idea. He did not think it possible that Aristotle wished "to harden men."[16] The playwright's son did not accept the medicinal metaphor that Dacier had offered: "When one hears [Aristotle's] interpreters explaining him in this way, wouldn't one think that, like those doctors who give smallpox by insertion [i.e., inoculation], the tragic poets give illnesses to the soul by insertion, in order then to cure them? This thought is so bizarre that I cannot attribute it to Aristotle." The young Racine asked, "And why seek to cure and even to moderate in men the passions more suited than others to bring them to virtue?"[17] He asserted, "Wanting to purge fear and pity from the hearts of men is wanting to dull the two needles of virtue."[18] Unlike other commentators, who made heroic efforts to reconcile the idea of the catharsis with their notions of morality, he hypothesized that the manuscript from which scholars had worked since Roman times was simply "corrupt."[19]

Another critic who grappled with Aristotle's theory of tragedy was Jean-François Marmontel, who laid out his views on the subject in his *Poétique française* (1763). According to Marmontel, "It is . . . natural that the ancients chose terror and pity as the springs of pathos: any other emotion is too strong or too weak, or is not mixed with any pleasure. That of hatred is sad and painful, that of horror is insupportable for us." Joy is "delightful" but passes quickly. Admiration "adds theatrical interest, but it does not suffice."[20] For Marmontel "it is only through terror and pity that pathos can be vivid and durable; it is only they that cause us sweet quivers [*de doux frémissemens*], and that cause us to taste without interruption, in the midst of pain itself, a pleasure more delicate and more sensitive than that of joy." But terror and pity were not merely pleasurable—they were moral. The effect of tragedy was "salutary," Marmontel claimed, using a word that we have already seen in numerous contexts associated with terror. It was salutary because it inured spectators to misfortune, so that when they met it in real life they were better equipped to face it. Marmontel acknowledged that for Aristotle the goal of tragedy was "to cure in us the very passions that it excites, and these passions, he said, are terror and pity," but by "cure" he did not mean remove or eliminate. Rather, he meant something like the inoculation that Racine *fils* ridiculed, or the stoic tempering that Dacier envisaged. Thus Marmontel wrote of tragedy as understood by Aristotle: "Its goal was not to moderate active passions in us, but to habituate the soul to impressions of terror and pity, to load it with a weight that exercises its power, and to make the weight of its own misfortunes seem lighter."[21]

A particularly interesting window onto eighteenth-century French interpretations of Aristotle's catharsis is provided by an anonymous article from 1740 in the Jesuit journal *Mémoires de Trévoux*. The author assured readers that Aristotle's view on terror, pity, and purgation was compatible with the requirements of morality: "Purging passions is nothing else, in the language of Aristotle, than giving them a brake." We have seen the idea that the terror conveyed by public executions would similarly act as a brake on dangerous impulses. The author added that Aristotle "wants tragedy, through the impressions of terror and pity, to serve to produce happy effects in the souls of spectators," and promised to "unveil . . . the mechanism and the secret springs by which theatrical terror and pity become instruments suited to contribute to the regulation of our morality and make men more virtuous." In particular, "theatrical terror is that which inspires in the spectator the sight of the punishments and the misfortunes that one draws upon oneself when giving oneself to one's passions." Moreover, "the natural and immediate effect of this terror is to induce the spectator to repress in himself the transports of these dreadful passions." The author gave the examples of Racine's tragic heroine Phèdre, who, after allowing herself to be overcome by illicit love for her stepson, embarks on further crimes until she is driven to suicide; and of Athalie (also a Racinian heroine), who "sacrifices to her ambition to reign alone in Judah and in Israel, an entire generation of infants, issued from her own blood, in the cradle" and ends up being executed.

Significantly, the author went on to compare the effect of viewing a tragedy to that of watching an execution. It was not necessary to pore over Aristotle's texts or those of his commentators to understand the philosopher's intention. One needed only consult "the wife of the artisan and of the plowman, who, guided by instinct, leads her child to the foot of the scaffold, where the malefactor expires; in order to protect, through the impression of this spectacle, this heart, which is still tender and flexible, against the reefs where the violence of inclinations, bad examples, in a word, the passions of a stormy youth could later cause his weak virtue to run aground." And indeed other writers on tragedy would make the same comparison.[22] The author of the article in *Mémoires de Trévoux* acknowledged that "the impressions . . . which produce theatrical terror are not at all equal to those that come from reality; but they are superior to those [impressions] that the simple recounting of similar events makes." In this way "the theater will . . . become a school of virtue, and the terror that the tragic action inspires will calm, will purge the tumultuous passions."[23] Thus the idea of the catharsis remained, but it was emotions other than terror and pity that tragedy purged. Terror and pity themselves remained, and indeed were heightened, as spectators to the tragedy improved morally.

Thus the French writers who dealt explicitly with Aristotle's concept of the catharsis interpreted it in such a way as to keep terror (and pity) in the "souls" of viewers even after the tragedy had ended. This is because they valued these emotions as both pleasurable and virtue-inducing. Other writers simply left out the catharsis entirely when defining tragedy. We have already seen this interpretive move in Terrasson and in Batteux's early work. But many other theorists of tragedy omitted any mention of the catharsis. Thus the Oratorian priest Bernard Lamy wrote in 1712, "Tragedy contains terror and compassion. The goal of the one and the other is to horrify [*d'épouvanter*] and instruct the people, by changes in fortune, and by the punishment of crime."[24] In his *Dialogues sur l'éloquence* (1715), Archbishop Fénelon had one speaker assert that "the ancient authors . . . wanted tragedy to turn on two passions: that is to say, terror, which shows the dreadful consequences of vice; and compassion, which persecuted and patient virtue inspires."[25] Neither this speaker nor his interlocutor said anything about purging. Abbé Jean-Baptiste Dubos also left out the catharsis when he wrote in 1740 that "the goal of tragedy" was "principally to excite in us terror and compassion."[26]

Other commentators used similar formulations, typically employing the verb *exciter*. In 1745 Edmé-François Mallet adapted Aristotle to define tragedy as "the imitation of a complete heroic action in which numerous persons contribute in the same place, on the same day, and whose principal end is to form or to rectify morals by exciting terror and pity."[27] In his 1751 treatise on poetry written for the education of Louis XV's daughters, Jacques Hardion wrote, "Tragedy is the imitation of a great and important act in which the poet has characters act and speak without appearing himself, and whose goal is to excite terror and pity in the souls of the spectators."[28] A 1776 textbook on literature by Antoine-Hubert Wandelaincourt contained a sort of catechism in which the instructor asked the student, "What is tragedy?" to which the student was supposed to answer, "Tragedy is the representation of a heroic action capable of exciting terror and pity. *Phobos, kai Éleos.*"[29] In 1786 the *Encyclopédie méthodique* defined tragedy as the "representation of a heroic action whose object is to excite terror and compassion."[30]

Writers on the subject of tragedy therefore either explained away Aristotle's view of catharsis or simply ignored it. One might say that they purged the purgation from Aristotle. This is because of the high value eighteenth-century French writers placed on the emotions of terror and pity, which they believed to be stimulants to moral behavior. The moral implications of terror in this context contributed to the word's positive emotional connotations.

ASSESSING THE GREEKS

Armed with a quasi-Aristotelian definition of tragedy that highlighted terror, critics assessed specific playwrights and specific tragedies according to this standard. They praised those authors who "excited" terror (and sometimes pity) and criticized those who failed to do so. They applied this test to every major tragedian, from Aeschylus, Sophocles, and Euripides to Corneille, Racine, and eighteenth-century playwrights, and they judged minor playwrights according to the same yardstick. In very few cases did they mention the catharsis. It was assumed that spectators of successful tragedies left the theater with feelings of terror, and perhaps also pity, still affecting them.

Assessments of Sophocles are a case in point. Fénelon lauded him for inspiring terror and compassion.[31] Voltaire, writing in 1748, contended that not only the Greeks of the fifth century BCE but also "all of posterity" considered Sophocles the greatest of tragedians. As proof, he wrote that *Elec-*

tra provoked "terror and pity to the extreme."[32] In 1765 the *Journal des sçavans* claimed that *Oedipus* provoked "commiseration and terror."[33] In 1777 *L'année littéraire* wrote that in *Antigone* "terror and pity are carried to their furthest extent."[34] That same year Batteux gave a lecture at the Académie Royale des Inscriptions et Belles-Lettres praising Sophocles for the terror and pity he inspired in audiences.[35] In 1784 Jean Marie Bernard Clément approved of the dénouement of Sophocles' *Electra*: "It is thus that the spectacle . . . adds to the terror and to the pathos."[36] Even critics who objected to Sophocles nevertheless recognized his ability to instill terror and pity; they simply thought he misused this talent. Terrasson objected to the fact that Oedipus committed his offenses unwittingly, thus making his punishment unjust. If he had been warned by an oracle of the danger of committing parricide and incest, Terrasson argued, and done so anyway, then the tragedy "would have legitimately and usefully excited compassion and terror."[37] Similarly, an article in the *Journal encyclopédique* in 1756 argued that in Sophocles' hands "this subject [of Oedipus's transgressions], so suited to inspire terror and pity, can only authorize despair and make the gods appear unjust."[38]

French writers also praised Euripides for the terror and pity that his plays inspired. Racine himself—the playwright, not the critic—who took the subject of *Phèdre* from Euripides' *Hippolytus*—wrote in a much-reprinted preface that the character of Phèdre "has all the qualities that Aristotle asks in the hero of tragedy, and which are suited to exciting compassion and terror."[39] Fénelon also approved of Euripides' plays for inspiring "terror" and "compassion."[40] The classicist Pierre Brumoy, writing in 1732, agreed with Aristotle that Euripides was (in Brumoy's wording) " 'the most tragic of all the poets.'" Brumoy acknowledged that Euripides had "a careless air" whereas Sophocles exhibited "regularity," and he conceded that "one will find in [Euripides] certain defects that [Sophocles] avoided with care." But "one cannot help pardoning" these shortcomings "in favor of the sentiment of pity and of terror with which the soul feels itself agitated."[41] In his *De l'homme* (1773), Helvétius approved of "the terror" in Euripides' *Medea* and *Seven against Thebes*, though he did not say anything about pity or compassion.[42]

The reputation of Aeschylus was similarly built upon his supposed ability to incite terror (and, to a lesser extent, pity). Mallet wrote that "it is said of Aeschylus that in one of the choruses of his tragedy of the Eumenides, he excited such a great terror that children fainted and pregnant women miscarried out of fright [*de frayeur*]." This might seem to have been a criticism, but Mallet contrasted the power of Greek tragedies (including the

work of Euripides) with the tepid plays of his own day.[43] Mallet omitted
pity or compassion from his discussion of Aeschylus, as did the playwright
and critic François d'Arnaud, who wrote in 1764, "If this *terror* must be the
soul of the dramatic machine, shall I be excused for regarding Aeschylus
as the only *tragedian* in this genre whom we can propose as a model?"[44]
In 1770 the marquis de Pompignan, who translated the Greek playwright's
tragedies, concurred, praising Aeschylus as "the most sublime of the Greek
tragic poets," and praising his *Seven against Thebes* as a play in which "terror and pity are carried to their limit." He added that "there are in this poem
two invisible characters who fill it from the beginning to the end: terror
and pity."[45]

ASSESSMENTS OF CORNEILLE AND RACINE

Critics also judged the great tragic playwrights of the seventeenth century—
Pierre Corneille and Jean Racine—according to the terror and pity that
their plays "excited" in audiences. Racine fared better than Corneille in
this respect. Critics tended to see Corneille's tragedies as lacking in terror
and pity. The poet and critic Nicolas Boileau-Despréaux, who famously advised those with ambitions to write tragedy to "fill" spectators with "sweet
terror" (*une douce terreur*) and to "excite . . . charming pity" (*une pitié
charmante*) in their "souls,"[46] wrote in 1700 to the Academician Charles
Perrault that Corneille had invented "a new genre of tragedy unknown
to Aristotle" and had "not cared, like the poets of ancient tragedy, to stir
pity and terror." Boileau did not fault Corneille for this, and elsewhere he
praised "the sublimity of [his] thoughts."[47] Other critics took the lack of
terror and pity in Corneille's plays to be a serious failing.

The most relentless of Corneille's critics was Voltaire. His three-volume
Commentaires sur le théâtre de Pierre Corneille (1761) went through the
playwright's oeuvre play by play, act by act, scene by scene, and in many
cases Voltaire found it lacking in terror and pity. For example, Voltaire
faulted Corneille for scene 2 of the second act of *Polyeucte*, in which the
emperor Severus tries unsuccessfully to seduce Pauline, the faithful wife
of the soon-to-be-martyred Christian Polyeucte. This was more suitable to
comedy than to tragedy, according to Voltaire, because there was "no pity,
no terror, nothing tragic" in the scene.[48] Similarly, when Cleopatra, in Corneille's *Death of Pompey*, confesses to her lady-in-waiting that she is in love
with Julius Caesar, Voltaire protests that the scene is "very cold, and against
the laws of tragedy" insofar as "it inspires neither terror nor pity."[49]

Voltaire was likewise critical of *Héraclius*, a play that hinges on mistaken identities. He began by faulting Corneille for the play's slow start. Four scenes into the first act, according to Voltaire, none of the characters "inspired terror." As late as scene 6 of the second act the play was still lacking "that terror, that pathos, which are the soul of true tragedy." At the end of act 2 there was still "neither pity nor terror." Elsewhere Voltaire wrote simply of "terror" as the requisite emotion lacking in Corneille's work, or he mixed terror with other emotions. "Genius," Voltaire wrote, "carries terror to the soul," but Corneille did not have this ability. He asserted that "everything that is not sentiment, passion, pity, terror, horror, is coldness in the theater." He added that the complicated plot of *Héraclius*, involving indeterminate family relationships, could "never [inspire] any trouble, any terror."[50] When a surprising family relationship was revealed, it "cause[d] neither terror nor trouble."[51]

Similarly, Voltaire criticized *Nicomède*, a play about thwarted Roman attempts at imperial conquest, for having "neither the terror, nor the pity of true tragedy." When the title character lectures his half-brother on the duties of leadership, Voltaire complains that this speech fails to do what it should, namely to "say things that . . . increase terror." When, at the close of the play, the Roman ambassador makes a speech indicating his refusal to take part in a planned takeover of Nicomède's kingdom, Voltaire laments that "political arguments do not have great effect in the fifth act, where everything should be action or sentiment, where terror or pity should take hold of all hearts."[52]

Voltaire also chided Corneille for the low level of terror present in his *Œdipe*. (Voltaire himself had adapted Sophocles' story for the stage, to great critical and popular acclaim, and perhaps felt the need to defend his position by diminishing Corneille's version.) When Oedipus realizes that he has killed his father and married his mother, "what is missing are these great emotions of terror and pity that accompany such a frightful [*affreuse*] situation." By act 5, scene 5, there is "no more surprise, no more terror," as "the author falls back into his miserable dissertations" and Oedipus speaks in dispassionate tones about his fate.[53]

Voltaire applied the same standard to other plays by Corneille. When a Roman general, the eponymous hero of *Sertorius*, is the object of a rivalry between two women, Voltaire quotes Aristotle in Greek, noting that "this is not *phobos kai eleos*, terror and pity." When Sertorius is assassinated in the final act, the audience is unaffected, because "that which is not at all prepared with terror does not cause any." Frustrated with *Othon*, a tragedy complicated by numerous marriage negotiations, Voltaire declared that it "excites laughter rather than terror."[54]

Other writers criticized Corneille for a lack of terror and pity in his plays. In 1770 the playwright Pierre-Laurent Belloy praised Corneille as "this great poet" but claimed that he was nevertheless guilty of "having mixed admiration [for his heroes] with a too-weak terror; of not having placed his heroes Nicomède, for example, and Sertorius in peril sufficiently imminent and present to the eyes of the spectator to produce that lively interest that tragedy demands."[55] The following year Batteux wrote of audience reactions to Corneille's *Cinna*: "The spectator feels the liveliest worry [*les plus vives inquiétudes*]; but he does not feel pity or terror, neither for Augustus [the target in an assassination plot], nor for Cinna [the plotter]." He added that *Rodogune* was similarly incapable of exciting these requisite passions.[56]

Corneille had his defenders, and they expressed their approval by noting the terror in his plays. In 1770 d'Arnaud wrote of the fifth act of *Rodogune*, "where the great Corneille struck all the blows united with terror," that "it is there that he makes himself my master, makes me fear [*me fait craindre*], shudder."[57] Interestingly, d'Arnaud mentioned terror but not pity. In 1773 the literary critic Antoine Sabatier de Castres also praised Corneille, writing that the playwright's "intrigues are so skillfully managed, conducted with such dexterity, terminated by an explosion (allow us to use this term) so luminous, so striking; that the terror and the pity that are born at the poet's will, and seize the spectator, are never weakened by the sentiment of admiration."[58]

Racine was far more enthusiastically embraced by French critics, who as usual used terror and pity as measures of effective tragedy. Indeed, this was how the playwright himself wished to be judged. In the preface to his *Phèdre* (1677) he reminded readers that the play had "such a happy success in the time since Euripides," from whom he took the story, and that "it has still succeeded so well in our century, because it has all the qualities that Aristotle demands in the hero of the tragedy, and which are suited to excite compassion and terror."[59] Early commentators agreed and judged Racine as skilled in bringing out these emotions. In 1686 the baron de Longepierre praised Racine's *Iphigénie*, writing that it "has the same effects on its spectators, as that of Euripides [from whom Racine again borrowed] had on the Athenians, that is to say, that it excited in them compassion and terror, which are . . . *the veritable effects of tragedy.*"[60] In 1717 Abbé Jean-François de Pons reminded his readers that Racine "wanted to please [audience members] by exciting in their souls these lively emotions that are born of admiration, compassion and terror."[61]

By the middle of the eighteenth century Racine's reputation was still strong. The marquis d'Argens wrote in 1744, "No one has yet stirred pity and terror as Racine did." Answering the objection that the love stories characteristic of modern French theater made it less "terrible" than Greek tragedy, he asked rhetorically, "Doesn't the love of Phèdre excite pity and terror?" He maintained, "Terror and pity being the principal passions that a tragic author must excite, nothing is more suited to produce them than the effects that an unhappy love affair ordinarily causes." In d'Argens's opinion Racine had "found the means of painting in his pieces a simple and ordinary love affair, such that all hearts could feel it, and a theatrical love made for exciting pity and terror. Thus in *Phèdre*, the love of Hypolite [*sic*] and Aricie is an ordinary love, and that of Phèdre is a theatrical love, which produces the greatest movements and which excites pity and terror by turns."[62]

Other critics expressed similar praise for Racine. In 1745 Mallet, who generally preferred the ancients, nevertheless conceded of "our modern tragedies," that "the best infallibly excite terror," and he offered Racine's *Phèdre* and *Athalie* as examples.[63] In 1746 Pierre-Antoine de La Place, who typically thought that French theater was overly attached to love stories, felt that Racine was at his best when he depicted uncontrolled passion; thus it is the "unbridled passion of Phèdre, it is her rage, her jealousy, the consequences and punishment of her crime, and the misery of the virtuous Hippolyte," her stepson, with whom she is in love, "that excite by turns terror and pity, [and] cause the great shocks that are required by dramatic poetry to be interesting."[64] Voltaire added his approval of Racine. On the subject of *Iphigénie*, he wrote in 1761, "Do you want grandeur? You find it in Achilles . . . Do you want real politics? The character of Ulysses has it in full; and it is perfect politics, truly founded on love of the common good; it is adroit; it is noble; it does not waste time with dissertations; it augments terror."[65]

CRÉBILLON "LE TERRIBLE"

Eighteenth-century critics applied the same standard of terror (and to a lesser extent, pity) to tragedies written by their contemporaries. The eighteenth-century tragedian with the greatest reputation for instilling terror was without a doubt Prosper Jolyot de Crébillon. He was most famous for his tragedy *Atrée et Thyeste*, first performed in 1707 and published in 1709 but republished more than twenty-five times before the Revolution.[66] The plot is as follows. Atrée, the king of Argos, and Thyeste, the king of Mycenae, are brothers. Thyeste kidnaps Atrée's wife Érope and forces her to marry him. They have a child, Plisthène, but Atrée has Érope murdered and abducts the child to raise as his own. Atrée has the opportunity to kill Thyeste as well but spares him only for the sake of wreaking a terrible vengeance upon him later in life. Atrée meets Thyeste twenty years later. He (Atrée) has secretly killed Plisthène and has the young man's blood poured into a cup which he then serves to his brother, who believes it is wine offered as a sign of reconciliation. Upon realizing that he has drunk the blood of his murdered son, Thyeste commits suicide.

In the preface to the published version of the play, Crébillon defined "tragedy" as "a disastrous action that . . . must conduct [audience members] by terror to pity, but with movements and with features that do not injure either their delicacy or their propriety." He wrote, "It only remains to be seen if I observed it, this propriety that is so necessary. I believed that I could flatter myself for having done so."[67] The predominant view of Crébillon was that his shocking scenes, including the dénouement of *Atrée et Thyeste*, were justified because of the salutary emotions they provoked. D'Argens wrote in 1745, "Those who have blamed M. de Crébillon for having made Atrée deceitful and cruel have doubtless not reflected that tragedy is the representation of an action that must excite pity and terror."[68] That same year Abbé Jean-Bernard Le Blanc wrote in an open letter to Crébillon, "You are the first, among us, who have known how to bring to [their] highest point terror and pity, the two great objects of tragedy." He added, "In *Atrée et Thyeste*, one of the masterpieces of our theater, terror and pity succeed each other by turns, and sometimes walk at an equal pace." Crébillon had the "superior taste" to know that "there is a point at which the emotion could be too strong and consequently disagreeable," and he therefore "brought terror only as far as it is permitted to be brought."[69] In his *Poëtique françoise, à l'usage des dames* (French poetry for the use of ladies) (1749), Gabriel-Henri Gaillard devoted an entire chapter to the passion of *terreur*. It begins with an homage to Crébillon: "It is in the tragedies of M. de Crébillon that one has to look for examples of this passion. One will find more striking examples there than anywhere else."[70] In a review of two books of English poetry in French translation, a writer for the *Bibliothèque impartiale* (1750) took issue with the Anglophile editor's claim that "'the genius of invention is rare among us [the French],'" responding, "Has not Crébillon, who is still quite alive, drawn from his own breast the principles of that terror that characterizes his tragedies[?]"[71] The reviewer said nothing about pity. Nor did the editors of the *Journal encyclopédique*, who in 1756 laconically praised Crébillon by writing that "he inspires terror."[72]

Crébillon's reputation outlived him. When the author died in 1762, an obituary appeared in the *Année littéraire* lamenting that "we have lost a poet who was the honor of his art, his nation, and his century." Crébillon was "the creator of a part [i.e., a character] that belonged to him alone, and that distinguishes him from all who preceded or succeeded him." The eulogist explained, "I mean that *terror*, little known by the great *Corneille*, absolutely unknown to *Racine*," and added that Crébillon was "perhaps the only tragic poet that France has produced."[73] Again, and by now characteristically, nothing was said of pity. Similarly, in an "Ode on the Death of Crébillon" an anonymous poet wrote: "You thus know how to make us love / The terror, so fatal to humans, of sepulchral pomp."[74]

A member of the Académie Française, Crébillon was replaced after his death by Claude Henri de Fusée de Voisenon. It was customary for a new member to present an inaugural discourse that praised his predecessor. Voisenon's included this allegory:

> The great Corneille and the tender Racine had just been plunged into the darkness of the tomb; their mausoleums were placed on the two sides of the throne that they had occupied; the Muse of tragedy . . . had fallen into a profound lethargy; her soul, worn out by pain, no longer had the strength that despair gives; in the excess of her dejection, her dagger had escaped from her hands. A proud and courageous mortal, draped in mourning, advances intrepidly, picks up the dagger and cries: *Muse, come back to life, I shall return your splendor to you.* Terror heard his voice, and appeared on the stage: *You are bringing me back to light, and your genius is giving me a new being,* she said with delight. With these words, she seized a bloody cup [the cup of Atrée], walked before him, and let the name of Crébillon ring out from the sacred mountain. The Muse recovered her senses, the ashes of Corneille and Racine came to life, and their successor was placed on the raised throne between the two tombs.[75]

The duc de Saint-Aignan, a fellow academician, responded with his own speech. He declared that Crébillon, "disdaining a rivalry of simple imitation" with his predecessors, "dared to create by himself a genre that had not yet appeared on our stage; and, through the lively impressions of terror, he obtained the same applause that we have accorded him." He added, "Thus had Michelangelo attained the highest reputation by only applying himself to give his brush a power . . . a pride that the experts have believed could not be better defined than by the epithet of *terrible*."[76]

Admiration of Crébillon continued to be strong among playwrights long after the writer's death. Among those who posthumously praised him

explicitly for the terror that his work incited were the playwrights Belloy
and Michel de Cubières-Palmézeaux;[77] the novelist, poet, and critic Nicolas Bricaire de la Dixmerie;[78] the jurist and anti-*philosophe* Jean-Antoine
Rigoley de Juvigny;[79] and the encyclopedist and Académie Française member d'Alembert.[80]

The verdict on Crébillon was not unanimous. In an anonymous letter to
the comic playwright Michel Guyot de Merville, published in an anthology
of Guyot's works in 1742 and possibly by Guyot himself, the correspondent
wrote that Crébillon had "sometimes left the nature of the tragic . . . by
pushing terror as far as the horrible [*l'horrible*]."[81] D'Arnaud advanced a
similar opinion in 1770, when he wrote that Crébillon was the forebear of
"this *terrible* genre" that he, d'Arnaud, was trying to further with his own
plays, but he added that "the vengeance of Atrée, devised over a long time
and executed in cold blood, inspires more *horror* than *terror*."[82] In his 1784
treatise *De la tragédie*, Clément was particularly critical of *Atrée et Thyeste*. He paraphrased Boileau's maxim and wrote that at the theater "*terror*
itself must be *sweet*." He thought it wrong "to attract respectable people to
the pleasures of the theater to present them with atrocious pictures," and
that "the Athenians would never have suffered that horrible situation of a
father who is offered the blood of his son to drink by his own brother." He
speculated that, "wanting to go farther than Racine, [Crébillon] went too
far," but he tempered his criticism by judging that in the later tragedies,
particularly in *Électre* and *Rhadamiste*, Crébillon "contained himself . . .
within the proper borders that separate terror from horror" and gave "more
energy to tragic terror."[83]

Crébillon's greatest critic was Voltaire, who appears to have been quite
jealous of his fellow playwright's popularity and took the occasion of
Crébillon's death to write a "eulogy" that attacked his rival more than it
praised him. Voltaire was particularly harsh in his assessment of *Atrée et
Thyeste*, though his criticism was idiosyncratic: "It is not because a cup
full of blood is a horrible thing that this piece is no longer staged: on the
contrary, this excess of terror would strike many spectators and would fill
them with that somber and painful attention that creates the charm of true
tragedy; but the great flaw of *Atrée* is that this piece is not interesting. No
one cares about a horrible [*horrible*] vengeance, meditated in cold blood,
without any necessity. An outrage done to Atrée twenty years ago does not
touch anyone."[84] Significantly, Voltaire suggested that Crébillon was on the
right track when he introduced terror into his play. Even an "excess" of
this emotion was warranted, provided that something was at stake. Since
the king's vengeance was not "necessary," however, terror was ineffective.

Similarly, Voltaire was willing to concede to Crébillon a scene of terror in his *Électre* (1708), when the title character berates her mother, Clytemnestra (who has killed Electra's father, Agamemnon); but he ridiculed the playwright for following the provocation of "these emotions of terror and pity" with a banal scene in which Electra's brother, Orestes, declares his love for "the insignificant Iphianasse."[85] Finally, Voltaire's criticism of Crébillon's *Sémiramis*—a subject Voltaire himself treated in a tragedy—was that the illicit love of the title character for her stepson was "without terror and without interest."[86]

Despite the misgivings of Voltaire and some other critics, then, Crébillon enjoyed the reputation for being *terrible*. Significantly, most of the commentators who elevated him to the status of France's greatest eighteenth-century tragic poet focused on the terror his plays produced but said nothing about that other "spring" of tragedy: pity. Nor did they say anything about catharsis. This indicates that for many critics the principal goal of tragedy was to instill or "excite" terror, plain and simple.

TERROR AND PITY IN VOLTAIREAN TRAGEDY

Voltaire was not merely a judge of tragedy. As a playwright himself, he was subject to criticism on the basis of the very standards upon which he insisted. He was well aware of this. For example, in 1719 he responded to critics of his *Œdipe*, the tragedy in verse he had written the previous year, at the age of nineteen, with a series of letters explaining his thinking before, during, and after the play's first performances. Specifically, he acknowledged that he had initially included a forty-line section describing the suicide of Jocasta (Oedipus's mother and wife) and the self-blinding of Oedipus. But this scene left the audience cold. Voltaire humbly wrote that "perhaps the mediocrity of the verse was the cause," but he also hypothesized that "perhaps terror having been pushed to its limit, it was impossible for the rest [of the description] not to seem boring." Therefore he cut the anticlimactic lines from future performances.[87] This self-critical revision was based on the conviction that terror must come at the right moment in a tragedy in order to have its maximum effect, a standard that, as we have just seen, he would apply to Crébillon's *Électre*.

Thirty years later Voltaire wrote an essay titled "Dissertation on the principal tragedies, ancient and modern, which have appeared on the subject of Electra, and in particular, on that of Sophocles," which was, among other things, a vehicle for commenting on his own *Oreste*. He wrote under the pen name of "M. Du Molard, member of numerous academies."

"Du Molard" complimented Voltaire for his introduction of a scene (not in Sophocles) in which Orestes, in disguise, presents Aegisthus with an urn supposedly containing the ashes of Aegisthus's son. This present "inspires terror in the heart of the spectator who is aware" of the ruse. The invented critic also approved of the introduction of the ghost of Clytemnestra, absent from Sophocles but present in versions by Aeschylus and Euripides. He wrote that "these *coups*, when well managed, are veritable tragedy, which does not consist of gallant sentiments, or of arguments, but of affecting [*pathétique*], terrible, theatrical action such as this."[88]

On other occasions as well Voltaire expressed the hope that his audiences would feel terror while watching or reading his tragedies. In 1730 he wrote to the actress Marie-Anne Dangeville, who was playing the role of Tullie (Tullia) in his play *Brutus*. He advised her to "put terror" into her last scene, where she tries to convince Titus to join in a conspiracy against the Roman Republic.[89] In 1749 he sent Frederick the Great a copy of his *Sémiramis*, writing, "I tried to spread all the terror of Greek theater and to change the French into Athenians."[90]

Many readers believed that Voltaire had succeeded in his goal. One of his greatest admirers was Frederick the Great. In 1738 Frederick (then crown prince) wrote to Voltaire praising his as yet unpublished *Mérope*, a play about a queen whose son kills her husband, as "one of the finest tragedies that has ever been written" and adding, "terror increases at each scene." Though this letter was meant to be private, it was published by Beaumarchais and Condorcet in their complete edition of Voltaire's works in 1785.[91] As king, Frederick lauded Voltaire in similar terms, and his praise reached eighteenth-century French readers in published editions of Voltaire's works. In 1749 Frederick wrote that *Sémiramis* "inspires terror mixed with pity."[92] When Voltaire died in 1778 the Prussian king wrote a eulogy in which he declared of the tragedy titled *Zaïre* (1732), about a murderous and unjustifiably jealous husband, "the interest, the pity, the terror that this great poet has the skill to excite in such a superior way, carries the auditor away."[93]

Other enthusiasts described Voltaire's tragedies in similar terms. For example, the historian and literary critic Gabriel-Henri Gaillard approved of *Zaïre*: "Jealous, furious Orosmane, stabbing with his own hand a wife whom he adores, by whom he is loved, by whom he believes he has been betrayed, carries trouble, terror, and pity to the depths of one's heart."[94] Gaillard also applied the standard of terror to Voltaire's *Électre*. He congratulated Voltaire for the ending, asking, "What is more striking . . . than to see in . . . the dénouement the sisters of Orestes flying full of joy into the arms of their brother to congratulate him on his victory; and this brother, overcome, trembling . . . telling them of his misfortune and his crime in mysterious, terrible terms, and interspersed with accents of desperation?" He added, "What surprise, what terror, what a *coup de théâtre!*"[95] A contributor to Louis Petit de Bachaumont's *Mémoires secrets* (1781) wrote of Voltaire's *Orphelin de la Chine* (1755) that "as it excites terror and pity, it has been raised to the rank of tragedy."[96] Indeed, Voltaire's tragedies were formative to the education of actors, according to Charles Palissot de Montenoy, who wrote in a 1779 *éloge* that "it is only through *Mahomet*, through *Sémiramis*, through *Tancrède*, that our actors, instead of declaiming, learned to become living pictures, and . . . to express, as they should, these great movements of pathos and of terror."[97]

Voltaire's critics, for their part, used the language of terror and pity to justify their judgments. For example, the *Almanach des muses* dismissed Voltaire's tragedy *Le triumvirat* (1764) with the single line: "These are scoundrels without energy who excite neither terror nor pity."[98] D'Arnaud objected to the exposure of the bloody body of Caesar in *Le mort de César*, writing, "This is the border where we must stop, where *terror* becomes *horror*,"[99] and thus recalling the very criticism Voltaire had directed at Crébillon. A reviewer for the *Année littéraire*, a journal edited by Voltaire's archrival Élie Catherine Fréron, objected to *Dom Pèdre, Roi de Castille* (1775), writing that "in the soul of the reader it produces . . . neither terror, nor pity."[100] Thus the very expression Voltaire used to disparage Corneille's plays came back to him.

TERROR VS. HORROR, OR
THE PROBLEM OF SHAKESPEARE

As we have seen, critics often distinguished between terror and horror, viewing the former as a key "spring" of tragedy and disparaging the latter as a defect. The notion that some writers went too far and crossed the line between terror and horror sheds light on the boundaries that critics attempted to draw around their ideal of terror. Uncertainty over just how far a playwright was permitted to go in the service of terror is most evident in debates over the value of Shakespearean tragedy and its influence on French theater.

Voltaire was particularly instrumental in articulating a view of "English" or Shakespearean tragedy as more horrible than it was terrible. In his *Discours sur la tragédie* (1731), addressed to the English statesman and political philosopher Bolingbroke, Voltaire insisted that terror not be "carried to excess." He acknowledged that even the Greeks, whom he admired,

included "revolting" scenes such as Oedipus ripping out his eyes and Orestes cutting his own mother's throat. Thus the "Greek tragedians . . . erred
by often taking horror for terror." Shakespeare was also guilty of this error,
Voltaire claimed, though he was quick to mollify his English correspondent by observing that "the art [of tragedy] was in its infancy at the time of
Aeschylus, as it was in London at the time of Shakespeare." He chastised
his own countrymen for condemning English drama without qualification,
and wrote that "if the English have mounted frightful plays [des spectacles
effroyables] when they wanted them to be terrible, we French playwrights,
as scrupulous as you have been bold, have held back too much . . . and
sometimes out of fear of crossing the line we do not arrive at the tragic."[101]

Other eighteenth-century French writers repeated Voltaire's criticisms,
often without his caveats. For example, in 1744 the marquis d'Argens
railed, "Let us leave to the English the genre of tragedy that only excites
terror by the view of cadavers, daggers, and poisons. The theater, made to
soften morals, then becomes the school of harshness, of barbarism and of
inhumanity." He added, "Let us never expose anything odious and frightful
[d'affreux] under the eyes of the spectators. Inspire terror and pity by the
power of thoughts, feelings and situations, and leave it to the people whose
heart is as hard as their genius the feeble talent of moving the spectators
with horrible images."[102] Belloy similarly sought to police the border between the terrible and the horrible. In the preface to his tragedy Gabrielle
de Vergy (1770) he wrote, "One of the great defects of the majority of English tragedies, that which most characterizes the genius of that nation, as
opposed to that of the Athenians, is terror carried to excess, terror degenerating almost always to horror, and leading rarely to tears."[103]

French critics continued to lament the influence of English horror in
the 1780s. In 1782 a writer for the Journal encyclopédique complained that
"our authors, forgetting the chefs-d'oeuvre of our masters, have wished to
seek [their] models in Great Britain." Consequently "they have multiplied
massacres, tombs . . . they have substituted horror for terror."[104] Rigoley de
Juvigny echoed this view in 1787, when he asked, "To what has the French
stage in effect been reduced today?" He replied, "Terror and Pity are banished from it; but dark HORROR reigns." He blamed the influence of the
English: "Melpomene appears now only to be covered by the disgusting rags
of Shakespeare."[105]

English drama in general and Shakespeare in particular had their French
defenders, however, and they invoked terror as well as pity to support their
arguments. Specifically, Pierre-Antoine de La Place was a critic and translator whose eight-volume Théâtre anglois (1745–49) made the case for En-

glish theater to French readers. In his "Discours sur le théâtre anglois," he defended the English for the violence of their theater: "If we see scoundrels, and poisoners, in history, why not present in the theater actions capable of augmenting the terror and pity that one seeks to produce . . . ?" De La Place also defended the English use of "ghosts, witches, and demons," and insisted that the "marvelous" had its place in theater, since it could "augment terror, pity, or interest." As to the relative lack of love in English tragedy, de La Place argued that subplots involving love only distracted from the "truly theatrical passions" of "terror and pity," which in turn worked toward the "correction of morals."[106]

D'Arnaud, writing in 1770, also praised Shakespeare, lamenting that "we do not have in any of our pieces a tableau of the effects of the terror that follows the crime," as Shakepeare included in *Macbeth*. Elsewhere, when describing *le genre terrible*, which he also called *la tragédie par excellence*, he wrote that "*terror* [is] unquestionably one of the most powerful springs of theatrical action," and that "the Greeks, and the English alone after them, have achieved this goal."[107] Similar reasoning guided a positive review in the *Almanach des muses* (1771) of a French version of Hamlet: the reviewer affirmed that "this piece excites profound terror."[108] Other promoters of Shakespeare included a correspondent for the *Année littéraire* (1776) who wrote that the bard's "details" "always produce terror and pity, the goal of all tragic authors,"[109] and Marmontel, who wrote in 1787 that Shakespeare "knew how to spread profound terror."[110]

Those critics who accused Shakespeare and *le théâtre anglois* of crossing the line from terror to horror reveal an attempt to keep terror pure, dignified, and moral, and this attempt in turn discloses a widespread feeling that theatrical terror was a good thing, worthy of being protected. Shakespeare's supporters were less worried about terror "degenerating" into horror, but they shared with his detractors the belief that terror in tragedies led to moral improvement in audiences.

Despite the controversial position of Shakespeare in French theater, and perhaps because of it, playwrights in the quarter century before the Revolution continued to test the boundaries between terror and horror. The best-known among them was Pierre-Laurent Buirette de Belloy. In 1765 he enjoyed great success with *Le siège de Calais*, a patriotic subject well suited to the political atmosphere in the aftermath of the Seven Years' War.[111] Belloy was nevertheless subject to criticism for this work. The *Année littéraire* published a review that claimed, "There is neither *terror* nor *pity* in the piece; it is therefore not a *tragedy*."[112] He also failed to inspire terror in his *Gaston et Bayard* (1770), a play about the famous knight Bayard who fought under Gaston de Foix in the Italian campaigns of Louis XII, at least according to the *Journal des beaux-arts et des sciences*, which published this critique: "One will find that M. de Belloy might have made his heroes too grand for their assassins, which lessens the terror that the latter should inspire in the most critical moments." It added that the treacherous character Avogare "is more capable of inspiring contempt than terror."[113] The *Année littéraire* was even harsher, writing that the play was "more suited to make sane spectators laugh than to inspire them with terror."[114]

With his tragedy *Gabrielle de Vergy* (1777), however, Belloy took such care to inspire terror that he was accused of crossing the line into horror. In this grim story, which Belloy himself called "tragedy of the most terrible genre," the eponymous heroine is forced by her jealous husband to eat the heart of her lover. Belloy acknowledged that with this subject "one believes oneself threatened with being taken all the way to horror." But he assured his readers that "for the past few years the public has gotten used to strong situations which Racine and Corneille had not deployed on the French stage." He asserted, "You will hardly find in the masterpieces of the two fathers of our theater those violent blows of terror . . . which seemed to constitute the tragedy of the Greeks."[115] Yet Sabatier de Cavaillon, a "former professor of eloquence" writing in 1779, denounced the "atrocious" heart-eating episode as a scene that provoked "more horror than terror." He wrote of "tragedy" more generally that "its greatest power consists of terror taken to the limit," but he warned that "often it is only separated from horror by a line."[116] A contributor to the *Correspondance secrète* (1787) felt similarly, seeing Belloy's tragedy as one of a series of plays that have "displayed horror where terror used to reign."[117] Yet the *Bibliographie parisienne* gave *Gabrielle de Vergy* a positive review: "All the furies of jealousy, all the painful sentiments and all the horrors of which love . . . is perhaps capable, fill this piece with compassion and terror."[118] This was a rare example of horror—or, more precisely, horrors, in the plural—carrying positive connotations. But it is the exception that proves the rule. In almost every case, in the context of theater criticism, *terreur* was a good thing and *horreur* was a bad thing.

CONCLUSIONS

There are many other examples of critics using the term *terreur* to approve of tragedies and noting its absence to chastise playwrights. Thus d'Arnaud enjoyed the approbation of the *Journal des beaux-arts et des sciences* for his *Euphémie, ou Le Triomphe de la Religion* (1768), which according to the author of the review included both pity and terror.[119] And he must have been gratified by the review of his tragedy *Fayel* in *L'année littéraire*, which used the word *terreur* seven times, each time as a compliment, to describe the play.[120] Jean-François Ducis earned plaudits from the *Journal politique* for his version of Romeo and Juliet, which had "more terror" than Shakespeare's original and was "a very great success."[121] The editors of *Histoire de la république des lettres et arts en France* approved of his election to Voltaire's *fauteuil* at the Académie Française in 1779, writing that the "tragedies that he has given where terror breathes have shown that Melpomene gave him the scepter of tragedy."[122] This list of positive and negative reviews could be extended. Among those playwrights who received praise for the terror their plays instilled were Henri Richer, Sébastien-Roch-Nicolas Chamfort, and Dubois de Rochefort.[123] Among those criticized for lacking terror in their plays were Scipione Maffei, Madeleine-Angélique de Gomez, Charles-Pierre Colardeau, Jean-François de la Harpe, Bernard-Joseph Saurin, and Nicolas Fallet.[124] But by now the point should be clear that in the context of theater criticism *la terreur* was an unquestionably positive component of any tragedy. It was an indication that a play was effective, that it instilled in the minds of viewers and readers an emotion at once pleasurable, salutary, and productive of virtue. If Aristotle had a different view of terror, seeing it (together with pity) as a passion that needed to be purged, his French interpreters in the century prior to the Revolution either explained the catharsis away or simply declined to mention it. For them it was important for spectators to retain feelings of terror and pity long after the play ended, and even here many critics focused on terror without mentioning the role of pity. Taken together, the many writings—difficult and easy, ponderous and light, systematic and impressionistic—that used *la terreur* as a critical measure for theatrical success helped to give the word positive emotional connotations. They contributed to the moralization of terror, making it a salutary emotion for the viewer, whom it improved, and for society, which it protected.

CHAPTER FIVE

Terror and the Sublime

INTRODUCTION

The last chapter explored a strand of aesthetic thought that promoted terror as a sign of theatrical success. This chapter examines a strand of aesthetic thought that characterized terror more generally as a precondition of "the sublime." It focuses on the ideas of Edmund Burke and their reception in France from the middle of the eighteenth century, though it considers other sources of the belief that "the terrible" in art and nature was worthy of respect and admiration. There were important differences between the theater criticism that exalted terror and the aesthetic reflections on the sublime and the terrible. To begin with, the cult of the sublime went beyond the stage to consider the place of terror in the arts more generally and even in nature. Moreover, whereas theater critics typically had an ethical message to convey, the advocates of a sublime sensibility were more interested in the intrinsic value of terror, regardless of its moral implications. Finally, while theater critics were usually careful to guard the frontier between the "terrible" and the "horrible," reflections on the sublime were more likely to conflate the two. Despite these differences, both fields of aesthetics characterized terror as a praiseworthy force and contributed to the word's positive emotional connotations.

FROM LONGINUS TO BURKE

If Aristotle provided a model—more or less loosely followed—for French theater critics who promoted "terror and pity" as prerequisites for tragedy, Longinus supplied a way of thinking about terror as a component of the sublime. His treatise *Peri Hypsous* (*On the Sublime*), written in the first or third century CE (scholars disagree on this matter), was designed to teach rhetoric to public speakers, though for eighteenth-century writers the concept also came to describe features of other art forms as well as the natural world.[1] The French knew their Longinus via Nicolas Boileau-Despréaux, whom we saw in the previous chapter recommending "sweet terror" in tragic poetry. Boileau translated *Peri Hypsous* in 1674 as *Traité du sublime, ou Du merveilleux dans le discours* (Treatise on the sublime, or On the marvelous in speech). In Boileau's version, Longinus wrote that "the sublime is in effect what forms the excellence and the sovereign perfection of speech." It is through the sublime "that the great poets and the most famous writers won prizes and filled all of posterity with their reputation for glory." The sublime "does not persuade, properly speaking, but it ravishes, it transports, and it produces in us a certain admiration mixed with astonishment and surprise, which is something altogether different from persuading." Unlike mere persuasion, it "gives to speech a certain noble vigor, an invincible force that raises the soul" of the listener and "overthrows everything like a thunderbolt."[2]

For Longinus the characteristics of the sublime were clearest when writers failed to exhibit them. He gave examples of poets who were deficient in producing sublime verse, and he faulted them strongly for using imagery that was not *phoberos* or *deinos*, which Boileau translated as *terrible*. When one unnamed poet used such expressions as "entangled torrents of flames" and "vomiting against the heavens," for Boileau's Longinus "all these phrases thus encumbered with vain imaginings disturb and spoil a discourse more than they serve to elevate it, such that when one looks at it up close and in the light of day, what initially appeared so terrible suddenly becomes stupid and ridiculous."[3] Similarly, Homer received disapproval for writing of "the goddess of darkness" that "a stinking humor ran from her nostrils." By doing so he "does not make this goddess properly terrible, but odious and disgusting.[4] Elsewhere the poet Aratus was criticized for writing in relation to sailors threatened by a storm at sea, "A thin and light pole defends them from death." Of this formulation the reader of the *Traité du sublime* learned, "But in so varnishing this thought, [Aratus] rendered it low and flowery from the terrible [thought] that it was."[5]

Boileau's version of Longinus was republished more than forty times before the Revolution.[6] In addition to any direct influence it may have had on French writers, it exerted an indirect impact in the person of Edmund Burke, who undoubtedly did more to promote the aesthetic value of terror, on both sides of the Channel, than any other single writer. Burke's *Philosophical Enquiry into the Origin of Our Ideas of the Sublime and the Beautiful* (1757), which French readers knew as *Recherches philosophiques sur l'origine des*

idées que nous avons du beau & du sublime (1765), argued that terror or
"the terrible" was a precondition of the sublime.[7] (The following analysis
is based on the French translation by Abbé des François, and where I refer
to "Burke" I mean des François's rendering in *Recherches philosophiques*.)
Burke paid his debt to Longinus when he wrote of the "pride" that people
experience "when without running any danger we can familiarize ourselves
with terrible objects," and when "the mind . . . arrogates a part of the dignity and importance of these same objects." He noted, "This is what called
Longinus's attention to that glory, and to that feeling of grandeur with which
one is always filled inside when one reads sublime passages in the poets and
orators."[8]

Yet if Burke acknowledged the importance of "terrible objects" for
Longinus, he shifted the emphasis to place terror at the very center of any
sublime experience: "Whatever is suited in any fashion to excite ideas of
pain and danger, I mean all that is in any manner terrible, horrible [*épouvantable*], that which turns only on terrible objects, or that which acts in
such a way as to inspire terror, is a source of the sublime; that is to say that
it results in the strongest emotion the mind can feel."[9] Burke also departed
from Longinus (and other writers on the sublime) by distinguishing between
the sublime and the beautiful. For Burke the beautiful (*le beau*) inspired
love rather than terror. Moreover, it produced pleasure (*le plaisir*), a positive emotion which Burke distinguished from the relative emotion that he
called "contentment" (*le contentement*). One felt contentment upon the
diminution of any pain, including pain caused by terror.[10]

In a chapter devoted specifically to terror Burke elaborated, writing that
"everything that is terrible, with regard to sight, is likewise sublime, whether
this cause of terror be accompanied by greatness of dimensions or not."
Thus snakes and "venomous animals of all species" were among those creatures capable "of producing ideas of the sublime, because they are regarded
as objects of terror." Larger objects could be sublime, but only if they (like
snakes) were dangerous. One could imagine "a single plain of vast extent"
that could "equal the immensity of the ocean," but the ocean would be more
sublime because of "the terrible, horrible [*épouvantable*] idea presented by
this vast collection of water that covers the terrestrial globe." Burke therefore reiterated, "In effect terror in every case whatsoever is the first principle of the sublime, whether one perceives it or not."[11]

Darkness contributed further to the sublime, according to Burke, because it increased danger and therefore terror. Burke affirmed, "Darkness
appears in general necessary when it is a matter of adding to the terror that
any given thing inspires." He asked his readers "to examine to what extent

the night adds to terror, in all cases of danger," and to reflect on "how far notions of spirits and specters, of which no one can form clear ideas, affect those who believe in popular stories about these types of beings." He observed that "in despotic governments that are founded on the passions of men, and principally upon fear," thinking no doubt of Montesquieu's definition of the "principle" of despotism, "the ruler is hidden, so far as it is possible, from the eyes of the public." He added that "even today the savages of America keep their idol in a dark corner of the hut that is consecrated to its cult," and recalled that "the druids performed their ceremonies in the midst of the thickest and darkest woods, and in the shadow of the oldest and many-branched oaks."[12]

Elsewhere Burke promoted his view of darkness by contending with Locke. He wrote, "M. Locke believes that *darkness* is not naturally an idea of terror," and "once a nurse and an old woman have allied the ideas of ghosts and revenants with that of darkness, the night then always becomes painful and horrible [*horrible*] for the imagination." But for Burke darkness was a real source of danger and therefore of terror, and he answered Locke's claim about ghosts and revenants by postulating that it is "certainly more natural to think that *darkness*, which has been since the beginning an idea of terror, was chosen as the condition suited to these terrible representations, than to believe that these representations made darkness terrible."[13]

The role of terror in the sublime could also be seen in the realm of power, according to Burke, who claimed to know "of nothing sublime that is not a modification of power." He wrote that power "comes . . . naturally from terror" and explained that power was linked in every person's mind with pain and death; thus, "ideas of pain, and above all those of death, affect [us] to the point that insofar as we are in the presence of anything that is supposed to have the power of inflicting the one or the other, it is impossible for us to be completely sheltered from terror." He invited his reader to imagine "a man, or above all an animal of prodigious power," and asked what emotion this thought would provoke. His answer was: "The emotion that we feel will be an effect of the fear that we initially have that this enormous power might be employed for rapine or destruction," adding, "This power draws all its sublimity from the terror that generally accompanies it."[14]

But power alone was not enough to produce terror. If power was tamed and thereby lost its ability to harm, it would lose its terribleness together with its sublimity. To prove this point, Burke compared the emotional effect of an ox with that of a bull. An ox, he wrote, "is an extremely powerful animal, but it is an innocent animal, and very useful; it is not at all dangerous," and "this is also the reason why the idea of an ox is not at all a sublime idea." By contrast, "the bull is an equally powerful animal, but its power is of another sort; most of the time it is very destructive." Accordingly, "the idea that one has of a bull is sublime." Similarly, the horse, "when seen as a useful animal, fit to pull the plow, . . . has nothing of the sublime," whereas with the wild horse described in the book of Job, " 'whose bristling mane makes a sound like thunder, who by the proud breath of its nostrils spreads terror, who foams, trembles, and seems to devour the earth,' " all thoughts of utility disappear as "the terrible and the sublime are present together, and strike alone."[15] Once again Burke recalled that "wherever we find power . . . we notice that the sublime always accompanies terror."[16]

Political power, on the other hand, was always terrible and hence sublime. Burke wrote, "The idea of power established in a king, in a chief, is connected in the same way to the idea of terror." He recalled that "often when speaking of sovereigns, one gives them the title of terrible Majesty, of fearsome princes [*de princes formidables*]," a phenomenon that we considered in chapter 2. He also observed that "there are many young persons who have little experience with the world, and who not having been in the habit of approaching the great, [or] ministers, when they appear before them, are seized with fear and respect, lose the use of their faculties, or at least that free and easy air that is natural to them."[17]

If political power was terrible, majestic and sublime, divine power was all the more so. Burke rejected the claims of "people who believe that the idea of power is never accompanied . . . with terror" and who "go so far was to say that we can contemplate the idea of God without feeling any emotion of this nature." After all, "When we contemplate an object so vast, so immense, before the eyes of this all-powerful God, whose universal presence surrounds us from all sides, we tremble to see the smallness of our being, we are as annihilated before him." Though reflecting on God's mercy might reduce our fears, "we cannot entirely rid ourselves of the terror that a force which nothing can resist inspires."[18] Burke provided evidence from the Bible, observing that "wherever God is represented as appearing in his glory, and making men hear his word, all that is terrible in nature is assembled to augment the respect mixed with fear that the presence of the Divine Majesty inspires."[19] He also drew on secular writers to make his point, noting that for Horace it took "the greatest effort of philosophical courage to look without terror . . . on this universe that certainly proves the immensity, the glory of him who made it." Even Lucretius, "whom one could not suspect of ever having given himself over to those terrors that superstition engenders," betrayed the "secret horror and terror with which he [was] seized."[20]

Burke affirmed that many other writers, "both sacred and profane," affirmed "inseparable union of respect with fear of the Divinity with the ideas that we have of that same Divinity." This assertion brought Burke uncomfortably close to "a maxim we seemingly owe to these ideas, and which I believe quite false with regard to the origin of true religion," namely Petronius's claim that " '*Primus in orbe Deos fecit timor,*' " or, " 'Fear first made the gods in the world.' " For Burke it was the other way around, since "the notion of a supreme power must always precede the terror that it inspires"; yet it was also true, in Burke's opinion, that "that this terror must absolutely be the consequence of the idea of such a power, once the mind has formed it."[21]

There were other sources of sublime terror, according to Burke. Specifically, certain sounds were capable of producing the terror that the sublime required. Burke wrote, "An excessive *noise* suffices to stun the mind, to suspend its action, and to fill it with terror," and he gave as examples waterfalls, storms, thunder, and artillery. Loudness was not the only feature of sounds that could produce terror. For example, "a sudden beginning, or the sudden cessation of sound" had the same effect, whereas "everything that by sight or by sound eases the transition from one extreme to another does not cause any terror, and consequently cannot produce the sublime." Likewise, "a single sound of a certain power, though it may not be of a long duration, if it is repeated at intervals, produces a sublime effect." Examples of this phenomenon were clock towers striking the hours at night, "a single stroke of the drum, repeated from one time to another," and distant cannon fire.[22]

In addition to being majestic, terror was also healthful, according to Burke, who saw it as affecting the mind in much the same way that physical exercise affected the body. He observed that "rest" and "relaxation" prevented the "natural and necessary secretions" from taking place in the fibers of the organs, which in turn dried out. This led to nerve pain as well as "melancholy, depression, despair, and often suicide." The cure was "exercise, or labor."[23] Just as "ordinary labor" constituted "the exercise of the grossest parts of the body [i.e., the muscles]," "terror" was "the exercise of the most delicate ones [i.e., the nerves]."[24] Provided that the terrified person was not in danger of imminent "destruction," the emotion of terror could remove "a dangerous and uncomfortable encumbrance" from the nerves and thereby "produce . . . a type of satisfying horror [*une espèce d'horreur qui satisfait*], a sort of tranquility mixed with terror."[25]

For Burke, then, terror had an array of positive meanings. As a precondition of the sublime, it connoted power, majesty, and the divine, and it was also salutary in the medical sense of the term. Burke did not make an explicitly moral case for terror. Indeed, his remarks on despotism suggested an amoral interpretation of the passion. In this respect he parted ways with the theater critics I examined in chapter 4 who insisted on the positive ethical effects of terror-inducing tragedies. But his identification of terror with magnificence, including God's magnificence, combined with his conviction that the emotion was good for the human body, contributed to a more general valorization of terror. It reinforced—and was in turn reinforced by—theatrical, legal, political, and theological terror speech.

BURKE'S CRITICAL RECEPTION IN FRANCE

French readers were aware of Burke's ideas even before the 1765 translation of his *Philosophical Enquiry* appeared. In 1757 a lengthy review of the first edition appeared in the *Journal encyclopédique*, the periodical edited by the journalist-*philosophe* Pierre Rousseau of Toulouse and published in Liège to avoid censorship by the French monarchy. The reviewer lavished Burke with praise, calling him "a *philosophe*" who had been "raised up by the force of his genius . . . to plumb the depths of his existence, to analyze his faculties, to trace them back to their origin," and compared him to "those bold navigators who are too restricted within the limits of the continent and brave the reefs and storms to discover a new world." The reviewer also placed this "English *philosophe*" among the ranks of "the *Descartes*, the *Newtons*, and the *Lockes*" for his work on the beautiful and the sublime.[26]

The review, which went on for sixteen pages and over three thousand words, provided an extensive summary of Burke's arguments, and it affirmed his thesis: "When surveying all . . . sources of the sublime in relation to our senses, we shall find that it is born of causes that inspire a kind of terror."[27] The review contained criticisms as well. Specifically, Burke "seem[ed] sometimes to confuse astonishment with terror [*l'étonnement avec la terreur*]." For the reviewer, "astonishment" occupied a midpoint between admiration—which in Burke's theory stimulated love—and terror. Since astonishment could "participate" in either the sublime or the beautiful, the two principles could "become confused." Moreover, "above terror, there is a violent impression which suspends all the movements of the soul; this is horror [*l'horreur*]."[28] As we have already seen, Burke occasionally conflated terror and horror, ignoring a distinction that many theater critics, particularly those who objected to "English" tragedy, considered important. Here he was taken to task for that shortcoming; but by policing the border between terror and horror, the critic writing for the *Journal encyclopédique* reaffirmed the aesthetic value of terror. All in all, the review encouraged readers who could understand English to delve more deeply into the work of the genius Burke and, perhaps more important, summarized and promoted the argument for those who could not read English and propagated the idea that terror was a precondition of the sublime.[29]

If the pro-Enlightenment publicist Pierre Rousseau was enthusiastic about Burke's views on terror and the sublime, so did the "enemy of the Enlightenment" Élie-Catherine Fréron also eagerly endorse Burke's work.[30] In the January 1765 issue of his *Année littéraire*, Fréron included a review of Abbé des François's translation. The article, which took the form of a letter to an unnamed correspondent, was nearly as long as the review in the *Journal encyclopédique*, and it concluded, "The little that I have cited of this production suffices, Monsieur, to inspire you to read it." The reviewer asserted that "writers and artists will profit from this writing" and that "this profound and luminous work is destined to take its place among the small number of truly useful books."[31] The review reported on the linkage in Burke's mind between the sublime and the terrible, informing the reader that "all general *privations* are sublime, because they are all terrible; such are voids, darkness, solitude, silence," and it relayed Burke's admiration for "majestic and terrible images."[32]

One month later it was the turn of pro-Enlightenment editors to praise the translation of Burke's *Philosophical Enquiry*. In the February issue of the *Gazette littéraire de l'Europe*, published by the philosophes Abbé Arnaud and Jean-Baptiste Suard, a brief (five-hundred-word) review of the *Recherches philosophiques* asserted that Burke "proves that the sublime is always the effect of a vivid impression of astonishment or of terror." (Unlike the 1757 article in the *Journal encyclopédique*, this review did not distinguish between astonishment and terror.) The reviewer was more critical of Burke's analysis of the beautiful, writing that "this part [of the book] appears to us greatly inferior to the first."[33] But this criticism only highlights the positive effect that Burke's valorization of terror had on the reviewer.

The French edition of Burke's treatise was reviewed yet again in 1767, this time by the *Journal des sçavants*, in a substantial article of roughly thirteen hundred words, which began with the judgment, "This Work is well-reasoned, and deserves our attention." According to the reviewer, Burke "finds that [the passion] which the sublime produces is astonishment mixed with terror." Therefore "all the ideas of danger, of power insofar as it can destroy us, of immensity insofar as it astonishes our weakness and seems ready to crush or devour [us] . . . are the most common sources of the sublime." The reviewer had "only one objection to this general system." Specifically, "The author gives the terrible as the basis of the sublime. According to this principle, M. de Crébillon . . . is more sublime than Corneille;

he is even the only sublime one, and Corneille is not." We have seen in the previous chapter how common it was to use the terms "terror" and "terrible" when describing the work of the playwright Crébillon. By contrast, Corneille was known not for his terribleness but for the admiration his characters and stories inspired. For the reviewer, the feeling of admiration justified classifying Corneille and his work as sublime. The review concluded that "perhaps the defect in M. Burke's system comes from a too-restrictive idea of the sublime, whereas it would be necessary to understand it not as a single kind of astonishment, but as astonishment in general, whether it derives from admiration or from terror." In this case "the sphere of the sublime extends and embraces Corneille and Crébillon at the same time."[34] The more capacious interpretation of the sublime offered by the reviewer thus muted the importance of terror by allowing for alternative forms of "astonishment," but it nevertheless agreed that terror was often a source of the sublime. More important, the review, appearing two years after the publication of the French translation and a full decade after the article on the English edition in the *Journal encyclopédique*, attests to the continuing interest in Burke's argument about the role of terror in the production of the sublime.

THE SUBLIME AND THE TERRIBLE IN ART
CRITICISM AND NATURE WRITING

The French writer who most enthusiastically adopted Burkean ideas about terror and the sublime was Denis Diderot. Commissioned by Friedrich Melchior Grimm to write for his manuscript newsletter, *Correspondance littéraire*, Diderot supplied reports on the biennial royal art expositions held in the *salon carrée* at the Louvre palace. Just as theater critics praised tragedies that instilled terror and critiqued those that failed to do so, Diderot applied the same standard to painting. He began writing his reports in 1759, before the *Recherches philosophiques* appeared, and it was not until 1767 that he explicitly linked terror and the sublime. But even in his earliest art criticism he promoted the aesthetic valorization of terror.

In his report on the Salon of 1759, for example, Diderot chastised Carle (Charles-André) van Loo for his painting of Jason and Medea (see fig. 1) because it lacked the capacity to induce terror in its viewers. He addressed Grimm, "Oh, my friend. [It's] a bad thing . . . a little Medea, short, stiff, constrained, overloaded with fabric . . . not a drop of blood falling from the tip of her dagger or dripping onto her hand; no disorder; no terror." Similarly, when evaluating *Carthusians Meditating* (see fig. 2), by Étienne Jeaurat, he

Fig. 1. *Jason and Medea* (1759), by Carle [Charles-André] van Loo,
was not sufficiently terrifying for Diderot's taste.

faulted the artist for failing to induce terror: "nothing wild; nothing that
recalls divine justice; no idea, no profound adoration; no inward contempla-
tion; no ecstasy; no terror."[35]

By contrast, in his *Salon* of 1761, Diderot praised Jean-Baptiste-Henri Deshays as "the best painter in the nation." Commenting on *The Martyrdom*

Fig. 2. *Carthusians Meditating* (1759), by Étienne Jeaurat,
lacked terror, in Diderot's view.

of Saint Andrew (see fig. 3), he described Saint Andrew rising from a kneeling position and enduring the stroke of an executioner's whip while a mother tries to shield her frightened child from the sight: "The saint has his arms raised, his head back, and his eyes turned heavenward; a bushy beard covers his chin. Constancy, faith, hope, and pain are cast onto his face, which has a simple, strong, rustic, and moving character; one suffers greatly seeing him. . . . It is impossible to look for long without terror at this scene of inhumanity and furor.[36] Similarly, "one of the greatest compositions of the [1761] *Salon*" was *The Combat of Diomedes and Aeneas* (see fig. 4), a painting by Gabriel-François Doyen based on the fifth book of Homer's *Iliad*. It was "full of fire, grandeur, movement, and poetry." Diderot particularly approved of the inclusion of a warrior pierced by a javelin, as he "inspires terror."[37]

Fig. 3. *The Martyrdom of Saint Andrew* (1761), by Jean-Baptiste-Henri Deshays,
inspired terror in the viewer, according to Diderot.

Fig. 4. Diderot approved of *The Combat of Diomedes and Aeneas* (1761),
by Gabriel-François Doyen, noting that the warrior pierced by a
javelin "inspires terror."

At the same exposition Diderot registered his disappointment with Simon Challe's painting of Cleopatra dying. Specifically, he questioned the
choice of the moment depicted on the canvas. Challe displayed the snake
on Cleopatra's breast after it had bitten her and she was dying. It would
have been preferable, in Diderot's opinion, to depict the moment when
"this haughty woman . . . uncovers her breast, smiles at the snake, but with
a disdainful smile that will fall onto the victor from whom she is going to
escape, and has it bite her breast." He added, "Perhaps the expression would
have been more terrible and stronger if she had smiled to the snake attached
to her breast." Choosing the "moment in which she expires" meant not depicting Cleopatra but rather "a woman dying of a snakebite."[38] Diderot was
even more dismissive of Louis-Jean-François Lagrenée's *Joshua Fighting the
Amoreans and Ordering the Sun [to Stop]*, directly addressing the author,
"You have neither the variety of thoughts, nor that passion, nor that terrible
quality [*ce terrible*] appropriate to a painter of battles."[39]

When Lagrenée exhibited his work again in 1765, Diderot was similarly
critical. Remarking on *The Sacrifice of Jephtha*, he conceded that Jephtha
"does not lack expression," but wondered whether it was the expression
"of a father who is about to slit his daughter's throat." A more realistic and
more terrifying Jephtha would have his "eyes closed, his mouth clenched,

his face muscles convulsed, and his head turned toward heaven." In the painting Jephtha is accompanied by "three old men, calm and idle spectators of the scene," who make him look like "an assassin," and the young man who serves him "without lifting an eyebrow" is "atrociously insupportable and false." Diderot added, "In a word, ask the indulgent admirers of this piece if it inspires any of that terror, that shuddering, that pain which one feels from the [Bible] story alone."[40]

Diderot also faulted Jean-Baptiste-Henri Deshays (whom he had praised in 1761) for two paintings exhibited at the 1765 Salon. Both lacked the requisite terror, in Diderot's opinion. Commenting on the artist's *Conversion of Saint Paul*, Diderot advised painters not to undertake this subject unless they were sure they could depict "fire raining down from heaven" and "men and horses falling over in fear [*d'effroi*]." He asked an imagined painter, "Do you have in your imagination the various faces of terror?" He also emphasized the importance of "the terrible effect of light" in a painting of that subject, noting that Deshays "did not think of this." He did include "frightened [*effrayés*] soldiers" among the figures in his painting, but they were "cold and mediocre."[41] Diderot likewise judged Deshays's *Saint Jerome Writing about Death* (see fig. 5) as a missed opportunity to convey terror. It would have been appropriate to show the saint's "face, his arms, his position, his attitude, [to] show the terror that all must feel when exposed to the miseries present at the end of their lives," but Deshays did not achieve this effect.[42]

Diderot admired one of the paintings Deshays exhibited at the 1765 Salon, praising it highly for the terror it conveyed. This was *Artemisia at the Tomb of Mausolus*. Mausolus had been the tyrant of Caria in the fourth century BCE, and Artemisia had been his sister and wife. When Mausolus died, Artemisia wished to have him with her always and therefore drank a potion containing his ashes. Deshays's painting depicted the moment just before she consumes the contents of Mausolus's urn. Diderot wrote, "This whole composition is very sad, very lugubrious, very sepulchral. It inspires admiration, pain, terror, and respect."[43]

It was in his commentary on the 1767 Salon that Diderot first explicitly linked the terrible to the sublime, and a close examination of his writing leaves no doubt that he made liberal use of Burke's ideas, which had appeared in Abbé Des François's French translation of the *Philosophical Enquiry* two years previously. Gita May has shown how extensively Diderot made use of Burke, even to the point of nearly plagiarizing him.[44] Diderot's praise of terror in the works of artists at the Salons between 1759 and 1765 suggests some reasons for this affinity. Diderot was predisposed to adopt a work that made terror into a standard of aesthetic judgment.

Fig. 5. *Saint Jerome Writing about Death* (1765), by Jean-Baptiste Deshays,
failed to inspire terror, in Diderot's opinion.

Burkean ideas are evident in Diderot's extensive commentary on a series
of paintings by Claude-Joseph Vernet. In analyzing a painting titled *Claire
de Lune* (Moonlight), he expressed doubts about his ability to "render [in
words] the effect and the magic, that stormy and obscure sky, those thick
and black clouds, all that depth, all the terror that they gave to the scene."[45]
When discussing an unidentified painting of a nocturnal scene on the water, he wrote of "the terror and the truth of that august scene."[46] Diderot

ascribed terribleness not only to the artist's work, but to the artist himself, apostrophizing him as "this Vernet, this terrible Vernet."[47] All this could have been written without the help of Burke, but when Diderot outlined some general principles about the relationship between terror and the sublime, his debt to the Anglo-Irish *philosophe* became clear. "Everything that astonishes the soul," he wrote, "everything that imprints a sentiment of terror leads to the sublime." He added that "a vast plain does not astonish like the ocean does, nor does a tranquil ocean [astonish] like an agitated ocean does," thus recalling the very imagery Burke used to support his view of the sublime. He went on to write that "darkness increases terror," and though this might have seemed to be a commonsense idea, it is one to which Burke had devoted several chapters. Indeed, the wording he used— *l'obscurité ajoute à la terreur*—mimicked the wording in Des François's rendering of Burke's contention that *la nuit* [night] *ajoute à la terreur.*[48]

Moreover, Diderot's elaboration on the effect of darkness owed much to Burke. In a digression to his commentary on Vernet, Diderot wrote, "Temples are dark," echoing Burke (in Des François's version). "Almost all the pagan temples were dark." Similarly, Diderot wrote, "Tyrants show themselves rarely; they are not seen at all," which was simply a more succinct version of this statement in the *Recherches philosophiques*: "In despotic governments that are founded on the passions of men, and principally on fear, the ruler is hidden, insofar as it is possible, from the eyes of the public." He adjured priests, "Place your altars, build your edifices in the depths of the forest," advice he no doubt drew from Burke's report that "the druids performed their ceremonies in the midst of the thickest and darkest woods, and in the shadow of the oldest and many-branched oaks."[49]

Continuing his excursus with a commentary on terrible sounds, Diderot wrote, "Great noises heard from a distance . . . the noise of muted drums, drumbeats separated by intervals, interrupted strokes of a bell tower . . . there is in all these things a certain quality that is terrible, great, and dark." Again he was drawing on the *Recherches philosophiques*, which reported that "there are few things more majestic than the sound of a great clock tower when the hour sounds" and that "one can say the same thing about a single stroke of the drum, repeated from one time to another."[50]

Finally, Burke's oft-quoted remarks about the difference between oxen and bulls, tame horses and wild horses, and so on found their way, with little transformation, into Diderot's advice to artists in his 1767 *Salon*: "Ideas of power also have their sublimity, but power that threatens is more moving than power that protects. The bull is more beautiful than the cow; the bellowing horned bull than the bull walking and grazing; the wild horse, its mane floating in the wind, than the horse under its rider; the wild donkey than the domesticated donkey; the tyrant than the king; crime, maybe, than virtue, cruel gods than good gods, and the sacred legislators knew it well."[51]

Diderot's position was much more radical than Burke's. The atheist *philosophe* drew distinctly irreligious conclusions from the idea of the sublime and the terrible, whereas Burke saw terribleness as a laudable attribute of God. Moreover, it is clear that Diderot conflated the beautiful and the sublime by saying that a bull was "more beautiful" (*plus beau*) than an ox and that other threatening things were similarly more beautiful than their protective counterparts. Thus he strangely missed the entire point of Burke's book, which was precisely to prevent commentators on aesthetics from treating the sublime and the beautiful as synonymous. Nevertheless, Diderot was using Burke to elevate the terrible as an aesthetic category, to make it a standard against which art could and should be judged. He therefore contributed to the positive connotations of the words *terreur* and *terrible*.

Claude-Adrien Helvétius similarly made use of Burkean conceptions of terror and the sublime. In his *De l'esprit* (1758), Helvétius wrote at length about the frightening things that incite pleasurable feelings. In a passage that recalled Burke's distinction between a large plain and the open ocean, Helvétius wrote that "if the sight or description of a large lake is agreeable to us, that of a calm sea without limits is without doubt more agreeable still; its immensity is a source of great pleasure for us." Soon, however, this spectacle would become boring. It would therefore be preferable to add a storm, "enveloped in black clouds" and "rolling before it mobile mountains of water." Helvétius asked, "Who doubts that the rapid, simple and varied succession of frightening images [*tableaux effrayants*] . . . would make at every instant new impressions on our imagination, that it would strongly fix our attention . . . and consequently please us even more?" It would be still more pleasurable if "night [came] to increase even further the horrors [*les horreurs*] of this same storm," and if lightning bolts turned the ocean into "a sea of fire." When narrated by the poet, who makes us hear the "roaring of the water, the whistling of the wind, and the crashing of thunder," this imagined event would "add still more to the secret terror and, consequently, to the pleasure that we feel."[52] Helvétius did not yet explicitly connect terror to the sublime, but his oceanic imagery, his love of "immensity," and his promotion of terror as a suitable subject for artists and poets nevertheless qualify him as Burkean as early as 1758.

In Helvétius's *De l'homme* (1773), a "forbidden best-seller" published two years after the author's death, the imprint of Burke was unmistakable.[53]

In it Helvétius devoted an entire chapter to "the sublime." After acknowledging the importance of such theorists as Longinus and Boileau for an understanding of this concept, he stressed the role of terror, asserting that "the sublime is always the effect of the feeling of an incipient terror."[54] It could be felt in "the depths of the heavens, the immensity of the seas, irruptions of volcanoes, etc." Helvétius asked, "What is the source of the lively impression these grand objects excite in us?" His answer: "From the grand forces in nature that they proclaim and from the involuntary comparison that we make between these forces and our weakness." "At the sight of this," he added, "one feels seized with a certain respect that reveals in us the sentiment of fear and of incipient terror."[55] This observation recalled Burke's claim that terror manifested itself in a feeling of "smallness."[56]

Helvétius illustrated his point with art criticism. He wrote that he would grant the word "sublime" to the sixteenth-century artist Giulio Romano, in particular his fresco depicting the combat between the gods and the titans (see fig. 6), while "refusing" the same term to *The Toilet of Venus* by the seventeenth-century artist Francesco Albani (see fig. 7). He admitted that it was no less difficult to paint the latter than the former, but "when Albani transports me to the toilet of the goddess, nothing awakens in me the feeling of respect and terror." When Romano, on the other hand, transported the viewer "to that place where the sons of the earth [i.e., the titans] piled [Mount] Ossa onto [Mount] Pelion" in their attempt to destroy the gods, Helvétius continued, "I automatically compare myself and my strength to that of those giants." And further: "Convinced then of my weakness, I feel a kind of secret terror, and I give the name of sublime to the impression of fear that this painting makes on me."[57]

Other examples of terrible imagery came from ancient sources, both Hebrew and Greek. Although a materialist and an atheist, Helvétius paid the Old Testament a compliment by attributing sublimity to some of its passages. "When God said, 'Let there be light,' and there was light," he wrote, "this image is sublime. What a picture this is of the universe suddenly pulled from nothingness by light!" He asked, "But should such an image inspire fear?" and responded, "Yes; because it necessarily recalls in our memory the idea of a being capable of creating such a wonder." Again linking power, respect, and terror, he added, "seized despite oneself with a fearful respect [*d'un respect craintif*] for the author of the light, one experiences the feeling of an incipient terror." Helvétius repeated the phrase "incipient terror" when describing the emotions incited by the "sublime" productions of Homer, and he wrote simply of the "terror" imparted by

Fig. 6. *Fall of the Giants* (1530–32), a fresco by Giulio Romano, inspired a "secret terror" in Helvétius and was therefore worthy of the adjective "sublime."

Euripides' tragedies, especially *Medea* and *Seven against Thebes*.[58] He was more critical of Aeschylus, who in his view went too far by creating a "lively impression" on the Greeks which was "perhaps horrible for some," thus reiterating the distinction between terror and horror that we have seen other eighteenth-century theater critics make. Nevertheless, he believed that if sufficiently "softened" this same impression "would have been generally recognized as sublime."[59] In addition to high culture, popular culture confirmed Helvétius's view. He asked, "Of what kinds of stories are men, women and children most avid?" His answer: "Those involving thieves and vampires. These stories frighten; they produce . . . the feeling of an incipient terror and this feeling is the one that makes the . . . most vivid impression." Helvétius concluded his chapter by noting that "the beautiful . . . makes a strong impression on most people" but "the sublime . . . makes an even stronger impression on us," and he reiterated that it was "always mixed with a certain feeling of respect or of incipient terror."[60]

It is possible that Helvétius derived his Burkean ideas from Diderot. After all, Helvétius was a subscriber to Grimm's *Correspondance littéraire* and therefore likely read Diderot's reports on the biennial art exhibitions.[61] He may also have learned his Burke through Des François's 1765 translation. And he may have been influenced by both sources. In any event, ultimately

Fig. 7. Francesco Albani's *The Toilet of Venus* (c. 1625) inspired neither "respect" nor "terror" in Helvétius and for that reason was not sublime.

Helvétius was more Burkean than Diderot, because the latter conflated the beautiful and the sublime whereas the former insisted on their distinctness. Nevertheless, by connecting the terrible and the sublime, both *philosophes* contributed to the aesthetic valorization of terror in eighteenth-century France.

Yet another French writer who commented on Burke's view of terror and the sublime was the sculptor and classicist Étienne Falconet. His initial remark on that view appeared in a footnote to his 1772 translation of books 34–36 of Pliny's *Natural History* and was little more than an erudite aside, but it tells us something about the impact of Burke's ideas in France. In it Falconet objected to Burke's explanation of the sublime, and in particular his view that it derived from terror: "M. Burke defines *the sublime* in material objects as *everything that imprints terror.*" He asked a series of rhetorical questions designed to cast doubt on this idea: "Would it not result from this too vague definition that the gibbet, that a roué, would be sublime? That phantoms, any kind of apparitions, would be sublime? That the robber who at the corner of the woods places a pistol at the throat of a passerby would be sublime? That mice and spiders would be sublime to those in whom they *imprint terror?*" He noted that "there are men who without being stupid coolly envisage danger" and that not everyone was afraid of revenants, mice, and spiders. For Falconet "the true sublime is essential; it is real, it is absolute." For example, "The ocean is sublime; habit, stupidity, deafness, blindness alone can diminish or prevent its effect on our *sensorium commune.*"[62] Despite these objections, the very fact that Falconet was attempting to refute Burke suggests that he expected others to take a Burkean position on the sublime. Clearly there was an ongoing discussion about the sublime and the role of terror in it.

By 1781 Falconet modified his position to include more "particular cases" of the sublime. In volume 5 of his *Œuvres* he recycled the observations just quoted but added a paragraph in which he used the terms "horror" and "terror" interchangeably:

A vast forest fire, the burning of a great city, a frightful [*effroyable*] rock whose steep summit covers the abyss of the seas, and which the furious waves appear at every instant to cause to crumble into the whirlpools; storms, hurricanes, typhoons, the eruption of a volcano combined with the earthquake that swallows up cities and causes them to disappear, [these] are sublime horrors. A broken dike in Frisia or in Zealand is a sublime horror. The physical and moral [i.e., psychological] effects of thunderbolts cast by the hand of atrocious kings and tyrants imprint the same terror; for just as there are sublime virtues, there are sublime atrocities. In order for an action to be [sublime], it does not necessarily have to conform with reason, order and our duties.[63]

With these observations Falconet was no longer arguing with Burke, who would have agreed wholeheartedly with this catalog of instances of the sublime. His observations also conformed to Diderot's view that the sublime could frequently be seen in amoral forces. Yet this more capacious sense of the sublime only added to its appeal. It made the sublime, and the terror that engendered it, all the more powerful. As we shall now see, it lent emotional force to descriptions of the sublime and the terrible in the natural world.

The French valorization of terror in nature precedes Burke. One sees it, for example, in a prose translation of James Thomson's poem *The Seasons* (1730) by Marie-Jeanne de Chatillon Bontems, which included an apostrophe: "Nature, great author whose indefatigable hand ceaselessly directs the seasons of the year, how your works are powerful and majestic! With what agreeable terror they penetrate the soul that sings of them with astonishment and admiration!" Bontems continued by celebrating the winds and "the violence of the storms" that they provoked.[64] This version of Thomson's poem was quite popular, appearing in ten editions between 1769 and 1789.[65] Although it did not use the word "sublime," it celebrated nature and its "violence" in much the same way Burke (and later Diderot and Helvétius) would do.

Other writers linked terror and the sublime in their celebrations of nature, and though it is hard to say with certainty how influential Burke was in their conception, they shared with him a belief in the positive aesthetic value of natural terror. For example, in *Les styles* (1781), a book-length poem in four cantos (*chants*) by the future revolutionary Antoine de Cournand, the sublime and the terrible are evident in the mountains. In the fourth *chant* the protagonist, a sensitive Rousseauian soul weary of hypercivilized hypocrites, flees to the Alps, where he proclaims:

RECEIVE ME beneath your sacred shadows,
Frightful rocks!
Whose sublime horror
Still inspires holy terror in me.[66]

This kind of rhapsodic veneration of the terrible sublime was not restricted to poetry. In fact, it was most common in travel writing. In *Les*

soirées helvétiennes, alsaciennes, et fran-comtoises (1771), the marquis
de Pezay wrote of his initial encounter with the Alps, "One does not see
without a sentiment of terror boulders suspended above one's head like
clouds, nor the fathomless gulfs at one's feet and the torrents whose noise
alone strikes with consternation; yet this terror is but an additional pleasure."[67] A glowing review in *L'année littéraire* reproduced lengthy passages
of Pezay's book, including the sentence just quoted, no doubt expanding
its readership.[68] One did not have to visit the Alps personally in order to
experience the simultaneous terror and pleasure felt by travel writers, according to a review of another work of travel literature. A reviewer for the
journal *L'esprit des journaux* praised an account of Alpine glaciers, writing
that "one peruses this book with that pleasure mixed with terror that the
voyagers themselves felt at the sight of the magnificent precipices of which
the vast extent of the Alps offers the image."[69] The most famous alpinist
of all, Horace Bénédict de Saussure, did his best to convey the pleasure and
terror he felt when visiting the Alps, though he doubted his ability to do so:
"How [can I] depict to the imagination objects that have nothing in common with everything one sees in the rest of the world; how [can I] transmit
to the reader's soul that mixed impression of admiration and terror inspired
by those heaps of ice surrounded and topped by those even more immense
pyramid-shaped rocks[?]"[70]

The valorization of sublime terror penetrated deeply into the shared ro-
mantic culture of eighteenth-century writers on both sides of the Channel.
One even finds it in Thomas Whately's *Observations on Modern Gardening* (1770), translated as *L'art de former les jardins modernes, ou L'art des
jardins anglois* (1771). The English statesman and gardener explicitly connected terror and the sublime when he maintained that "the noise and the
rage of a torrent, its force, its violence, its impetuosity inspire terror, that
terror so tightly linked with sublimity."[71] Elsewhere Whately commented
specifically on the effect of the river Derwent on those who witnessed it
rushing past. In an allusion to the theatrical genre that we have seen promoted by Crébillon, the French translation affirmed: "A river like the Derwent would be infinitely better suited to a scene of a *genre terrible* which is
the effect of grandeur combined with power; it is always animated and interesting by virtue of the astonishment and the uneasiness that it casts into
the soul." The analogy to theater continued: "One could compare the terror
that a scene of nature inspires to that which is born of a dramatic scene. The
soul is strongly shaken: but the sensations are only agreeable when they
pertain only to terror, without having anything horrible or shocking [*sans
avoir rien d'horrible ni de choquant*]."[72]

CONCLUSIONS

A particularly tantalizing source of praise for the pleasures of nature-induced terror comes from the writing of Jacques-Pierre Brissot de Warville. In his posthumously published *Mémoires* the Girondin leader wrote:

> I love the terror that a dark forest inspires in me, and those lugubrious sepulchral vaults where one only encounters bones and tombs. I love the whistling of the winds that announce the storm, those agitated trees, that thunder that bursts or rumbles, and those torrents of rain that drive in great streams. My heart quivers, moved, bruised, distressed; but this is an emotion that appears sweet to it, for it [my heart] cannot detach from it [the emotion]. For me in that instant there is a horrible charm, a pleasure that I am better able to feel than to define.[73]

Brissot wrote his memoirs shortly before his death in 1793, but he was describing feelings that he also claimed to have experienced when watching Shakespeare plays in Paris in the 1770s. As we saw in chapter 4, Shakespeare was a controversial figure in eighteenth-century France, though he had his defenders. Brissot was clearly untroubled by the worry that Shakespearean tragedy crossed the border between the terrible and the horrible, as he saw these concepts as synonymous. In any case, he was reporting a Burkean sensibility and a love of both natural and theatrical terror. Ironically, Brissot would become one of the first and most prominent victims of the Terror in the French Revolution and was reviled by the Montagnards who initiated that phase of the Revolution. It is no less ironic that Burke praised terror as sublime in the 1750s and rejected revolutionary terror in the 1790s. But Brissot's love of terror and Burke's praise of the emotion, in a very different context, of course, are vivid reminders of how ecumenical the valorization of terror was prior to the Terror of 1793–94. Under the Old Regime the word contained positive emotional connotations for atheists and believers, *philosophes* and anti-*philosophes*, just as during the Revolution it was uttered enthusiastically by royalists and republicans, Girondins and Montagnards. Part of that word's distinguished genealogy came from the aesthetic writings of Longinus (via Boileau), Burke, and the French exponents of the sublime.

CHAPTER SIX

Terror and Medicine

INTRODUCTION

In 1747 the materialist philosopher and physician Julien Offray de La Mettrie wrote in his *Histoire naturelle de l'ame* (Natural history of the soul), "Terror, that passion that by shaking the [human] machine, places it so to speak on guard for its own defense . . . sometimes suddenly cures paralysis, lethargy, gout, pulls a sick person away from the gates of death, produces apoplexy, kills with sudden death, and in a word causes the most terrible effects."[1] How could the same force alternately cure and kill? As with other medicines—and here it is important to note that terror *was* a medicine for many early modern physicians—terror produced a sense of wonder in its mysterious capacity to help and harm. In this respect it was very much like God, the ultimate arbiter of life and death, and the sovereigns who claimed the deputized right to lift up and strike down. Insofar as it was curative, it recalled other kinds of salutary terror. If the terror of the laws could save lives and the terror of God could save souls, the physical experience of terror could literally produce *salut* or health. Insofar as terror was harmful, the terror portrayed in medical writing was nevertheless a powerful force and therefore an object of respect. In this chapter I summarize the state of eighteenth-century French medical knowledge regarding the impact of terror on the human body. I will examine claims about the reputedly harmful effects of terror and then turn to the idea of healthful terror. Finally, I will consider the possibility that these medical ideas had political implications.

PATHOGENIC TERROR

The eighteenth-century physician who had the most to say about the effects of terror on the human organism was Friedrich Hoffmann (1660–1742). Pro-

fessor of medicine at the University of Halle and Royal Physician to the king
of Prussia, Hoffmann wrote voluminously. Many of his works appeared in
French over the course of the eighteenth century. The most popular was a
nine-volume compilation, *La médecine raisonnée* (Systematic medicine),
translated from the Latin by Jacques-Jean Bruhier and appearing in numerous
editions between 1738 and 1763. In volume 4 French readers could consider
Hoffmann's most extensive reflections on terror.

Hoffmann characterized terror as a cardiovascular episode. He wrote that
"a sudden and violent terror causes a contraction of all the substance of the
body; which causes the vessels to deflate and the veins to disappear entirely,
or almost entirely, causes the face to become pale, and causes the chilling
and trembling of the exterior parts." Blood gathered in the lungs, and "the
pressure exerted in these viscera produces cruel disquiet, difficulty in breathing, weakness, and rapid heart rate." Worse still, "as the heart tries to relieve
itself of the burden with which it is overloaded, it happens at once that the
spirits enter impetuously into its muscles and produce there a convulsive
movement called palpitation, which is an occurrence almost inseparable
from terror."[2] In case one questioned "the energy of terror in producing con-
densation, and precipitation, in the blood," Hoffmann referred the reader to
the Bolognese physician Marcello Malpighi, who reported the case of "a robust man who [was] suddenly precipitated by terror into an irregularity, and a
concentration of the pulse." This unfortunate patient immediately began to
spit "lumps" of blood and "whitish concretions" and then died, "suffocated
by the swelling of the vessels of the superior parts [of the body]."[3] Hoffmann
also drew on the authority of Gottfried Möbius, the Jena professor who "also
remarks that terror makes the heart lose its strength, and produces tremors
similar to those of a fever." Hoffmann found this claim reasonable because
"terror, and the beginning of an attack of fever, resemble one another in that
a spasmodic contraction of the exterior parts prevents the blood from entering freely and obligates it rather to flow toward the heart, where, having
stopped there, it causes inexpressible suffering."[4]

The effect of terror went beyond the heart, according to Hoffmann: "The
spasmodic contraction of the parts produced by a violent terror is also the
cause of the slowing, or of the total suppression of all sorts of excretions." It
also "diminishes perspiration, and often causes a sudden suppression of the
menstrual flow, of evacuations . . . even of urine." The same phenomenon
of contraction resulted in the coagulation of milk in the breasts of nursing
women, the emergence of purple specks on the skin, and "eruptions" of
smallpox and measles. It could also lead to asthma and "convulsive colic."[5]
Moreover, "by repulsing the blood toward the internal parts, and by making

circulation entirely irregular," terror "produces congestions," including in
the head, where it could lead to "apoplexies, hemiplegia [i.e., paralysis on
one side], paralysis, epilepsy, and convulsive movements." Citing Hippoc-
rates, he claimed that "terror can cause delirium and cause one to see
specters." For pregnant women, terror could result in blood settling in the
womb, leading to miscarriage, and "when terror is felt during menstruation,
it causes spasmodic symptoms," including "breathing trouble, pain in the
lower back and feet, fainting spells, and other infirmities." Hoffmann added
that "the breasts of pregnant women, and women in childbed, feel particularly the impressions of terror, which often causes tubercles that sometimes
degenerate into ulcers of a bad character, and even into carcinomas."[6]

Yet "the bad effects of terror," in Hoffmann's view, were not restricted
"to the illnesses that it produces": it was also sometimes "a very efficient
cause of sudden death." That it need not work through the intermediary of
any particular illness to lead to death was proved by the testimony of physicians through the ages: "Long ago Galen remarked that terror caused the
death of many persons." For additional support he cited the Bible, Pliny the
Elder, Valerius Maximus, the sixteenth- and seventeenth-century Florentine
forensic scientist known as Fortunatus Fidelis, the seventeenth-century Genevan doctor Théophile Bonet, the Hungarian physician Carl Rayger (1675–
1731), and his Danish contemporary Thomas Bartholin. He concluded, "It is
not difficult to discover the reason for these dire and sudden accidents. The
blood, amassing by the effect of terror in the vicinity of the heart and lungs,
coagulates quickly, especially if the subject is weak; therefore one perceives
that this coagulation is necessarily mortal."[7]

Hoffmann's ideas about the effects of terror were widely quoted. In particular, the French physician and medical journalist François Planque, whose
ten-volume *Bibliothèque choisie de médecine* appeared between 1748 and
1770, liberally reproduced Hoffmann's theories, at times to the point of pla-
giarism. Planque repeated the story, drawn from Malpighi, about the "robust
man" who was "suddenly precipitated by terror into an irregularity" of the
pulse, spat blood, and died, "suffocated by the swelling of the vessels of the
superior parts." He repeated Möbius's claim "that *terror* makes the heart lose
its strength, and produces tremors similar to those of a fever." He added that
"*terror* suppresses the menstrual flow," as well as the flow of urine, "coagulates the milk in the breasts," and provokes "eruptions" of smallpox and
measles. He repeated Hoffmann's claim that Galen "remarks that terror
caused the death of many persons."[8]

Another medical writer who drew on Hoffmann's ideas about terror was
the English physician Robert James. In the article on epilepsy in volume 3

(1747) of his *Dictionnaire universel de médecine*, the French translation of his *Medicinal Dictionary*, James cited Hoffmann when noting that in the case of epileptics "it is necessary to avoid above all every occasion for terror, fear, or anger, since these passions are capable of renewing paroxysms."[9] Similarly, people suffering from melancholy were advised "to avoid all the violent passions, such as anger and terror, because the violent motions that accompany them cause the blood to enter with difficulty into the small vessels where it is seized due to its thickness; which often causes considerable damage to [the vessels]."[10] James did not cite Hoffmann, but his view bore the imprint of Hoffmann's ideas about the role of blood in the emergence of illness.

Hoffmann was not the only source of beliefs regarding the baneful effects of terror. In his *Lettres sur le pouvoir de l'imagination des femmes enceintes* (Letters on the power of the imagination in pregnant women), the French obstetrician Isaac Bellet opposed the long-standing belief that a pregnant woman could imprint characteristics on the fetus by force of imagination, yet he insisted that "disturbance of the child's brain is in truth the consequence of the terror with which the mother has been struck."[11] Worse still, in the case of "disproportionate terror, the child could be suffocated by an overly long suspension of the blood flow."[12]

Other mid-century medical writings confirmed the notion of terror as a dangerous passion. François Chicoyneau, physician to Louis XV and a doctor who had made his name by treating plague victims in Marseilles in the 1720s, wrote in 1744 that "terror is, so to speak, the seed of the plague," since it "prepares the body for the impressions of the pestilential venom."[13] The pulmonologist François de Paule Combalusier wrote in 1754 that "windy colic" could come from "sudden terror."[14] Joseph Lieutaud, pediatrician to the court of Louis XV, and subsequently Louis XVI's personal physician, wrote of "malignant fever" in 1761: "We have seen that *mental suffering*, and above all terror, often give rise to this cruel illness."[15] He also identified terror as one of the causes of heart palpitations,[16] and elsewhere he wrote that it (along with "sorrow and adversity") "often causes *memory loss* and makes one *stupid*."[17] The next year the Austrian physician Anton von Störck reportedly treated a woman who "having had, while she was giving birth, a sudden terror, immediately felt a violent pain in her right breast, then the breast became red and very hard." (He cured her by applying bandages soaked in hemlock.)[18] That same year Mazars de Cazelles, a physician from Toulouse, wrote an article attributing a case of catalepsy to terror.[19] Toussaint Bordenave, director of the French Academy of Surgery, wrote in his *Essai sur la physiologie* (1764) that "terror causes pallor, palpitations, tremors of the lips, etc."[20] In 1766 Jean Ferapie

Dufieu identified "terror" as one of the things that "diminish and retard the menses."[21] Also in 1766, Antoine Petit, of the faculty of medicine at the University of Paris, wrote that "this terror" which the rumor of a smallpox epidemic excited was actually a factor in spreading the disease.[22]

Medical writings appearing in French in the 1770s confirmed the view that terror prompted or exacerbated many illnesses. Boissier de Sauvages de Lacroix, whose *Nosologie méthodique* offered a classification of diseases, referred repeatedly to the effects of terror on the human body. He blamed it for memory loss, convulsions, "lassitude," hallucinations, "hysterical vertigo," fainting, and nightmares resulting in suffocation.[23] Francis Home, the Scottish physician whose *Principia medicinae* was translated from the Latin by the Montargis physician (and future member of the revolutionary Legislative Assembly) René Gastellier in 1772, wrote that "in fear and in terror, the solids are weakened; the movement of fluids is stopped; trembling seizes all members, the whole body is covered in cold sweat; the heart and lungs are overloaded with the blood that accumulates in them; excrement and urine flow involuntarily; finally the entire machine falls into the greatest looseness, and from there [come] palpitations of the heart, weakness, anxiety, difficulty breathing, lethargy, fainting, mania, and death."[24] Terror could also cause fever, and in adult men it could lead to "paralysis in the natural parts" and therefore to impotence.[25] Home's compatriot Robert Whytt, whose 1765 work on "nervous, hypochondriac, or hysteric" illnesses appeared in French translation in 1777, wrote that terror could lead to "attacks of hysteria or the vapors" as well as "convulsions or syncope."[26] He also cited the cases of "delicate women and children whom sudden terror caused . . . [to be] subject all their lives to attacks of epilepsy."[27]

The 1770s saw many other publications confirming the role of terror in provoking illness. Among the authorities represented in this corpus were the Lyonnais surgeon Jean-Baptiste Pressavin (who reported cases of paralysis resulting from terror); the Dutch physician and botanist Cornelius Pereboom (who also attributed paralysis to terror); the Swiss physician, naturalist, and philosopher Johann Georg von Zimmermann (who saw terror as a cause of arterial collapse and apoplexy); the French physician Jean-Gaspard d'Ailhaud (who confirmed Chicoyneau's belief that terror facilitated the spread of plague); the University of Geneva medical professor Daniel de La Roche (who believed that terror made people susceptible to smallpox as well as plague); the French pediatrician Joseph Raulin the Elder (who wrote a textbook chapter on "miscarriages caused by terror"); and the University of Nancy medical professor Michel du Tennetar (who wrote of "cases of sudden death" attributable to "the lively passions of the soul," including terror).[28]

This trend continued into the 1780s. In 1782 the Russian epidemiologist Danilo Samoilovich repeated what by then had become a standard interpretation of the role of terror in the spread of the plague, writing that it was "justifiable to search for the cause of these popular ravages in despair and terror, which suffocate courage and beat down the soul of each individual." Generalizing his point beyond the case of the plague, he wrote, "A capital goal in *contagious illnesses* appears therefore to be to remove terror, despair, pusillanimity."[29] The following year the *Dictionnaire universel des sciences morale, économique, politique et diplomatique* reported in the entry for *sens interne* (internal feelings), "In terror . . . is born palpitation, pallor, sudden chills, trembling, paralysis, epilepsy, change in hair color, sudden death."[30] In 1787 the *Encyclopédie méthodique*, published by Félix Vicq-d'Azyr (the anatomist and physician to Marie-Antoinette), reported in the article "Affectations de l'âme" (Affects of the soul) that "terror and fear [*la terreur & la peur*] cause paralysis."[31] That same year a French translation of William Cullen's *First Lines of the Practice of Physic* revealed to French readers the Edinburgh professor's belief that terror could cause syncope, epilepsy, asphyxia, and death.[32]

The extensive catalog of ills believed to be caused or exacerbated by terror is in tension with the main thesis of this book, namely that terror had largely positive connotations in prerevolutionary France. In the medical writing surveyed so far, terror was a thing to be avoided, a danger and source of suffering to all people, not merely "scoundrels" or criminals. Could terror under these circumstances have positive connotations? Perhaps. One way of interpreting the evidence would suggest that terror, as conceived by medical writers, was a powerful force and deserving of respect. Like God, the state, and the law, terror had the power to harm or kill, even if this power was not backed by morality. In this respect it might have been sublime in the sense elaborated by Burke, Diderot, and Helvétius and discussed in chapter 4. Yet medical thinking on terror was not so simple. Competing with the idea of terror as a danger was the contradictory notion of terror as a remedy.

SALUTARY TERROR

Many early modern physicians believed that under certain circumstances terror could cure illnesses. Some of the very doctors who warned against the dangers of terror also argued for its curative properties. Sometimes they even believed that terror could cure the same illness it supposedly caused.

Consider the idea that terror could cure mental illness, which arguably goes back to Aurelius Cornelius Celsus (25 BCE–50 CE), whose *De medicina* was widely cited throughout the early modern period. The work was known to French readers via a 1753 translation by Henri Ninnin, doctor to the comte de Clermont and regent of the medical faculty at Reims. According to Ninnin's version, patients suffering from "frenzy" were to be subjected to "certain corrections," for example withholding food, tying and beating the patient, and forcing him or her to memorize "certain things, and to recite them." In addition, Celsus/Ninnin explained, "Terrors, sudden fears, in a word, all that can considerably disturb the mind, bring relief in this malady."[33]

Eighteenth-century medical writers also drew on the authority of the German physician Werner Rolfinck (1599–1673) when arguing for terror as a cure for mental illnesses. In his *Bibliothèque choisie de médecine* (1766), François Planque wrote that "despite an infinity of examples of the bad effects of terror, we learn from other observations that it has cured many illnesses." As an example, he recalled Rolfinck's account of "a maniac" who had been "cured by the fright [*la frayeur*] that a masked man had caused in him."[34] This story was repeated verbatim and again attributed to Rolfinck in 1771 in the Belgian *Gazette salutaire*.[35]

Francis Home—whom we have also seen reporting on the baneful consequences of terror—reinforced the idea that terror could be effective in the treatment of mental illness. Home distinguished between melancholy and mania and prescribed widely divergent treatments for the two disorders. According to a French edition of his *Principia medicinae*, "It is necessary to employ different means for restoring the bewildered mind of melancholics and maniacs: raise that of the former with hope, trust, games, music, and stories. Depress, on the contrary, that of the latter by terror, darkness, chains, and sudden frights [*les frayeurs subites*]."[36]

On the eve of the Revolution belief in the power of terror to cure "maniacs" was present on both sides of the English Channel. A 1787 translation of William Cullen's *First Lines in the Practice of Physic*, a book that otherwise warned of terror's harmful effects, affirmed the need to diminish the "excitement" of manic patients and recommended "inspiring them with respect and terror for particular persons, especially for those who are constantly near them." In order "to inspire this respect and this terror," the physician was advised "to have recourse to the whip and to blows."[37] In 1788 the English physician William Falconer wrote that in treating such patients "the aim is to eradicate the former false impressions by others still more violent. Hence the casting of such people into the sea and detaining them under the water until they are nearly drowned, recommended by [the Dutch physician Herman] Boerhaave, and the impressions of terror and perturbation of mind advised by Celsus."[38] The French edition, the work of the poet and translator Pierre de La Montagne and published that same year, repeated this advice and referred positively to "les effets de la terreur."[39]

Eighteenth-century medical writers likewise asserted that terror could cure rabies, which they classified as a mental illness. Joseph Lieutaud, who otherwise noted the negative effects of terror, nevertheless recommended its use in the treatment of hydrophobia. In his *Précis de médecine pratique*, an enormously popular digest that was published at least sixteen times between 1759 and 1789,[40] he wrote, "Everyone knows that *immersion in sea or river water* is considered one of the best remedies" for hydrophobia. He acknowledged that this was a controversial treatment: "many have attempted to decry this practice" on the grounds that not everyone who had been immersed in seawater avoided rabies. But Lieutaud explained that this had to do with "the manner in which they were bathed." It was "less the bath that cures than the surprise, or the terror that one has the skill of inspiring in those who are roughly cast into the sea." One dunking treatment was not sufficient, however, and Lieutaud advocated "keeping the patient under water for around half a minute," "many times each day" and "for ten to twelve days" altogether. He assured his readers that he had "never seen this remedy fail."[41]

One source for eighteenth-century ideas about the efficacy of such terrifying immersions was the Flemish chemist and physician Jan Baptista van Helmont (1579–1644), who had written that "terror through submersion removes rabies."[42] Van Helmont's theory had adherents in France as late as 1787. In that year Vicq d'Azyr's article in the *Encyclopédie méthodique*— the same article that saw terror as a cause of paralysis—maintained that "the passions of fear, of terror have sometimes been salutary." Evidence came from Van Helmont, who "reports that numerous hydrophobes have been cured with cold water by being plunged into it without warning." The article claimed that "the sudden fright and fear of death [*l'effroi subit & la crainte de la mort*] altered the *sensorium commune*," the Aristotelian organizing principle of the soul that by the end of the eighteenth century had come simply to mean the brain.[43] How these emotions "altered" the brain was not explained. The article cited Van Helmont again when asserting that "maniacs, and those who are attacked by an amorous delirium," could also be cured by immersion.[44]

Lieutaud provided additional evidence that terror could cure excessive libidinousness. He recounted the "very remarkable story," first reported by the seventeenth-century French physician Gabriel Naudé, of a doctor who discovered that his wife had been cheating on him. The cuckolded physician determined that "the strength of her temperament was the cause of her il-licit lovemaking" and sought "a sufficient means of changing her manner of living." His solution was to terrify her. One night after he had slept with her—how this intercourse affected the treatment of the supposed disorder was not explained—the doctor jumped up and began "shouting that there were robbers in their room." He armed himself, discharged "two or three pistol shots, struck his sword on the tables and the andirons, and spread ter-ror and horror [la terreur & l'épouvante] in his house." The next morning he resumed the regime of terror. He measured his wife's heart rate and declared that she had a dangerously high fever which could only be cured by an im-mediate bloodletting. She was bled "seven or eight times," leeches were applied to her, and she was given laxatives repeatedly. All the while her hus-band continued to claim that she was sick and confined her to her bed for six months. "By this means he so cooled her temperament and made her so thin, so pale, so exhausted, that he extinguished in this poor woman the fire of love."[45] This empathetic remark raised the question of just how ill the "poor woman" had been before her husband applied his extreme treatment to her and at what price she had been "cured," but the article nevertheless reinforced the impression that terror could remove undesirable symptoms (even if what constituted "undesirable" was a matter of perspective).

Just as terror could cure mental disorders or cool torrid "temperaments," according to early modern doctors, it could also cure paralysis. The most frequently cited authority for this claim was the sixteenth-century physi-cian François Valleriola of Montpellier. In his 1573 work, *Observationum medicinalium libri sex* (Six books of medical observations), Valleriola told the story of a patient from Arles who had been paralyzed on one side for many years, "destitute of all human help." Neither the "skillful hands of doctors, nor suitably applied remedies, nor the cautious observation of diet was able to relieve this dire illness." It was a "truly miraculous accident" that saved the man. A fire broke out in his house, "the beams caught fire, and the flame crawled on as far as the room in which the sick man was ly-ing." Eventually "everything was filled by the fire," and "this patient, trem-bling with fear and anger [metu & ira], and struck with grave fear [grauique timore perculsus], suddenly roused himself and tried with the utmost effort to stand upright: soon, aroused with truly great bodily strength collected together, he threw himself from the top of the building." The patient was unhurt and, even more astonishingly, he was "suddenly free from the ill-ness." He now had full use of the "senses and motions" that had previously been inactive and "lived in good health."[46] Elsewhere in his book Valleriola repeated the story to demonstrate the "power of terror and anger" (*terroris ac irae potentia*) in curing paralysis.[47]

Valleriola's story reached the French of the eighteenth century through numerous sources. Some medical writers cited the sixteenth-century authority directly. For example, the 1742 French translation of works by Hoffmann—the same Hoffmann who wrote so extensively on the harmful effects of terror—revealed that "Valleriola attests that a man who had remained paralyzed on one side, without having been able to receive any help from any remedy over the course of many years, was suddenly cured by the terror of a fire."[48] In 1748 the French translation of Robert James's *Medicinal Dictionary* similarly cited Valleriola as having reported the case of "a man who was cured by the force of terror and anger of a paralysis in one of his sides that had resisted all remedies."[49] François Planque repeated the story as well, plagiarizing the French edition of Hoffmann and writing that Valleriola reported the case of a paralytic "on one side" who was "suddenly cured by the terror of a fire."[50] The same wording appeared in an excerpt from Planque's book in a 1771 issue of the *Gazette salutaire*.[51] Also in 1771 Boissier de Sauvages de Lacroix, whose theories on the many ailments produced by terror we have already encountered, wrote of "anger and terror curing" paralysis, and he duly cited Valleriola's sixteenth-century book as evidence.[52]

Other eighteenth-century French readers knew Valleriola's story via the sixteenth-century German physician Johannes Schenck von Grafenberg. Specifically, Mazars de Cazelles, in a 1762 article (discussed earlier) about terror as a *cause* of catalepsy, recalled that Schenck reported the case of the paralyzed man who threw himself from his roof to escape from fire. This proved to the French physician that "if terror is capable of producing paralysis . . . it can also dissipate it."[53] Another writer who attributed the story to Schenck was Joseph Aignan Sigaud de la Fond, author of a 1781 *Dictionnaire des merveilles de la nature* (Dictionary of the wonders of nature). This reference book had an entry titled "terreur" in which the author claimed that Schenck "reports that a man who had long been paralyzed threw himself from the top of his house to escape the flames that were devouring it, and that the terror which he then felt cured him of his paralysis." The author added that the man "lived a long time afterward free from this infirmity."[54]

Another story of paralysis cured by terror originated with the seventeenth-century Dutch medical professor IJsbrand van Diemerbroeck. In his 1672 work, *Anatome corporis humani* (Anatomy of the human body), he recalled the case of a woman (his own patient) who had been paralyzed on the left side "until finally one night she was struck by the immense Terror [*immenso Terrore percussa*] of a most horrendous storm with lightning and thunder, which made her believe the world was coming to an end." The "obstructive matter" that had caused the paralysis was "suddenly expelled," and Diemerbroeck's patient "was freed and remained free from paralysis."[55] This story reappeared in the 1762 article by Mazars de Cazelles (cited above). There the author affirmed that "one reads in Diemerbroec [*sic*] that in the height of a violent storm, accompanied by lightning strikes, a woman, paralytic for thirty-eight years, who was enveloped in the fires of this terrible meteor, was instantly cured of her stubborn illness." For those who would attribute the cure to the electricity, Mazars insisted that "terror" was responsible for "dissipating" the malady.[56] Diemerbroeck's story also appeared in the article on *terreur* in the *Dictionnaire des merveilles de la nature.*[57]

Other medical writers confirmed the power of terror to cure paralysis. We have seen that La Mettrie listed paralysis as one of the ills cured by terror.[58] Boissier de Sauvages de Lacroix concurred, writing in 1776 of "hemiplegic patients" who emerged from this condition "at the sight of danger." He wrote that "numerous patients of this kind escaped from a hospital in which a fire had broken out." He also told the story of an elderly paralytic man whose children left him to his own devices during the Lisbon earthquake of 1755. The man persuaded a sympathetic shop boy to carry him out of the house and into the street, at which point the boy ran away. Much to his astonishment, the boy saw the man "running after him and crying for him to wait for him." The explanation for this extraordinary phenomenon was that "terror had given him back the use of his strength and of his legs."[59]

Similarly, patients immobilized by inflammatory illnesses suddenly regained mobility from the experience of terror, according to numerous early modern doctors. An oft-repeated story from the Dessau physician Philipp Salmuth (d. 1626) appeared to confirm this belief. In a case history titled "Arthriditis curatio per terrorem" (Cure of arthritis by terror), Salmuth wrote of "a certain arthritic" whose hands and feet were wrapped in poultices that had been prepared with flour, milk, and turnips. One day when the servants were away, a pig smelled the comestibles, entered the man's house, tried to eat the bandage, and knocked the patient over. He called out for the servants, who finally arrived and removed the pig from the house. In this case the man did not recover his health and strength suddenly, but his "pains diminished, little by little until they ceased entirely, nor did they ever return." Salmuth asserted that in cases of "mixed arthritis" (where inflammation accompanies joint damage), bile is to blame for the fluid build-up and hence the inflammation, and he concluded with the question, "Can it therefore be that by terror [*per terrorem*] bile is removed, and together with it [other] peccant [i.e., harmful] humors?"[60]

Salmuth's story was repeated, with some modification, in 1787 in Vicq d'Azyr's *Encyclopédie méthodique* to prove the thesis that terror could be "salutary." The article described Salmuth's patient as "gouty" and noted that only his feet were bandaged. It also altered the story to make the cure more sudden than in Salmuth's version: now the pig's attempt to eat the bandages provoked "such a fright [*une telle frayeur*]" that the patient "began to jump and run, and his pains vanished." No mention was made of Salmuth's humoral explanation, and in fact no explanation was offered at all. Rather, the article simply adduced another story to prove that terror could cure gout. This one recalled the Siege of Siena (1553–55), when "a bullet that passed very close to the marquis of Marignac gave him such a fright [*lui donna tant d'effroi*] that he was cured of the gout with which he had been tormented."[61]

Another tale of severe inflammation cured by terror came from a letter written in 1607 by the theologian Hermann Lignaridus of Bern to the German surgeon Guilhelmus Fabricius Hildanus (1560–1634) and published in the latter's posthumous *Opera* in 1646. The letter recounted an intractable case of gout that was cured only when a man wearing an "Ethiopian" mask sneaked into the patient's house at night, crept up to his bed, woke the patient, and carried him down the stairs. The patient was so "terrified" (*perterritus*) that he ran up the stairs and called out the window for help. It was "by means of fear" (*metu*) that the gouty man was permanently healed.[62] Falconer repeated this story in 1788, changing the "Ethiopian" mask to that of a ghost, and in the French translation of this later work the reader learned that "the gouty man, seized with terror, rose up, recovered the use of his legs, and climbed into his room with the greatest speed." Moreover, "since that moment, he was cured of his gout and lived many years without feeling any attacks."[63]

This was not the only case of gout cured by terror, according to Falconer, who wrote of a "person who for forty years had been tormented by gout" and was "condemned to capital punishment." Just as he was about to be executed, he was informed that he had been pardoned, but in the meantime the terror of dying on the scaffold had cured him of his gout, and he went on to live "many years without experiencing any fits of this cruel malady."[64] In the French edition of Falconer's book La Montagne added a footnote that recounted an additional case of terror curing gout: "At Bordeaux a lion of a monstrous size was displayed. Suddenly the rumor spread that the animal had escaped. A gouty man, who, not being able to make use of his legs, was attending Mass in a litter, stood up, and, running with ease, ascended an altar, where he climbed into a niche. When the alarm was over," La Montagne added playfully, "it was necessary to use a ladder to retrieve this new saint from the place where he had been exposed to the veneration of the faithful."[65]

Among other eighteenth-century doctors who believed that terror could cure gout was Boerhaave's pupil (who was also Maria Theresa's physician) Gerard van Swieten. In a book written in Latin and published in Paris, van Swieten maintained that patients suffering from gout could be cured by "powerful terror" (*terrore valido*).[66] Gout was also on the list of diseases that La Mettrie believed terror capable of curing.[67]

The application of terror had similarly positive effects on epilepsy, according to numerous early modern physicians. The most famous case of such a cure was attributed to Boerhaave. A 1745 book by his nephew, Abraham Kaau-Boerhaave, recalls a case of contagious epilepsy that broke out at a Haarlem orphanage. First a girl fell into convulsions, and soon thereafter other children, one at a time, were "seized by the same illness," until "nearly all" were afflicted with epilepsy, and "skilled doctors applied in vain the most salubrious antiepileptic medicines that the art [of medicine] prescribes." In desperation, the physicians sent for Boerhaave in Leiden; his solution was to apply terror to the children. Upon arriving at the orphanage, Boerhaave had stoves filled with glowing coals and irons and announced that the next child who had a seizure would be burned "to the bone" on his or her arm. The orphans were "all terrified [*perterriti*] by this cruel remedy." Therefore, at "the onset of a paroxysm," all would be "impressed by painful fear" (*metudolorificae* [sic] *inustionis*), and "with all the concentration of their minds" they would "greatly resist" the seizure. Kaau-Boerhaave concluded that "terror itself [*ipse terror*] cured various forms of epilepsy."[68]

The story about Boerhaave and the epileptic orphans made its way into French publications. Zimmermann, who also believed that terror could cause arteries to collapse and could incite apoplexy, nevertheless believed that it could cure epilepsy, and he recounted the story of Boerhaave and the Haarlem orphanage to prove his point. He quoted Kaau-Boerhaave at length and concluded that terror was one of the remedies that had "cured epilepsy in the past."[69] An article titled "terreur panique," or "panic terror," published in 1772 in the *Nouveau dictionnaire universel et raisonné de médecine, de chirurgie, et de l'art vétérinaire* (New universal and reasoned dictionary of medicine, surgery, and the veterinary art), put it this way: "Panic terror can sometimes do good, and calm convulsions by producing more violent ones." To support this claim, the author recalled that

"Boerhaave reports to have seen children who were attacked by convulsions cured of this illness by the fright [*par la frayeur*] of the threats that had been made against them."[70] Cullen also referred to Boerhaave's cure as "remarkable proof" that "fear [*la peur*] or a certain degree of terror can be useful in preventing epilepsy."[71]

Another account of epilepsy cured by terror came from the November 1778 issue of *L'esprit des journaux, françois et étrangers* (The spirit of journals, French and foreign). There it was reported that a certain Hannes, a "savant doctor from Wesel" (a Prussian enclave in northwestern Germany), claimed "a cure produced by terror." Specifically, "a twelve-year-old girl experienced periodic convulsions every day." She was treated with vermifuges, or medicines designed to eradicate worms (presumably a possible cause of her epilepsy), as well as quinquina wine, which contained the antimalarial cinchona bark (evidently in case malaria was at the root of her convulsions). These medicines only served to increase the frequency of the fits, "but after a fire broke out at night in her neighborhood, she escaped with a fright [*une frayeur*] that was salutary to her; for from that moment, she was exempt from all attacks." Hannes also "makes mention of a charlatan who promised a certain cure to epileptics, and whose entire art consisted in imprinting in them a strong terror or another strong passion." Any scorn implied in the use of the term *charlatan* may have stemmed from the fact that the writer for *L'esprit des journaux* felt that it was wrong to promise a "certain cure" to epileptics or to have only one remedy for their disease.[72] Yet both Hannes and the article's author believed that terror could cure epilepsy, as seen in the effect of the fire on the epileptic girl. In any event, the fact that the activity of the "charlatan" was reported suggests a popular belief in the efficacy of such medicinal practices, and it is unlikely that the belief stopped at Wesel, a town on the Rhine that was close enough to France to have been occupied by French forces during the Seven Years' War.

Moreover, the article in *L'esprit des journaux* cited sources other than Hannes as evidence that terror could cure epilepsy. It reported that "Bartholin . . . assures that epilepsies have been cured by terror."[73] This was a reference to the seventeenth-century Danish anatomist Thomas Bartholin, who claimed that just as terror could be a cause of epilepsy, it was also possible that "by means of another terror the first illness would be dislodged." He reported having treated a boy in the midst of convulsions by soaking him unexpectedly with a great deal of cold water, thereby curing the "terrified" patient.[74]

Terror could alleviate a variety of other medical complaints, according to early modern doctors. Just as today the popular belief persists that an unexpected fright can stop the hiccups, Valleriola reported personally having been cured of a "serious and stubborn case of the hiccups" that had "ceded to no remedies" thanks to the "unexpected terror" of encountering a Knight Hospitaller.[75] Drawing on Valleriola, Hoffmann claimed that "a very stubborn case of the hiccups was cured by sudden terror," a phenomenon he explained by the theory that "the nervous and muscular parts that form the hiccup, being restricted by the terror, prevented the violent onset of nervous fluid."[76] In 1777 the French translation of Whytt's book on "those disorders which have been commonly called nervous, hypochondriac, or hysteric" reported that "one cures a person of the hiccups by instilling in his soul terror, fear, surprise, or any other violent passion."[77] As has been shown, Whytt believed terror to be at the root of a wide variety of illnesses, but in at least one case he thought it could be curative.

Terror could also allegedly cure fevers. Planque reported the case of a servant who had been subject to tertian fever, a malarial fever that produces spikes in body temperature every third day. His employer cured the fever by firing at him a rifle loaded only with powder. Planque noted that this was one of those cases in which "terror produced a salutary effect."[78] Lieutaud concurred, writing of "*la terreur*" that it was one of those passions that could "produce fever and cure it."[79] To prove that "the passions of fear, of terror," could be "salutary," Vicq d'Azyr told the story of sailors who ran aground during Vasco da Gama's voyage to India. This event produced "such a fright" (*une telle frayeur*) that those who had been suffering from fever "were all cured."[80]

The list of illnesses subject to cure by terror could be extended. To demonstrate that "panic terror can sometimes do good," the article "Terreur panique" in the *Nouveau dictionnaire* noted, "One has often seen terrible dental pain calmed at the telling of some frightening [*effrayante*] news."[81] In his description of whooping cough Cullen wrote that "terror has often cured this illness."[82] Cullen also remarked that "in order to stop hemorrhages, many superstitious remedies and charms have been recommended, [and] some have even claimed to have used them with success," but the appearance of a cure was "due to the terror of the spectators who took the spontaneous cessation of the hemorrhage for the remedy's effect." Cullen reasoned that "remedies of this type may have been useful by imprinting on the mind feelings of horror, fear, or terror [*d'horreur, de crainte, ou de terreur*]."[83] One piece of evidence supporting the claim "that terror has cured many illnesses," according to Hoffmann, was the fact that "it is an experience known to everyone that one stops and even cures nosebleeds by throwing cold water at the patients without their expecting it, and this is due to the fear [*la peur*] with which they are struck."[84] Another was that "a uterine prolapse was cured" when the woman suffering from it witnessed a fire.[85]

CONCLUSIONS

Eighteenth-century medical texts in French displayed ambivalence about the effects of terror on human health. For the most part they regarded terror as dangerous and even potentially fatal, attributing to it the power to provoke many illnesses. Yet many of them also believed that terror could restore health. This chapter began with a quote from La Mettrie affirming at once the positive and negative consequences of terror. Other authors expressed the paradox as well. Lieutaud wrote that "terror" could "produce fever and cure it."[86] Vicq d'Azyr's *Encyclopédie méthodique* informed readers that "terror and fear [*la terreur & la peur*] cause paralysis" but also affirmed that "this passion cures the same illness."[87] Hoffmann wrote that "though nothing is a greater enemy to life, and to health, than the movement that terror imparts to the blood, by repulsing it from the circumference to the center . . . and though its effects are uncertain, we learn nevertheless by observations that terror has cured many illnesses.[88] The Swiss physiologist Albrecht von Haller listed the dramatically divergent effects of terror: "Violent terror augments strength to the point of exciting convulsions, it excites the pulse, it destroys obstructions and paralyses, it suppresses the movement of the blood, it causes sudden death."[89] Zimmermann reported in the same sentence that terror could provoke apoplexy and impart "incredible vigor to the body."[90]

One source attesting to ambivalent attitudes toward terror is particularly tantalizing because it might suggest a link between prerevolutionary medical writing and revolutionary politics. In 1775 a young physician wrote:

> Terror, that terrible emotion that produces tremors of horror [*de l'épouvante*], cries of fury, or the prospect of imminent danger, this passion always composed of the fear [*la crainte*] of the object that frightens us [*qui nous effraie*], and the inseparable desire to avoid it, produces very different effects on the body. Sometimes one feels a universal trembling, an extreme weakness, a general torpor that removes from the members the faculty of obeying the soul, suspends the use of the senses, causes the voice to expire on the lips; and this torpor of the organs even goes, though rarely, to the point of destroying its functions. At other times in place of stupor, there is a new vigor that makes us agile, fit and well, capable of prodigious efforts, and raises us above ourselves.[91]

That young doctor was none other than Jean-Paul Marat. Was Marat drawn to the Terror during the Revolution because he had seen the "prodigious" effects of terror in the human organism and wished to apply that "new vigor" to the body politic? This is conceivable, as it was common to think of the state as an organism.[92] Or perhaps Marat was more attracted to the harmful effects of terror, seeing it as a means of disabling the nation's enemies. Maybe both aspects of terror made it appealing as a concept that could be applied to political life.

Marat did not explicitly link medical and political terror, but such a linkage was conceivable in prerevolutionary France. Specifically, one sees it in an article published in the *Mercure historique et politique* in 1766. The report discussed riots that had recently taken place in Madrid against the unpopular Neapolitan diplomat the marquis of Esquilache and by implication against King Charles III, a Bourbon monarch and France's ally.[93] It took the side of the Spanish crown and called for harsh measures against the "ill-intentioned ones," who should be made "to tremble." This would "divert others . . . [who had] the intention of stirring up trouble." The article added, "It is necessary to imprint terror, when one cannot do otherwise, to restore political order. Certain maladies in states, like certain ills in the human body, can only be extirpated by extraordinary remedies."[94]

The implication in this political comment, as in the writings of physicians, was that terror could rightfully be imposed under emergency circumstances, when all other remedies had been exhausted and the "patient" faced imminent death. We see this kind of caution in a remark by Cullen on the treatment of whooping cough in young children. The Scottish physician advised that "terror might be a very powerful remedy," but it was "difficult to fix the degree." If the terror was "light" it "could be ineffective," but if it was "too strong" it would be "dangerous." Therefore he "would not advise it."[95] In this respect he was following a long tradition of medical thinking on terror, one that went back at least to 1733, when Leonard Stocke, a doctoral candidate at Utrecht University, wrote his *Dissertatio medica inauguralis de terrore ejusque effectis in corpus humanum* (Inaugural medical dissertation on terror and its effects in the human body). After enumerating the many ills that terror could cure, Stocke was careful about recommending it. "Unless one is despairing of [the patient's] health, one should not have recourse to the remedy," he wrote, noting that it was "unpredictable and dangerous." It did "not always remove the morbific material" and sometimes led to illnesses becoming "worse . . . even incurable."[96] Stocke's dissertation was written in Latin and therefore inaccessible to most readers in eighteenth-century France, though medical professors and other well-educated physicians would have been able to read it. But Stocke's thinking on the subject was in line with many of the writings I have considered in this chapter that depicted terror as a dangerous force that could nevertheless produce a salutary change at a time of crisis.

It was easy to transfer the concept of crisis from medicine to politics, as Reinhart Koselleck has shown.[97] Antoine de Baecque has shown more generally how political ideas in eighteenth-century France drew on metaphors from the body.[98] For those revolutionaries who saw an analogy between medical and political terror, the application of terror, however dangerous, might have appeared justified in dire cases, when the body politic was at great risk of dying otherwise. If one was "despairing of [the patient's] health," whether the suffering body was a person or a nation, the use of dangerous methods might have seemed warranted.

The significance of the writings examined in this chapter, however, does not depend on a direct correlation between medical ideas about terror and the belief that the body politic must experience terror in order to purge itself of its own "morbific material." Rather, these medical texts are more significant in that they reveal a respectful attitude toward terror. Whether it was "salutary" or harmful, terror was a powerful force, with the capacity to inflict sudden and dramatic changes on human bodies and minds.[99] Like God and the earthly rulers who drew their legitimacy from him, it had the capacity to hurt or spare the human beings under its control. In this respect it was sovereign and therefore an object of veneration.[100]

CHAPTER SEVEN

Terror before "the Terror":
June 1789–August 1793

INTRODUCTION

The principal argument of this book is that terror, whatever it meant to revolutionaries in September 1793, was appealing in large measure because of the positive emotional connotations historically attached to the words *terreur* and *terrible*. Traditionally God was conceived of as "terrible," and the terror he instilled in his creatures highlighted his power, glory, and majesty. Old Regime kings sought the status of "terror of their enemies," and with the growth of nationalism in the eighteenth century it was also possible to characterize nations as the terror of *their* enemies.[1] That the laws, especially those governing the application of punishments, needed to instill terror in malefactors was a truism of eighteenth-century judicial thought. In the realm of theater criticism, terror became a requisite quality of tragedies, and for aesthetic theorists it was a precondition of the sublime. Terror could even have positive effects on the human body, though physicians advised employing it only as a last resort. Yet to understand more fully the effect that these ideas might have had on the Montagnards of 1793 and 1794, it is necessary to explore terror speech in the first four years of the Revolution. When Claude Royer called for terror as "the order of the day," he was drawing both on prerevolutionary traditions and on more recent, revolutionary-era precedents.

In some respects, as will be apparent in the final chapter of this book, the Montagnards skipped over the years 1789 to 1793 and embraced discourses of terror that the early revolutionaries did not deploy. For example, during the Year II revolutionaries expressed their enthusiasm for terror in language that mirrored Old Regime traditions of theology, aesthetics (especially of the sublime), and medicine, which are not in evidence during the constitutional monarchy and the first year of the Republic. In other respects, however, the

Montagnards repeated elements of terror speech that were common in the earlier revolutionary years. As this chapter will argue, between 1789 and 1793 revolutionaries repeatedly spoke or wrote, as had prerevolutionary legal commentators, of the terror of the laws. Moreover, they frequently expressed the wish to impose terror on their military enemies (including domestic rebels), even to the point of praising generals as "the terror of [their] enemies," in much the same way as Old Regime kings and commanders had been praised. This military discourse gained strength as France waged war on an increasingly formidable array of foes and left the idea of the terror of the laws in the background, though never fully discarding it.

In this chapter I will make two additional arguments. First, terror speech was not a monopoly of the Left. It was the common property of Montagnards, Girondins, and even monarchists. Indeed, its ecumenical character was a large part of its appeal. Those who invoked it could not be accused of addressing a faction of the population. They were using a term that held positive emotional connotations for the entire political spectrum. A second argument concerns what I will call the therapeutic purpose of terror speech. Revolutionaries imputed terror to their enemies as a means of reducing their own terror. The thought of enemies rendered disabled by terror was literally encouraging in the sense of raising the courage of revolutionaries, who had many reasons, some imaginary but many real, to be terrified. The ecumenical character of terror speech and its therapeutic benefits, combined with longstanding positive emotional connotations associated with the word "terror," help to explain why the Montagnards called their cherished political platform *la terreur*.

LAW, ORDER, AND TERROR

On October 19, 1789, a crowd of women berated a baker named François for allegedly gouging the people. Then a group of men seized the hapless François, beheaded him and impaled his head on a pike as a warning to others. According to the pro-revolutionary newspaper *Le moniteur universel*, this "horrible murder, committed practically under [the] eyes [of the National Assembly], excited its indignation and obliged it to deploy all the rigor of the laws to assure the lives of citizens by the punishment of the guilty, and to repress by terror the audacity of the disturbers of public tranquility." The murderers were tried, convicted, and executed on the very same day, and the Assembly declared Paris to be under martial law.[2] Thus, quite early in the Revolution the concept of terror was connected with the swift and rigorous but legal repression of crime. The law itself was terrible, and by extension the national legislature was an organ of terror. Potential "disturbers of public tranquility" would presumably think twice before violating the law.

This was only one of many instances in which revolutionaries or their supporters used the language of terror to delineate the proper function of legal punishment. Early in the Revolution this language was ecumenical, appealing both to the democratically inclined and to the *monarchiens*, who sought to reconcile representative government with a powerful king, and even in the early months of the Republic the reputedly moderate Girondins shared terror speech with the more radical Montagnards. All were heirs to an established tradition (discussed in chapter 3) that viewed terror as necessary for law and order.

For example, when Deputy Jacques Duval d'Eprémesnil, a champion of monarchical power, opposed the February 1790 proposal of his fellow *monarchien* Pierre-Victor Malouet to accord municipal officers the power to declare martial law and summon the National Guard against "seditious gatherings," he asserted, "It is necessary to strike brigands with great terror." He predicted that municipal officers who confronted disturbances would be afraid to call in the National Guard (and he no doubt feared the reputedly democratic sympathies of the civic force), and he preferred "to invest the king with the plenitude of repressive power" over all troubled municipalities.[3] Ironically, it was Robespierre who spoke out against "authorizing the executive power to deploy the terror of arms," and who in a subsequent session insisted that "this revolution cannot be completed if the people are kept powerless by terror."[4] (Five years later Robespierre would argue that "overthrowing by terror the enemies of liberty" was precisely the hallmark of "revolutionary government" or "the despotism of liberty against tyranny.")[5]

Yet others on the left of the Assembly spoke in favor of terror when arguing about the status of another policing institution, the Assembly's own investigative body, known as the Comité des recherches.[6] This agency had the power to detain political suspects, and it had already incarcerated members of the nobility whom it alleged to be plotting against the state. Now it was the Right that decried perceived assaults on civil liberties, while the Left embraced terror speech to justify the pursuit of the nation's enemies. Duval d'Eprémesnil himself called for the abolition of the Comité. Pleading the case of the queen's secretary, Jacques-Mathieu Augeard, who had been arrested on suspicion of plotting with the counterrevolutionary émigrés to overturn the Revolution, he compared the national police force to the Spanish Inquisition.[7] To this Isaac Le Chapelier, who would later drift to the right but in March 1790 was still an ardent Jacobin, replied, "I consider [the Comité] more necessary than ever for the maintenance of the constitution;

I see it as a sure means of spreading salutary terror among those with bad intentions."[8] In August the Parisian municipality would endorse the Comité in similar terms, praising it as "the terror of the enemies of the fatherland."[9]

Terror speech was also deployed by supporters of yet another police force. In November the Assembly addressed the status of the *maréchaussée*, a kind of precursor to the *gendarmerie* but one that had long been associated with arbitrary power. Rabaut de Saint-Étienne, the Protestant pastor and moderate deputy from Nîmes who would later align himself with the Girondins, lauded this "completely prepared and organized force . . . the severe enemy of disturbers of the public peace . . . [a force] whose name alone inspires terror in malefactors and brigands."[10] The *Moniteur* paraphrased Rabaut, who proposed (in its words) "preserving the *maréchaussée*, assimilating it to the current regime and preserving in it all that can attract the trust of the people and make it the terror of malefactors."[11] This view was not restricted to the National Assembly. The utopian novelist and social commentator Mercier had written the previous year that "the brigand" who encountered an officer of the imposing force would feel "salutary terror."[12]

Just as terror justified police power, it was also invoked in debates about judicial institutions and practices. In August 1790 the Assembly considered whether the Old Regime office of public prosecutor would continue to exist. Some deputies on the left wished to emulate the Romans and allow any citizen to prosecute any other, whereas those on the right preferred to leave the job to royal appointees. Louis-Étienne Brevet de Beaujour, a moderate deputy from Angers who voted with the *monarchiens* but would later drift toward decentralized, Girondin-style republicanism, argued that "the origin of the right of accusation is found in the social contract itself." He reasoned that since "any infraction against the law . . . at once harms each individual and puts all of society in peril, it is in the interest of each of its members that public order be constantly maintained, that the law be religiously respected, and that salutary and ceaselessly menacing terror make crimes almost impossible." Ultimately Brevet called for a compromise by which the office of public prosecutor would be elective, but his reasoning rested on belief in the necessity of "salutary" terror.[13]

Bertrand Barère, a deputy in the National Assembly and future member of the Committee of Public Safety during the Terror, used similar language when defending his view of the proper role of criminal courts. On January 20, 1791, during a debate over whether there should be numerous local criminal courts or a smaller number but with larger jurisdictions, Barère argued for the latter. He made the case that criminal courts should be grand and intimidating and therefore few in number. Criminal justice, in his view, "must have its dignity, and it is only here that it [dignity] is a part of the criminal justice [system], which must inspire salutary terror in crime [i.e., criminals] by its pomp even more than by its judgments."[14] We saw in chapter 3 that prerevolutionary commentators disagreed about the effectiveness of "pomp," with Voltaire disparaging it and Mercier endorsing it; Barère was clearly more inclined to Mercier's view when he linked terror and "dignity."

The perceived need to impose terror on lawbreakers was also evident in discussions of three violent disturbances that took place in 1790. First, in June of that year Protestants in Nîmes murdered between two hundred and three hundred Catholics.[15] On October 30, in the midst of a lengthy investigation, the Assembly admitted a Catholic widow named Gas to the bar to describe what had happened to her husband and other coreligionists. Significantly, in her speech she invoked the terror of the law. She apostrophized "the directories of the department of the Gard and of the district of Nîmes," the authorities she accused of the murder of her husband, predicting that "soon you will be seen trembling, not with rage as you did when you led my husband to his death, not with satisfaction as you did when . . . you stepped on the corpse of my husband to enter my house which was being demolished, but with that profound terror that the pomp of justice impresses in the soul of the guilty one."[16] After hearing and reading numerous accounts of the events in Nîmes, in February 1791 the Assembly concluded that they were too "partisan" to lead to a verdict. The conservative deputy Jacques Antoine Marie de Cazalès, who would later that year go into counterrevolutionary emigration, protested against what he saw as the premature conclusion of the inquiry. Like *veuve* Gas, he invoked terror as a crucial feature of justice. He accused his fellow deputies of "refus[ing] to citizens the protection that the law owes them," noting that "this protection is only effective by the terror that punishment inspires in crime."[17]

A second serious disturbance that elicited terror speech in revolutionaries in 1790 took place in Nancy. On August 31 a mutiny of soldiers from three regiments garrisoned at Nancy ended with roughly one hundred killed in the fighting and more than twenty subsequently hanged. As the moderate deputy Charles-Alexis Brûlart de Sillery explained to the Assembly, tensions had been simmering throughout August as soldiers demanded back pay from their commanding officers. The dispute was not merely about money, however, as increasingly radicalized soldiers confronted aristocratic officers whose loyalty to the Revolution they questioned. After a series of instances in which the soldiers disobeyed their superiors, the Assembly sent General François Claude Bouillé to restore discipline. But his appearance convinced three regiments that a counterrevolution was imminent. Their armed resistance prompted a bloody suppression. Brûlart deftly and diplomatically assigned blame to soldiers as well as officers. He carefully endorsed the "patriotism" of misguided soldiers and questioned the degree to which the officer class understood the egalitarianism of the Revolution—and he conveniently shifted some of the blame to the municipal government of Nancy, which had refrained from intervening in some of the smaller confrontations leading up to the rebellion. But he was equally careful to condemn both major and minor acts of insubordination, which in his view revealed a failure to feel a proper terror of the law.

Brûlart described one event (a few days prior to the armed rebellion) in which members of the Swiss Guard publicly ridiculed their own regimental standard by tearing the red cover from a passing wagon and flying it as though it were a Swiss flag. The soldiers were "followed by a large number of people who applauded this pasquinade." At this point, Brûlart opined, the municipal authorities of Nancy should have stopped the troublemakers, but "the municipality not having dared punish them, it attenuated the respect and terror that this imposing [but] violated mark of the law [i.e., the regimental flag] should inspire in the hearts of all citizens."[18] More seriously, the mutinous soldiers ignored the orders of the National Assembly that obliged them to return to obedience. Bouillé "prescribed to them what they had to do to show their submission; it is at this price that he carries the sword of the law." Bouillé's tone was firm, according to Brûlart, but "that tone was the only one he could employ to inspire the respect and terror that must accompany one who marches by this sacred name [of the National Assembly]."[19] Bouillé would later be instrumental in the king's failed attempt to escape France in June 1791, and for this (and his conduct in the Nancy mutiny) he would appear as a villain in the "Marseillaise." Only his flight to England saved him from the Terror. Brûlart would go to the guillotine in October 1793, but in 1790 he could expect to convince members of the National Assembly of Bouillé's right to suppress the mutiny by linking the general's act of "terror" to "respect" for the legislature's "sacred name."

A third disturbance in 1790 prompted still another affirmation of the terror of the law. On November 30, 1790, the left-leaning deputy Pierre-Jacques Vieillard, speaking on behalf of the Committee of Reports, informed the Assembly of a revolt that had broken out recently in the town of Saint-Jean d'Angély (department of Charente-Inférieure).[20] The trouble began early in October, when a National Guard commandant named Arnault erroneously reported that the National Assembly had abolished the dîme, or tithe, and urged his fellow citizens to withhold payment. The departmental authorities called the maréchaussée to arrest Arnault and his followers for sedition, but Arnault's party violently resisted. In the ensuing melee four rebels were killed, and subsequently the mayor of a neighboring town was assassinated for his alleged support of the repression. At this point the municipal government of Saint-Jean d'Angély indicated its support of the tax revolt. The administrators of the Charente-Inférieure responded by calling in 150 men from the royal regiment of Agenais, 120 National Guardsmen, and 130 gendarmes. According to Vieillard, they asked the commandant of La Rochelle (the major port city and department seat) to send an infantry battalion to Saint-Jean d'Angély and four field canons to nearby Saintes "to impress salutary terror on the people who have strayed until they are disabused" of their false notions.

From the perspective of only three years in the future, this version of terror would have looked quite restrained. In 1790 the authorities used terror only "on the people who have strayed," not "enemies" or "monsters," and they were optimistic that the show of force would "disabuse" the misled townspeople and villagers. Indeed, Vieillard's report stresses the reconciliation that occurred after the authorities had brought in the might of the state. Terror worked, and the citizens who had revolted quickly recognized the error of their ways, at least in Vieillard's interpretation of events.[21] In this respect his understanding of "salutary" terror looked much like that of the prerevolutionary legal commentators examined in chapter 3.

Prerevolutionary understandings of terror likewise informed the debates that the National Assembly held on the death penalty. On May 23, 1791 Louis-Michel Le Pelletier de Saint-Fargeau presented to the Assembly a paper entitled "Report on the Project of a Penal Code." Le Pelletier would become famous as the first regicide martyr when he was murdered on January 20, 1793, for having voted in favor of the king's execution. Ironically, however, like Robespierre he began his revolutionary career opposing the death penalty. In the tradition of Beccaria, whom he cited in his report, he objected to capital punishment on the grounds that it was *insufficiently* terrifying. Le Pelletier argued that "punishments must be durable," explaining "that a prolonged series of painful privations, while sparing humanity the horror [*l'horreur*] of tortures, affects the guilty much more than a passing instant of pain too often braved with a sort of courage and philosophy." He insisted that long-lived punishments were "even more effective for the example" they presented: "The impression of the spectacle of a day is quickly erased," whereas "a slow punishment of lengthy labors ceaselessly renewing themselves before the eyes of the people, [and] the memory of the avenging laws, give birth again at every moment to salutary terror."[22]

Between May 31 and June 2 numerous deputies weighed in on the question of capital punishment. The first to do so, Louis-Pierre-Joseph Prugnon, a moderate deputy with a firm commitment to monarchy, affirmed that "the pomp of punishment, even viewed from afar, frightens [*effraye*] criminals and stops them," and he therefore urged his fellow lawmakers not "to break a spring such as that of the terror of punishment." He challenged the notion that the "loss of honor" could be a suitable substitute for the death penalty, arguing that "it is crime that has killed honor in the guilty person, not the punishment that you inflict on him." "Where honor is silent," he added, "the only thing that can be made to speak is terror."[23] On June 1 Jean Mercier-Terrefort, a conservative deputy who himself would be sentenced to death in December 1793 for counterrevolutionary activity, spoke in favor of maintaining the death penalty. He conceded that opponents of capital punishment had strong theoretical arguments on their side, but he maintained that French society was too unsettled to abolish the death penalty without incurring harmful consequences: "It is not at a time when minds are agitated by hatred, by intrigue, factions, vengeance, ambition, fanaticism, by all the passions that bring people to the cruelest excesses . . . it is not at such a time that it would be wise to relinquish the spring of terror."[24] On June 2 François-Jérôme Riffard de Saint-Martin (who would later oppose the death penalty for the king) argued against having a death penalty in the penal code, but in the spirit of Beccaria he affirmed that the principal object of punishment was terror. He recommended chain gangs, or "public works punishment," which "fulfills, as numerous legislators from Pennsylvania have recognized, the principal object of the punishment of crimes, which is to prevent them with terror."[25] On June 3 the left-wing deputy Tuaut de La Bouverie argued in favor of the death penalty. As in the arguments of other deputies, terror was central. "The interest of society is to provide a great example," Tuaut asserted. "It is extremely important that the man exposed to all the passions of humanity return home after an execution, his heart penetrated with terror and fright [*de terreur et d'effroi*]."[26] Ultimately the Assembly decided not to abolish capital punishment, but the debate surrounding the death penalty reinforced the venerable prerevolutionary idea that "salutary terror" of the law prevented crime and kept society safe. It was an idea shared by the Left and the Right, by defenders of capital punishment and by its opponents.

In October 1791 a Legislative Assembly succeeded the National (Constituent) Assembly, and the newly elected lawmakers inherited their predecessors' concern for law and order. They also shared the belief that terror was a key element in making the law and judicial institutions respectable. The first such call for terror came in October from Deputy Fauchet, a bishop in the reorganized "constitutional" church, who explained that the best way to persuade his fellow clerics to take the required oath to the nation was through "some great examples of legal justice against the instigators of the troubles," which would "strike their foolish disciples with useful terror." He was speaking of imprisonment rather than execution, but his successors in the Convention would apply the same principle of exemplary terror in their calls for executions.[27]

When discussing judicial terror, the Legislative Assembly and its supporters often focused on government officials, who might otherwise be considered beyond the reach of the laws. In January 1792 the Jacobin deputy Claude-Bernard Navier of Dijon pressed his fellow legislators to work towards the creation of a High Court (Haute Cour), which the Constitution of 1791 authorized as a tribunal designed to judge high officials and which Navier believed would be able "to inspire salutary terror in the enemies of liberty."[28] When in March the Assembly brought accusations against two ministers, Delessart and Duport, and sent them before the High Court, a businessman from Dunkirk wrote to the legislature, congratulating it for having provided "a great example which has imprinted terror into the souls of great criminals." Lessart and Duport allegedly "believed that the laws could not reach them," but fortunately "the throne will cease to be surrounded by perverse men when ministers see the sword of the law suspended over their heads."[29] Similarly, in July the Feuillant (moderate monarchist) deputy Louis-Michel Demées of the Orne department called for a law requiring ministers to submit their accounts to the Assembly and face punishment for any irregularities, insisting that "if they are truly citizens, they must call for this law themselves, for if it is the terror of the wicked one, it can only be favorable to him who acquits himself faithfully of his duties."[30] In August 1792, in the very last days of the constitutional monarchy, the Girondin deputy Armand Gensonné insisted on the creation of the High Court as a means of creating "the terror of the example"—in other words, producing exemplary terror among the government officials in its purview.[31]

Deputies similarly conceived of other courts in terms of the terror they could instill. Military courts in particular could accomplish this goal. In March 1792 the Legislative Assembly considered the question of whether the crime of *embauchage*, or recruiting soldiers for émigré armies, should be reserved for the National High Court. The Feuillant François Alexandre Tardiveau of Rennes argued that requiring the High Court to handle the many cases of *embauchage* would be impracticable and ineffective: "Punishments that the laws have pronounced against the guilty do not only have for their object the punishment of the crimes committed; they have another goal as well, that of preventing new crimes by example and by the terror of punishment." Yet this goal "is totally missed if the application of the punishment does not follow the crime immediately, [or] if the judgment is rendered far from the place that served as the theater of the misdeeds." There were too many cases of *embauchage* to be heard quickly by the High Court, and many *embaucheurs* had committed their crimes in distant provinces. Tardiveau, who believed that the death penalty applied to anyone who "removes defenders from the *patrie* . . . to double the forces of exterior enemies," proposed "that a court-martial apply [the penalty]; that the punishment be prompt; that the guilty be punished in the place of the crime, in order that the example of the necessary punishment finally stop, by terror, the enemies of the Revolution."[32] Yet even courts-martial could be slow, as the anti-Jacobin Joseph-François Dupont-Grandjardin (who himself would be executed in 1793 for having supported the marquis de Lafayette) argued on September 15, 1792. Speaking for the military committee, Dupont-Grandjardin proposed simplifying the court-martial process (mainly by reducing the number of jurors). His reasoning was similar to Tardiveau's: "The object of the law in establishing punishment is to inspire salutary terror in those who would be capable of troubling the order of society. If the application of punishments is too slow, it does not produce the same effect, and the accused, far from exciting just indignation, only inspires pity."[33]

Like courts, prisons could also spread salutary terror of the law. On April 21, 1792 two members of the directory of the Seine-et-Oise department (comprising Versailles and other locales near Paris) came to the bar of the Legislative Assembly to request a prison for their department. Charles-François Lebrun (future consul under Napoleon) spoke on behalf of both of them. He complained about "the anarchy and the ills" that were afflicting the provinces. He acknowledged that with the Revolution "justice has risen up and the sword of the law is weighing down on the head of the guilty one," adding that "already salutary terror has given remorse and maybe virtue to men whom the example of crime had corrupted and the hope of pardon was about to lead to more crimes." But in order for punishment always to be "present before the eyes of citizens," leading them "to respect and fear of the law," a prison needed to be built.[34]

Although there were many possible sources for Lebrun's mental association of prison and exemplary terror—Le Pelletier's argument against the death penalty stands out here—Jeremy Bentham may also have played a role. On November 25, 1791, the English reformer and utilitarian philosopher had addressed a letter to the Legislative Assembly in which he offered to design a new prison for the French. Referring to his *Panopticon*, a French translation of which he was sending as a separate package, he wrote, "Let me construct a prison according to this model, and I will make myself its jailer." He even offered to manage the prison free of charge.[35] The deputies did not hire Bentham, but they did order his book to be published by the Assembly's own press. *Panoptique* stated, "What must a prison be? A place where those who abused their liberty are deprived of it, in order to prevent new crimes for their part and to divert others from [crime] by the terror of the example."[36] Bentham proposed that the panopticon, the central tower from which the prisoners could all be seen, be transformed every Sunday into a "chapel" in which "the public" could view the prisoners as well. He wrote, "This would be a moral theater whose productions imprint the terror of crime."[37]

THE PEOPLE OR THE LAW?

On August 10, 1792, a massive insurrection overthrew the monarchy and the short-lived Legislative Assembly, and on September 21 yet another legislature, the National Convention, took on the task of making laws for what was now a republic. The Convention faced the challenge of sansculottes claiming for themselves the right to impose laws based on what they deemed to be the general will, as well as the right to judge and punish malefactors. This competitor to sovereignty—the people—naturally sought one of sovereignty's chief attributes: terror or terribleness. Champions of the people therefore highlighted this quality. For example, on August 28, while France was ruled by an interim government and it was often unclear who was in charge, the *Moniteur* printed a letter from Robespierre in which he endorsed the newly established tribunals appointed by the Parisian National Guard: "The people's justice must bear a character worthy of them; it must be imposing as well as prompt and terrible."[38]

The implication of Robespierre's message was that anything "the people" deemed to be just was legitimate. It was in the context of such a general dispensation that the September Massacres took place. On September 2 sansculottes, convinced that inmates of Parisian prisons were preparing to massacre the people as Prussian forces crossed the border and headed for the capital to join in the slaughter, engaged in their own preemptive slaughter of fourteen hundred prisoners. The response of Minister of the Interior, Jean-Marie Roland de la Platière, is revealing of the new way of conceptualizing terrible justice. Roland expressed some misgivings about the extent of the killings, which were still taking place when he declared, "Yesterday . . . was a day the events of which should perhaps be left veiled"; but he nevertheless affirmed that "the people, terrible in its vengeance, still exercises a sort of justice." Excusing the butchery, he affirmed that the people "does not take as its victim each one who presents himself to its fury." Rather, "it directs it to those who it believes have been too long spared by the sword of the law, and who the peril of circumstances persuades must be immolated without delay."[39] The idea that the massacres were only "a sort of justice" hinted at the need to replace summary killing with a more authentic system of justice, but the suggestion that those killed had "been too long spared by the sword of the law" gave the impression that "the people" were only doing what the law itself should have done long before. Indeed the adjective *terrible* itself lent legitimacy to the killings, since the law, after all, was supposed to be terrible. It is worth emphasizing that this justification, though mirroring Robespierre's idea of "the people's justice," was the product of a leading Girondin and therefore a mortal enemy of Robespierre. Indeed, Roland would certainly have faced execution at the hands of Robespierre and the Montagnards if he had not robbed them of that satisfaction by committing suicide following the anti-Girondin insurrection of May 31–June 2, 1793. Yet in September 1792 both men endorsed the justice of "the people" by pronouncing it "terrible." The *Moniteur* similarly legitimized the September Massacres by reporting the supposedly salutary effects of the judicial terror: "Those who were only mildly guilty were brought before the expiring criminal, and the spectacle of terror to which they were witnesses preceded the moment of their deliverance." The *Moniteur* reinforced the message by claiming, in language similar to Roland's, that "the people's justice is terrible."[40]

Despite their praise for "the people," lawmakers sought to regain control of the Revolution, and this meant replacing "terrible" acts of popular "justice" with the terror of the laws. Thus on September 21, 1792, the very first day of the new republican legislature, Minister of Justice and Deputy Georges Danton declared, "Now the laws must be as terrible against those who attack them as the people have been in blasting tyranny."[41] He reiterated this imperative the following day when the Convention received a deputation from Orléans claiming that the municipality had threatened citizens who were asking for bread and had surrounded the town with cannon. Danton proposed that three members of the Convention go to the scene of the accusations, and if the municipal officers were trying to turn the department against the Revolution, he said, "their heads must fall under the sword of the laws." He added, "Let the law be terrible, and order will be restored."[42] The implication was that law without terror would not be respected, that it would be ineffective, that it would scarcely be law at all.

As the legislators formed the institutions designed to keep law and order in the new Republic, they likewise used terror speech to describe and legitimize them. On March 10, 1793, Danton was one of the first to propose new "judicial measures to punish the counterrevolutionaries." Troubled by the "popular vengeance" enacted by crowds, especially the September Massacres, which had occurred while he was Minister of Justice, Danton sought to place terror back into the law, where he believed it belonged. He enjoined his colleagues in the Convention, "Let extraordinary laws, taken outside the social body, horrify [*épouvantent*] the rebels and reach the guilty." For the sake of the *salut du peuple*, Danton argued, "terrible measures must be taken." He urged the Convention, "Let us do what the Legislative Assembly did not do; let us be terrible so that the people does not have to be [*soyons terribles pour dispenser le peuple de l'être*]," and he called for his colleagues to "organize a tribunal . . . so that the sword of the law weighs heavily over the heads of all its enemies."[43] The Convention responded by creating an institution that would be central to the Terror: the Revolutionary Tribunal.

When the architects of another crucial institution of the Terror, the Committee of Public Safety, sought to persuade their colleagues of its value to the nation, they used similar language. According to Danton, on April 3, 1793, the Convention had "the duty to create a terrible authority." "Such is the violence of the storm that rocks the ship of state," he warned, that only a small committee endowed with emergency powers to execute the law quickly could guarantee what he variously called *salut public* and the *salut de tous*.[44] That same day Barère observed that the local surveillance committees recently authorized by the Convention had "the terrible right to issue arrest warrants" and that lawmakers "on mission" in the departments had "the frightful authority [*l'effrayante autorité*] to deport enemies of liberty and equality." A *Comité de salut public* was only the logical extension of these other measures.[45]

THE KING'S TRIAL

The most immediately pressing judicial matter that faced the Convention, and one that predated the establishment of the Revolutionary Tribunal and the Committee of Public Safety, was the fate of the king. Louis XVI—or Louis Capet, as he was now typically called—had been arrested during the insurrection of August 10 and was imprisoned in the Temple fortress. Discussions of his judicial status and of the Convention's rightful power to punish the king frequently included invocations of terror. In this respect revolutionaries were honoring a long-standing tradition of justifying punishment on the basis of the terror it would convey to others. Here the "others" were foreign monarchs and the people who supported them. Thus on November 27, 1792, Deputy Lepelletier, now considerably less squeamish about the death penalty than he had been only eighteen months earlier, reported that the Convention had recently received a letter from a Jacobin club in Auxerre. He paraphrased it: "The nations, these citizens say, are awaiting the judgment that you are going to pass on the crimes of Louis XVI; may it be terrible, may it be prompt, may it make the tyrants of the earth quiver."[46]

On December 3 the Convention considered the question of whether the king could be legally punished, and those who argued in favor used terror speech to justify their position. The first to do so was Robespierre, who, like the Jacobins of Auxerre, legitimated the king's execution by referring to the terror it would provoke. He asked the Convention to "give a great example to the world at the same site at which the generous martyrs to liberty died on August 10," and he further asked "that for these memorable events a monument be consecrated, [a monument] destined to nourish in heart of peoples the sentiment of their rights and a horror of tyrants, and in that of tyrants the salutary terror of the people's justice."[47] Like Robespierre, Pierre-Arnaud Dartigoeyte, of the Landes department, conceived of the king's punishment as exemplary and called for "a terrible example."[48] Léonard Bourdon, of the Loiret, concurred. "May [the king] appear before this august and terrible tribunal," he urged, linking the Convention's terribleness with its respectability, and added that "by pronouncing the penalty [of death] . . . we will augment the terror and consternation that our victorious armies have already spread."[49] Nicolas Hentz, from Metz, made a similar connection: "Republicans, the terror of your arms has spread throughout Europe and given hope to peoples; may the terror of your judgment spread equally, and overturn the despots' thrones."[50] Alexandre Deleyre, deputy from the Gironde (but a regicide nonetheless), asked rhetorically, "Would you dare show mercy to those who never showed it to the human race?" He answered, "No, no: since pardon would be an encouragement to breach of duty, it is necessary for punishment to become its terror."[51]

After having tried the king in December, in January the Convention discussed his culpability and appropriate punishment. Three addresses delivered in written form on January 7 reveal the continuing prominence of the language of terror. Jacques-Léonard de La Planche called for "a great example for the justice of peoples and the terror of tyrants."[52] Jean-Louis Seconds declared that it was only possible to have "peace with tyrants . . . through terror and the force of arms."[53] Jean-Paul Marat anticipated "the terror that this spectacle [of the king's execution] will cast into the souls of schemers."[54]

More written endorsements of terror appeared in a collection of addresses deposited at the Convention on January 15. Paul-Augustin Lozeau, of the Charente-Inférieure, responded to those deputies who feared that the execution of the king would incite additional countries to wage war on France. He insisted that the king's death "will diminish the interest they have in attacking us. It will annihilate their hopes, it will be able to cast terror . . . among them."[55] Charles-Nicolas Beauvais de Préau, of Paris, believed that "[the king's] punishment must inspire a just terror in the despots who fight for him,"[56] and his fellow Parisian François Robert wrote that the death penalty was necessary "to imprint terror on all the crowned brigands."[57]

During the dramatic roll call on the night of January 16–17, numerous deputies used terror speech to describe, embellish, or justify their regicidal votes. Alexandre Besson, of the Doubs, urged his colleagues, "Let us never hope or try to inspire in tyrants sentiments other than that of terror," and therefore voted for the death penalty.[58] The Parisian deputy Antoine Louis François Sergent likewise proclaimed, "The head of a tyrant only falls with a crash, and his execution inspires salutary terror."[59] Similarly, many deputies used the word *terrible* to describe the king's punishment or their vote for it. Louis Marie Turreau-Linières, of the Yonne, felt that killing the king would provide "the great and terrible lesson that we are going to give to usurpers of the inalienable rights of nations."[60] Barère believed "that the punishment of Louis, which will be the lesson of kings, will also be the terrible lesson of factious ones, anarchists, pretenders to dictatorship or to any other power like royalty."[61] Thomas-François-Ambroise Jouenne-Longchamp, of the Calvados department, declared "a terrible judgment" against the king whom he condemned to death,[62] Jean-Baptiste Cavaignac, of the Lot, relayed his "terrible wish" that the king face the executioner,[63] and Mathieu Guezno, of Finistère, called his regicidal vote "this terrible vow."[64]

At the same time, terror speech was not the monopoly of regicides. Deputies who wished to save the king, or at least submit his death sentence to a national referendum, also frequently invoked terror. Charles-François Dupont, of the Hautes-Pyrénées, used a Beccarian conception of terror to defend his proposal for keeping the king incarcerated. An imprisoned king, he asserted, "will be the terror of kings . . . and the consolation of nations."[65] Jean-Baptiste Louvet, of the Loiret, favored a referendum on the king's sentencing and personally called for the king's imprisonment for life, yet he used terror speech in his argument. Whatever decision the people reached, according to Louvet, the exercise of its collective will would be "a terrible lesson for despots" and leave them "frozen with terror."[66] Philippe Charles François Séguin, of the Doubs, argued that "the existence of Louis" would be "for all the despots an infinitely more terrible example than his death would be."[67] The ecumenical character of terror speech helps to explain its allure later in 1793, when Montagnards called for terror à l'ordre du jour.

The execution of the king took place on January 21, 1793. Soon thereafter the Convention received confirmation from revolutionary citizens that this event inspired terror in the nation's enemies. Supporters typically used terror speech to legitimize the execution. For example, on January 29 the mayor and six municipal officials from the village of Criqueboeuf-sur-Seine (Eure) wrote to the Convention congratulating the deputies on their decision and assuring them that the execution of Louis "will cast terror into the hearts of kings."[68] On February 10 the Convention read a letter from the Jacobin club in the newly "liberated" municipality of Annecy, in the former duchy of Savoy. These revolutionaries exulted, "Louis the last is no more; his criminal head has just fallen under the sword of the law. Terror seizes the souls of despots."[69] On February 28 the Convention received a letter signed by sixty-two "republicans" from the village of Saint-Gengoux (Saône-et-Loire) who declared, "You have just put terror into the souls of the tyrants of all Europe."[70]

THE TERROR OF THE CONSTITUTION

If the law was terrible, in the logic of the revolutionaries, then the Constitution was more terrible still. Even during the period of the National Assembly, the Constitution (of 1791) was described in terms of the terror it was capable of instilling in "tyrants" or "despots." The municipality of Avallon (Yonne) wrote on March 23, 1790, more than a year before the first revolutionary Constitution was completed, "Already its foundations, established upon eternal truths, have carried terror into the souls of tyrants."[71] On June 11, 1791, Fréteau de Saint-Just—a moderate deputy, not to be confused with the terroriste Louis-Antoine de Saint-Just—described the still-incomplete Constitution as "the terror of tyrants."[72] During the brief period in which the Constitution of 1791 was operative—in other words, during the tenure of the Legislative Assembly—the founding document was depicted as a source of terror. In October 1791, for example, in a speech demanding intervention in the German states that were harboring émigrés, Pierre-Louis

Sissous, of the Aube department, lauded the French kingdom as "the terror of all the despots by virtue of . . . the energy that its Constitution gives it."[73]

Members of the Convention inherited the habit of depicting the Constitution as a source of terror. This was the case even before the republican Constitution of 1793 was completed in June. During the late spring, as the Convention was considering various constitutional proposals, the Girondin Pierre-Claude-François Daunou, of the Pas-de-Calais, presented his plan, which involved a considerable degree of autonomy for the departments and municipalities. In his conclusion he promised his fellow legislators, "By discussing constitutional laws, you will invest yourselves with all the dignity that belongs to these laws; you will receive from your own work an august brilliance that, . . . surrounding you more and more with national trust, will soon command respect and terror from your enemies."[74]

The theme of the terrifying Constitution enjoyed still greater prominence during the summer of 1793, as communes, districts, departments, popular societies, and army units assented to it. On July 13 the Convention received a letter from the general council of the district of Saint-Omer (Pas-de-Calais) affirming that the citizens there had joyfully assented to the Constitution and predicting that it would be "the terror of tyrants."[75] On July 14, the fourth anniversary of the storming of the Bastille, a deputation representing several communes in the department of Paris came to the Convention to declare its support of the Constitution. The speaker praised "this constitutional code" as "the terror of the enemies of the Republic."[76] Also on July 14 a deputation from the Droits de l'Homme section of Paris came to the bar to declare its adhesion to "a popular and republican Constitution" that would be "the terror of tyrants."[77]

In the following weeks still more patriotic acclamations linked the Constitution with terror. On July 15 the secretary of the Convention read a letter from the Jacobin club of La Roche-Chalais (Dordogne) predicting that "the completely republican Constitution" would "soon bring terror and fright to the souls of the despots."[78] On July 24 the Montagnard deputy Billaud-Varennes read an address from the Jacobins of Châtillon-sur-Chalaronne (Ain), who called the Constitution "the terror of the malevolent ones."[79] On August 4 the *procureur syndic* (chief executive) of the district of Vic (Hautes-Pyrénées) wrote to the Convention in praise of "the Constitution, which will shake the thrones of the coalition despots and fill their satellite slaves with terror."[80]

THE TERROR OF THEIR ENEMIES

From the earliest days of the Revolution through the summer of 1793, then, the laws and the institutions that made or enforced them were justified by

their capacity to instill terror in the wicked, and in this respect revolutionaries were drawing on an Old Regime discourse of the "terror of the laws."
Furthermore, they made liberal use of a militaristic discourse, also inherited
from the Old Regime, in which they praised the Revolution for instilling terror in their enemies. The border between these two discourses was porous, as
one sees in the utterances surrounding the king's execution. The punishment
was meant to impart "salutary terror," but since the king's most obvious
crime was simply to have been a king, the intended recipients of the exemplary message of his execution were other monarchs. Of course, their "satel-
lites" or minions constituted another audience for this terrible lesson, and
here many of the malefactors were foreigners, though already in January 1793
revolutionaries perceived a threat from domestic royalists. This blending of
lawbreakers and "enemies" is hardly surprising, since, as Dan Edelstein has
shown, the revolutionaries had a very expansive view of "the law," one that
went beyond the notion of positive legislation and rather drew on the tradition of natural law. According to this way of thinking, anyone who proved
to be an "enemy of the human race" was subject to annihilation; nationality
played no role in that designation.[81] Still, it is worth examining the revolutionaries' tendency to identify a wide variety of enemies on whom terror was
to be inflicted, even when the laws played no role in the act of terrifying,
since this militaristic discourse helped to make terror speech attractive to
those who endorsed and enacted the Terror of September 1793–July 1794.

War was a natural stimulus for calls to strike the enemy with terror,
and for this reason one finds few such utterances prior to April 1792, when
France declared war on Austria. Yet even before war broke out, civilians
and soldiers alike spoke of the need for terror against France's enemies. On
January 28, 1791, the National Assembly ordered reinforcements along the
border with Belgium (the Austrian Netherlands). The previous summer
Austrian forces had suppressed a pro-French revolution in Belgium, and
they were now preparing to cross French territory in order to reinforce that
suppression. Following a rousing speech by Mirabeau in favor of mobiliza-
tion, Deputy Goupil de Préfeln spoke to the legislature. Though a monarchist who had tried and failed to make Catholicism the official religion of
France, he nevertheless seconded Mirabeau's proposal, calling it "indispensable to the salvation of the *patrie*," and added, "There is not an instant to
lose; we must inspire salutary terror in the enemies of the *patrie* for their
own good."[82] This utilitarian approach was similar to the deterrent strategy
of using harsh punishments against criminals. The assumption was that the
enemy, being rational and envisaging the consequences of aggression, would
refrain from causing harm.

The idea of using military terror as a means of dissuading enemies from attacking was suggested again at the end of 1791. On August 27, 1791, the Austrian emperor and the king of Prussia had issued the Declaration of Pillnitz, in which they offered "the most effective means for enabling the king of France to consolidate with complete freedom the foundations of a monarchical government" and hinted that they would use force if necessary.[83] On December 26, 1791, the Girondin deputy Armand Gensonné responded to this threat by proposing that the Legislative Assembly allocate twenty million *livres* "for military preparation commanded by the [current] circumstances." Gensonné wanted the Assembly to prepare for war, but he also noted that "it is possible that the proud and imposing stance that the nation is going to take will imprint salutary terror on our enemies, and that their interest in their own security will force them to respect ours."[84]

The outbreak of war provided more occasions for using the word *terreur* to describe a means of discouraging the enemy from attacking. On May 4, 1792, two weeks after the declaration of war, the foreign minister, General Dumouriez, informed the Legislative Assembly that he had ordered General d'Elbecq "to bring a corps of twelve hundred men to Furnes [in Belgium] to inspire . . . terror in the government at Brussels."[85] Dumouriez would defect to the Austrians in 1793, but at the outset of the war he expressed the belief that a terrifying display of force would prevent the enemy from harming France.

Even children used military terror speech. On May 22, 1792, a group of pupils from a local school came to the bar of the Assembly to deliver an address. The orator praised the "forces, more thundering than lightning bolts," with which their fathers would "bring terror and fright into the souls of the despots." Should their fathers die in battle, the speaker continued, "may their infamous victors tremble! It is on our parents' funeral urn that the most terrible of oaths will be pronounced."[86]

The use of military terror speech only increased with the establishment of the Republic. On October 28, 1792, the Girondin Gensonné reported to the Convention that General Custine's recent invasion of the Palatinate had "cast terror into all of Germany."[87] In fact, Custine had withdrawn his forces soon after invading, thereby incurring the suspicion of Montagnard deputies and prompting Gensonné's defense. (Both the deputy and the general would be guillotined as traitors the following year.) But as we have already seen, praise of terror was an ecumenical practice, and in 1792 it was common to Girondins and Montagnards alike. One Montagnard who agreed with Gensonné on the need to impose terror on the enemy was Jean-Jacques Bréard, of La Rochelle, who assured the Convention on December 24 that

"our intrepid warriors, after having chased from our borders the henchmen
of those despots . . . have carried terror to them."[88] His fellow Montagnard
Silvain-Phalier Lejeune, of the Indre, agreed, and in a speech to the Convention on January 7, 1793, he spoke of "the brilliant successes of French
arms . . . which have struck tyrants with terror and fright."[89] On February 13,
less than two weeks after the French declaration of war against Britain, the
procureur-syndic of the Calvados department spoke at the bar of the Convention. He requested arms for the defense of his department and boasted,
"The sons of the Normans have not at all forgotten how to subdue arrogant
England." All the Convention had to do was give its assent, and "soon we
will once again bring terror and death to it."[90] On February 24, 1793, the
procureur (roughly equivalent to a mayor) of Charleville wrote to the Convention of "the terror that the proud French Republic inspires" in "despots."[91] Robespierre confirmed on March 2 that "the patriotism of our brave
brothers in arms is carrying terror abroad."[92]

The image of a terrified foreign enemy was similarly prominent in a letter that Pierre-Joseph Duhem and Gaspard-Jean-Joseph Lesage-Senault, deputies who had been sent as commissioners to the Army of the North, wrote to
the Convention on July 17, 1793. The commissioners informed the lawmakers that the citizens of Lille, a front-line city on the Belgian border, had resolved to combine the forces of the Nord department with those of the four
nearest departments. At an agreed-upon but unspecified date, a general call
to arms would be heard, cannons would be fired and the tocsin sounded, and
"in an instant" a levy of "300,000 men, free and guided by the intrepid Army
of the North, . . . will open to them the path to honor and victory, fall *en
masse*, in the manner of the ancient Gauls, on those hordes of brigands, and
exterminate them, and thus bring terror and consternation to an astonished
Europe."[93] Interestingly, here the object of terror was not merely enemies but
"an astonished Europe." This is because terror was not simply a military
tactic to discourage the enemy. It was also a sign of France's power and glory.
Therefore, the more people who were terrified, the more powerful and glorious the French nation was.

Even the bellicose cries of soldiers at patriotic festivals were believed
capable of inciting terror in the enemy. An account of a festival on July 14,
1793, at the military camp of Iocrim, near Landau in the occupied German
Palatinate, reported that as soon as General Ferrier finished reading the new
Constitution of 1793, "cries a thousand times repeated of 'Long live the
Constitution! Long live the Republic one and indivisible! [and] Long live
the National Convention!' resounded in the surrounding forests and were
capable of bringing terror and desperation to the despots' camps around

us."[94] The *avant-garde* of the Army of the Ardennes, celebrating the one-year anniversary of the overthrow of the monarchy on August 10, similarly engaged in a festival honoring the new Constitution, and an "address" to the National Convention signed by eighty-eight soldiers reported that their "cries of happiness brought terror to all [the enemy's] lairs."[95]

Of course, foreign enemies were not the only threat to the Republic. Domestic enemies were in full-scale rebellion in 1793, and the military terror speech that applied to the Prussians, Austrians, and British also applied to counterrevolutionaries and "federalists" in the provinces, though it was sometimes mixed with the discourse of legal terror. For example, on March 22, 1793, Deputies Billaud-Varenne and Sevestre de la Metterie wrote from Brittany, where a guerrilla-style royalist uprising was under way, and reported that "an extraordinary tribunal" was going "to punish the hordes of seditious people and counterrevolutionaries whose liberticidal furor can only be stopped by the terror of judgment [i.e., punishment]."[96] Shortly thereafter the Convention received a letter from the directory of the Côtes-du-Nord department informing the legislature that, "wanting to contain the rebels and conspirators by terror," it had arrested six "guilty ones," condemned them to death, and scheduled their executions in six separate towns, no doubt to spread the exemplary terror more widely.[97]

An even larger royalist rebellion in the Vendée prompted further endorsements of terror. Deputy Anne-Pierre Coustard, who had been sent to Nantes to observe the unrest there, wrote to the Convention on May 24, 1793, boasting, "My expedition in the Prinée forest . . . cast salutary terror among the rebels."[98] Montagnards in Bordeaux felt similarly about the suppression of the Vendée rebellion. On August 10 the president of the department of the Gironde spoke at the Festival of Unity and Indivisibility, assuring the National Guardsmen who were about to be deployed to the Vendée, "You are going to impress a new terror into the enemies of our happiness and repose."[99]

Despite the appeals to the law in the suppression of rebellion, revolutionaries ultimately depended on military force to accomplish their goals, and they consequently made use of the language of military terror that, as we have seen, had enhanced the majesty of Old Regime sovereigns. Often revolutionary generals were depicted as the agents of this terror against the nation's enemies. Consider the case of François-Joseph Westermann, whose suppression of the Vendée rebellion was notoriously brutal, but who was nevertheless under suspicion of having conspired with Dumouriez against the Republic. A letter from the municipality of Poitiers, sent to the Convention on July 16, 1793, was used in his defense. The citizens of this city who had been embroiled in the Vendée fighting declared that Westermann was "innocent and incapable of having betrayed the interests of the Republic." They noted that "his rapid march from Saint-Maixent all the way to Châtillon, the victory that accompanied him, the terror [that he] spread all around, prove authentically that he did not spare" the rebel forces.[100] Deputy Louis Legendre defended Westermann in similar terms, informing his colleagues on July 26 that "Westermann had the reputation of being the scourge of brigands and that his name alone carried terror among them."[101] Jean Julien, speaking on behalf of the Committee of General Security, reported on July 30 that the commune of Poitiers had defended Westermann by claiming that "his name alone spread terror" among the Vendean rebels.[102] Three weeks later Julien said similar things about Jean-Michel Beysser, a general in the Vendée who had also come under suspicion. Julien told the Convention, "His [Beysser's] name alone inspired the greatest terror in the brigands of the Vendée."[103] This was enough to convince the Convention to send Beysser back to the front, though both he and Westermann would be executed (for their affiliation with Danton) in April 1794.

TERROR AS AN IDENTITY

As the praise for Westermann and Beysser demonstrates, the perceived ability to strike terror into enemies could become a crucial component of a person's identity. Thus terror, or terribleness, was more than an instrument of legal or military force. It was also a personality trait. Danton had famously urged his colleagues to be terrible. It was a short step from being terrible to being a terror, and in many cases during the first year of the Republic revolutionaries praised each other for being the terror of their enemies. In this respect they conformed to a pattern established under the Old Regime of rulers acquiring legitimacy by embodying the principle of terror.

The most obvious candidates for this distinction were generals, who were often in desperate need of such validation. The case of the ill-fated General Custine is instructive here. Following the battle of Neerwinden (March 18, 1793), which ended the French occupation of Belgium and prompted Dumouriez's treason, Nicolas Haussmann, Commissioner to the Armies of the Rhine, Vosges, and Moselle saw the bright side of Custine's continued occupation of Mainz. He wrote, "Custine is the terror of the Germanic aristocracy; he has the trust of the army and the inhabitants, and I believe I can say that he deserves yours . . . you can count on his courage, abilities, and patriotism. If he is well supported, and if he is given new forces, he will be able to compensate for the misfortunes of Belgium."[104] The Convention agreed, and on May 13 Custine was promoted to commander of the Army of the North and the Army of the Ardennes.[105] Yet within a few days Custine raised doubts about his fitness for that position. On May 17 his forces suffered a serious defeat in Alsace,[106] and Custine was called to Paris to account for himself. Among his supporters were the municipal authorities of Saint-Omer in the embattled Pas-de-Calais department, who sent the Convention an account of a meeting at which the commune had donated clothing for Custine's troops. At that gathering the mayor had praised Custine, declaring, "'Citizen, . . . at the head of the brave soldiers of liberty, you have become the terror of tyrants.'"[107]

Even a dead general could be the terror of his enemies. At least that is what Deputy Jean-Marie Lequinio, commissioner of the Army of the North, said of General Dampierre when eulogizing him. Dampierre had been killed in an attempt to raise the siege of the fortress of Condé on May 8, 1793. Speaking beside Dampierre's grave on May 10, Lequinio promised the bereft French troops that the general's "shade" would be "the terror of the horde of slaves armed against you."[108]

If generals could embody terror, so could their troops. The deputies visiting the departments on the Swiss border assured the Convention on November 1, 1792, that the troops recruited from the area "want to be at once the terror of tyrants and the friends of humanity."[109] On June 19, 1793, Agricole Moreau, "deputy extraordinary" from newly annexed Avignon, boasted of the local battalions that were "the terror of the Piedmontese" enemy.[110] On August 5, 1793, a proclamation by the directory of the department of the Haute-Marne addressed soldiers preparing for battle as "the terror of the coalition powers."[111]

Civilians were also distinguished by the name "terror." In July 1793 the administrators of the district of Haguenau in the Bas-Rhin department wrote to the Convention assuring the lawmakers that "the French, rallying around a republican Constitution, are becoming the terror of tyrants and the friends of suffering humanity."[112] On August 20 the Jacobin club of Pontarlier (Doubs) wrote in support of the Convention, which it called "the terror of [its] enemies both within and without."[113]

Still other groups of French citizens earned the title of "terror." In a speech of January 15, 1793, Camille Desmoulins declared Paris "the terror of intriguers." He added that the Jacobin societies were "the terror of kings."[114] Danton declared on May 28, 1793, "Paris will always be the terror of the enemies of liberty."[115] And on August 9, 1793, just one day before the first anniversary of the overthrow of the monarchy, Deputy Gossuin proclaimed that "this astonishing city, [the] cradle of liberty, will always be the terror of the wicked."[116] Even a militant neighborhood could acquire the respectable designation, as when the sansculottes of the Faubourg Saint-Antoine, speaking to the Convention on March 24, 1793, declared themselves "the terror of [their] enemies."[117]

THE CONSERVATION OF TERROR

How did revolutionaries feel when they imputed terror to those they considered capable of harming the French nation? Brissot gives us some indication of his emotional response to the prospect of terrified enemies. On July 26, 1792, he declared, "I admit it, as I contemplate the dangers that surround us, as I see the terror that agitates all the thrones of Europe, the numerous armies that they have assembled to destroy us, I feel a kind of pride at belonging to the people that is going to fight them."[118] Pride was a respectable feeling in the emotional regime of France in the summer of 1792. But lurking behind this avowed emotion was a hint of fear that could not be openly acknowledged. Brissot was "contemplat[ing] the dangers that surround[ed]" France and believed that the nation's enemies would be satisfied with nothing short of destroying him and his compatriots. These perils would have instilled fear into practically anyone. Moreover, the word "terror" itself suggests the possibility that Brissot was feeling the emotion he attributed to "all the thrones of Europe." Perhaps he was projecting his own terror onto his enemies and using that very fantasy to alleviate his fear. After all, a terrified enemy was a disabled one, and the thought of that must have been reassuring. Finally, if we inquire into Brissot's choice of the word "pride" to describe his emotional condition, we might infer that the Girondin leader was precisely proud of his ability to overcome the terror he was experiencing.

If this interpretation is correct, then Brissot was practicing a kind of therapy, for himself and for any of his compatriots who were terrified by the prospect of defeat—and perhaps death—when he postulated the enemy's feelings of terror. Something similar might have been going on in the mind of an unnamed army officer whose letter to the Legislative Assembly was read aloud by the Montagnard Deputy Robert Lindet on August 3, 1792. The officer was stationed near Maubeuge, on the Belgian border—in other words, on the front facing the Austrian forces—and according to his optimistic bulletin, written on July 30, "Not a day passes without our patrols cutting down some Austrians. Terror has spread among them; they flee at the first sight of a Frenchman."[119] Perhaps this was true, but it is also likely that, true or not, this image helped the officer cope with his own terror of being killed in battle. Lindet's recitation of the letter in the Convention was similarly meant to be reassuring, both to Lindet himself and to his fellow lawmakers.

The function of terror speech, at least in part, as a means of reassuring terrified patriots would also help to explain the tendency of numerous revolutionaries to place the word "terror" in close proximity to an antonym or near-antonym. For example, when in February 1790 Barnave called for concluding the investigation into the massacre of Catholics by Protestants in Nîmes, he argued for the importance of unity among the deputies: "It is when one sees at the center of the Assembly, when in the face of all powers one sees unity, constancy, invariable firmness, [and] severity against those who fight against the general will, it is then that the good will have confidence and the wicked will have terror."[120] This parallel construction suggested that only if "the wicked" experienced terror could good Frenchmen feel "confidence." Another example of such parallelism is evident in a speech of May 19, 1792, in which the Jacobin deputy Marc-David-Alvin Lasource complained that "it is not with three little armies that can hardly go on the offensive that we will inspire confidence in the French nation and terror in its enemies."[121] During the session of January 16–17, 1793, the Girondin Nicolas-Joseph Marey, of the Côte-d'Or, similarly paired terror and confidence. Seeking to spare the king but participating in an ecumenical discourse of legal terror, he declared, "When our Constitution, . . . lifting its august and imposing head, imprints confidence within and terror without . . . then we will be able without danger to banish from the land of liberty the one who made himself unworthy to inhabit it."[122]

The need for revolutionaries to be relieved of terror is also suggested in statements that juxtaposed this emotion with references to courage. For example, on the night of January 16–17 the Parisian deputy Fabre d'Églantine imagined the emotional and cognitive condition of unnamed "kings" and affirmed that "the death of their accomplice will inspire them with no less terror than perspicacity." And since he subscribed to the belief that the terror felt by despots was in direct proportion to the courage experienced by the people, he added that the king's death would inspire "audacity among the peoples [whom the kings] oppress."[123] Was he thinking of his own need for audacity in the face of the dangers he was experiencing? Likewise, on February 28, 1793, General (and minister of war) Beurnonville triumphantly announced the surrender of Breda in the Netherlands, asserting, "The frightened Orangist party [backed by Prussia] is trembling," and further boasting, "The terror of our arms is spreading everywhere; the courage of the [French] soldier enables him to defeat all the obstacles that nature and artifice can put in his way."[124] The proximity of terror and courage suggests that it was precisely the enemy's feelings of terror that gave courage to the French.

A most revealing hint of revolutionary courage stemming from the terror imputed to the enemy appears in a speech made by a child. On April 29, 1792, a deputation of schoolchildren "of both sexes from the free national schools of the Saint-Louis parish" in Versailles came to the bar of the Legislative Assembly. A speaker from the school affirmed that the children "burn with an ardent desire . . . to see again all of our young heroes [in the army] crowned with the laurels of victory." The orator continued, "Their intrepid courage inspires terror in our enemies, our generals are guided by prudence and the purest patriotism . . . what have they to fear? They only have tyrants and courtiers to fight; they are incapable of defeating free men." Once again, picturing the terror felt by the enemy appears to have assuaged French fears. The question "What have they to fear?" betrayed a real anxiety behind the rhetorical bravado; picturing an enemy incapacitated by terror worked toward easing that anxiety. A condition of fearlessness, projected onto warriors displaying "intrepid courage," itself seemed to explain the terror felt by "our enemies," but that presumed terror in the minds of France's foes was equally a source of courage in the young patriots.[125]

This dynamic pre-dates the revolutionary wars, which began in April 1792, and indeed goes back to the very beginning of the Revolution. On June 15, 1789, the comte de Mirabeau urged the representatives of the Third Estate to take a daring step. Rather than abide by the antiquated and unfair procedures of the Estates General, he called on them to declare themselves a "National Assembly" uniquely qualified to reform the kingdom. He told the representatives that while they temporized, "the usurpations of the [first] two orders have accumulated," and insisted, "Now is the moment to reassure your minds and to inspire wariness [la retenu], fear [la crainte], I almost said respectful terror [la terreur du respect] in your adversaries by showing, from your first operations, competent prudence joined with the sweet firmness of reason."[126]

Mirabeau's words reveal that terror speech was present in the Revolution from the very start. In fact, properly speaking, the Revolution had not even begun when Mirabeau spoke. Only after he and others finished their speeches on June 15 did the members of the Third Estate vote to call themselves the National Assembly, and they did not officially convene in this capacity until two days later. Truly it was one of the utterances that inaugurated the Revolution. This does not mean that the Terror of 1793–94 was inevitable. But it does mean that Claude Royer and the advocates of terror "as the order of the day" were not inventing a new way of expressing political goals. They were drawing on an uninterrupted tradition that began under the Old Regime with acclamations of terrible sovereigns and continued with the earliest acts of revolutionary defiance.

Mirabeau's invocation of terror also serves as a reminder that terror speech was ecumenical. It was not the exclusive property of radical Montagnards, nor even of republicans. Mirabeau was truly a monarchist. Indeed, he advised the king to support the Revolution as a means of buttressing the monarchy itself. The availability of terror speech to those of all political persuasions also helps to explain the decision by Montagnards in 1793–94 to use the word "terror" in their rallying cries. They were not invoking a partisan ideal but rather appealing to a universal value.

Finally, Mirabeau's speech of June 15 reveals a psychological dynamic at play in revolutionary terror speech more generally, one that helps to explain its appeal across the political spectrum and from the very outset of the Revolution. Let us look more closely at Mirabeau's declaration. Its invocation of terror was cautious. The words "almost said" (*presque dit*) are an example of paralipsis, the rhetorical device by which a speaker claims not to say something that she or he in fact says. As in the expression "needless to say," it calls attention to a putatively unutterable word or phrase. If Mirabeau had truly "almost said" terror, he would not have said it. But Mirabeau was not merely being coy. He was acknowledging that terror was a problematic concept, especially in politics. In some contexts it was reminiscent of the despotism that he and his fellow revolutionaries were trying to overthrow. At the same time, his use of the term indicated a desire to tap into the power and legitimacy that the Old Regime had long enjoyed. After all, Mirabeau invoked *terreur du respect*. As we have seen, terror and respect were intimately connected in prerevolutionary understandings of power. Indeed, terror was often a sign of respect.

Similarly, Mirabeau drew on familiar conceptions of terror by placing it near the word *retenu* (wariness). Derived from the verb *retenir*, which is translated literally as "retain" but suggests holding back or restraining, *retenu* pointed to a long-standing goal of terror: preventing someone from carrying out an undesirable act. Like its synonym *contenir* (contain), which we have seen in prerevolutionary reflections on crime and punishment,[127] *retenir* signaled a preventive approach in which a potential malefactor would view or imagine negative consequences for a particular behavior and therefore refrain from engaging in it. In this scenario the threat of violence was implicit, but ideally violence could be avoided. The object of terror—here

tactfully labeled "your adversaries"—was seen as reasonable, capable of assessing the consequences of their actions and of avoiding suffering through
restraint or *retenu*. In future years some revolutionaries would call their
opponents "enemies," or, worse still, depict them as monsters with whom
any reasoning was pointless. But at this point it was still politically possible to conceive of antagonists as capable of responding prudently to threats
of force. Of course, the question of force at this point was entirely abstract,
and one of the most obvious ways in which Mirabeau's invocation of terror
differed from that of later revolutionaries was that Mirabeau did not have
a guillotine at his disposal. If anything, he had more reason to fear violence
than to plan violent acts against "adversaries."

This aspect of fear is also important to understanding the significance
of Mirabeau's words. The call for terror against adversaries was not merely
a statement; it was a speech act by which Mirabeau dealt with and tried
to overcome his fear. It is revealing that he prefaced his injunction "to inspire . . . terror" with the declaration, "Now is the moment to reassure your
minds." This much-needed reassurance was itself produced in the moment
of uttering a threat, and Mirabeau deflected the very real fear of punishment
and projected it onto those who were in a position to punish. A little more
than a week later, confronted by the king's master of ceremonies and the
demand that the National Assembly disperse, Mirabeau would utter the
defiant words so often reproduced in histories of the Revolution: "Go tell
your master that we are here by the power of the people and will only be
dislodged by the force of bayonets."[128] We can see his prior terror speech as
psychological preparation for his later, risky act of disobedience. Nor is it
an accident that revolutionaries would frequently pair the concepts of terror (for others) and reassurance (for themselves). They reassured themselves
by imagining the terror experienced by others.

This habit of juxtaposing the enemy's terror with the revolutionaries'
courage, confidence, or reassurance illustrates what might be called the
principle of the conservation of terror, according to which the enemy was
imagined to be as terrified as the French were courageous or fearless. (The
corollary of this principle was that if the enemy did not feel terror, the revolutionaries would.) Even from the beginning, the emotional regime of the
Revolution discouraged overt confessions of fear, but if we read between the
lines we can see that the revolutionaries were frightened, indeed terrified,
and that their fantasies about terrified enemies were meant to alleviate their
own terror.[128] Ultimately, however, this dynamic was self-perpetuating and
self-defeating, since the image of enemies fleeing in terror depended on the

extension and intensification of hostilities at home and abroad. This in turn created new enemies and additional terror, which the revolutionaries felt compelled to assuage through still more aggressive threats and the actions that made them credible. The temporary relief that terror speech brought to frightened revolutionaries came at a high price.

CHAPTER EIGHT

Terror Speech in the Year II

INTRODUCTION

At this point it is clear that Claude Royer's invocation of terror on September 5, 1793, did not come out of a vacuum. Although shocking to our sensibilities today, "terror" was an appealing word in many contexts in eighteenth-century France. It connoted power, justice, legitimacy, and majesty; it was "salutary" in both the religious and medical senses of the word; and it had moral as well as aesthetic appeal. A long history of the word's meanings and the emotions attached to them was necessary in order for Royer's words to be comprehensible and attractive. A still clearer picture of the allure of terror emerges if we examine the use of the word during the period known to historians simply as the Terror. What did "terror" mean in the Year II, and how did revolutionaries feel when using it?[1] This chapter will show that from September 1793 through July 1794 republicans drew on many of the traditions of terror speech discussed in previous chapters, and that they did so in large measure to comfort and reassure themselves. The idea that the enemy experienced terror was reassuring and encouraging to revolutionaries who themselves were frightened or even terrified.

TERROR AS LEGAL, EXEMPLARY, AND UTILITARIAN

As under the Old Regime and during the first four years of the Revolution, terror during the Year II was often conceptualized in legal terms. Advocates of punishing malefactors referred to the terror of the laws. Thus, for instance, the Jacobins of Saint-Puy (Gers) wrote in praise of the Law of 14 Frimaire (December 10), which created a "revolutionary government" by concentrating power in the Committee of Public Safety, "You have struck the malevolent ones with terror and the law that you have just decreed, by suspending the sword over the heads of intriguers, is going to dissipate them like timid doves."[2] On February 26 (8 Ventôse) the Popular Society of Ambronay (Ain) likewise exulted that France's enemies "are perishing under the sword of the law" and congratulated "the revolutionary government" for "imprinting salutary terror on the brows of the malevolent ones."[3] In April the Popular Society of Cieux (Haute-Vienne) expressed its "appreciation and fidelity" following the execution of the Dantonists and asserted, "All eyes are open and fixed on the impure remains of the traitors and false patriots. They are struck with terror; the sword of the law is weighing on their heads."[4]

These were largely utilitarian pronouncements revealing a belief that "the wicked" could be prevented, by the sight or prospect of punishment, from acting according to their inclinations. A key word in this context was "restrain." On December 21 Collot d'Herbois, in his capacity as a member of the Committee of Public Safety, complained to his fellow deputies that the punishment of the federalists in Lyon was not proceeding quickly or thoroughly enough and insisted on employing "useful and salutary terror that restrains the rage of the conspirators."[5] Similarly, at a festival in celebration of the retaking of Toulon from the British, a member of the municipal council of Belley (Ain) spoke enthusiastically of terror's utility, "Terror, that useful terror which has restrained all the enemies within, terror restrains all the enemies without."[6] In April 1794 the Popular Society of La Roumieu (Gers) likewise wrote to the Convention, "May salutary terror restrain the malevolent ones."[7]

This conception of terror represented punishment as instructive or exemplary. Just as regicides of late 1792 and early 1793 used the word "example" to legitimize the terror of the king's execution—and just as Old Regime jurists from the time of Francis I used it to justify the terror of the laws—so too did Montagnards of the Year II deploy this term in their terror speech. On October 4 (13 Vendémiaire) Deputies Lacoste, Peyssard, and Duquessnoy, commissioners with the Army of the North, issued a decree, which they subsequently sent on to the Convention, establishing an ad hoc military commission "to judge all the leaders and employees in the army administrations." They stipulated that "any leader of the administration or employee" whom "three unimpeachable witnesses" accused of "peculation" or "negligence in the deposit, transport, and supply of the army" would be publicly executed in front of his division. Their reasoning was that "it is only through striking examples that one can carry terror into the souls of these true conspirators."[8] The Committee of Public Safety explained the collective punishment of Lyon in similar terms, advising deputies *en mis-*

sion Maignet and Chateauneuf-Randon, "If you wish, as we do, to give a great example of terror and national justice to the counterrevolutionaries, strike hard at Lyon and at the core of aristocrats and emigrés armed against the *patrie*."[9] Presumably the example of Lyon would prevent other cities from engaging in, or persisting in, their rebellions. Montagnards also viewed the punishment of the Girondins in terms of the example their execution would set for counterrevolutionaries. On November 6 (16 Brumaire) the Popular Society of Saint-Calais (Sarthe) wrote to congratulate the Convention on "the great and terrible example" it had set in decapitating the alleged traitors and urged it to maintain "that imposing stance which strikes our enemies with terror."[10] Revolutionaries also pronounced or wrote the word "terror" in close proximity to "example" when celebrating the punishment of Hébert, Danton, and other perceived traitors in the spring and early summer of 1794, indicating that the idea of exemplary terror persisted for most of the Year II.[11]

The utilitarian thinking behind comments on exemplary terror reveals a significant degree of optimism concerning the efficacy of punishment. It indicates a belief that witnesses to executions, either in person or through secondhand accounts, could be dissuaded by terror from giving in to their inclinations and harming the *patrie*. The use of the conditional mood in the articulation of this conviction highlighted the sense of optimism. For instance, when the Jacobins of Castelnau-Montratier (Lot) congratulated the Convention on purging itself of the "vile intriguers" (Girondins), they warned, "It is not enough to have unraveled the horrible plots of the conspirators; it is necessary that by a great example you carry terror and fright into the souls of those who would be so cowardly as to wish to imitate them."[12] That such souls "would be" capable of imitating the Girondins suggests that they also had the capacity to refrain from doing so, hence the need "for a great example." Similarly, on January 11 (22 Nivôse) Charles Cochon-Lapparent, representing the joint committees of war and legislation, reported on the need for severe measures against "squanderers" (*dilapidateurs*) in the army. The committees proposed an elaborate system of tribunals combining elements of criminal and military justice, but the main point was "to frighten [*d'effrayer*] the malevolent ones and to restrain, by the terror of example, the weak men who could allow themselves to be carried away by the perfidious suggestions of enemies of liberty."[13] This conditional clause left room for rehabilitation, which the prospect of the guillotine was believed to facilitate. Even relatively late into the Terror it was possible to use the conditional mood and thus to leave open the possibility that would-be counterrevolutionaries might be dissuaded by exemplary terror from carrying out their nefarious designs. On April 23 (4 Floréal) the municipality of Ingrandes (Indre) wrote to thank the Convention for having executed the Dantonists. The officials made the tautological claim that "this terrible example, thus made on the chiefs of the party, on the guiltiest ones, produces the double advantage of imprinting terror on all those who would be tempted to imitate them and destroying the dangerous coalition that they had formed."[14] Enemies "would be" dangerous but for the terror that restrained them.

VENGEANCE AND EXTERMINATION

Although terror speech during the Year II often drew on optimistic discourses of utility and exemplarity, it even more frequently displayed the killing of enemies as an open-ended project of extermination in which vengeance took the place of deterrence. Here revolutionaries harkened back to a pre-Enlightenment ethos of vendetta that eighteenth-century jurists had tried to supersede. Enemies were to be killed because they were bad, because they deserved it, because they had killed first, or, in what was seen as equivalent, because they had plotted against or failed to defend the Republic. Alternatively, and in a departure from Old Regime conceptions of terror, enemies were to be killed because they were monsters, ferocious or "unclean" beasts, or because they collectively constituted a disease to which the nation was vulnerable.

The language of vengeance is present in the founding document of the Terror. In his speech calling for terror as "the order of the day," Royer appealed to "the vengeance of the laws."[15] Other revolutionaries followed his example by invoking vengeance in close proximity to their calls for terror. "General" Ronsin of the "revolutionary army" addressed the Convention on October 20 (29 Brumaire), congratulating the deputies on having "made terror the order of the day" and noting that if some traitors had escaped the destruction of Lyon, "national vengeance will be able to reach them everywhere."[16] On November 18 (28 Brumaire) Billaud-Varenne presented a report to the Convention on behalf of the Committee of Public Safety in which he affirmed that "when the course of the revolution forces the legislator to make terror the order of the day, it is to avenge the nation on its enemies."[17] On January 17 (28 Nivôse) the sansculottes of Dolus-d'Oléron (Charente-Maritime) wrote to the Convention, which they called "the terror of the aristocracy," and fondly recalled the day when it "made [the Girondins'] guilty heads fall under the avenging sword of the law."[18] In some cases revolutionaries were so avid for vengeance that they repeated the word in their calls for terror. The Popular Society of Valence (Drôme) wrote to the Convention on March 21 (1 Germinal) with a suggested response to the persistence of conspiracies against the Republic: "Vengeance, legislators, vengeance! May terror and fright [*la terreur et l'effroi*] be your only watchwords in this moment of crisis."[19] On May 28 (9 Prairial) a speaker representing the municipality of Belleville (Seine) addressed the Convention. Indignant at the traitors who had recently tried to assassinate Robespierre and Collot d'Herbois, the orator proclaimed, "May their punishment strike the crowned scoundrels with terror. Vengeance! Vengeance!"[20]

One document in particular reveals the extent to which revolutionaries favoring terror could be beholden to Old Regime understandings of vengeance. On October 24 (3 Brumaire) the Popular Society of Saint-Gaudens (Haute-Garonne) wrote to the Convention concerning Deputy Beauvais-Préau, who had been imprisoned by the British following the surrender of Toulon but was believed to have been assassinated. (Beauvais-Préau died the following spring from mistreatment at the hands of his jailers.) Regarding the alleged assassination the Popular Society wrote, "You must avenge in a striking manner this insult to the majesty of the French people. The brother-in-law of George [III],[21] it is said, is in your power[;] may he perish from the same punishment that Beauvais was forced to undergo; may the English tyrant be struck with terror as he fixes his eyes on his brother-in-law attached to the gibbet."[22] The use of terms such as "insult" and "majesty" in a fantasy of terror-inducing vengeance against a single person suggested that revolutionaries had not discarded the Old Regime idea of revenge as a means of restoring injured honor.[23]

When connected to vengeance, the violent acts that characterized the Terror lost much of their utilitarian meaning. Enemies suffered punishment not simply in order to deter others, but because of the exigencies of national honor, or because they were deemed incapable of restraining their inclination to harm the nation. The emphasis in Year II terror speech was more on killing than on frightening counterrevolutionaries or "moderates" into changing their behavior. One sign of this emphasis is the frequency with which revolutionaries called for "terror and death." For example, on November 17 (27 Brumaire) the artist and deputy Jacques-Louis David, in his capacity as a member of the Committee of Public Instruction, announced a contest for a monument celebrating France's victory over despotism. A colossal statue was to be made of "a metal [i.e., bronze] that is precious and necessary to [the Republic's] defense, a metal destined to bring terror and death to the enemy phalanxes."[24] When seen as a utilitarian expedient, "terror" would naturally follow rather than precede "death." Death would have been the means by which to incite terror. But when seen as punishment or retribution, terror could precede death because death itself was part of the punishment that began with the terrible realization of its imminence.

Similarly, on March 20 (30 Ventôse) a member of the government office in charge of "the revolutionary fabrication of powders and saltpeter" boasted to the Convention of the fifty thousand pounds of saltpeter (an essential ingredient in gunpowder) that had been produced by volunteers throughout the country and predicted, "Soon the Republic, bristling with cannon, will carry terror and death among those hordes of slaves that dare fight against her."[25] Again, the addition of "death" to "terror" suggests that terror was not designed to restrain, since there would be no point in killing an enemy who had been terrified to the point of inaction. The placement of death at the end of the sentence revealed its primacy in the terror/death dyad. Many other revolutionary groups paired "terror" and "death" (in that order) when speaking or writing of their enemies' envisaged fate.[26]

That terror meant more than frightening through the selective use of examples can also be seen in the exterminationist language that characterized much terror speech in the Year II. Indeed, the verb *exterminer* was common in letters that the Convention received from popular societies, provincial officials, and Parisian sansculottes and was often in close proximity to the word *terreur*. For example, the Society of the Friends of Liberty and Equality of Saint-Amand (Cher) wrote to the Convention on September 29 to urge the lawmakers not to disperse "at a moment . . . when you have made terror the order of the day," adding, "Remain at your post, may the day of exterminating all the conspirators not be put off any longer."[27] Similarly, the Popular Society of Simandre (Nièvre) wrote to the Convention, "Terror has been made the order of the day, [and] since then . . . the Vendéans [have been] exterminated and the perfidious Lyonnais punished."[28] On February 12 (24 Pluviôse) the Popular Society of Bonnefoy-sur-Commune-Affranchie (formerly Sainte-Foy-lès-Lyon), just outside the infamous federalist city, reassured the Convention, "We shall maintain terror as the order of the day for as long as traitors and rich egoists exist," and urged the lawmakers, "Exterminate the dirty debris of royalism and federalism."[29] Many other groups wrote to the Convention in praise of terror and extermination.[30]

Exterminationist terror was often justified by the dehumanization of the enemy. Many of the demands the Convention received in support of terror depicted the Republic's foes as dangerous animals or monsters that needed to be destroyed. Royer's famous speech introducing the slogan "Make terror the order of the day" portrayed France's enemies as "tigers."[31] Other revolutionaries made use of similar imagery, which also would have been familiar from the "Marseillaise," in their calls for terror. On March 20 (30 Pluviôse) the Popular Society of Vouziers (Drôme) wrote to the Convention to urge it to continue the fight against the nation's enemies. Using the now-familiar pairing of terror and death, the address exhorted, "May terror, may death be the order of the day for these monsters[;] no peace, no truce with these tigers"; and, using equally familiar exterminationist language, it added, "War to the death with tyrants, until the last one is exterminated, until the seed itself and the seed's seed [le germe même et l'arrière-germe] of their execrable race is annihilated."[32] On April 15 (26 Germinal) the members of the Popular and Republican Society of Marolles (Oise) entreated the Convention, "Give terror to those whose perfidious feelings would induce them to favor the infernal plots of our enemies," but they could not decide whether these targets were "tigers" or "lions." They finally settled on "these animals blackened by crime," an interesting way of dehumanizing the enemy while simultaneously making it accountable for its actions.[33]

Other dangerous animals appeared in calls for terror. On October 12 (21 Vendémiaire) the legislators received an address from the municipality of Saint-Yrieix that called them "the terror" of conspirators and advised, "It is necessary to kill rabid dogs to avoid their bites."[34] The Popular Society of Aides-Saran (Loiret), after celebrating the fact that the "henchmen of despotism" had been "struck by terror" from Republican troops, described the nation's adversaries alternately as "bloodthirsty tigers," "unclean animals," and "poisonous insects."[35] The Popular Society of Cirey (formerly Château de Cirey, in the Haute-Marne) expressed its frustration that "the party that terror caused to return to the dust has risen," and it adjured, "Destroy . . . all these vile insects."[36] Other revolutionaries preferred reptilian imagery. The Popular Society of Roquebrune (Alpes-Maritimes), writing to the Convention on April 6 (17 Germinal) in favor of "terror . . . on the agenda," was pleased that "the Rolandins, the Brissotins, the Girondins, all these impure reptiles of the swamp, have been suffocated in the mire."[37]

Of course, it made more sense to exterminate dangerous or pestiferous animals than to make examples of a restricted number of them, since such creatures could not reason. The same could be said of "monsters," a favorite epithet for counterrevolutionaries. Again Royer's speech was paradigmatic. It characterized Brissot as "this monster" who was "vomited by England."[38] Other revolutionaries similarly linked terror with the killing of monsters. On October 29 (8 Brumaire) François-Xavier Audouin, secretary of the Jacobins of Paris, came to the Convention to lobby for swifter procedure in the revolutionary tribunals "in order for these monsters [i.e., federalists] to perish," arguing that "then, and only then, will the traitors will be foiled and terror be the order of the day."[39] On November 13 (23 Brumaire) Deputy Marc-Guillaume Vadier, speaking for the Committee of General Security, praised the Parisian militants who had discovered treasures hoarded by aristocrats, and he called for pitiless punishment of the latter: "The force and energy that they opposed to all seductions [by the aristocrats] have made terror the order of the day. Beware of pitying the monsters who have made the blood of republicans flow."[40]

More calls for terror against monsters appeared in March and April as high-profile executions of alleged conspirators took place. On March 20 (30 Ventôse) the Revolutionary Committee of Meaux (Seine-et Marne) wrote to congratulate the Convention for having dispensed with "those monsters," by which it meant the popular sansculotte journalist Hébert and his followers, and in the very next sentence the Committee declared that "it is necessary that . . . terror remain constantly the order of the day."[41] After Danton and his followers went to the guillotine, the Popular Society of Cieux (Haute-Vienne) observed, "All eyes are open and fixed on the impure remains of the traitors and false patriots. They are struck with terror; the sword of the law is weighing on their heads and soon they will have disappeared like the monsters that preceded them on the dark path of treason."[42]

By envisaging terror as extermination, supporters of the Montagnards departed from Old Regime and early revolutionary understandings of the term as indicating selective, exemplary punishment—though they recalled biblical models of annihilationist terror. What they shared with all prior apologists for terror was a feeling that imposing the force on "the wicked" would keep "the good" safe.

SUBLIMITY AND *SALUT*: THE MOUNTAIN AS A SOURCE OF TERROR

Many of the meanings of "terror" as it was understood in the Year II can be seen with particular clarity when looking more closely at how revolutionaries portrayed its principal agent: the Mountain (*la Montagne*). All students of the French Revolution know that "the Mountain," a term designating the radical deputies in the Convention, derived from the fact that these deputies sat in the upper seats of the assembly hall. But the name quickly came to mean much more than that. Adapting the popular eighteenth-century imagery of the sublime (discussed in chapter 5) to the current political situation, revolutionaries who explicitly called for terror spoke and wrote of the Mountain as though it were a real landform with a foot, "heights," and a "summit," as well as the capacity to engender terrifying storms, and they often portrayed it as a volcano. Drawing on discourses of health (discussed in chapter 6), they depicted it as a "salutary" geographical feature, bringing fresh air, and contrasted it with the miasmic "swamp" in which the nation's enemies dwelled. At the same time, they gave it agency by attributing to it (or to the deputies who "resided" on it) the ability to cast thunderbolts or spew lava at the nation's enemies at will. Finally, they sanctified it, repeatedly calling it "holy" or "sacred" and likening it implicitly or explicitly to Mount Sinai.

Many advocates of revolutionary terror described the Mountain as a force of nature capable of going on the offensive. In particular, they frequently depicted the Mountain as a volcano directing its lava at counterrevolutionaries. In a letter affirming that "terror and victory are the order of the day," the Popular Society of Palaiseau (Seine-et-Oise) fondly recalled the insurrection of May 31–June 2 when "all these monsters brought together were suffocated by the volcanoes of this revered Mountain."[43] On January 29 (10 Pluviôse) the administrators of the district of Brignoles (Var) wrote of "the august Mountain," "The ardent and volcanic lava that it vomits from its belly furrows everywhere, in flaming arrows, the salutary marks of terror."[44] On April 8 (19 Germinal) the commune of Uzès-la-Montagne (Gard) addressed its namesake in the Convention, urging it to remain "the terror of despots" and "not to abandon the fearsome [redoutable] summit of the Mountain," and concluded with the promise, "For as long as you direct the revolutionary volcano . . . we shall shed our blood if necessary for the triumph of the Republic."[45]

Even nonvolcanic depictions of the Mountain portrayed it as an active force capable of terrorizing enemies. According to many revolutionaries, it had the capacity to conjure storms and cast thunderbolts at the nation's foes. On December 4 (14 Frimaire) the municipal authorities of La Rochelle (Charente-Inférieure) and the city's popular society sent an address, signed by 187 citizens, to the Convention to express their approval of the execution of the Girondins: "Satisfied with your menacing attitude and convinced that terror must be the order of the day, they [the Rochellais] invite you not to put down the thunderbolts that you are casting from the heights of the Mountain until there are no more enemies left to blast."[46] The municipal officers and the Jacobins of Saint-Porquier (Haute-Garonne) wrote to the Convention on January 9 (20 Nivôse), "You have saved the Republic by making Terror the order of the day. The confounded conspirator has hidden himself in the shadow, the malevolent ones have been dispersed by the thunderbolts that burst from the Mountain."[47] On March 19 (29 Ventôse) a deputation from the Popular Society of Montagne-du-Bon-Air (formerly Saint-Germain-en-Laye, in the Seine-et-Oise) came to the Convention to congratulate the deputies on having foiled the most recent "infamous plots hatched by scoundrels." The speaker declared, "It is always from the Mountain, citizen representatives, that the thunderbolts destined to remove the despots must come. Here it is from the judgment of the Mountain that the decrees come which carry terror into the souls of all the enemies of Liberty."[48]

These many vivid depictions of the Mountain as a violent force of nature highlight the degree to which terror speech in the Year II drew on the imagery of the sublime.[49] In fact, many revolutionaries used the word "sublime" when advocating terror. For instance, on November 20 (30 Brumaire) the municipality of Provins (Seine-et-Marne) wrote to congratulate the Convention on the execution of the Girondins and the Lyonnais federalist leaders: "This beautiful and great act of justice has struck all their henchmen with terror, and the rolling of their heads is making all the enemies of the Republic tremble. It [the Republic] is saved, thanks to you, sublime and pure Mountain."[50] The Popular Society of Pagny-la-Ville (Côte-d'Or) wrote to the Convention on January 4 (15 Nivôse), "Terror is wisely the order of the day, the provisional and revolutionary government . . . is going to hasten the days when the sublime Constitution . . . will make the happiness of all the French and then of the entire world."[51] On April 1 (12 Germinal) the Popular Society of Lacaune (Tarn) wrote to praise the Convention for its decree making "justice and probity the order of the day." Speculating on the effect of this decree on France's enemies, the group affirmed, "It is this sublime promulgation that is going to bring terror and shame to their souls."[52] In its letter to the Convention, the Popular Society of Luxeuil (Haute-Saône) linked the imagery of thundering terror with the language of the sublime: "With your thundering decrees you are annihilating the counterrevolutionaries and carrying terror to the despots [who are] frightened by the immensity of our resources and by this sublime national *élan*, which will infallibly overthrow the tyrants and tyranny."[53] In some cases "sublime" might simply have been a generic term of acclamation akin to "great" or "magnificent," and it would be a mistake to assume that revolutionaries using this language were necessarily thinking of the ideas promoted by Burke, Diderot, and Helvétius and discussed in chapter 5. Still, the convergence of the word "sublime" with the imagery of lightning, thunder, volcanoes, and, indeed, the language of terror itself suggests that the aesthetic of the sublime was very much in force during the Year II.

Some of the features attributed to the terrible Mountain are also found in the discourse of the sublime and that of health. On November 6 (16 Brumaire) the Surveillance Committee of Bayeux (Calvados) wrote to the Convention to complain about the "agitators" who had tried "to shake the rock of Calvados and to detach it from the indissoluble Mountain." It praised "the mass of the people," whose "constant firmness made the rash and vile children of the swamp tremble," and it praised the Convention for having engendered surveillance committees that "make the terror and the desperation of the parricides as far as their darkest lairs," adding, "It is for you . . . to support this salutary torch."[54] One cure for the infectious miasma of the "swamp" was fresh air, which emanated from the terrible Mountain. Thus on November 21 (1 Frimaire) the Popular Society of Florac (Lozère) wrote to the Convention, "It is necessary for the fresh air of the mountain to chase away all the fog of our horizon and revive our souls," clarifying in the following sentence, "May a revolutionary tribunal organized in each department make terror the great order of the day."[55] The contrast between a health-giving, terrible Mountain and a toxic *marais* can also be seen in an address by the Popular Society of Riverols (Puy-de-Dôme) in praise of "the revolutionary government, the terror of our enemies." The members asserted, "We too, legislators . . . we are Montagnards," which they meant both literally and figuratively, as they lived in the vicinity of the Puy de Dôme volcano. They added, "And from the summit of our sterile rocks we have an eye on the swamp so that its pestilential vapors do not poison us."[56] The linkage between terror and health recalls Old Regime medical understandings of terror discussed in chapter 6. It also suggests that the revolutionary keyword *salut* connoted not only safety but health.

Yet *salut* could also mean "salvation," and the imagery of the Mountain that terrified the enemy while providing health to patriots cannot be fully understood without attention to its religious meanings. In this respect it is important to note that the Mountain was frequently characterized as "holy." I have found 877 instances of the expression "holy mountain" in the *Archives parlementaires* (though not all of these are in texts that used the term "terror").[57] The expression predated the Year II: it appeared on March 17, 1793, when the Society of Friends of Liberty and Equality of Marseille wrote a letter to "the forty-eight sections of Paris, to the Jacobins, to the Cordeliers, to the faubourgs Saint-Antoine and Saint-Marceau," urging them to decree that the "scoundrels" who had voted to submit the king's sentence to a referendum were "traitors to the nation" who "must no longer occupy places near the deputies of the Holy Mountain."[58]

Almost all of the documents invoking the *sainte Montagne* or *Montagne sainte* are from the Year II, however. In many of these there is also an explicit endorsement of *terreur*. On October 10 the administrators of the department of the Lozère wrote, "The holy Mountain has followed the hypocrites into their sinuous detours; it has vanquished despotism, destroyed royalty, and it has just enchained federalism, [the] hideous monster of civil war. . . . The imposing attitude that you have taken has carried terror into the souls of tyrants."[59] On March 5 (15 Ventôse) the Parisian section of Brutus assured the Convention "that it continues to make terror the order of the day against the moderates and pitiers [les apitoyeurs] who would like to turn the attention of the Holy Mountain away from the interests of the people."[60] On March 14 (24 Ventôse) the Popular Society of Loudun (Vienne) wrote to the Convention to congratulate it on the abolition of slavery and to declare, "Terror is the order of the day, and it will stay so until . . . all the despots and their henchmen have come to prostrate themselves before this holy mountain."[61] Dozens of other letters to the Convention combined valorization of "terror" with invocation of the "holy Mountain."[62] In still other cases revolutionaries used terror speech while calling the Mountain "sacred."[63]

By calling the Mountain "holy" or "sacred," revolutionaries likely conjured in the minds of their listeners or readers the image of Mount Sinai. Moreover, the association of the Mountain with lightning and thunder was reminiscent of Sinai, as these atmospheric conditions occurred in the Book of Exodus precisely when God was giving Moses the Ten Commandments.[64] But in some cases the Old Testament imagery was explicit. For example, on September 29 a Citizen Musset gave a speech at a republican festival in Machecoul (Loire-Inférieure) in which he lauded the "brave Montagnards" for having "saved the Republic by casting terrible thunderbolts down onto faithless and factious colleagues" in order "to give us a Constitution which, like the tablets of Moses, could only come down from the Mountain in the midst of thunder and lightning." Elaborating on the metaphor of the mountain, Musset portrayed the Constitution as "the boulder of liberty and equality which this holy mountain has just rolled onto the enemies of free France, and which brings terror and fright to the souls of despots and federalists."[65] Similarly, on November 12 (22 Brumaire) the General Council, Revolutionary Committee, and Popular Society of Ham (Somme) wrote to the Convention, "Oh, Mountain, hope of those who cherish liberty and terror of our enemies of all kinds! Continue to be an Aetna for the ones [the enemies] and a Sinai for the others."[66] On January 11 (22 Nivôse) a "Citizen Mulard" wrote to Jacques-Louis David (who was president of the Convention at the time) simultaneously praising "the Mountain which, similar to Mount Sinai, brought forth a republican constitution in the midst of thunderbolts," and the Committee of Public Safety, which "quickly became the terror of the aristocrats."[67] As late as July 9 (21 Messidor), during the "Great Terror" that produced the majority of the guillotine's victims, the administrators of the Department of the Somme were using Sinaitic imagery. They wrote to the Convention with news of a subscription for the construction of "a frigate that carries terror and fright to the infamous English, and to all those who would dare insult the tricolor flag," and declared, "It is . . . true in politics as in physics that Mountains dominate, shelter and protect the most beautiful countries of the globe. Winds, storms, tempests break apart against their majestic immobility. It is on the august flanks of the French Sinai that patriotism bubbles up, that this all-powerful genius resides, this sacred love of liberty."[68]

THE SANCTIFICATION OF TERROR

In addition to the Sinaitic imagery of the holy mountain, revolutionaries of the Year II employed other expressions suggesting a sanctification of terror. For example, they frequently described the targets of terror as "impious." On March 10 (20 Ventôse) the "republicans of Pacy-sur-Eure" (Eure) pictured the response of the "despots" to the *levée en masse* (universal conscription) of August 23: "terror took hold of them and their impious souls."[69] The Popular Society of Blain (Loire-Atlantique) likewise claimed that "terror and severity" were necessary to "extinguish that impious race of conspirators and Machiavellians."[70] Other revolutionaries similarly advocated or celebrated the use of terror against "impious" enemies.[71] Alternatively, revolutionaries used the religiously charged word "sacrilegious" to describe the intended targets of terror. For example, on September 30 the "Society of Republican Sansculottes of Dunkirk" (Nord) wrote to the Convention, which it called "the terror of the wicked" and "the Holy Ark," "Woe to him who would be tempted" to touch the legislators with "a sacrilegious hand."[72] On March 27 (7 Germinal) the Popular Society of Neuvy-la-Loi (formerly Neuvy-le-Roi, in the Indre-et-Loire) urged the Convention to "make terror the order of the day" and congratulated the legislators on the execution of the Hébertists, that "faction of scoundrels" who had plotted "to put their sacrilegious hands on the founders of the Republic."[73]

Other instances of terror speech characterized the Revolution as a divinely ordained event and its enemies as rebels against God. On December 27 (7 Nivôse) the French Ambassador wrote from Basel rejoicing in "the terror and the horror [*l'épouvante*]" that counterrevolutionaries were displaying in their flight from Alsace and depicting them as "wandering the roads and woods," and claiming that "the fugitive priests, packs on their backs, shout their blasphemies against a democratic and vengeful God who has abandoned their cause."[74] On December 4 (14 Frimaire) the Revolutionary Tribunal in Commune-Affranchie (formerly Lyon) sent the Convention a list of the *guillotinés* in what the judges were calling "the new Sodom" and expressed the wish that "this festival [*fête*] forever imprint terror in the souls of scoundrels and confidence in the hearts of republicans!"[75] The Commune of Blain, writing to the Convention on March 28 (8 Germinal), noted that the "infamous Vendée" had been "treated like a Sodom" and justified this by observing that "you can only arrive at peace through terror."[76]

A particularly noticeable feature of the sanctification of terror was the tendency to invoke the "shades" (*mânes*) of martyred revolutionaries who could not rest until they were avenged. In many cases such appeals accompanied explicit calls for terror.[77] According to the version of Royer's September 5 speech in the *Moniteur universel*, the Jacobin justified his call for terror with the claim, "The shades of the victims piled up by treason ask you for striking vengeance."[78] On November 2 (12 Brumaire) the "sansculottes composing the provisional administration of the district of Orgelet [Argelet]" (Jura) recalled May 31, "that day of terror for the conspirators and of triumph for liberty," urged the Mountain to remain at its post, and ended their letter with "homage to the shades of the virtuous Marat."[79] On November 17 (27 Brumaire) the Montagnard and Revolutionary Society of Moissac (Tarn-et-Garonne) held a memorial for Beauvais, Marat, Le Pelletier, and "other martyrs to liberty." According to a description of the festivities, a department administrator proclaimed that "vengeance and terror are the order of the day" and swore "to avenge the shades of all the republican martyrs."[80] There are many more examples of revolutionaries evoking the shades of martyrs while calling for vindictive terror.[81]

18 FLORÉAL AND THE RETURN OF RELIGIOUS TERROR

The sanctification of terror is perhaps clearest in commentary on the Law of 18 Floréal (May 7). Sponsored by Robespierre, this law contained fifteen articles, mostly dealing with revolutionary festivals, but it was the first article that inspired the most subsequent discussion: "The French people recognizes the existence of the Supreme Being and the immortality of the soul."[82] Many revolutionaries praised the Convention for this law, which they believed would strike terror into their enemies. The Popular Society of Commune-Affranchie wrote, "Thanks be to you, wise legislators! In a single stroke you have blasted both grievous atheism and hideous fanaticism; you have brought consolation to the hearts of all the citizens, you have struck the wicked with terror."[83] The Revolutionary Committee of Saint-Omer echoed this view, writing on May 27 (8 Prairial), "This solemn decree has struck all the conspirators with terror and despair."[84] On May 30 (11

Prairial) the administrators of the Department of the Côtes-du-Nord wrote of the decree, "What sweet consolation these sentiments bring to honest souls, and what salutary terror they inspire in scoundrels [and] conspirators, who are enemies of liberty and equality."[85] The Convention received other, similarly worded outpourings of gratitude.[86]

Why should the Republic's recognition of a Supreme Being and the immortality of the soul have been so terrifying to counterrevolutionaries? In the speech in which he called for the law, Robespierre argued that "the idea of the Supreme Being and of the immortality of the soul is a continual reminder of justice: it is therefore social and republican."[87] By contrast, kings and counterrevolutionaries, according to Robespierre, endorsed atheism because it reduced people to their animal instincts of seeking pleasure and avoiding pain and discouraged them from engaging in any altruistic actions.

But Robespierre did not use the word *terreur* in his speech, though he did recall that Cicero (whom he admired) "invoked against traitors both the sword of the laws and the thunderbolts of the gods." He did not say anything about heaven or hell or mention any future rewards or punishments, and the law that emerged from his proposal was similarly silent on these matters. Robespierre did envisage fear overtaking France's enemies at the prospect of revolutionary festivals in which patriots vowed to emulate the nation's martyrs: "May they tremble, all the tyrants armed against liberty, if they still exist! May they tremble on the day when the French come to your tombs swearing to imitate you!"[88] But this imputed fear was based on the supposed realization that belief in immortality made the French unafraid. There is no sense that the tyrants were trembling because they anticipated their own punishment in the afterlife.

Yet some of the addresses the Convention received in appreciation of the Law of 18 Floréal suggested that it was effective precisely because it would induce the terror of posthumous punishment in counterrevolutionaries. On May 25 (6 Prairial) the Popular Society of Neufchatel (Seine-Inférieure) wrote to the Convention, "These two great principles [belief in the Supreme Being and immortality of the soul] recognized by all civilized peoples have always been the terror of crime and the triumph of virtue; they spread sweet consolation to the pure souls of the unfortunate while they . . . announce inevitable punishment to the perverse and the scoundrels."[89] "Inevitable punishment" in this context could only have meant suffering in the afterlife, since it was clear to any observer that some "scoundrels" were escaping human punishment. Similar reasoning informed the May 25 (6 Prairial) address by the Popular Society of Orbec (Calvados): "Any law that brings mortals back to the divinity necessarily exercises an empire that prepares them to respect the laws, either by the terror that it [the divinity] inspires in them or by the hope that it gives virtue."[90] "Hope" clearly refers to a happy afterlife, leaving the "terror" that God instills in human beings to suggest suffering after death.

In still other addresses the connection between the terror of the Law of 18 Floréal and punishment following the death of the "scoundrel" was explicit. On May 30 (11 Prairial) the Popular Society of Vic-sur-l'Osse (formerly Vic-Fezensac, in the Gers) wrote to "bless" the Convention for "having consecrated this consoling truth [of posthumous rewards and punishments] that the just one always finds at the bottom of his heart, this truth which is the terror and the eternal punishment of the scoundrel."[91] Here they drew on a centuries-old tradition of threatening "scoundrels" with "eternal punishment" should they escape human justice. For these Jacobins, belief in hell was revolutionary.

A similar eschatology underlay a letter from the Popular Society of Bouquenom (Bas-Rhin) to the Convention. The missive depicted a "defender" of the *patrie* imbued with the principles of the Law of 18 Floréal and consequently saying to himself, "Kings . . . will be the damned of the future life: by fighting against them . . . I am serving the supreme being . . . [and] if I die on the battlefield, an eternal and blessed life will be the recompense for my actions." The Jacobins further imagined a husband saying to his wife, regarding "the scoundrels who wanted to introduce atheism into the Republic," "Already their souls must be feeling the punishment that is reserved for the wicked. Let us raise our children to love the *patrie*, let us practice virtue; we will have fulfilled the duty that the author of nature has prescribed to us and he will reward us in the future life." The letter concluded, "This, Citizen Representatives, is the salutary effect that your decree of 18 Floréal has produced. It is the consolation of good citizens and the terror of counterrevolutionaries, conspirators, and intriguers."[92]

The revolutionaries of Vic-sur-l'Osse and Bouquenom thus explicitly articulated a view of terror, punishment and theology that was implicit in many other affirmations of the Law of 18 Floréal. This view was strikingly similar to the throne-and-altar ideology of the Old Regime (discussed in chapters 1 and 2). It served as a divine supplement to the "terror of the laws" that police and judicial institutions could only imperfectly execute. It was a set of claims that made religion once again into a source of coercion through the terror that its threats of damnation inspired in the people. Ironically, this return to religious terror took place precisely at the moment when the church, denounced as fanatical, was in the process of being overrun.

TERROR SPEECH AS THERAPY

At this point we can identify the continuities and discontinuities in terror speech from the Old Regime, the first four years of the Revolution and the Year II. Though the word "terror" continued to denote exemplary and utilitarian legal punishment, it increasingly referred to premodern values of vengeance and biblical concepts of extermination and purification. It described the actions and essence of the "holy Mountain," which was at once sublime and health-giving, thereby recalling Old Regime understandings of aesthetics and medicine. It even appeared in religiously charged affirmations of eternal punishment for the wicked, thus resuscitating a form of threat that Enlightenment writers had denounced in the church. Finally, the habit of referring to individuals or groups metonymically as "the terror" of their enemies, a practice that had largely gone dormant during the first four years of the Revolution, flourished again during the Year II.[93]

How did revolutionaries of the Year II feel when they spoke or wrote the word *terreur* in the contexts delineated above? It is hard to know precisely, but the revolutionaries left clues regarding their own emotions even as their focus was ostensibly on the emotions (and especially the terror) of others. These clues suggest that the revolutionaries who invoked terror felt good while doing so. More specifically, using the language of terror made them feel powerful and safe. It functioned as a kind of therapy by which revolutionaries tried to overcome their own feelings of terror.

The pleasure revolutionaries took in reporting or anticipating the terror of their opponents is evident in many descriptions of military action. As in the earlier phases of the Revolution, and particularly since the outbreak of war, descriptions of such action made abundant use of the word *terreur*. Inevitably it was the enemy that was depicted as terrified—I have not encountered any documentation admitting that French troops suffered from terror—and the agents of terror were just as inevitably brave republican soldiers and their commanders. This pairing of characteristics—a terrified enemy and fearless defenders of the *patrie*—is not accidental. It illustrates the idea (introduced at the end of the previous chapter) of the conservation of terror, according to which the French were as courageous as their enemies were terrified.

An abundant source illustrating this dynamic is the correspondence of generals with their military superiors and the civilian authorities. In these letters generals reliably painted a Manichean picture of courageous French troops and cowardly enemies. For example, on September 11, 1793, Barère read before the Convention a letter that General Leclerc had sent to General Carion regarding the aftermath of the battle of Hondschoote (September 8) at which republican forces liberated Dunkirk from a two-week British siege. Leclerc had written, "We have just learned that at the camp of Afrenoue the enemy had abandoned fourteen pieces of twenty-four-pounder cannon and a great quantity of oats." Leclerc added, "Terror is with them: *Vive la République!*"[94] This letter, which was reprinted in the *Moniteur* and clearly intended for wide distribution, interpreted the small French victory in terms of terror that had seized the enemy, and news of this (both the terror and the victory it allegedly produced) was designed to be reassuring. Similarly, on September 13 the Convention received a letter from General Rossignol that explained that two days of fighting in the Vendée had "produced a good effect by casting terror and horror [*l'épouvante*] at the enemy."[95] On October 9 General Chalbos, also fighting in the Vendée, boasted that his army routed "an enemy struck with terror and whose hordes were dispersed."[96] Other letters followed the same pattern of interpreting French victories in terms of the terror that allegedly seized the enemy. Among these were an account by Eustache-Charles D'Aoust of his victory in Spain, Jourdan's depiction of his troops' success against the Austrians, Delatre's explanation of his incursions into Catalonia, Michaud's letter concerning the recovery of Fort-Vauban in Alsace, Lacombe-Saint-Michel's description of the defeat of Corsican counterrevolutionaries, Bonnet's account of a victory in Spain, Dumerbion's narrative of the surrender of Saorgio in Piedmont, and Jourdan's characterization of the fall of Namur in Belgium.[97] To be sure, these communications were formulaic. Reporting terrified enemies was a way of underscoring the bravery of the French troops (and by implication the inspiring character of their generals). And of course enemies feeling terror was simply good news, since terrified troops tended to flee, leaving easy victories (and often caches of weapons) to the victorious republicans. But the very predictability of the bulletins reveals the extent to which revolutionaries sought reassurance in the image of a terrified enemy.

Generals were not alone in describing military victories in terms of terrified enemies. Civilians were as eager, if not more so, to envisage terror-stricken "slaves of despotism" fleeing advances by fearless French soldiers. The most prolific generators of this discourse were those of the Convention's deputies who had been commissioned to observe and follow the Republic's various armies. For example, on September 13 Pierre Bourbotte, one of the commissioners with the anti-Vendean army, began a letter to the Convention with the declaration, "It is today that we can truthfully assure that terror and fright are pursuing the rebels of the Vendée." The word "assure" had a double meaning, indicating both certainty and comfort. As was typically the case, the terror of the enemy implied the [re]assurance of the Republic.[98] The very next day Joseph-Étienne Richard, another deputy commissioned with observing the military situation in the Vendée, wrote to the Convention with good news from the rebellious region: "We are assured [*On nous assure*] that terror is spreading among [the rebels]."[99] Again the word "assure" was not accidental, and again the prospect of the enemy's terror was meant to reduce the fear that the revolutionaries themselves undoubtedly felt. Other commissioners with the anti-Vendean forces provided similar accounts of terrified rebels in the coming months.[100]

Meanwhile, commissioners with other armies provided similar accounts. On September 20 the Convention read a letter from Jean-Baptiste Massieu, commissioner with the Army of the Ardennes. Massieu reported "that terror reigns among the Austrians," who were "so horrified" (*si épouvantés*) by General Hilaire and his sixteen thousand men advancing on them in Belgium that they were fleeing the city of Dinant.[101] On April 8 (19 Germinal) Augustin Robespierre (Maximilien's younger brother) and Antoine Saliceti, commissioners with the Army of Italy, wrote to the Committee of Public Safety to announce the taking of the strategically important town of Oneglia in Piedmont. The assault began with French forces seizing the nearby hamlet of Sant-Agata. This "put terror among the slaves," who quickly fled the scene.[102] Later that month the younger Robespierre, together with Saliceti's successor Jean-François Ricord, announced the acquisition of the Piedmontese town of Saorgio, writing that they had witnessed "terror spread in all [the enemy's] camps, and then horror [*l'épouvante*]."[103] On July 24 (6 Thermidor) Deputy Richard, commissioned with the Army of the North, wrote to the Committee of Public Safety to announce the surrender of Antwerp to the French: "The terror with which the armies of the coalition tyrants are struck appears to be forever growing; the vile slaves are finding no other means of escaping the blows of the republicans than a shameful and precipitous flight."[104] Other deputies reinforced the message that terrified enemies were fleeing.[105] Jacobin clubs expressed themselves in similar terms.[106]

That revolutionaries took pleasure in describing or imagining their enemies' terror is clear from their tendency to linger over the physical symptoms of that terror. The word most frequently used to depict terror was the verb *trembler*. Famously employed in the *Marseillaise* ("Tremblez, tyrans!"), it was extremely popular in the terror speech of the Year II. Often it appeared in close proximity to the word *terreur*. For example, the Republican Society of Saint-Maximin (Var) wrote to the Convention, "Citizen representatives, may terror therefore [be] the order of the day; may they tremble, the traitors!"[107]

Closely related to trembling was shuddering, and revolutionaries repeatedly pictured their enemies shuddering with terror. To cite just one example, early in April the Popular Society of Annecy (Mont-Blanc) congratulated the Convention on the execution of the Dantonists: "The foreigners, the intriguers, all the disguised enemies are shuddering with terror [over this]."[108] Yet another symptom of the enemies' terror, according to numerous revolutionaries, was turning pale. On March 24 (4 Germinal) the Revolutionary Committee of Bordeaux wrote to congratulate the Convention on the execution of the Hébertists, adding the wish that "this terrible example of an outraged nation imprint such terror in the souls of their accomplices that they can be recognized by the pallor of their brows."[109]

The use of *terreur* alongside images of trembling, shuddering, and pallor suggests pleasurable lingering over the enemies' supposedly terrified condition. But there is still more evidence that revolutionaries took pleasure in uttering or writing the word "terror." Specifically, when republicans of the Year II called for or celebrated terror in their enemies, they frequently referred to positive emotions that they themselves felt or wished to feel. The most prominent of these were consolation, encouragement (or a feeling of courage), hope, confidence, and a sense of safety.

Revolutionaries repeatedly envisaged terror in their enemies while reporting or predicting consolation in themselves or their compatriots. For instance, following the liberation of Toulon in December the Popular Society of Parthenay (Deux-Sèvres) held a celebration in which a Citizen Thibault carried a tricolor flag and proclaimed, "May it [the flag] be the terror of brigands, the support and the consolation of good citizens."[110] On March 5 (15 Ventôse) the commune and the Popular Society of Saint-Quentin (Aisne) sent a letter thanking the Convention for a decree that had released eight citizens whose arrests had been the result of "intrigue": "This act of justice will be the terror of the wicked; it has brought consolation to our commune."[111] On April 4 (15 Germinal) the Popular Society of Libreval, formerly Saint-Amand-Montrond (Cher), wrote to urge the Convention, "Continue to cast terror into the souls of the traitors and consolation into the souls of the Republicans."[112] Calls for consolation implicitly acknowledged suffering on the part of the revolutionaries. That suffering might have been from privation or grief. It might also have stemmed from feelings of fear or terror.

A clearer indication that revolutionaries themselves were fearful or terrified comes from the many references they made to courage or encouragement when speaking or writing of their enemies' terror. On September 23 the Surveillance Committee of Essay (Orne) wrote to the Convention boasting that it had "taken all the measures that it considered suited to carry terror to the aristocrats and reanimate the courage of the patriots."[113] That it was necessary to "reanimate" (*ranimer*) the patriots' courage hinted at the possibility that even patriots could be prevented by fear or terror from doing their duty. Similarly, the need for courage is seen in a letter by the administrators of the district of Montfort-l'Amaury (Seine-et-Oise) to the Convention. Focusing on the French response to the setbacks of 1793, the officials wrote that disasters in Mainz, Valenciennes, Lyon, Toulon, and the Vendée "have not weakened the courage of the French; on the contrary, they have only augmented it and made it become an object of terror for the enemies." The administrators claimed that French courage produced terror in the enemy, but the causality might have been reversed: the belief that the enemy was terrified *encouraged* the French. At least it gave courage to the authors of this optimistic address.[114]

More evidence that revolutionaries needed relief from their own feelings of terror and sought it in the prospect of their enemies' terror comes from Barère, who spoke to the Convention on November 25 (5 Frimaire) on behalf of the Committee of Public Safety. Barère insisted that only the Republic's enemies need feel terror, but he hinted that revolutionaries might be experiencing this emotion and contrasted it with courage and encouragement. He declared, "It is not at all in the temple of liberty, in the center of the Revolution, that terror must live, that courage must be frozen, that speech must be paralyzed; it is not at all here that souls must be timid, energy dulled, and that the character of the free man must be effaced." On the contrary, it was "from this sanctuary that terror must go to restrain domestic enemies" and "from this tribune that must come rewards and encouragements for the armies of the Republic and fright for the foreign cohorts."[115] Barère's words suggested that terror and "fright" themselves, insofar as they affected France's enemies, engendered courage in patriots who might otherwise experience fear.

Similar reasoning can be seen in a report of December 14 (24 Frimaire) by the Legislation Committee. Presented to the Convention by Deputy Merlin (de Douai), it contained a bill concerning people who had been declared "outlaws" by the decrees of September 7 and 17, 1793. Among these were Frenchmen who had taken public positions in areas of France that had been invaded by foreign enemies. Some deputies had asked whether nonsalaried officials in such areas were to be considered outlaws. The Legislation Committee proposed closing this loophole. Its language is telling: "Let us declare that in the future, any nonsalaried public official will be, in execution of the decree of September 17, treated as a salaried public official or state pensioner; and we shall be as sure in this way to inspire salutary terror in the malevolent ones as to raise the courage of patriots." One can easily see why this decree, which would subject more people to the death penalty, would inspire terror "in the malevolent ones." But why would it "raise the courage of patriots"? Because notwithstanding the possibility of fewer enemies (some having been executed), terrified enemies were less effective than fearless ones.[116]

One component of courage was hope, which in some ways was the opposite of terror. If terror implied the anticipation of future suffering or unhappiness, hope involved envisaging a future that was happy and free from suffering. It is therefore revealing that "hope" (*espoir* or *espérance*) often appeared in close proximity with "terror" in the political speech of the Year II. Again the principle of the conservation of terror was operative. Insofar as the enemy was terrified, the French could feel hope. For example, in an undated letter (received by the Convention on November 21 [1 Frimaire]) the Republican Society of Grasse (Var) praised the planned "criminal code, hope of the innocent and terror of the guilty."[117] On January 17 (28 Nivôse) a deputation of the Popular and Republican Society of the Arts came to the bar of the Convention and declared of the deputies: "Your energy, carrying terror to the tyrants and rebels, at the same time carries the hope of happiness to all the peoples of the world."[118] On February 18 (30 Pluviôse), according to the minutes of the Popular Society of the canton of Mello (Oise), a festival inaugurating a Temple of Reason had taken place in which the leader of a procession of "young boys" carried a banner with the inscription, "Hope of the *patrie* and terror of kings."[119] Many more examples of hope/terror parallelism appear in the *Archives parlementaires*.[120]

Closely related to hope, and equally important for courage, was confidence, thus we sometimes find *confiance*—which can also mean "trust"—as a foil for *terreur* in many revolutionary documents from the Year II. On March 8 (18 Ventôse) the administrators of the district of Le Dorat (Haute-Vienne) wrote to the Convention in praise of the Ventôse decrees (on the redistribution of property confiscated from suspects and émigrés), predicting that "you will make terror the order of the day among all the rich aristocrats of the land, and . . . inspire confidence in the sansculottes of all nations."[121] Similarly, on March 20 (30 Ventôse) the Popular Society of Auxonne (Côte-d'Or) wrote to the Convention in praise of the Committee of Public Safety, "whose revolutionary energy inspires as much confidence in the Republic as terror in tyrants."[122]

Words such as "shield," "safeguard," "protection," "security," and "safety," though they did not, strictly speaking, describe or name emotions, also indicate a desire on the part of revolutionaries to feel safe and as such reveal much about the fear they were experiencing. These words also appear in close proximity to "terror." On October 13 (22 Brumaire) the Popular Society of Lure (Haute-Saône) wrote to the Convention, "Courage, saviors of the *patrie*, continue to deploy that manly energy that was always the terror of tyrants and the shield of free men."[123] The image of a "safeguard" functioned similarly to that of a shield. Thus on June 24 (6 Messidor) the Popular Society of Omont (Ardennes) wrote to the Convention, "May your measures and your energy be the terror of the intriguers and traitors, and your justice the safeguard of the true children of the *patrie*."[124] Revolution-aries also juxtaposed terror for enemies with protection for themselves, thereby revealing their own fears. For instance, the Popular Society of Lan-gres (Haute-Marne) urged the Convention, "Leave terror constantly as the order of the day for the conspirators, and protection for the patriots."[125] In other cases they referred to "security" for themselves while advocating ter-ror for their enemies. Thus on January 18 (29 Nivôse) the General Council of Montlieu (Charente-Inférieure) wrote to the Convention in praise of the Law of 14 Frimaire. The officials explained, "Terror will now only be the order of the day for traitors, for negligent or perfidious public officials; good citizens will give themselves over with security to the sweetness of society, fraternity, equality, and liberty, without fearing [*sans redouter*] the effect of hatred or the vengeance of the wicked."[126] Here the authors of the letter im-plicitly acknowledge the fear that citizens felt in the absence of institutions that terrorized their enemies. The Popular Society of La Guerche (Cher) used the word *sûreté* to convey the same idea (and feeling) when it informed the Convention, "Your Revolutionary measures will be our strength, our security, the terror and vexation of our enemies."[127]

The most famous of the "safety" words employed by revolutionaries was *salut*, which could also mean salvation, and it too appeared in calls for terror against the enemy. Thus when Robespierre promoted the Law of 22 Prairial (June 10)—a measure that would extend the reach of the revolution-ary tribunals, empower all citizens to seize suspected counterrevolution-aries, limit the ability of suspects to defend themselves, and make death the only penalty available to the revolutionary tribunals—he justified it by noting that there was nothing in it that was "not written for the *salut* of the patriots and the terror of the aristocracy."[128]

We have now seen considerable evidence that revolutionaries in the Year II displayed a desire for—and likely a dearth of—consolation, courage, hope, con-fidence, and security, and that they simultaneously called for counterrevolu-tionaries to feel the opposite, namely terror. They evinced the belief that the republic's leaders, laws, institutions, citizens, and actions were the source of both the positive emotions (in themselves) and terror (in their enemies).

Moreover, in some of their statements they indicated a belief that the terror experienced by their enemies was precisely the source of courage, hope, confidence, and security in good citizens. In this respect they clearly revealed a belief in the conservation of terror. Consider the letter of November 14 (24 Brumaire) from Deputy Hérault de Séchelles, on mission in the Haut-Rhin, to his colleagues in the legislature. Writing of the sad state of affairs in the department, where "sansculottes" were being "insulted," he opined, "Only terror can establish the Republic here and give courage to the small number of patriots."[129] Here Hérault made the connection unambiguous: a terrified enemy gave courage to the republicans. Similarly, on February 26 (8 Ventôse) Danton called for a decree requiring all revolutionary committees to submit a list of their members (to avoid false accusations): "It is thus that the revolutionary instruments will become still more useful and that, terror remaining constantly the order of the day against the enemies of the Revolution, the patriots will be able to be secure [sûrs] in peace and liberty."[130] Yet another explicit link between the enemy's terror and revolutionary courage appears in a letter of April 16 (27 Germinal) in which the Popular Society of Souillac (Lot) congratulated the Convention on the execution of the Dantonists: "Representatives, the striking justice that you have just exercised toward these audacious criminals, by imprinting terror on the brow of the guilty, emboldens, raises the souls of true republicans."[131] The corollary of this message was that as long as "the guilty" did not experience—and indeed did not make apparent through facial expressions or the blood draining from the face—the terror imposed by the revolutionary government, the "true republicans" could not feel bold. In other words, it would be good citizens who were disabled by their own feelings of terror.

CONCLUSIONS

In some respects the revolutionaries of the Year II followed uninterrupted traditions of terror speech. Like commentators under the Old Regime and the first four years of the Revolution, they characterized terror as a property of the law, deeming it exemplary, restraining, and therefore "salutary." They also employed a familiar pattern of characterizing terror as a legitimate resource to be directed against "enemies" and even represented themselves *as* the terror of those enemies, elaborating on a trope that had once been reserved for kings but now belonged to the sovereign nation and its institutions. In other respects they attached meanings to the word "terror" that were absent during the earlier days of the Revolution. For instance, they associated terror with vengeance and even extermination. In this respect they skipped over their revolutionary forebears and drew on biblical imagery. They identified their cause with that of God and even revived the idea of eternal punishment for the wicked, despite the Enlightenment anathema on using the terror of hell for political advantage, so tempting was it to imagine their enemies punished. Their vivid descriptions of a "holy Mountain" endowed with the capacity to cast thunderbolts at the nation's foes further served to present terror as a sacred, divine force. It also recalled elements of the sublime ironically promoted by a man (Edmund Burke) who later famously railed against the Revolution, and which we do not see in the period from June 1789 through August 1793. The same imagery associated terror with fresh air and health, and much as the medical literature of the Old Regime had presented terror (under certain circumstances) as beneficial to the human organism, the revolutionaries who saw terror as a miasma-dispersing force suggested that it preserved the health of the body politic.

Given the many positive associations of the word "terror," we can see why revolutionaries uttered and wrote it again and again with the greatest pleasure. Moreover, in light of the contextual readings of terror speech offered in this chapter, we can see precisely *how* the word functioned in the emotional experiences of its users. William Reddy has shown that emotion claims can transform the condition of the person making them.[132] Though his study is restricted to first-person claims, such as "I am angry," the claims that revolutionaries made about *other* people's emotions suggest that those statements could also be transformative to the people making them. In the process of acknowledging one's anger via a statement such as "I am angry," one might become even angrier or, alternatively, might recognize an exaggeration in the claim and consequently feel relief. Similarly, claims about one's enemies' misfortunes can serve to cheer the person making them. More particularly, if the enemies are said to be incapacitated by the emotions attributed to them—such as fear or terror—then the persons speaking on their behalf can feel relief from their own fears or terrors. Here we see the emotional appeal of terror speech to the revolutionaries. Insisting that the enemy was terrified, or needed to be terrified, eased the revolutionaries' own fears. It is for this reason that pro-Montagnard republicans so frequently described revolutionary terror as consoling, reassuring, hopeful, emboldening, and encouraging.

The process I have just described not only explains the proliferation of speeches and written communications that advocated and celebrated "terror" in its many forms. It also helps to explain the Terror itself. Beginning with Royer's speech, "terror" came to describe a specific set of practices, policies, laws, and institutions. It became a shorthand term for revolutionary tribunals; the Committee of Public Safety; the cataloguing, incarceration, and execution of "suspects"; and the suspension of due process, even of the much-revered Constitution of 1793, and its replacement by "revolutionary government." These were new and controversial measures; yet, although it is impossible to gauge the popularity of any policy under a repressive regime, the Terror had its sincere advocates. What motivated their support? Many things, to be sure, but the name attached to the policies had something to do with their popularity. When republicans declared that terror was "the order of the day," or that it should be, they were honoring a set of dangerous innovations with a venerable and reassuring name. The appeal of "terror" therefore helps to explain the appeal of the Terror.

W here does the story I have just told fit into the historiography of the Terror? That scholarship is vast, and I do not pretend to have mastered it. A WorldCat search for the Library of Congress subject heading "France—History—Reign of Terror, 1793–1794" yields the titles of 4961 books. Not included in this corpus are books about the French Revolution more generally, which typically have something to say about the Terror. WorldCat yields 91,669 book titles for the subject "France—History—Revolution, 1789–1799." Given this insuperable body of commentary, the best I can do is review some trends that have captured historians' attention in recent decades.[1]

It is conventional to divide historians of the Terror into two parties: those who see it as the product of ideology, and those who understand it as the result of circumstances. The first to focus on ideological origins were conservatives such as the Abbé Barruel and Joseph de Maistre, contemporaries of the Revolution who saw it as the disastrous product of Enlightenment thought.[2] In the late nineteenth and early twentieth centuries the like-minded historians Hippolyte Taine and Augustin Cochin revived the idea of the Revolution as the work of Enlightenment-besotted men.[3] More recently François Furet, partly inspired by Cochin's work, characterized the Terror as the product of a Rousseauian ideology of the "general will" combined with the Old Regime precept of indivisible sovereignty. This lethal combination, according to Furet, made loyal opposition look like treason and gave the power of life and death to anyone who could claim to represent the general will.[4] Keith Michael Baker similarly supports an ideological interpretation of the Terror. Examining the available ideological options in terms of Foucauldian discourses, he argues that revolutionaries combined "a discourse of the political, grounded on the theory of a unitary political will," with discourses of "civic virtue" and "absolute sovereignty," which in turn justified government by terror.[5] Simon Schama attributes the mentality of the Terror largely to such ideological developments as the cult of *sensibilité* and the revival of classical republicanism.[6] Patrice Gueniffey, a former student of Furet, also stresses the role of ideas, in particular maintaining Furet's belief that the revolutionaries inherited a view of sovereignty that precluded compromise.[7] Dan Edelstein sees the Terror as emerging largely out of an Old Regime view of natural law according to which enemies of the human race could rightfully be killed without the benefit of a trial.[8] In a recent intellectual history of the French Revolution, Jonathan Israel traces the Terror to Rousseau.[9]

Other historians emphasize contingency, or circumstances, over ideology. Over a century ago Alphonse Aulard, the first chair of the history of the French Revolution at the Sorbonne, used the word "circumstances" repeatedly to explain the violent or undemocratic actions of revolutionaries. Writing on the proclamation of "revolutionary government" (October 10, 1793), Aulard observed that it was necessary to consolidate the various institutions of government "to adapt them better to the circumstances" of a prolonged war. On the decree of 14 Frimaire (December 4, 1793), which placed representatives *en mission* under the authority of the Committee of Public Safety, Aulard wrote that "circumstances led [the revolutionaries] to strengthen centralization further." Elsewhere he claimed that if the Convention "employed means so contrary to the principles of the Revolution, it was because circumstances forced it" to do so.[10]

Aulard's successors at the Sorbonne promoted what Cochin derided as *la thèse des circonstances*.[11] Albert Mathiez described the Terror as a necessary response to the circumstances of the war against the Austrians, Prussians, British, and Spanish; the civil war in the Vendée; the "federalist" uprisings in Lyon and other French cities; and the presence of "masked aristocrats" posing as good republicans. It was "to cut [this] danger," Mathiez wrote, that the Convention created the institutions of the Terror.[12] Similarly, Mathiez justified the acceleration of the Terror after 22 Prairial (June 10, 1794) by pointing to plots by *citras* and *ultras*, or successors to Danton and Hébert, respectively.[13] Georges Lefebvre in turn saw "revolutionary government" as responding to "the pressure of events."[14] Its uneven application was evidence for him that "circumstances exerted a more considerable influence" than the character of the revolutionary leaders themselves." Citing the statistics compiled by Donald Greer, Lefebvre affirmed, "It was in the two areas where counterrevolutionaries took up arms and committed open treason that [the Terror] raged with the greatest fury."[15] Albert Soboul agreed: "In the departments, the Terror was a function of the seriousness of [counterrevolutionary or federalist] revolt." No doubt influenced by Greer's statistics and Lefebvre's interpretation, he added, "The regions untouched by civil war most often were unfamiliar with [the Terror]."[16] Michel Vovelle explicitly opposed Furet's critique of the "circumstance" thesis, asking rhetorically whether the revolutionaries had merely "dreamed" of such dangers as foreign enemies and domestic counterrevolution.[17] The current chair of the history of the French Revolution, Jean-Clément Martin, similarly sees the violence of the Terror as the result of circumstances, namely the presence of real foreign and domestic enemies.[18]

In addition to the paradigms of ideological origins and circumstantial explanations, the historiography of the Terror has recently taken an "emotional turn."[19] While the recognition of emotions in the French Revolution is not in itself new, the habits of analyzing the Revolution in terms of ideology and events were so ingrained, particularly in professional academic history, that the recent return to emotion as a category of analysis has attracted notice.[20] With respect to the Terror in particular, Sophie Wahnich posits an "emotional economy of the Terror" in which the revolutionaries' own fright (effroi) played a decisive role. Drawing on the work of Jacques Guilhaumou, Wahnich argues that the assassination of Marat, which revolutionaries regarded as an act of profanation of a sacred body, provoked effroi. Rather than succumbing to this emotion, however, Marat's supporters responded by sublimating it and calling for "vengeance and terror."[21]

Other historians have similarly seen the Terror as a response to revolutionaries' fears. Arno Mayer writes that "much of the revolutionary violence and terror" (in the French and Bolshevik revolutions alike) were "fear-inspired."[22] Patrice Higonnet interprets the Terror in terms of trauma provoked not by enemies per se but rather by the "violent collapse of a . . . world view."[23] Marisa Linton argues that fear of counterrevolutionary plots was not only crucial in provoking calls for terror but also in maintaining the Terror: "There is evidence that some of the Jacobins were looking for a way out of terror in the spring of 1794, but one of the things that made this difficult was the atmosphere of fear itself."[24] Timothy Tackett concurs that the revolutionaries' own emotional condition was crucial for understanding their decisions in 1793 and 1794: specifically, he argues that "fear was one of the central elements in the origins of Revolutionary violence."[25] David Andress also sees the fear that revolutionaries experienced as an explanatory factor in the Terror. "Without going so far as to say that the Jacobins were literally psychologically traumatized by their experiences," Andress claims that "for Robespierre at least, the movement from 1789 to 1792 seems to have been akin to a long, slow descent toward an abyss of real fear and suffering."[26]

At the risk of appearing indecisive, I contend that all three of the explanatory models of the Terror are valid. The Terror had ideological antecedents and circumstantial catalysts, and the emotional condition of its leaders and supporters helps to explain their actions. I believe that my study of terror speech confirms each of the three paradigms. Specifically, the history of statements in which terror appears as a sign of sacrality, a mark of legitimacy, a characteristic of the sublime, or a "salutary" response to disruptions in bodies (including bodies politic) can be seen as revealing a specifically pro-terror ideology. More than any doctrine of Rousseau—who, as we have seen, opposed terror—or Montesquieu or Mably, this ideology united and inspired advocates of the Terror in the Year II.

Yet it would be wrong to see this ideology alone as explaining the Terror. After all, as we have seen, pro-terror ideas were the common heritage of Europe, and indeed the Western world, whereas the Terror took place only in France. The Bible promoted the idea of a "terrible," hence majestic, God, as it continues to do for Jews and Christians throughout the world. French kings were not the only monarchs to be flattered as "the terror of their enemies."[27] Jurists in countries other than France recommended punishment as a means of instilling terror in malefactors.[28] The idea that effective tragedy must instill terror came from Aristotle, and it appeared in modified form in British and German writers such as Addison and Lessing.[29] The connection between terror and the sublime originated in Longinus and entered France mainly via the Anglo-Irish writer Edmund Burke, as we have seen in chapter 5. It was also a staple of Kant's aesthetics, first articulated in the 1764 treatise "On the Feeling of the Beautiful and Sublime."[30] Medical writers praising the effects of terror on the human organism, as mentioned in chapter 6, included Italian, British, German, and Dutch physicians, not to mention ancient Greek authorities such as Galen. The fact that terror was only "the order of the day" in France proves that other factors—in other words, other *circumstances*—were necessary. An ideological predisposition to approve of terror in many different contexts only explains why the slogan was thinkable, and why revolutionaries chose to call their favored policies "terror."

Among the circumstances that helped determine French political behavior in 1793 and 1794 was precisely the fear, indeed the terror, that the revolutionaries themselves experienced. In this respect historiographical works taking the "emotional turn" can be seen as a subset of the "circumstantial" interpretations of the Terror, especially insofar as the emotion under examination is fear. When describing the revolutionaries' own feelings of fear, Wahnich, Mayer, Linton, Tackett, and Andress attribute that emotion to the menacing presence of counterrevolutionaries, and in this way they continue in the tradition of Aulard, his successors at the Sorbonne, and others who emphasize the role of circumstances.[31] Their point is that the revolutionaries were right to be afraid: counterrevolutionary conspiracies were real.[32] As Rebecca Spang colorfully puts it, "It probably isn't paranoia if there really are people out to get you."[33]

I would like to bracket the question of how justified the revolutionaries were in feeling afraid—since the consequences of that fear were the same whether it was rational or irrational—and simply proceed from the fact that they were truly frightened. This knowledge does not come from the presence or strength of counterrevolutionaries, but rather from the statements of the revolutionaries themselves. To be sure, it is hard to find revolutionaries directly admitting their fear. It is far more common to find them attributing it to their enemies. This is because the "emotional regime" of the Terror discouraged people from acknowledging fear, as Linsday A. H. Parker has shown.[34] Consequently, historians' claims regarding the emotional condition of revolutionaries are frequently inferences based on how they *should have felt* given the dangers they faced. But clues to their frightened condition are evident in the emotives they uttered or wrote when describing or prescribing the emotional state of their enemies.[35] As we have seen in chapters 7 and 8, these emotives were often projections of the revolutionaries' own feelings, as revealed in repeated calls for or celebrations of "encouragement."

What I have added to the historiography of the Terror, then, is a neglected but crucial ideological component dating from the Old Regime and even earlier, together with additional evidence for the psychological circumstances that made both terror speech and advocacy of the Terror thinkable and pleasurable. This is not a totalizing interpretation. It does not even come close to exhausting the myriad causes of the Terror, about which historians will continue to argue.

In this book I have also described, at least in part, the emotional dynamic of the Terror, which helps to explain the source of the energy that sustained it for ten months. Those revolutionaries who found the terror speech of Royer and other Montagnards convincing and motivating, and who therefore "chose Terror," to paraphrase Marisa Linton, created new enemies among all who questioned their extreme measures. Those enemies then became a source of anxiety for the revolutionaries that could seemingly be assuaged only by more terror, both in language and action. This circular process of (1) threatening and attacking, (2) fearing the enemy, and (3) threatening and attacking once again provided emotional energy that sustained the Terror. As with any explanation of the origins of the Terror, this explanation of its energy can only be partial.[36] After all, despite the power of the dynamic I have just described, the Terror *did* end, and not because revolutionaries stopped using terror speech.[37] If anything, it was the ending of the Terror that put a stop to terror speech, not the other way around.

Ultimately, if my explanations of the cause and character of the Terror are limited, there are two reasons for this. First, as I have already suggested, any explanation for a phenomenon as complex as the Terror must be eclectic, drawing on multiple interpretations and in some cases synthesizing the findings of historians who are methodologically or politically hostile to one another. Any one study can only serve as a partial explanation. Second, the genealogical method I have employed in this book is better suited to what Clifford Geertz called "thick description" than it is to causal explanations.[38]

In the event, the ancient practice of referring to terror as a good thing disappeared with remarkable rapidity, and it did so precisely as the Terror in the French Revolution ended. On July 29, 1794 (11 Thermidor), only one day after the execution of Robespierre, Deputy Marc-Antoine Jullien declared on the floor of the Convention, "You have put an end to tyranny, which reigned by terror; it is no longer terror that reigns, it is justice."[39] In this sentence terror displayed radically different meanings from those it had held two days earlier. It was no longer the weapon of free citizens, but the tool of tyranny. It had ceased to be a sign of justice; it was now the opposite of justice. This was a sharp contrast from Robespierre's definition of terror in his famous speech of February 5 (17 Pluviôse): "Terror is nothing but prompt, severe, inflexible justice."[40] Furthermore, in Jullien's rendering terror was a thing of the past. It reigned—past tense—but was "no longer" in force. The Terror suddenly became the name of a historical period.[41]

On August 1 Bertrand Barère reinforced the sense of terror as a detestable thing, and as a thing of the past. He began his speech with the assertion, "Citizens, three days ago everything happily changed around us." "The tyrant" Robespierre was overthrown, and now it was time for "inflexible justice" to replace "stupid terror." Interestingly, he used Robespierre's term "inflexible justice" but now contrasted it with terror. He reiterated the contrast when he proclaimed, "Terror was always the arm of despotism; justice is the arm of liberty."[42] Moreover, the distinction between "was" and "is" highlighted the sense that terror was no more. It is striking that these words came from Barère, the deputy who had been more prolific in his praise of terror than had any of his colleagues. How he managed to get away with this about-face need not concern us here. The point is that the Barère of August 1 lived in a different historical period from the Barère of July 27, at least insofar as the meaning of terror was concerned. Terror, which had been such a positive force for so long, was suddenly a bad thing.

Condemnations of terror came quickly after that. On August 2 (15 Thermidor) two citizens came to the bar of the Convention to denounce Joseph Le Bon, the deputy who had been sent *en mission* to the Pas-de-Calais department and who "reigned by terror."[43] That same day the Popular Society of Cambremer (Calvados) wrote to congratulate the Convention on the execution of Robespierre, whose "favorite means [of government] was terror,"[44] and the administrators of the district of Saint-Flour (Cantal) repudiated the slogan of the Terror, announcing in their letter to the Convention that "terror and oppression will no longer be the order of the day."[45] On August 7 (20 Thermidor) the Jacobins and the municipality of Viry-Châtillon (Seine-et-Oise) denounced "the terror universally spread by this tyrant," Robespierre.[46] On August 10 (23 Thermidor) the Commune and the Jacobins of Bruyères-Libre (formerly Bruyères-le-Châtel, Seine-et-Oise) acknowledged what would have been virtually impossible two weeks prior, namely that "the most zealous partisans of the revolution were trembling in silence" while Robespierre, "making terror the order of the day, let heads fall at will."[47]

A heated exchange at the Convention on August 19 (2 Fructidor) reveals the extent to which "terror" had lost its status as a legitimate political rallying cry. Deputy Louis Louchet was calling for the arrest and imprisonment of all former nobles of military age who were not already incarcerated, being "keenly aware of the magnitude of the perils that still threaten public liberty and of the necessity to dry up as soon as possible the source of our domestic troubles; [and] persuaded that there is no other means of maintaining terror everywhere as the order of the day." At that point, according to the *Archives parlementaires*, he was interrupted by "violent murmurs," and "from everywhere in the hall burst these words: *'justice! justice!'*" Aware of his faux pas, Louchet tried to explain, "What I mean by the word terror is the most severe justice." His colleague Louis-Joseph Charlier came to his aid, declaring, "Justice for patriots, terror for aristocrats." But this distinction did not satisfy the rest of the Convention, and "a great number of voices" called out, "Justice for everyone," which prompted applause. At this point Louchet took back the now-unacceptable expression, claiming, "It never entered my heart to make terror the order of the day."[48]

Thus in an astonishingly short period of time, terror came to stand for injustice, tyranny, and the discredited Robespierre. On August 26 (9 Fructidor) Deputy Louis-Marie Stanislas Fréron called the suddenly maligned entity a "system," perhaps unintentionally attributing to it a coherence that it had never truly had.[49] Others seized on the expression "system of terror," most notably Tallien, who denounced it repeatedly.[50]

Tallien even coined a word to express the idea that terror was above all a system: *terrorisme*. Denouncing Robespierre on August 28 (11 Fructidor), one month after the "tyrant's" execution, Tallien proclaimed, "When terrorism had ceased for a moment to make [people] tremble, he could only tremble himself."[51] Inevitably this neologism was followed by *terroriste*, which first appears in the *Archives parlementaires* in the pages covering October 12 (21 Vendémiaire Year III). On that date the Parisian section Mutius-Scaevola praised the Convention for a proclamation issued on August 2 (15 Thermidor) that explained why Robespierre had been arrested and executed. This proclamation would "foil the projects of the terrorists."[52] The next day the members of the tribunal of the fifth arrondissement in Paris declared "war to the death on the heirs to the crimes of Robespierre, on the terrorists."[53] On October 16 (25 Vendémiaire Year III) the civil tribunal of the district of Laval (Mayenne) wrote to the Convention, "We . . . declare eternal war . . . on the terrorists, on those monsters who, covered in blood, would like to be soaked in it again."[54] On October 20 (29 Vendémiaire) the Popular Society of Lepellier-les-Bois (Eure) "vow[ed] public execration for the drinkers of blood and the terrorists [who are] vile henchmen of the tyrant Robespierre."[55] The following day the company of cannoneers of Lorient (Morbihan) urged the Convention to "annihilate . . . the terrorists," whom they also called "men of blood."[56]

It is this "climate of opinion," to adapt a phrase by Carl Becker, that we inhabit today.[57] We have a post-Thermidorian sensibility toward terror and terrorism. Though these concepts have evolved over more than two centuries to focus on violence perpetrated by enemies of the state rather than by the state itself, we identify much more easily with post-Thermidorian denunciations of terror than with the idea that it is salutary, majestic, and divine.

The transition from revering to reviling terror is a good example of what Nietzsche called the "transvaluation of values."[58] But how did it happen? What accounts for this sudden and enduring shift? A thorough explanation may not be possible. After all, when producing a "genealogy," as Nietzsche understood it, one must be prepared to find contingency.[59] Perhaps a stroke of genius (or luck) on the part of Thermidorians such as Barère and Tallien enabled them to condense the traumatic experience of the previous months— and shield themselves from their own complicity in the violence—into a single, memorable term. There is no reason to believe that the momentous cultural shift that took place after 9 Thermidor was inevitable.

Still, the new association of terror with injustice is explicable. Though terror meant many things in the Year II, in many instances it simply meant what historians have since called "the Terror." In other words, it largely referred to the policies of the Committee of Public Safety, which in turn came to be identified with Robespierre alone. Thus the word was bound up with the fate of Robespierre. Once he was executed and posthumously reviled, what seemed to be *his* terror lost legitimacy and indeed became a term of abuse that could be used to discredit political adversaries. Much of this narrowing of the word's meaning took place in the days and weeks after Robespierre's death, as we have just seen. The conflation of "terror" and "terrorism" further hardened the meaning of the former, which was now a "system" that could be reduced to a set of policies that deprived people of their liberty and set the guillotine in continuous motion. When conceived of as a period, for many "the Terror" came to encapsulate a wide array of sufferings, from loss of property to grief over executed loved ones, not to mention fear of denunciation and death. In this respect *la Terreur* served as what Maurice Halbwachs called a "gripping abbreviation," or a "summary of collective reflections and feelings."[60] Why the transvaluation was so lasting is a question that far exceeds the capacity of this study, but the fact is that it has endured. It is in large measure thanks to the Thermidorians that we call almost anyone who kills for political reasons a terrorist and that a massive effort to thwart such killers has been dubbed a "war on terror."

The French Revolution was not that long ago, and the cultural environment in which "terror" has exclusively negative meanings is relatively new. There are people today who are only a few degrees of separation from witnesses to the Revolution. And when compared to the centuries-long period when "terror" had largely positive emotional connotations, our post-Thermidorian attitude toward the word is of particularly recent vintage. This is worth remembering at a time when our contemporaries treat the advocacy of terror as alien to the Western tradition.

ACKNOWLEDGMENTS

A fellowship at the Shelby Cullom Davis Center for Historical Studies at Princeton University gave me an uninterrupted academic year (2007–8) and a stimulating environment in which to research and begin writing this book. Sabbaticals from the College of William and Mary in 2008–9 and 2012–13 were likewise invaluable. The college also provided me with funds to attend meetings of the Society for French Historical Studies, the Western Society for French History, and the Consortium on the Revolutionary Era, 1750–1850, at which I gave papers on various aspects of terror in eighteenth-century France and benefited from my colleagues' comments. Numerous institutions generously invited me to speak on my work in progress: the history departments of Florida State University, the University of Pittsburgh, and the American University of Paris; the Center for Eighteenth-Century Studies at Indiana University; the Triangle Legal History Seminar at Duke University; and the Center for European Studies at Harvard University. Closer to home I benefited from workshopping portions of my project at William and Mary, at both the Lyon Gardiner Tyler Department of History and the Omohundro Institute for Early American History and Culture. Finally, both the history department and the office of the Dean of Arts and Sciences at the college provided a publication subvention for this book.

I wish to thank Alan Thomas, editorial director for humanities and social sciences at the University of Chicago Press, for his interest in my project. I am also grateful to the many people who read the book manuscript and provided me with helpful comments and criticisms. Among these are the acquisitions editor Priya Nelson at the University of Chicago Press, the two anonymous outside readers for the press, and the four equally anonymous referees for my promotion application. In addition, David Bell read several iterations of this book as well as numerous research proposals and unfailingly offered sage advice. Jeffrey Freedman read the entire manuscript and six days later sent me what was effectively a complete reader's report. Tom Phelps also took the time to read the whole manuscript and to discuss it with me. Tom Kselman read and commented on the introduction and the chapter "Holy Terror and Divine Majesty." I have done my best to respond to their suggestions for improving this book. In addition, I would like to thank the copyeditor Barbara Norton for catching errors in the manuscript and the project editor Mary Corrado for overseeing the complex logistics of publication.

Conversations with the following people over the past decade have helped me clarify the ideas presented in this book: Alvaro Acuña, Jeremy Adelman, Jim Allegro, David Andress, Tim Barnard, Tuška Beneš, Mike Blum, Gail Bossenga, Julian Bourg, Chandos Brown, Nina Caputo, Jeremy Caradonna, Roy Chan, Linda Colley, Magali Compan, Kate Cooper, Fred Corney, Bob Darnton, Julia Douthwaite, Dan Edelstein, Alexander Etkind, Jack Farraj, Sergio Ferrarese, Bill Fisher, Jeffrey Freedman, Jonathan Glasser, Jan Goldstein, Leonard Groopman, Lisbeth Haas, Ruth Harris, Mitchell Hart, Patrice Higonnet, Dale Hoak, Rhys Isaac, Dominic Janes, Colin Jones, Arthur Knight, Tom Kselman, Michael Laffan, Kris Lane, David Lederer, Christina Lee, David Leheny, Rob Leventhal, Sara Lipton, Melani McAlister, Terry Meyers, Phil Nord, Mark Olsen, Julia Osman, Derek Penslar, Jan Plamper, Jeremy Popkin, Adam Potkay, Gyan Prakash, Richard Price, Sasha Prokhorov, Meghan Roberts, Brett Rushforth, Michael Saman, Arthur Schechter, Ute Schechter, Christopher Schmidt-Nowara, Pierre Serna, Rebecca Spang, Miranda Spieler, Marla Stone, Carl Strikwerda, Ravi Sundaram, Fredrika Teute, Judith Vishniac, Max Weiss, Sibel Zandi-Sayek, and Naama Zahavi-Ely.

As the above list shows, I talked a lot about my book before completing it. Some people endured more of my observations about terror in eighteenth-century France—or about my own terror of failing to complete the book—than others: my spouse, Ute Schechter; my son, Arthur Schechter; and my friends Rob Leventhal, Arthur Knight, and Jean-Pierre (J-P) Babka, who all generously supplied helpful ideas, moral support, or both. Over the last two years J-P in particular has been a kind of counselor, therapist, and life coach, but above all a friend who has always had a knack for saying the right thing to motivate me. I therefore dedicate this book to him.

NOTES

INTRODUCTION

1. On this revolutionary institution see Richard Cobb, *The People's Armies: The Armées Révolutionnaires, Instrument of the Terror in the Departments, April 1793 to Floréal Year II*, trans. Marianne Elliott (New Haven, CT: Yale University Press, 1987).

2. Jérôme Mavidal et al., eds., *Archives parlementaires de 1787 à 1860, première série (1787–1799)* (Paris: 1867–2005), vol. 73, 419. On Royer see Dan Edelstein, *The Terror of Natural Right: Republicanism, the Cult of Nature, and the French Revolution* (Chicago: University of Chicago Press, 2009), 137–38 and 138n. Jean-Clément Martin notes that the Convention did not make an official decree declaring terror "the order of the day," as historians have long reported: *Violence et révolution: Essai sur la naissance d'un mythe national* (Paris: Seuil, 2006), 188; and *Nouvelle histoire de la Révolution française* (Paris: Perrin, 2012), 395. Nevertheless, the frequent repetition of the phrase "la terreur à l'ordre du jour" and the belief that terror was (or ought to be) the order of the day constituted a cultural reality that was at least as significant as any piece of legislation.

3. *Archives parlementaires*, vol. 73, 425.

4. *Archives parlementaires*, vol. 75, 437. Emphasis in the original.

5. *Archives parlementaires*, vol. 75, 441.

6. *Archives parlementaires*, vol. 75, 573. To place this statement in its proper context, it must be acknowledged that Boilleau was defending himself as an accused Girondin deputy. (He was unsuccessful and went to the guillotine on October 31, 1793.) But what is important to our inquiry is the fact that he used the image of terror as the order of the day to establish his radical credentials.

7. *Archives parlementaires*, vol. 73, 419 and 425; vol. 75, 437, 441, and 573; vol. 76, 84, 420, and 596; vol. 77, 30, 355, 543, and 559; vol. 78, 22, 37, 121, 350, 647, and 705; vol. 79, 81, 120, 157, 167, 317, 366, 387, 391, 441, 456, 558, 566, 634, 645, and 663; vol. 80, 57, 84, 112, 155, 164, 190, 218, and 532; vol. 81, 9, 20, 396, and 469; vol. 82, 40, 108, 121, 170, 185, 287, 328, 365, 487, 556, and 647; vol. 83, 82, 221, 303, 354, 627, and 668; vol. 84, 74, 458 and 589; vol. 85, 6, 243, 451, 472, 494, 499, 520, and 551; vol. 86, 129, 194, 206, 281, 300, 366, 370–71, 574, 691, and 696; vol. 87, 68, 93, 323, 393, 423, 427, 429, 523, 550, 587,

618, 620, and 690; vol. 88, 109, 128, 135, 161, 177, 260, 273, 313, 330, 520, 553, 554, and 627; vol. 89, 17, 45, 104, 150, 275, 294, 312, 325, 363, 366, 441, 443, 467, 489, and 546; vol. 90, 431, 463, and 543; vol. 91, 120, 126, 567, and 601; vol. 92, 339, 391, 392, and 411; and vol. 93, 526.

8. The deputy who used the expression most frequently was Barère. *Archives parlementaires*, vol. 73, 425; vol. 82, 365; vol. 86, 129; vol. 92, 391; and vol. 93, 368. See also vol. 78, 647 (Barras and Fréron); vol. 79, 456 (Billaud-Varenne); vol. 75, 573 (Boilleau); vol. 78, 705 (Bourdon de l'Oise); vol. 80, 164–65 (Danton); vol. 76, 596; and vol. 83, 627 (Dartigoeyte); vol. 85, 472 (Dubarran); vol. 79, 167 (Dufourny); vol. 79, 645 (Forestier); vol. 79, 566 (Guimerteau); vol. 82, 487 (Hérault de Séchelles); vol. 82, 328 (Lanot); vol. 77, 30 (Laplanche); vol. 88, 330 (Louchet); vol. 88, 135 (Mallarmé); vol. 79, 120 (Milhaud); vol. 79, 366 (Prieur de la Marne); and vol. 79, 157 (Vadier).

9. *Archives parlementaires*, vol. 79, 81; vol. 80, 112; vol. 86, 281; vol. 87, 93; and vol. 92, 411.

10. *Archives parlementaires*, vol. 78, 22; vol. 78, 37; and vol. 82, 170. On March 26, 1794, the Convention also received a "numerous deputation of the Society of the Defenders of the Republic" (vol. 87, 393).

11. Though historians in the past decades have tended to be skeptical about positing Enlightenment influence on the French Revolution, Jonathan Israel has recently argued that the Enlightenment is indeed the root of the Revolution. Writing specifically of the "radical Enlightenment," exemplified by Diderot, Helvétius, and Holbach, Israel affirms that this intellectual movement was "incontrovertibly the one 'big' cause of the French Revolution." *Revolutionary Ideas: An Intellectual History of the French Revolution from the Rights of Man to Robespierre* (Princeton, NJ: Princeton University Press, 2014), 708. For a more nuanced approach to the role of the Enlightenment in the French Revolution, see Dan Edelstein, "Enlightenment Rights Talk," *Journal of Modern History* 86 (September 2014): 530–65. By contrast, Roger Chartier has memorably insisted that instead of asking whether the Enlightenment "produced" the Revolution, historians should "consider . . . that it was the Revolution that invented the Enlightenment." *The Cultural Origins of the French Revolution*, trans. Lydia G. Cochrane (Durham, NC: Duke University Press, 1991), 5.

12. Max Horkheimer and Theodor W. Adorno, *Dialektik der Aufklärung* (New York: Social Studies Association, 1944), 7. The authors wrote of "Enlightenment" rather than "the Enlightenment," as they sought to describe a mindset that was not limited to the eighteenth century.

13. Charles-Louis de Secondat de Montesquieu, *De l'esprit des loix . . .* (Geneva, 1748), vol. 1, book 3, chapter 9, 41–42.

14. Most of the work on the language of terror in eighteenth-century France has focused on the period of the Revolution itself. See, for example, Mona Ozouf, "War and Terror in French Revolutionary Discourse (1792–1794)," *Journal of Modern History* 56, no. 4 (December 1984): 579–97; and Jacques Guilhaumou, "La formation d'un mot d'ordre: 'Plaçons la terreur à l'ordre du jour' (13 juillet 1793–5 septembre 1793)," in Bertrand Conein and Jacques Guilhaumou, eds., *La rhétorique du discours, objet d'histoire (XVIIIᵉ–XXᵉ siècles)* (Lille: Presses universitaires de Lille, 1981), 149–96, and "*La terreur à l'ordre du jour*: Un parcours en révolution (1793–1794)," *Révolution Française.net*,

Mots, January 6, 2007, http://revolution-francaise.net/2007/01/06/94-la-terreur-a-lordre
-du-jour-un-parcours-en-revolution-juillet-1793-mars-1794; accessed February 3, 2016. The
lexicon entry by Gerd van den Heuvel, "Terreur, terroriste, terrorisme," in *Handbuch
politisch-sozialer Grundbegriffe in Frankreich, 1680–1820*, ed. Rolf Reichardt et al.
(Munich: Oldenbourg, 1985), vol. 3, 89–132, devotes eight pages to the Old Regime but
otherwise focuses on the Revolution itself. Annie Jourdan's comparative study of terror
discourse in France, the Netherlands, and the United States during the Age of Revolution allocates four pages to prerevolutionary French writing. "Les discours de la terreur
à l'époque révolutionnaire (1776–1798): Étude comparative sur une notion ambiguë,"
French Historical Studies 36 (Winter 2013): 52–81. For an article-length study devoted to
the language of terror in Old Regime France see George Armstrong Kelly, "Conceptual
Sources of the Terror," *Eighteenth-Century Studies* 14 (Autumn 1980): 18–36.

15. Arthur O. Lovejoy, *The Great Chain of Being* (Cambridge, MA: Harvard University
Press, 1936), especially 3–23 on "unit ideas"; and Daniel Wickberg, "In the Environment
of Ideas: Arthur Lovejoy and the History of Ideas as a Form of Cultural History," *Modern
Intellectual History* 11 (August 2014): 439–64. The "history of ideas" approach has long
been in disrepute among practitioners of the "linguistic turn" in intellectual history,
with Quentin Skinner and J. G. A. Pocock leading the charge against the supposedly naive
"reification" of unchanging ideas and insisting instead that historians carefully contex-
tualize statements as "language games" designed to produce specific political outcomes.
Quentin Skinner, "Meaning and Understanding in the History of Ideas," *History and
Theory* 8, no. 1 (1969): 3–53; and J. G. A. Pocock, "Political Languages and Their Implications," in *Politics, Language and Time: Essays on Political Thought and History* (Chicago:
University of Chicago Press, 1971), 3–41. For an application of the Cambridge School
approach (modified by Foucauldian methods) to eighteenth-century French intellectual
history, see Keith Michael Baker, "On the Problem of the Ideological Origins of the French
Revolution," in *Inventing the French Revolution: Essays on French Political Culture in
the Eighteenth Century* (Cambridge: Cambridge University Press, 1990), 12–27. More
recently, however, intellectual historians have shown that Lovejoy was not as naive or
indifferent to context as Pocock and Skinner made him out to be, and that it is possible to
undertake a responsible "neo-Lovejovian" approach to the history of ideas. See John P. Diggins, "Arthur O. Lovejoy and the Challenge of Intellectual History," *Journal of the History
of Ideas* 67 (January 2006): 181–208; and Darrin M. McMahon, "The Return of the History
of Ideas?" in *Rethinking Modern European Intellectual History*, ed. Darrin M. McMahon
and Samuel Moyn (Oxford and New York: Oxford University Press, 2014), 13–31.

16. "A word becomes—in our method—a concept when the plenitude of a socio-
political relationship of meanings in which—and for which—a word is used goes together
into a word." Reinhart Koselleck, "Einleitung," in *Geschichtliche Grundbegriffe: Historisches Lexikon zur politisch-sozialen Sprache in Deutschland*, ed. Otto Brunner, Werner
Konze, and Reinhart Koselleck (Stuttgart: Ernst Klett Verlag, 1972), vol. 1, xxii. For a helpful introduction to *Begriffsgeschichte* see Melvin Richter, *The History of Political and Social Concepts: A Critical Introduction* (New York: Oxford University Press, 1995).

17. On December 15, 1793 (25 Frimaire Year II), the Convention received a letter
from the administrators of the Department of the Gers containing the reminder, "You made
Terror the order of the day [*Vous mîtes la Terreur à l'ordre du jour*]" and requesting the

application of this principle to "those who would dare protest against the measures of the preserving genius of liberty." *Archives parlementaires*, vol. 81, 469.

18. Rudolf Walther, "Terror, Terrorismus," in *Geschichtliche Grundbegriffe*, vol. 6, 323–444.

19. Van den Heuvel, "Terreur, terroriste, terrorisme," in *Handbuch*, vol. 3, 89–132.

20. Koselleck, "Einleitung," xiv.

21. Koselleck wrote of "words . . . that are first promoted [*die erst . . . aufrücken*] to modern concepts." "Einleitung," xiv.

22. Occasionally I will analyze more than one lexeme. The principal one is *terreur*. On a few occasions, however, I will examine the meanings of the lexemes *terreurs, terrible*, and *terribles*.

23. On the distinction between semasiology and onomasiology see Dirk Geeraerts, Stefan Grondelaers and Peter Bakema, *The Structure of Lexical Variation: Meaning, Naming, and Context* (Berlin and New York: Mouton de Gruyter, 1994), 1–16.

24. Mary Ann Glendon, *Rights Talk: The Impoverishment of Political Discourse* (New York: Free Press, 1991).

25. Dan Edelstein, "Enlightenment Rights Talk," *Journal of Modern History* 86 (September 2014): 530–65.

26. Ferdinand de Saussure, *Course in General Linguistics* (1916), trans. Roy Harris (LaSalle, IL: Open Court, 1983).

27. Friedrich Nietzsche, *On the Genealogy of Morals and Ecce Homo*, trans., ed., and with commentary by Walter Kaufmann (New York: Random House, 1967).

28. Michel Foucault, "Nietzsche, Genealogy, History," in Paul Rabinow, *The Foucault Reader* (New York: Pantheon, 1984), 76.

29. The similarities between French and non-French conceptions of terror will be clear in those sections of the book analyzing texts that were translated into French. Also, for terror speech elsewhere in Europe, see my "Conceptions of Terror in Eighteenth-Century Europe," in *Facing Fear: The History of an Emotion in Global Perspective*, ed. Michael Laffan and Max Weiss (Princeton, NJ: Princeton University Press, 2012), 31–53; and "The Terror of their Enemies: Reflections on a Trope in Eighteenth-Century Historiography," in *Historical Reflections/Réflexions historiques* 36 (Spring 2010): 53–75.

30. For examples of *Umwerthung* (then spelled with an "h") see "Zur Genealogie der Moral," in *Nietzsche's Werke*, ed. Ernst Holzer and Otto Crusius (Leipzig, 1899), vol. 7, 313 and 315. See also Nietzsche's "Jenseits von Gut und Böse," in *Werke*, vol. 7, 71 and 138.

31. Foucault, "Nietzsche," 76.

32. J[ohn] L[angshaw] Austin, *How to Do Things with Words* (Cambridge, MA: Harvard University Press, 1962).

33. William Reddy, *The Navigation of Feeling: A Framework for the History of Emotions* (Cambridge: Cambridge University Press, 2001), 96–107.

34. Reddy asserts, "Claims about third persons who are not present are not emotives" but merely "descriptive or constative in form." *Navigation*, 107.

35. Jean-Baptiste Massillon, "Discours sur la nécessité où sont les ministres de se renouveler dans l'esprit de leur vocation," in *Conférences et discours synodaux sur les principaux devoirs des ecclésiastiques* (Paris, 1759), vol. 2, 179–80.

36. Massillon, "Discours," in *Conférences*, vol. 2, 318, 319, 321, 325, and 335.

37. *Archives parlementaires*, vol. 76, 671.

38. Baker, "Ideological Origins," 13.

39. Reddy, *Navigation*, 14–15, and "Historical Research on the Self and Emotions," *Emotion Review* 1 (October 2009): 302–15.

40. Peter N. Stearns with Carol Z. Stearns, "Emotionology: Clarifying the History of Emotions and Emotional Standards," *American Historical Review* 90 (October 1985): 813–36.

41. Rosenwein writes of "emotional communities": "These are precisely the same as social communities—families, neighborhoods, parliaments, guilds, monasteries, parish church memberships—but the researcher looking at them seeks above all to uncover systems of feeling. what these communities (and the individuals within them) define and assess as valuable or harmful to them; the evaluations that they make about others' emotions; the nature of the affective bonds between people that they recognize; and the modes of emotional expression that they expect, encourage, tolerate, and deplore." Barbara H. Rosenwein, "Worrying about Emotions in History," *American Historical Review* 107 (June 2002): 821–45 (quote on 842). For Rosenwein's views about the limits of historians' access to the emotions of others, see her "Problems and Methods in the History of Emotions," *Passions in Context: Journal of the History and Philosophy of the Emotions* 1 (2010): 11n, www.passionsincontext.de/uploads/media/01_Rosenwein.pdf, accessed March 23, 2013.

42. Lovejoy, *Great Chain*, 15.

43. I will occasionally have recourse to the inelegant "terribleness" to avoid ambiguity. Though it is unlikely that anyone would read "God's terror" as meaning "God's feelings of terror," in other cases where "terror" is used in the possessive it might be unclear whether the noun is meant to be an emotion or the source of that emotion (as in the metonym "the terror of his enemies").

44. Jean-Paul Marat, *De l'homme, ou Des principes et des loix de l'influence de l'âme sur le corps, et du corps sur l'âme* (Amsterdam, 1775), vol. 2, 54–55.

45. Peter E. Gordon, "Contextualism and Criticism in the History of Ideas," in *Rethinking Modern European Intellectual History*, ed. Darrin M. McMahon and Samuel Moyn (Oxford and New York: Oxford University Press, 2014), 32–55.

46. Montesquieu wrote, "The severity of punishments is more suited to the Despotic Government, whose principle is terror [*la terreur*], than to Monarchy and the Republic, which rely on [*qui ont pour ressort*] honor and virtue [respectively]." *Esprit des loix*, vol. 1, book 6, chapter 9, 130. This was the only reference to "terreur" as the "principle" of despotism. Otherwise Montesquieu referred to "fear" (*la crainte*): book 3, chapter 9, 41–42; book 3, chapter 11, 45; book 4, chapter 1, 46; book 4, chapter 3, 52; book 4, chapter 5, 54; book 4, chapter 7, 59; book 5, chapter 14, 93 and 95; book 6, chapter 18, 146; book 6, 21, 149; and book 12, chapter 30, 335. Nevertheless, other commentators preferred the word *terreur* when describing despotism. For example, Mirabeau wrote that the word "despotism" had "become in our languages the sign of tyranny and the warning of terror." [Honoré Gabriel de Riqueti, comte de Mirabeau], *Essai sur le despotisme* (London [i.e., Paris], 1776), 11–12.

47. Holbach described the world's first religions as the product of tyrants who "exercised the most absolute power" and "reigned by terror," and he condemned other "impostors" who "in all ages, in all countries" made use of "terror, ignorance and credulity" as

the "true supports of their power." Paul Henri Thiry, baron d'Holbach, *La contagion sacrée, ou Histoire naturelle de la superstition* (London [i.e., Amsterdam?], 1768), vol. 1, 1, 21. Helvétius similarly denounced "the one who in this century has wished . . . to reign by terror, establish the tribunal of the Inquisition, burn his fellows and appropriate their fortune." Claude-Adrien Helvétius, *De l'homme, de ses facultés intellectuelles, et de son éducation . . .* (London [i.e., Paris], 1773), vol. 1, 307–8. For more examples of negative Enlightenment attitudes toward religious terror, see my "Conceptions of Terror in the European Enlightenment," 35–38.

48. I borrow the notion of the "thinkable" from Roger Chartier, *The Cultural Origins of the French Revolution*, trans. Lydia G. Cochrane (Durham, NC: Duke University Press, 1991), 2.

49. Robert Darnton, *The Great Cat Massacre and Other Episodes in French Cultural History* (New York: Vintage, 1984), 5.

50. Johann Gottfried von Herder, *Auch eine Philosophie der Geschichte zur Bildung der Menschheit* ([Riga], 1774), 46.

CHAPTER ONE

1. We know much about "forbidden best-sellers" thanks to the work of Robert Darnton and, more recently, Simon Burrows. See Darnton, *The Forbidden Best-Sellers of Pre-Revolutionary France* (New York: Norton, 1996); and Burrows, "French Banned Books in International Perspective, 1770–1789," in *Experiencing the French Revolution*, ed. David Andress (Oxford: Voltaire Foundation, 2013), 19–45. We know less about authorized best-sellers, including, perhaps surprisingly, the Bible. Yet Jean-Noël Jeanneney writes that since the Middle Ages the Bible has been "of all books the most printed." Martine Delaveau and Denise Hillard, eds., *Bibles imprimées du xve au xviiie siècle conservées à Paris* (Paris: Bibliothèque nationale de France, 2002), ix.

2. Anne Sauvy, "Lecture et diffusion de la Bible en France," in *Le siècle des Lumières et la Bible*, ed. Yvon Belaval and Dominique Bourel (Paris: Beauchesne, 1986), 25–46.

3. Jean-Baptiste Malou, *La lecture de la Sainte Bible en langue vulgaire . . .* (Louvain, 1846), vol. 1, 17–18.

4. Cited in Sauvy, "Lecture et diffusion," 25–26. Cf. Guillaume Hyacinthe Bougeant, *Exposition de la doctrine chrétienne par demandes et par réponses* (Paris, 1741), 206.

5. Gen. 9:2 and 35:5; Exod. 20:20 and 23:27; Deut. 2:25, 11:25, and 28:34; Josh. 2:9 and 9:24; 1 Chron. 17:21, 14:14, and 15:5; Esther 8:17; Job 6:4, 13:11, 15:21, 25:2, 37:2, and 39:20; Pss. 9:21, 54:5, 54:15, 87:17, and 104:38; Prov. 1:33, 3:25, 20:2, and 28:1; Isa. 7:25, 8:13, 10:18, 10:33, 30:17 (twice), 30:30, and 31:9; Jer. 15:8, 20:10, 30:5, 32:21, 46:5, and 49:5; Ezek. 30:13, 32:24, 32:25, 32:27, 32:32, and 34:28; Dan. 10:7; and Luke 21:11.

6. Jer. 32:21.

7. 1 Chron. 17:21.

8. Ezek. 30:13.

9. Isa. 30:30.

10. Isa. 31:9.

11. Isa. 10:33.

12. Deut. 28:34.

13. Jer. 15:8.

14. Exod. 23:27.

15. Deut. 11:25.

16. Deut. 2: 25.

17. Josh. 2:9.

18. Esther 8:14.

19. Though Ezekiel typically spoke of Sheol or the Pit, Jerome christianized the location as *infernus* or hell.

20. Ezek. 32:24.

21. Ezek. 32:27.

22. Ezek. 32:32.

23. Exod. 28.17.

24. Exod. 15:10.

25. Deut. 7:21.

26. Deut. 10:17 and 10:21.

27. Ps. 46:3.

28. Ps. 65:3.

29. Luke 21:11.

30. Heb. 10:27.

31. François Dupuigrenet Desroussilles, "La production biblique catholique en France au XVIIIᵉ siècle," in Belaval and Dominique Bourel, *Le siècle des Lumières et la Bible*, 81.

32. Gen. 9:2 and 35:5; Exod. 19:18 and 23:27; Deut. 2:25 and 11:25; Josh. 2:29 and 9:24; Judg. 4:15; 1 Kings 7:10; 1 Chron. 15:5 and 17:21; 2 Chron. 17:10 and 20:29; Neh. 6:14, 6:16, and 15:5; Judith 2:18 and 11:9; Esther 8:17; Job 6:4, 9:34, 13:11, 13:21, 39:20, and 41:5; Ps. 87:17; Prov. 20:2; Ecclus. 36:1; Isa. 2:10, 8:13, 14:16, and 30:17; Jer. 15:8, 32:21, 46:5, 49:29, and 50:34; Ezek. 30:13, 32:23, 32:24, 32:25, 32:26, 32:27, and 32:32; Zech. 1:21; 1 Macc. 3:6 and 3:25; and 2 Macc. 12:22 and 15:23.

33. Gen. 9:2 and 35:5; Exod. 23:27; Deut. 2:25 and 11:25; Josh. 2:29 and 9:24; 1 Chron. 17: 21; 2 Chron. 15:5; Esther 8:17; Job 6:4, 13:11, and 39:20; Ps. 87:17; Prov. 20:2; Isa. 8:13 and 30:17; Jer. 15:8, 32:21, and 46:5; and Ezek. 30:13; 32:24, 32:25, 32:27, and 32:32.

34. *La Sainte Bible contentant l'Ancien et le Nouveau Testament, traduite en françois sur la Vulgate: Par Monsieur Le Maistre de Saci; Tome Premier* (Paris, 1742), 10.

35. Exod. 23:27.

36. Deut. 2:25.

37. Jer. 32:21.

38. Exod. 20:20.

39. Deut. 28:34.

40. Ps. 54:5.

41. Ps. 104:38; Prov. 3:25; Isa. 10:18 and 31:9; and Jer. 20:10 and 49:5.

42. 2 Chron. 14:14 and Job 13:11.

43. Exod. 19:18; Judg. 4:15; 1 Kings 7:10; 1 Chron. 15:5; 2 Chron. 17:10 and 20:29; Neh. 6:14, 6:16, and 15:5; Judith 2:18 and 11:9; Esther 8:17; Job 9:34, 13:21, and 41:5; Ecclus. 36:1; Isa. 2:10, 14:16, and 30:7; Jer. 49:29 and 50:34; Ezek. 32:23 and 32:26; Zech. 1:21; 1 Macc. 3:6 and 3:25; and 2 Macc. 12:22 and 15:23.

44. 2 Chron. 17:10.

45. 2 Chron. 20:29.

46. Ecclus. 36:2.

47. 1 Macc. 3:6.

48. 1 Macc. 3:35.

49. Jacques-Bénigne Bossuet, *Élévations à Dieu sur tous les mystères de la religion chrétienne* (Paris, 1727; reprint, Paris: Vrin, 1962), 463.

50. Augustine, Sermon 279, *Sermones*, in *Opera omnia: Patrologiae cursus completus . . . , Series Latina*, vol. 38, ed. J.-P. Migne (Paris: Migne, 1861), col. 1275.

51. René-Jean Hesbert, *Saint Augustin Maître de Bossuet* (Paris: Nouvelles éditions latines, 1980), 7.

52. Bossuet, *Élévations*, 265.

53. Augustine, *The Confessions of Saint Augustine*, ed. John Gibb and William Montgomery (Cambridge: Cambridge University Press, 1908), p. 333, 11.2.2.

54. Augustine, *De catechizandis rudibus*, in *S. Aurelius Augustinus episcopus Hipponensis: De catechizandis rudibus, De fide rerum quæ non videntur, De utilitate credendi . . . ,* ed. C. Marriott (Oxford: J. Parker, 1869), p. 11, para. 9, line 1.

55. Jeanne-Marie Bouvier de La Motte, Madame Du Chesnoy Guyon, *Lettres chrétiennes et spirituelles sur divers sujets . . .* (Cologne, 1717–18), vol. 1, 427–28.

56. Guyon, *Lettres*, vol. 2, 538–39.

57. Guyon, *Lettres*, vol. 2, 101.

58. Guyon, *Lettres*, vol. 2, 278.

59. Guyon, *Lettres*, vol. 3, 150–51.

60. Esprit Fléchier, "Poëme Chrétien sur la Béatitude, contre les illusions du Quiétisme," (1696–99) in *Œuvres complètes de Messire Esprit Fléchier* (Nîmes, 1782), vol. 9, 186. On the date range in which the poem was written see Abbé A[ntonin] Fabre, *La jeunesse de Fléchier* (Paris, 1882), vol. 2, 277.

61. Bridel Arleville, *Le petit rhétoricien françois . . .* (London, 1791), 261.

62. According to WorldCat, more than 130 volumes of Massillon's writings were published over the course of the eighteenth century. Compilations of his synodal addresses appeared in at least eleven editions published in 1746, 1752, 1753, 1759, 1761 (twice), 1764, 1765, 1771, 1775, and 1776.

63. Jean-Baptiste Massillon, "Discours sur la nécessité où sont les ministres de se renouveler dans l'esprit de leur vocation," in *Conférences et discours synodaux sur les principaux devoirs des ecclésiastiques, avec un recueil de mandemens sur différens sujets* (Paris, 1761), vol. 2, 179–80.

64. Massillon, *Conférences*, vol. 2, 196.

65. Massillon, *Conférences*, vol. 2, 221.

66. Massillon, *Conférences*, vol. 2, 268–69.

67. Massillon, *Conférences*, vol. 2, 279.

68. Massillon, *Conférences*, vol. 2, 318, 319, 321, 325, and 335.

69. Massillon, *Conférences*, vol. 2, 364–65.

70. Antoine Arnauld, *De la fréquente communion* (Paris, 1643), 430.

71. Arnauld, *De la fréquente communion*, 507.

72. Antoine de Malvin de Montazet, *Instruction pastorale . . .* (Paris and Lyon, 1776), 61–62.

73. Montazet, *Instruction*, 31.

74. Jean Antoine Gazaignes, *Manuel des pèlerins de Port-Royal des Champs* (n.p., 1767), 22; Bonaventure Racine, *Abrégé de l'histoire ecclésiastique, contenant les événemens considérables de chaque siècle* . . . (Cologne, 1767), vol. 11, 288; and Mlle. Poulain de Nogent, *Nouvelle histoire abrégée de l'Abbaye de Port-Royal* . . . (Paris, 1786), vol. 1, 196. Cf. Nicolas Petitpied, *Obedientiæ credulæ vana religio* . . . (n.p., 1708), vol. 2, 202. Petitpied observed that the nuns' prayer was *plena sacri terroris*, or "full of sacred terror."

75. Dale Van Kley, *The Religious Origins of the French Revolution: From Calvin to the Civil Constitution, 1560–1791* (New Haven, CT: Yale University Press, 1996).

76. Timoléon Cheminais de Montaigu, *Sermons du Père Cheminais, de la Compagnie de Jésus* (Paris, 1764), vol. 1, 192.

77. WorldCat lists editions of sermons by Père Cheminais from 1690, 1691, 1692, 1693, 1694, 1695, 1699, 1700, 1702, 1710, 1711, 1720, 1729, 1730, 1735, 1737, 1740, 1741, 1744, 1754, 1757, 1764, 1765, 1776, and 1778.

78. Jean François Copel, *Sermons du R. Père Élisée, Carme Déchaussé, Prédicateur du Roi* (Paris, 1785), vol. 3, 132.

79. Copel, *Sermons*, vol. 3, 171 and 189.

80. Jean Soanen, *Sermons sur différents sujets prêchés devant le Roi, par le Père Soanen, Prêtre de l'Oratoire* (Lyon, 1769), 273–74.

81. On Soanen see Kley, *Religious Origins*, 86–87, 94–96, 111, 113, and 171.

82. Pierre Pacaud, *Discours de piété sur les plus importans objets de la religion* . . . (Liège, 1762), vol. 1, 100. On Pacaud see *Dictionnaire de spiritualité: Ascétique et mystique; Doctrine et histoire* (Paris: Beauchesne, 1935–95), s.v. "Pacaud (Pierre), oratorien, 1682–1760."

83. Jean-Baptiste Surian, "Sermon pour le mardi de la cinquième semaine de Caresme," in *Sermons des plus célèbres prédicateurs de ce tems, pour le Caresme, & quelques autres tems de l'année* (Brussels, 1740), vol. 2, 334. On Surian's anti-Jansenist convictions see Théophile Berengier, *Notice sur Mgr. Jean-Baptiste de Surian, éveque de Vence, 1727–1754* (Marseille, 1894), 32.

84. Pierre-Anastase Torné, *Sermons prêchés devant le roi, pendant le Carême de 1764* (Paris, 1765), 394–95.

85. On Torné see Adolphe Robert, Edgar Bourloton and Gaston Cougny, eds., *Dictionnaire des parlementaires français* . . . (Paris: 1889–91), s.v. "Torné (Pierre-Athanase [*sic*])," vol. 5, 430. On the Doctrinaires see Sharon Kettering, *French Society: 1589–1715* (Harlow and New York: Longman, 2001), 99.

86. Soanen, *Sermons*, 309–10.

87. Soanen, *Sermons*, 258.

88. Denis-Xavier Clément, *Sermons de M. L'Abbé Clément: Mystères* (Paris, 1771), vol. 2, 113.

89. Paul César de Ciceri, *Sermons et panégyriques* (Avignon, 1761), 208. He declared later in the same sermon, "Let us return humbly to God, who only thunders in our ears today with the terror of his judgments to recall us to him" (209). On Ciceri, who was born in Cavaillon in the Comtat Venaissin in 1678 and died in 1759, see *Mémoires pour l'histoire des sciences et beaux-arts*, January 1762, 92–105.

90. Martin Pallu, *Sermons du père Pallu, de la Compagnie de Jésus: Avent* (Paris, 1759), 223.

91. François-Valentin Mulot, *Essais de Sermons prêchés à l'Hôtel-Dieu de Paris* (Paris, 1781), 6.

92. Bossuet, *Élévations*, 265.

93. For other positive valuations of *terreur* in eighteenth-century French sermons see, for example, Copel, *Sermons*, vol. 2, 215–18; Denis-Xavier Clément, *Sermons pour l'Avent* (Paris, 1770), 8–9; Louis Bourdaloue, *Sermons* (Lyon, 1770), vol. 1, 187 and 217; Charles Frey de Neuville, *Sermons du Père Charles Frey de Neuville . . .* (Paris, 1776), vol. 8, 74; *Sermons du Père Charles Frey de Neuville* (Paris and Lyon, 1777), 237–39; Angélique d'Alègre, *Sermons nouveaux . . .* (Avignon, 1778), 14; Nicolas-Louis Poulle, *Sermons . . .* (Paris, 1778), vol. 2, 323–24; and Étienne Hubert de Cambacérès, *Sermons . . .* (Paris, 1781), 240, 416, 422, 430–31, and 459.

94. William Reddy, *The Navigation of Feeling: A Framework for the History of Emotions* (Cambridge: Cambridge University Press, 2001), 96–107. See also my discussion of Reddy and emotives in the introduction.

95. Ronald Schechter, "Conceptions of Terror in the European Enlightenment," in *Facing Fear: The History of an Emotion in Global Perspective*, ed. Michael Laffan and Max Weiss (Princeton, NJ: Princeton University Press, 2012), 35–38.

96. Charles-Louis de Secondat de Montesquieu, *De l'esprit des loix, ou Du rapport que les loix doivent avoir avec la constitution de chaque gouvernement, les mœurs, le climat, la religion, le commerce, &c. . . .* (Geneva, 1748), vol. 1, book 3, chapter 9, 41–42; book 3, chapter 11, 45; book 4, chapter 1, 46; book 4, chapter 3, 52; book 4, chapter 5, 54; book 4, chapter 7, 59; book 5, chapter 14, 93 and 95; book 6, chapter 18, 146; book 6, chapter 21, 149; and book 12, chapter 30, 335.

97. *Esprit des loix*, vol. 2, book 24, chapter 18, 192.

98. Louis, Chevalier de Jaucourt, "Enfer," in Denis Diderot and Jean Le Rond d' Alembert, eds., *Encyclopédie, ou Dictionnaire raisonné des sciences, des arts et des métiers, par une société de gens de lettres* (Geneva [Paris and Neuchâtel], 1772), vol. 5, 711. Cf. Polybius, who wrote that "the multitude must be held in by invisible terrors and suchlike pageantry" and opined "not that the ancients acted rashly and at haphazard in introducing among the people notions concerning the gods and beliefs in the terrors of hell, but that the moderns are most rash and foolish in banishing such beliefs." *The Histories*, trans. W. R. Paton (Cambridge, MA: Harvard University Press, 1922–27), vol. 3, book VI, part VII, section 56, lines 6–12, 396.

99. Abbé Mably, "De la législation, ou principes des loix" (1776), in *Œuvres completes de l'abbé de Mably* (London, 1789–90), vol. 9, 323–24. On Mably's republicanism see Keith Michael Baker, "A Script for a French Revolution: The Political Consciousness of the abbé Mably," in *Inventing the French Revolution: Essays on French Political Culture in the Eighteenth Century* (Cambridge: Cambridge University Press, 1990), 86–106; and Johnson Kent Wright, *A Classical Republican in Eighteenth-Century France: The Political Thought of Mably* (Stanford, CA: Stanford University Press, 1997). The reader is not necessarily meant to take this evaluation at face value, and Mably includes in the conversation an English milord who argues that Christianity and its threats of posthumous punishments have not done a good job of restraining the wicked. But the Swede's position is presented as reasonable. Well-informed readers would have recognized the argument, and some would certainly have sided with it. More to the point, the expression "salutary terror" was used to justify it.

100. For example, Rousseau wrote that "civil religion" must affirm "the existence of a powerful, intelligent, beneficent Divinity that sees the future and provides for it, a future life, happiness for the just, the punishment of the wicked, the sanctity of the Social Contract and of the Laws." Jean-Jacques Rousseau, *Du contrat social, ou Principes du droit politique* (Amsterdam, 1762), book 4, chapter 8, 244–45.

101. Montesquieu, *Esprit des loix*, vol. 2, book 31, chapter 2, 493.

102. Jean Le Rond d'Alembert, "Éloge de Bossuet, Évêque de Meaux" (1772), in *Œuvres complètes de d'Alembert* (Paris, 1821), vol. 2, 268n.

103. Mathieu François Pidanzat de Mairobert, *Anecdotes sur M. la Comtesse Du Barri* (London, 1775), 268. *Anecdotes* is number 2 on Darnton's best-seller list. Robert Darnton, *Forbidden Best-Sellers*, 64.

104. Jean Pechméja, *Télephe en XII livres* (London, 1784), 43.

105. Pechméja, *Télephe*, 183.

106. Pechméja, *Télephe*, 201.

107. Pechméja, *Télephe*, 206.

108. Josephine McDonagh, "Child-Murder Narratives in George Eliot's 'Adam Bede': Embedded Histories and Fictional Representation," *Nineteenth-Century Literature* 56 (September 2001): 245.

109. For classic studies of the "radical Enlightenment" see Margaret C. Jacob, *The Radical Enlightenment: Pantheists, Freemasons, and Republicans* (London and Boston: Allen & Unwin, 1981); and Jonathan Israel, *Radical Enlightenment: Philosophy and the Making of Modernity, 1650–1750* (Oxford: Oxford University Press, 2001).

110. Darnton ranks Mercier the fourth best-selling author of forbidden books. *Forbidden Best-Sellers*, 63–64.

111. Louis Sébastien Mercier, *L'an deux mille quatre cent quarante: Rêve s'il en fut jamais* (London [i.e., Dresden?], 1772), 110–11.

112. Timothy Tackett, *Becoming a Revolutionary: The Deputies of the French National Assembly and the Emergence of a Revolutionary Culture, 1789–1790* (Princeton, NJ: Princeton University Press, 1996), 36.

113. Maurice Gontard, *L'enseignement secondaire en France de la fin de l'Ancien Régime à la loi Falloux (1750–1850)* (Aix-en-Provence: Édisud, 1984), 11.

114. Gontard, *Enseignement*, 10–11.

115. Timothy Tackett, *The Coming of the Terror in the French Revolution* (Cambridge, MA: Harvard University Press, 2015), 300.

CHAPTER TWO

1. Jacques-Bénigne Bossuet, *Politique tirée des propres paroles de l'Ecriture-Sainte . . .* (Brussels, 1710), 79 (book III, article 2, proposition 4). Elsewhere in the same work Bossuet described princes as "gods", 106 (Book IV, article 1, proposition 2) and 212 (Book V, article 4, proposition 1).

2. Antoine Furetière, *Dictionnaire universel* (The Hague, 1690), s.v. "Terreur." Emphasis in the original.

3. *Le dictionnaire de l'Académie françoise* (Paris, 1694), s.v. "Terreur." Emphasis in the original.

4. *Dictionnaire de l'Académie françoise* (Paris, 1762), s.v. "Terreur." Emphasis in the original.

5. *Le grand vocabulaire françois* (Paris, 1773), s.v. "Terreur," vol. 27, 502.

6. "A punir les méchants ta colère fidèle / Fait marcher devant elle / La mort et la terreur." ARTFL *Dictionnaire d'autrefois* database, http://artflsrv02.uchicago.edu/cgi-bin /dicos/pubdico1look.pl?strippedhw=terreur, accessed May 5, 2014.

7. Dominick LaCapra has warned against taking Furetière's dictionary as "canonical," and this caution is warranted when using other dictionaries as well. "Chartier, Darnton, and the Great Symbol Massacre," *Journal of Modern History* 60 (March 1988): 101.

8. "Aliisque insidiantibus sit pavor, terror et formido." Richard A. Jackson, ed., *Ordines coronationis Franciae: Texts and Ordines for the Coronation of Frankish and French Kings and Queens in the Middle Ages* (Philadelphia: University of Pennsylvania Press, 2000), vol. 2, 478. Cf. *Les efforts de la liberté & du patriotisme contre le despotisme* (London, 1772–73), vol. 4, 189n.

9. Jean Bodin, *Les six livres de la repvbliqve . . .* (Paris, 1576), 465.

10. Le Jeune, *Clovis, poeme héroi-comique, avec des remarques historiques et critiques* (The Hague, 1763), vol. 1, 112.

11. Denis Diderot and Jean Le Rond d'Alembert, eds., *Encyclopédie, ou Dictionnaire raisonné des sciences, des arts et des métiers* (Paris, 1751–80), vol. 2, s.v. "Alaric II, roi des Visigoths," 10.

12. Pierre Laureau, *Histoire de France avant Clovis* (Paris, 1789), 392. Although the book appeared in 1789, it received its royal privilege in 1786 and its "approbation" by the royal censor in 1788. It is therefore a product of the Old Regime and not the Revolution.

13. Henri de Boulainvilliers, comte de Saint-Saire, *État de la France . . .* (London, 1727–28), vol. 3, 13. Boulainvilliers was writing with an agenda: he was defending the privileges of the nobility against the encroaching power of absolutism and used Charlemagne's consultation with the aristocracy as a model for the young Louis XV, who he hoped would depart from the absolutism of his predecessor. Still, what is significant is that he underscored Charlemagne's greatness by pointing to the terror that the medieval king instilled in foreign powers.

14. Gabriel Daniel, *Histoire de France, depuis l'établissement de la monarchie françoise dans les Gaules* (Paris, 1713), vol. 1, 414, 433.

15. Gabriel-Henri Gaillard, *Histoire de Charlemagne* (Paris, 1782), vol. 2, 96.

16. See, for example, Vincent Houdry, ed., *La Bibliothèque des prédicateurs . . .* (Lyon, 1731), vol. 3, 382; and Esprit Fléchier, *Panegyriques et autres sermons* (Paris, 1741), vol. 2, 9, and *Œuvres complettes* (Paris, 1782), vol. 5, 206.

17. François de Salignac de La Mothe-Fénelon, *Œuvres spirituelles* (Antwerp, 1718), vol. 2, 9. This advice was quoted in Abbé Pierre Barral, *Manuel des souverains* (Paris, 1754), 8.

18. *L'Office de la nuit et des laudes, imprimé par l'ordre de Monseigneur l'Archevêque* (Paris, 1745), 740.

19. Christophe de Beaumont, Archbishop of Paris, "Mandement de Monseigneur l'Archevêque de Paris, qui ordonne des Prieres publiques pour le repos de l'Ame de feu

Monseigneur le Dauphin," in *Récit des principales circonstances de la maladie de feu Monseigneur le Dauphin* (Paris, 1766), 30.

20. Abbé Pierre Jaubert, *Éloges historiques et moraux de St. Denis, de Ste Geneviève, et de St. Louis, patrons de la France* (Paris, 1786), 55. Elsewhere in this book Jaubert praised Saint Louis for the terror he spread to enemies. *Éloges*, 205, 218, and 226. Among other eighteenth-century writers who praised Saint Louis in similar terms, see Abbé Edme Mongin, who called him "the terror or the admiration of his century." "Panégyrique de S. Louis, Roi de France, prononcé dans la chapelle du Louvre, en présence de Messieurs de l'Académie Françoise," in *Œuvres de Messire Edme Mongin . . .* (Paris, 1745), 150.

21. M. [Jean-François] Dreux du Radier, *Tablettes historiques et anecdotes des rois de France, depuis Pharamond jusqu'à Louis xiv* (London, 1766), vol. 2, 14. On Dreux's exile see Robert Darnton, "Policing Writers in Paris Circa 1750," *Representations* 5 (Winter 1984): 25.

22. Charles Geneviève Louis Auguste André Timothée d'Eon de Beaumont, *Mémoires pour servir à l'histoire générale des finances* (London [i.e., Paris], 1758), 124.

23. Augustin Simon Irailh, *Histoire de la réunion de la Bretagne à la France* (Paris, 1764), vol. 1, 15.

24. Dominique Bouhours, *The Art of Criticism, or the Method of Making a Right Judgment upon Subjects of Wit and Learning* (London, 1705), 77.

25. Gayot de Pitaval, *Causes célèbres et intéressantes, avec les jugemens qui les ont décidées . . .* (The Hague, 1750), vol. 14, 20.

26. *Anecdotes échappées à l'Observateur anglois et aux Mémoires secrets, en forme de correspondance; pour servir de suite à ces deux ouvrages* (London [i.e., Paris?], 1788), vol. 1, 112. On *libelles* such as this one see Robert Darnton, *The Forbidden Best-Sellers of Pre-Revolutionary France* (New York: Norton, 1995), especially 137–66.

27. Peter Burke, *The Fabrication of Louis XIV* (New Haven, CT: Yale University Press, 1992).

28. Mademoiselle de Montpensier, "Portrait du Roy, Écrit à Paris le septième Octobre 1658," in *Mémoires de mademoiselle de Montpensier* (London [Paris], 1746), vol. 7, 340.

29. *Recveil de harangves faites av roy, avx reynes, la reyne de svede, et avtres personnes de qualité, auec plusieurs lettres, odes & sonnets, sur toutes sortes de sujets* (Paris, 1668), 5.

30. *Procez Verbal de l'Assemblée générale dv clergé de France . . . és années 1665. & 1666* (Paris, 1666), 305. Cf. "Remonstrance du Clergé de France, assemblé à Paris, faite au Roi Louis XIV. le 6. octobre 1665. par . . . Jacques Adhemar du Monteil de Grignan . . ." in *Recueil des actes, titres et mémoires concernant les affaires du clergé de France . . .* (Paris and Avignon, 1771), 723.

31. Dominique Bouhours, *Pensées ingénieuses des anciens et des modernes* (Paris, 1698), 450.

32. Jacques Bénigne Bossuet, "Oraison funèbre de Marie Terese d'Austriche, Infante d'Espagne, Reine de France et de Navarre," in *Recueïl des oraisons funèbres* (Paris, 1699), 201–2. Cf. Bridel Arleville, *Le petit rhétoricien françois . . .* (London, 1791), 182.

33. [Henri Basnage de Beauval], *Histoire des ouvrages des savans . . . mois d'octobre 1688* (Rotterdam, 1697), 187.

34. Antoinette Deshoulières, "Ode sur le soin que le Roi prend de l'éducation de sa noblesse dans ses Places et dans Saint-Cyr, laquelle remporta le prix à l'Académie françoise. 168[7]," in *Œuvres choisies de Madame et de Mademoiselle Deshoulières* (London [i.e., Paris], 1780), vol. 2, 31. On Deshoulières see Siep Stuurman, "Literary Feminism in Seventeenth-Century Southern France: The Case of Antoinette de Salvan de Saliez," *Journal of Modern History* 71 (March 1999): 18; and English Showalter, Jr., "Writing Off the Stage: Women Authors and Eighteenth-Century Theater," *Yale French Studies* 75 (1988): 96.

35. Frédéric Léonard, "Au Roi," *Recueil des traitéz de paix* . . . (Paris, 1693), n.p.

36. "Observation CXCI. D'une femme sterile durant quinze ans, qui devint féconde après la conception de deux faux germes," in François Mauriceau, *Observations sur la grossesse et l'accouchement des femmes, et sur leurs maladies, & celles des enfans nouveau-nez* (Paris, 1694), 153–54.

37. "Oraison funèbre de très-haut, très-puissant et très-excellent Prince Louis XIV: Roy de France et de Navarre; Prononcée dans l'Église de l'Abbaye Royale de Saint-Cyr, le 6. Decembre 1715; par Monsieur l'Abbé Lafargue," in *Recueil des oraisons funèbres de Louis XIV* . . . (The Hague and Nancy, 1716), 69–70.

38. "A la mémoire de Louis XIV, surnommé Le Grand, lorsque le Prevôt des Marchands et les Echevins de la Ville de Paris dresserent à son honneur une Statue Equestre dans la Place auparavant nommée de Vendôme, et maintenant Place de Louis le Grand. Poeme," in Vincent-Claude de Châlons, *Règles de la poesie Françoise* . . . (Paris, 1716), 377. The reference to the Rhine is an allusion to the king's invasion of the Palatinate in 1688, allegedly to protect the claims of his sister-in-law.

39. "Discours prononcé par M. l'abbé de Rothelin, lors qu'il fut reçû à l'Académie Françoise, à la place de feu M. l'Abbé Fraguier, le lundi 28 juin 1728," in *Recueil des pièces d'éloquence et de poësie qui ont remporté les prix donnés par l'Académie Françoise en l'année MDCCXXIX* . . . (Paris, 1730), 29.

40. Voltaire, *Siècle de Louis XIV* (1752), in *Œuvres complètes*, ed. Louis Moland, vol. 14 (Paris, 1878), vol. 19, 440.

41. Marchands merciers, *Au roi* ([n.p.], [1758?]), 3.

42. Abbé Claude François Xavier Millot, *Élémens de l'histoire de France, depuis Clovis jusqu'à Louis XV* (Paris, 1770), vol. 3, 281.

43. The petition is reproduced in Henri de Boulainvilliers, comte de Saint-Saire, *État de la France* (London, 1727–28), vol. 3, 541.

44. Edme Mongin, "Oraison funèbre de Louis le Grand, Roi de France et de Navarre: Prononcée dans la chapelle du Louvre en présence de Messieurs de l'Académie Françoise," in *Œuvres*, 236.

45. Louis-Antoine de Caracciolli, *Dialogue entre le siècle de Louis XIV et le siècle de Louis XV* (The Hague, 1751), 97.

46. Barral, *Manuel*, 32.

47. *Remontrances du Parlement au Roi, du 4 août 1756* (n.p., [1756]), 22, 7.

48. [Charles Gabriel], abbé de l'Attaignant, *Poesies de M. l'Abbé de l'Attaignant* . . . (London [i.e., Paris?], 1756–57), 166.

49. Comte [Louis-Gabriel] Du Buat, *Les maximes du gouvernement monarchique, pour servir de suite aux Éléments de la politique* (London [i.e., Paris?], 1778), 472.

50. *Formule de cérémonies et prières pour le sacre de Sa Majesté Louis XVI, qui se fera dans l'Église Métropolitaine de Reims, le Dimanche de la Trinité, 11 juin 1775* (Paris, 1775), 37.

51. *Formule de cérémonies*, 42.

52. *Formule de cérémonies*, 61.

53. *Journal politique, ou Gazette des gazettes* (August 1775), 56.

54. Henri Boniface, "Au Roi Louis XVI pour le jour de son sacre," in *Le trésor des pièces rares et curieuses de la Champagne et de la Brie: Documents pour servir à l'histoire de la Champagne*, ed. Jean Baptiste Carnandet (Chaumont, 1863–66), 150.

55. Paul Henri Mallet, *Histoire de Dannemarc* (Geneva, 1763), vol. 3, 432.

56. Gabriel Bonnot, Abbé Mably, "Le droit public de l'europe," (1764) in *Œuvres complètes de l'abbé de Mably* (Loudon, 1789–90), vol. 5, 298–99.

57. Voltaire, *Le Siècle de Louis XIV*, in *Œuvres complètes*, vol. 14, 328. In his *Histoire de L'Empire de Russie sous Pierre le Grand* (1759) Voltaire wrote of Charles's campaign of 1703, "He spread terror in upper Poland, in Silesia, in Saxony." *Œuvres complètes*, vol. 16, 491.

58. Voltaire, *Histoire de Charles XII, roi de Suede* (1731), 11, 79, 80, 83, 138, 146, 264, and 306.

59. Mably, "Droit public," in *Œuvres completes*, vol. 6, 172 and 175.

60. Voltaire to Frederick, May 26, 1742, in *Les œuvres complètes de Voltaire/The Complete Works of Voltaire*, ed. Theodore Besterman (Geneva: Institut et Musée Voltaire, 1968), vol. 36, 129.

61. Voltaire, *Histoire de la guerre de mil sept cent quarante & un: Première partie* (London, 1756), 274.

62. Pierre Laureau, *Éloge de Frédéric II, Roi de Prusse, Électeur de Brandebourg* (Paris, 1787), 56.

63. *Collection universelle des mémoires particuliers relatifs à l'histoire de France* (London [i.e., Paris?], 1785–90), vol. 3, 347.

64. *Collection universelle*, vol. 4, 50.

65. *Collection universelle*, vol. 4, 373.

66. *Collection universelle*, vol. 4, 121–22.

67. *Collection universelle*, vol. 5, 13.

68. Philippe de Commynes, *Mémoires* (London [i.e., Paris], 1747), no page number. At the head of all four volumes.

69. "Vers sur le Maréchal de Richelieu," in [Louis-François Metra], *Correspondance secrète, politique & littéraire, ou Mémoires pour servir à l'histoire des cours, des sociétés & de la littérature en France . . .* (London [i.e., Paris?], 1787–90), vol. 16, 325. The entry is for July 12, 1784.

70. [Claude-Louis-Michel de Sacy], *L'honneur françois, ou Histoire des vertus et des exploits de notre nation, depuis l'établissement de la monarchie jusqu'à nos jours* (Paris, 1784), vol. 12, 417.

71. "L'arrivée de l'armée de M. le Comte de Rochambeau à Rhode-Island, y répandit la terreur . . ." Abbé Robin, *Nouveau voyage dans l'Amérique septentrionale, en l'année 1781: Et campagne de l'armée de M. Le Comte de Rochambeau* (Philadelphia [i.e., Paris?], 1782), 29.

72. Samuel, Freiherr von Pufendorf, *De officio hominis & civis, juxta legem naturalem libri duo* (Cambridge, 1682), vol. 2, 155.

73. Pufendorf, *Le droit de la nature et des gens* . . . (London [i.e., Paris], 1740), vol. 3, 389.

74. Gottfried Wilhelm, Freiherr von Leibniz, *Essais de Théodicée* (1710), 196.

75. Antoine de Pas, marquis de Feuquière, *Mémoires de M. le Marquis de Feuquière* (London [i.e., Paris?], 1736), 88.

76. Feuquière, *Mémoires*, 175.

77. Feuquière, *Mémoires*, 450.

78. Feuquière, *Mémoires*, 235.

79. Feuquière, *Mémoires*, 496.

80. Feuquière, *Mémoires*, 261.

81. Feuquière, *Mémoires de M. le Marquis de Feuquière* . . . *Nouvelle édition* (London [Paris?], 1740), vol. 1, lxxi.

82. David A. Bell calls Guibert "France's most influential pre-Revolutionary military reformer (and an habitué of 'philosophical' salons)." *The First Total War: Napoleon's Europe and the Birth of Warfare as We Know It* (New York: Houghton Mifflin, 2007), 79.

83. Jacques Antoine Hippolyte, comte de Guibert, *Éloge du roi de Prusse: Par l'auteur de l'Essai général de tactique* (London [i.e., Paris?], 1787), 189.

84. Guibert, *Essai général de tactique, précédé d'un discours sur l'état actuel de la politique & de la science militaire en Europe* (London [i.e., Liège], 1773), vol. 2, 38.

85. Guibert, *Éloge du Maréchal de Catinat* (Edinburgh [i.e., Paris?], 1775), 22.

86. Mably, "De l'étude de l'histoire: À Monseigneur le Prince de Parme," in *Œuvres complètes*, vol. 12, 109.

87. Girolamo Belloni, *Dissertation sur le commerce* (The Hague, 1755), 3.

88. Pierre Laureau, *Histoire de France avant Clovis* (Paris, 1789), 129, 63, and 28.

89. Pierre-Daniel Huet, *Mémoires sur le commerce des Hollandois, dans tous les états et empires du monde* (Amsterdam, 1717), vii–viii.

90. Jacques Savary des Brûlons, *Dictionnaire universel de commerce* (1723), vol. 4, 359.

91. Abbé Gabriel-François Coyer, "La noblesse commerçante" (1756), in *Œuvres de M. l'Abbe Coyer, de l'Académie Royale des Sciences & Belles-Lettres de Nanci* (London [i.e., Paris?], 1765), vol. 2, 65.

92. Philippe-Auguste de Sainte-Foy, chevalier d'Arcq, *La noblesse militaire, opposée à La noblesse commerçante, ou Le patriote françois* (Amsterdam, 1756), 127–28.

93. D'Arcq, *Histoire du commerce et de la navigation des peuples anciens et modernes* (Amsterdam, 1758), lvii.

94. P[ierre] Jaubert, *Éloge de la roture dedié aux roturiers* (London [i.e., Paris?], 1766), 74.

95. Alexis Piron, "Feu Monseigneur le dauphin, à la nation, en deuil depuis six mois," in *Œuvres complettes d'Alexis Piron* (Paris, 1776), vol. 6, 351–52.

96. De Sacy, *Honneur françois*, vol. 7, xiv.

97. Paul François Velly, Claude Villaret, and Jean-Jacques Garnier, *Histoire de France, depuis l'établissement de la monarchie jusqu'au regne de Louis XIV* (Paris, 1755–86), vol. 10, 365–66.

98. [Louis Mayeul Chaudon], *Nouveau dictionnaire historique* (Paris, 1772), vol. 2, s.v. "Charles VIII," 130.

99. Charles Jean François Hénault, *Nouvel abrégé chronologique de l'histoire de France* (Paris, 1749), vol. 1, 348.

100. De Sacy, *Honneur françois*, vol. 4, 70–71.

101. Antoine-Henri de Bérault-Bercastel, *Histoire de l'Église* (Paris, 1780), vol. 8, 33.

102. Abbé de Maugre, *Le militaire chrétien, ou Extraits des sermons de M. l'abbé de Maugre, prieur de Chablis, ci-devant curé de Givet* (Vienne and Paris, 1779), 48.

103. "Lettre d'un missionnaire d'Alep, sur le Ramadan des Turcs, sur la Pâque des Chrétiens, & sur les principales circonstances de son voyage," in *Nouveaux mémoires des missions de la Compagnie de Jésus dans le Levant* (Paris, 1745), vol. 8, 343.

104. Louis de Rouvroy, duc de Saint-Simon, *Mémoires de Monsieur le Duc de S. Simon . . .* (London [i.e., Paris?], 1789), vol. 1, 97.

105. Abbé Raynal, "Sur la marine," in [Alexander Scot], *Nouveau recueil, ou Mélange littéraire, historique, dramatique et poétique: Contenant le poème célèbre des jardins de Mons. l'Abbé de Lille* (London, 1785), 359–60.

106. Raynal, *Histoire du parlement d'Angleterre* (London [i.e., Paris?], 1748), 351–52 and 335–36.

107. *Le point d'appui entre Thérèse et Frédéric* (Frankfurt, 1758), no page number.

108. Voltaire, *Siècle de Louis XIV* (Geneva, 1769), 441.

109. Simon-Nicolas-Henri Linguet, *Considérations politiques et philosophiques, sur les affaires présentes du nord et particulièrement sur celles de Pologne* (London, 1778), 70.

110. *Histoire universelle, depuis le commencement du monde jusqu'à présent* (Amsterdam and Leipzig, 1780), vol. 42, 106.

111. Jean-Louis Castilhon, *Considérations sur les causes physiques et morales de la diversité du génie, des mœurs, et du gouvernement des nations . . .* (Bouillon, 1770), 25.

112. Nicolas Lenglet-Dufresnoy, *Tablettes chronologiques de l'histoire universelle, sacrée et profane, ecclésiastique et civile, depuis la création du monde jusqu'à l'an 1775 . . .* (Paris, 1778), vol. 1, clxxxvi.

113. Orazio Torsellini, *Abrégé de l'histoire universelle . . .* (Paris, 1757), vol. 3, 233n.

114. [Barnabé Farmian Durosoy], *Annales de la ville de Toulouse . . .* (Paris, 1776), vol. 4, 394.

115. Antoine Jacques Roustan, *Réponse aux difficultez d'un théiste . . .* (London, 1771), 184.

116. Nicolas Bricaire de La Dixmerie, *La Sibyle gauloise* (London [i.e., Paris], 1775), 5.

117. Charles Irénée Castel de Saint-Pierre, *Abrégé du projet de paix perpetuelle . . .* (Rotterdam, 1729), 59.

118. Victor de Riquetti, marquis de Mirabeau, *L'ami des hommes, ou Traité de la population* (Avignon, 1756), 111.

119. Jean Castillon, *Discours sur l'origine de l'inegalité parmi les hommes: Pour servir de réponse au discours que M. Rousseau . . .* (Amsterdam, 1756), 236.

120. There is a pun in the original French that is based on the double meaning of the word *répandre*, which means "to spread" and is used in the expression *répandre le sang* (roughly, "to spill blood"). D'Arcq writes: "Vous pouvez aller à l'Immortalité de deux

manières, l'une à force de répandre du sang, l'autre à force de répandre des bienfaits." D'Arcq, *Mes loisirs* (Paris, [1756]), 60.

121. D'Alembert, "Essai sur la société des gens de lettres et des grands, sur la réputation, sur les mécènes, et sur les récompenses littéraires," in *Mélanges de littérature, d'histoire, et de philosophie: Nouvelle édition, revue, corrigée & augmentée très-considérablement par l'Auteur* (Amsterdam, 1772), vol. 1, 324.

122. *Considérations sur l'influence des mœurs, dans l'état militaire des nations: Par l'auteur d'Azémor* (London, 1788), 14.

123. Mably, "Le destin de la France," in *Œuvres complètes*, vol. 13, 93–94.

124. Mably, "De l'étude de l'histoire: À Monseigneur le Prince de Parme" (1778), in *Œuvres complètes*, vol. 12, 270.

125. Mably, "Observations sur l'histoire de France" (1765), in *Œuvres complètes*, vol. 3, 267.

126. Jonathan Swift, *Voyages du capitaine Lemuel Gulliver, en divers pays éloignez* (The Hague, 1727), vol. 1, 43.

127. For example, William of Orange was described as "the terror of his enemies; and the delight of his subjects." John Lockman, *A New History of England* (Dublin, 1741), 234.

CHAPTER THREE

1. Michel Foucault, *Discipline and Punish: The Birth of the Prison*, trans. Alan Sheridan (New York: Vintage, 1995), 3.

2. *Histoire de Robert François Damiens, contenant les particularités de son parricide et de son supplice* (Amsterdam, 1757), 60.

3. Antoine d'Espeisses, *Œuvres de M. Antoine d'Espeisses, advocat et jurisconsulte de Montpellier* (Lyon, 1685), vol. 3, 154. WorldCat lists editions of the *Œuvres* from 1660, 1664, 1666, 1677, 1685, 1696, 1706, 1710, 1726, 1750, 1768, and 1778. D'Espeisses drew on Justinian, who authorized the display of the corpse "vt & conspectu deterrantur alii ab isdem facinoribus; & solatio sit cognatis" (in order that through the sight of it others be deterred [lit., "terrified from"] from the same crimes, and there be solace for the relatives)." Justinian, *Institutiones*, 19.28.15., ed. Paul Krueger (Berlin, 1905), vol. 1, 817.

4. Philippe Bornier, *Conférences des nouvelles ordonnances de Louis XIV . . .* (Paris, 1678), vol. 2, 334. WorldCat lists editions of this book from 1678, 1681, 1693, 1694, 1700, 1703, 1725, 1729, 1733, 1737, 1740, 1744, 1749, 1755, 1757, 1760, 1762, and 1767.

5. Jean Domat, *Les loix civiles dans leur ordre naturel* (Paris, 1689), vol. 1, xlviii. According to WorldCat, *Les loix civiles* was published in 1689, 1691, 1694, 1695, 1696, 1697, 1698, 1700, 1701, 1702, 1703, 1704, 1705, 1706, 1707, 1713, 1723, 1732, 1735, 1742, 1745, 1746, 1747, 1756, 1766, 1767, 1771, and 1777.

6. Domat, "Harangue prononcée aux assises de l'année 1666," in *Les lois civiles* (The Hague, 1703), vol. 1, 230.

7. Domat, "Le droit public, suite des loix civiles dans leur ordre naturel," (1697) in *Lois civiles* (The Hague, 1703), vol. 1, 22.

8. Domat, "Le droit public," 197.

9. In 1685 Claude de Ferrière, professor of law and barrister at the Parlement of Paris, explained why the customary law of Paris required the confiscation of a murderer's property after his execution. The intent was simply "to give terror to the wicked, and to divert them from committing similar crimes; the fear of leaving children who are miserable and without property being greater than that of losing one's life." Claude de Ferrière, *Corps et compilation de tous les commentateurs anciens et modernes sur la Coutume de Paris . . .* (Paris, 1685), vol. 2, 302. In 1694, in an essay that would be republished in 1721 and 1745, Jacques de Tourreil, of the Académie Française, wrote that a judge who possessed only "half-proof" should be authorized to impose a "half-punishment." Though he did not elaborate on what this meant, more important is his reasoning: "The terror that this full power to exercise public vengeance imprints, further bridles scoundrels; it suffocates their movements, it dissipates their projects, which a less terrible and more limited power would not at all guarantee." Jacques de Tourreil, "Si le Juge peut imposer une demi-peine, pour le crime dont il n'a qu'une demi-preuve," in "Essais de jurisprudence" (1694), in *Œuvres de Mr de Tourreil . . .* (Paris, 1721), vol. 1, 135.

10. Voltaire, *Le siècle de Louis XIV* (1733), in *Œuvres complettes de Voltaire* (Kehl, 1785), vol. 20, 80.

11. Henri-François d'Aguesseau, "II. Instruction: Étude de l'histoire" (1716), in *Œuvres de M. le Chancelier d'Aguesseau* (Paris, 1787), vol. 1, 327.

12. D'Aguesseau, "Essai d'une institution au droit public" (1716), in *Œuvres*, vol. 1, 482–83.

13. D'Aguesseau, "Méditations métaphysiques sur les vraies ou les fausses idées de la justice" (1722–26), in *Œuvres de M. le Chancelier d'Aguesseau* (Paris, 1779), vol. 11, 434.

14. "Discours prononcé à l'audience présidiale de Toulouse par M. de Morlhon, Juge-Mage, Lieutenant Général & Président Premier du Présidial," in D'Aguesseau, *Œuvres* (Paris, 1779), vol. 11, ci. Cf. *Le journal des sçavans: Octobre 1760*, 267.

15. See n. 9.

16. WorldCat lists editions of the *Dictionnaire* for 1740, 1749, 1754, 1755, 1758, 1762, 1768, 1769, 1771, 1778, 1779, and 1787.

17. Claude-Joseph de Ferrière, *Dictionnaire de droit et de pratique . . .* (Toulouse, 1779), s.v. "Peine," vol. 2, 308.

18. Ferrière, *Dictionnaire*, s.v. "Corps des criminels exécutés et mis à mort," vol. 1, 402.

19. Ferrière, *Dictionnaire*, s.v. "Lese-Majesté," vol. 2, 136. Elsewhere in the entry he reiterated that "this crime is so detestable and so contrary to the public good, that it is just that the penalty regard the criminal and his family, in order to divert by the terror of penalties those who would be wretched enough to have conceived the design of committing such a horrible crime" (137).

20. Guy Rousseaud de la Combe, *Traité des matières criminelles, suivant l'ordonnance du mois d'août 1670, & les Edits, Déclarations du Roi, Arrêts & Réglemens intervenus jusqu'à présent* (Paris, 1732), 375.

21. Pierre François Muyart de Vouglans, *Réfutation des principes hasardés dans le Traité Des Délits Et Peines* (Lausanne, 1767), 54–55.

22. François Serpillon, *Code criminel, ou Commentaire sur l'Ordonnance de 1670 . . .* (Lyon, 1767), vol. 3, 1199n.

23. Jean-Pierre Sartoris, *Elémens de la procédure criminelle* (Amsterdam, 1773), vol. 2, 538. Elsewhere Sartoris affirmed that "the principal object of Justice" was "to give examples capable of imprinting terror and of diverting those who would be disposed to commit crimes." *Elémens*, 580.

24. [Joseph Nicolas Guyot], *Répertoire universel et raisonné de jurisprudence civil, criminelle, canonique et bénéficiale . . .* (Paris, 1777), vol 16, 472.

25. [Guyot], *Répertoire universel* (Paris, 1778), vol. 24, 8.

26. Francis I, king of France, "Ordonnance qui rend la Tournelle Criminelle continuelle, et qui regle comment les Enquestes connoissent de l'incident criminel: Donné à Paris au mois d'avril 1515; Registrée en la Cour de Parlement le 3. may 1515," in Claude-Joseph Prévost, *De la manière de poursuivre les crimes dans les différens tribunaux du royaume avec les loix criminelles . . .* (Paris, 1739), vol. 2, 19.

27. *Les edicts et ordonnances des roys de France depuis l'an 1226 . . .* (Lyon, 1571), 276.

28. Louis XIII, king of France, "Edit du roy: Sur la prohibition et punition des querelles et duels; Donné à Fontaine Bleau au mois de juin 1609; Publié en parlement le 26. du même mois," in *Recueil des édits, déclarations, arrests, et autres pièces concernant les duels & rencontres* (Paris, 1699), 16.

29. Louis XIII, "Declaration du roy, pour la défense du port d'armes: Du 27 may 1610," in Prévost, *De la manière de poursuivre les crimes*, vol. 2, 117.

30. Louis XIII, "Déclaration de Louis XIII: Portant Règlement sur l'ordre qui doit être observé en la célébration des mariages; et contre ceux qui commettent le crime de rapt; Du 26 novembre 1639," in Daniel Jousse, *Commentaire sur l'édit du mois d'avril 1695: Concernant la juridiction ecclésiastique . . .* (Paris, 1764), 117 and 119.

31. Serpillon, *Code criminel*, vol. 3, 959. This maxim had been written by the fourth-century jurist St. Optatus, and it was invoked by other eighteenth-century French jurists. Bornier, *Conférences*, vol. 2, 340; and Rousseaud de la Combe, *Traité*, 410.

32. Louis XV, king of France, "Declaration du roy: Concernant les billets ou promesses causez pour valeur en argent; Donnée à Versailles le 22 septembre 1733; Registrée en Parlement les 14 octobre 1733, et 20 janvier 1734," in Bornier, *Conferences des ordonnances de Louis XIV. . . , nouvelle éd. . . . augmentée . . . des édits, déclarations et ordonnances, donnez par Louis XV . . .* (Paris, 1744), vol. 1, xxx.

33. Louis XVI, king of France, *Déclaration du roi, relative à l'ordonnance criminelle* (Versailles, 1788), 4.

34. [François Gayot de Pitaval], *Continuation des causes célèbres et intéressantes, avec les jugements qui les ont décidées* (Amsterdam and Liège, 1775), vol. 4, 368–69. Cf. Antoine Court de Gébelin, *Les toulousaines, ou Lettres historiques et apologétiques en faveur de la religion reformée* (Edinburgh [Toulouse?], 1763), 414.

35. *Arrest du Parlement . . . du trois mars mil sept cent soixante-quatre . . .* (Paris, 1764), 48.

36. *Arrêt de la Cour de Parlement, qui ordonne qu'un imprimé . . . intitulé: Mémoire justificatif, pour trois hommes condamnés à la roue . . . seront [sic] lacérés [sic] & brûlés [sic] . . .* (Paris, 1786), 100. The condemned book was Charles-Marguerite-Jean-Baptiste Mercier Dupaty, *Mémoire justificatif pour trois hommes condamnés à la roue* (Paris,

1786). The quotation from Accorso appears to be a variation on a maxim from the Code of Justinian: *"ut unius poena metus possit esse multorum* (that the punishment of one might be the fear of many)." *Codex Iustiniani,* 9, 27, 1. This saying was popular with authors who defended punishment by referring to the terror it instilled. See Domat, *Les loix civiles,* vol. 1, 216; and Vouglans, *Réfutation,* 54n. Another saying, equally popular, was Cicero's "Ut metus ad omnes, pœna ad paucos, perveniret" (that fear may come to all, punishment to few). *Pro Cluentio,* 46. This was quoted by Bodin, *Six livres de la repvblique* (Paris, 1576), 394 (book 3, chapter 7). Cf. the Latin version, *Ioannis Bodini andegavensis, de repvblica libri sex . . .* (Paris, 1586), 341; and Bornier, *Conférences,* vol. 2, 318.

37. *Arrêt,* 131.

38. *Arrêt,* 253–54.

39. *Arrêt,* 255.

40. *Remontrance du parlement de Dauphiné, concernant la lettre de cachet* (Grenoble, 1788), 8.

41. Voltaire, *Histoire d'Elizabeth Canning, et de Jean Calas . . .* (London, 1762). Cf. Voltaire, *Traité de la tolérance, à l'occasion de la mort de Jean Calas* (s.l., 1763).

42. Historians disagree about whether the abolition took place in 1741, upon Elizabeth's accession to the throne, or at some later date, with some claiming that it never actually took place. Cyril Bryner, "The Issue of Capital Punishment in the Reign of Elizabeth Petrovna," *Russian Review* 49 (October 1990): 389–416.

43. Voltaire, "Histoire de l'empire de Russie" [1759–63], in *La Henriade, divers autres poèmes* ([Geneva], 1775), vol. 22, part I, chapter 8, §353.

44. Cesare, marchese di Beccaria, *Dei delitti e delle pene* (Haarlem and Paris, 1766), 70.

45. Beccaria, *Traité des délits et des peines, traduit de l'italien, d'après la troisième édition revue, corrigée & augmentée par l'auteur . . .* (Philadelphia [i.e., Paris], 1766), 59. On Morellet's role as translator, see Dorothy Medlin, "André Morellet, Translator of Liberal Thought," *Studies on Voltaire and the Eighteenth Century* 174 (1978): 189–201. On the number of reprints and Morellet's estimate of the number of people who read his translation, see Medlin, 197 and 197n.

46. Beccaria, *Traité,* 63. Cf. *Dei delitti,* 122.

47. Beccaria, *Dei delitti,* 121. Cf. *Traité,* 100.

48. Beccaria, *Dei delitti,* 81.

49. Beccaria, *Traité,* 70.

50. Beccaria, in Jacques-Pierre Brissot de Warville, *Bibliothèque philosophique du législateur, du politique, du jurisconsulte . . .* (Berlin and Paris, 1782), vol. 1, 76, 117. On Lisy, see Renato Pasta, "*Dei delitti e delle pene* et sa fortune italienne," in *Beccaria et la culture juridique des lumières,* ed. Michel Porret (Geneva: Droz, 1997), 129.

51. Charles Duclos, *Essais sur les ponts et chaussées, la voirie et les corvées* (Amsterdam, 1759), 233. On the other hand, Victor Riquetti, marquis de Mirabeau (the noted physiocrat and father of the revolutionary comte de Mirabeau), disagreed with Duclos, writing that "the sight of death strikes brutal souls" and that executions rather than chain gangs should be used to punish criminals. *Réponse à l'essai sur les ponts et chaussées, la voierie et les corvées* (Avignon, 1761), 90.

52. Jean-Nicolas Démeunier, *L'esprit des usages et des coutumes des différens peuples* . . . (London [i.e., Paris?], 1776), vol. 3, 146. On Démeunier, see George B. Watts, "Thomas Jefferson, the *Encyclopédie* and the *Encyclopédie méthodique*," *French Review* 38 (January 1965): 318–25.

53. William Coxe, *Voyage en Pologne, Russie, Suède, Dannemarc, &c* . . . (Geneva, 1786), vol. 1, 363. In the original Coxe wrote that "the horror of dissolution has been repeatedly observed in the generality of mankind to preponderate beyond any other terrors." *Travels into Poland, Russia, Sweden, and Denmark* . . . (Dublin, 1784), vol. 2, 299n.

54. Robert Darnton, *The Forbidden Best-Sellers of Pre-Revolutionary France* (New York: Norton, 1995), 63–64.

55. Louis-Sébastien Mercier, *L'an deux mille quatre cent quarante: Rêve s'il en fût jamais* (London [i.e., Paris?], 1771), 84–101.

56. According to Robert Darnton, the *Histoire philosophique* was the number 5 "forbidden best-seller" of prerevolutionary France. *Forbidden Best-Sellers*, 65.

57. Cf. Serpillon's observation: "It is very advantageous for the benefit of Justice that the condemned be made to endure, at the locations [of their crimes], the punishments pronounced against them, which has the intention of inspiring terror in the wicked at the very location where the crime was committed." François Serpillon, *Code criminel* (Lyon, 1767), vol. 3, 959.

58. Abbé [Guillaume-Thomas-François] Raynal, *Histoire philosophique et politique, des établissemens & du commerce des Européens dans les deux Indes* (Amsterdam, 1770), vol. 4, 84–85. Emphasis added.

59. Raynal, *Histoire philosophique*, vol. 4, 85.

60. Louis Philipon de La Madelaine, *Discours sur la nécessité et les moyens de supprimer les peines capitales* (n.p., 1770), 55.

61. Jacques Accarias de Sérionne, *L'ordre moral, ou Le développement des principales loix de la nature* . . . (Augsburg, 1780), vol. 1, 126.

62. Accarias de Sérionne, *L'ordre moral*, vol. 1, 129.

63. Antoine-Nicolas Servin, *De la législation criminelle* . . . (Basel, 1782), 54–56.

64. "Vienne (le 20 Septembre)," *Journal politique, ou Gazette des gazettes: Année 1782; Octobre; Premiere Quinzaine*.

65. On Mably, see Johnson Kent Wright, *A Classical Republican in Eighteenth-Century France: The Political Thought of Mably* (Stanford, CA: Stanford University Press, 1997). I referred to this dialogue in chapter 1 in the context of a discussion of Mably's views on theological terror.

66. Abbé de Mably, *De la législation, ou Principes des loix* (Amsterdam, 1777), 91–93.

67. Mably, *De la législation*, 95–96. The marquis de Condorcet, the *philosophe*-turned-revolutionary whose refusal to vote for the execution of Louis XVI would lead indirectly to his own death, reasoned similarly, and in 1781 he argued that punishments that were "too severe" had "a certain quality of injustice that causes men to rebel against the law, diminishes the horror of crime, and [reduces] the terror of punishment." Jean-Antoine-Nicolas de Caritat, Marquis de Condorcet, *Recueil de pièces sur l'état des protestans en France* (London [i.e., Paris?], 1781), 110.

68. Mably, *De la législation*, 94.

69. The brother of the sensationalist philosopher Condillac, Mably shared the episte-
mological belief that the mind was like wax and bore "traces" of impressions. This does
not mean that he subscribed to the view of the "milord," only that he could conceive of
an argument in which the waxlike nature of the mind was operative.

70. Mably, *De la législation*, 94.

71. Louis-Jean Lévesque de Pouilly, *Théorie des sentimens agréables* (Geneva, 1747), 232.

72. Jean Castilhon, *Discours qui a remporté le prix, par le jugement de l'Académie
des Jeux Floraux, en l'année M.DCC.LVI . . .* ([Toulouse], 1756), 27. On the Jeux Floraux
see Jeremy Caradonna, *The Enlightenment in Practice: Academic Prize Contests and
Intellectual Culture in France, 1670–1794* (Ithaca, NY: Cornell University Press, 2012),
15–16, 21, 26, 35–36, 38, 50–51, 54, 56, 58–59, 66–67, 71, and 107. Montesquieu saw
fear (*la crainte*) as the principle of despotism and virtue as the principle of the republic.
Charles-Louis de Secondat de Montesquieu, *De l'esprit des loix . . .* (Geneva, 1748), vol. 1,
book 3, chapter 9, 41–42; book 3, chapter 11, 45; book 4, chapter 1, 46; book 4, chapter 3,
52; book 4, chapter 5, 54; book 4, chapter 7, 59; book 5, chapter 14, 93 and 95; book 6,
chapter 18, 146; book 6, chapter 21, 149; and book 12, chapter 30, 335. He saw honor (not
love) as the principle of monarchy. *Esprit des loix*, book 3, chapter 7, 39.

73. Pierre-Jacques Changeux, *Traité des extrêmes, ou Éléments de la science de la
réalité* (Amsterdam, 1767), vol. 2, 66.

74. Paul Henri Thiry, baron d'Holbach, *Système de la nature, ou Des loix du monde
physique & du monde moral* (London [i.e., Amsterdam], 1770), 249.

75. Denis Diderot and Jean Le Rond d'Alembert, eds., *Encyclopédie, ou Dictionnaire
raisonné des sciences, des arts et des métiers, par une société de gens de lettres* (Paris,
1772), s.v. "Vertu," vol. 17, 179.

76. Jean-Jacques Rousseau, "Discours sur l'économie politique" (1755), in *Œuvres choisies
de J. J. Rousseau de Geneve [sic] . . .* (London [Paris?], [1785?]), vol. 2, 190. For Rousseau's views
on the death penalty, see *Du contrat social . . .* (Amsterdam, 1762), book 2, chapter 5, 53–57.

77. Honoré-Gabriel de Riqueti, comte de Mirabeau, *Errotika Biblion* (Rome [i.e.,
Paris?], 1783), 121–22.

78. Abbé Gabriel Brizard, "Éloge historique de l'abbé de Mably, discours qui a partagé
le Prix au jugement de l'Académie Royale des Inscriptions et Belles-Lettres, en 1787," in
Mably, *Observations sur l'histoire de France* (Kehl, 1788), vol. 1, 95.

79. Theodore Besterman, ed., *The Complete Works of Voltaire* (Banbury, Oxfordshire:
Voltaire Foundation, 1972), vol. 106, 261, letter D9367.

80. Frederick II, king of Prussia, *Les raisons d'établir ou d'abroger les loix* (Utrecht,
1751), 51.

81. On the fate of this phrase, and its frequent misquotation, see Richard Bellamy,
"Introduction," in Beccaria, *On Crimes and Punishments and Other Writings* (Cambridge: Cambridge University Press, 1995), xviii–xxiii.

CHAPTER FOUR

1. Aristotle, *Poetics*, VI. 2. Quoted and translated from S[amuel] H[enry] Butcher,
*Aristotle's Theory of Poetry and Fine Art, with a Critical Text and Translation of the
Poetics* (London: Macmillan, 1895), 23.

2. André Dacier, *La poëtique d'Aristote, traduite en françois* (Paris, 1692), 70–71. This book was republished in 1733 and 1735, and the definition was excerpted in anthologies and other publications. See, for example, Denis Gaullyer, *Règles de poëtique, tirées d'Aristote, d'Horace, de Despreaux, et d'autres célèbres auteurs* (Paris, 1728), 265; and *Dictionnaire universel françois et latin, vulgairement appelé Dictionnaire de Trévoux . . .* (Paris, 1743), vol. 6, s.v. "Tragédie," 381.

3. Dacier, *Poëtique d'Aristote*, 78.

4. Dacier, *Poëtique d'Aristote*, 79–80.

5. Dacier, *Poëtique d'Aristote*, 81.

6. Jean Terrasson, *Dissertation critique sur l'Iliade d'Homère . . .* (Paris, 1715), vol. 1, 174–77.

7. Charles Batteux, *Cours de belles lettres distribué par exercices* (Paris, 1750), vol. 4, 35.

8. Batteux, *Cours de belles lettres*, vol. 4, 274.

9. Batteux, *Cours de belles lettres*, vol. 4, 277–78. Emphasis in original.

10. Batteux, *Les quatre poëtiques: d'Aristote, d'Horace, de Vida, de Despréaux* (Paris, 1771), vol. 1, 55–57.

11. Batteux, *Quatre poëtiques*, vol. 1, 269–70.

12. Batteux, *Quatre poëtiques*, vol. 1, 276.

13. Batteux, *Quatre poëtiques*, vol. 1, 280–81.

14. Louis Racine, *Remarques sur les tragédies de Jean Racine . . .* (Amsterdam, 1752), vol. 3, 83.

15. Racine, *Remarques*, vol. 3, 84–85.

16. Racine, *Remarques*, vol. 3, 102.

17. Racine, *Remarques*, vol. 3, 108–9.

18. Racine, *Remarques*, vol. 3, 111.

19. Racine, *Remarques*, vol. 3, 114.

20. Jean-François Marmontel, *Poétique françoise* (Paris, 1763), vol. 2, 96–97.

21. Marmontel, *Poétique françoise*, vol. 2, 103–4 and 106.

22. A contributor to the *Journal encyclopédique* wrote that "the scaffold is the tragedy of the populace." *Journal encyclopédique . . . Année 1778: Tome III; Partie III* (Bouillon, [1778]), May 1, 1778, 411–12. A contributor to the journal *Pot-pourri* similarly wrote, "What barrier does human Justice oppose to crime? Scaffolds, Torments, Shame. Tragedy spares these frightful Scenes [*ces Sçenes effrayantes*], but it shows crime suffering from remorse; the guilty one falls under the blows of vengeful Justice, [and] she [Justice] teaches [us] to respect Heaven whose eye pursues the guilty one. These are the effects of the tragic Spectacle." *Pot-pourri* 3, no. 13 (1782): 9–10.

23. *Mémoires pour l'histoire des sciences & des beaux arts, commencés d'être imprimés l'an 1701 à Trévoux . . . Janvier 1740* (Paris, 1740), 31–35.

24. Bernard Lamy, *La rhétorique, ou L'art de parler* (Amsterdam, 1712), 537.

25. François de Salignac de La Mothe-Fénelon, *Dialogues sur l'éloquence en général, et sur celle de la chaire en particulier . . .* (Amsterdam, 1718), 19–20.

26. Abbé Jean-Baptiste Dubos, *Réflexions critiques sur la Poésie et la Peinture* (Paris, 1740), 109.

27. Edme-François Mallet, *Principes pour la lecture des poëtes* (Paris, 1745), vol. 2, 15.

28. Jacques Hardion, *Nouvelle Histoire poëtique . . .* (Paris, 1751), 54.

29. Antoine-Hubert Wandelaincourt, *Cours de littérature . . .* (Bouillon, 1776), 194.

30. *Encyclopédie méthodique: Grammaire et littérature . . .* (Paris, 1786), vol. 3, s.v. "Tragédie," 551.

31. Fénelon, *Dialogues sur l'éloquence*, 19–20.

32. François-Marie Arouet de Voltaire, "Dissertation sur les principales tragédies, anciennes et modernes, qui ont paru sur le sujet d'Electre, et en particulier sur celle de Sophocle," ed. David H. Jory, in *Les œuvres complètes de Voltaire* (Banbury: Voltaire Foundation, 1973), vol. 31A and 571–72. Voltaire was not uniformly positive in his assessment of Sophocles, but even his critiques reveal adherence to the twin goals of eliciting terror and pity in the audience. For example, Voltaire criticized the Greek playwright for a "very long description" of the Pythian Games at which Orestes had allegedly died. This recounting "produces neither pity nor terror," Voltaire complained. "Dissertation," 575.

33. *Le journal des sçavans, pour l'année M.DCC.LXV. Avril* (Paris, 1765), 225–26.

34. *L'année littéraire: Année M.DCC.LXXVII . . .* (Paris, 1777), vol. 3, 35.

35. *Journal encyclopédique . . . Tome I; Partie 1* (Bouillon, [1777]), January 1, 1777, 145.

36. Jean Marie Bernard Clément, *De la tragédie, pour servir de suite aux lettres à Voltaire* (Amsterdam, 1784), 165.

37. Terrasson, *Dissertation*, vol. 2, 193–94.

38. "Nouvelles, relations, avis divers," in *Journal encyclopédique . . .* (Liège, 1756), vol. 8, part 2, 129–30.

39. Jean Racine, "Préface," in *Phèdre et Hippolyte: Tragédie* (Paris, 1677), no page number. This comment reappeared numerous times in the seventeenth and eighteenth centuries. Cf. "Preface," in *Œuvres de Racine . . .* (Lyon, 1781), vol. 2, no page number. Cf. also Adrien Baillet, *Jugemens des savants sur les principaux ouvrages des auteurs* (Paris, 1722), vol. 5, 443.

40. Fénelon, *Dialogues sur l'éloquence*, 19–20.

41. Pierre Brumoy, *Le théâtre des grecs* (Amsterdam, 1732), vol. 4, 91.

42. Claude-Adrien Helvétius, *De l'homme, de ses facultés intellectuelles, et de son éducation: Ouvrage posthume de M. Helvetius* (London [i.e., Paris?], 1773), vol. 2, 345–46.

43. Mallet, *Principes*, vol. 2, 23.

44. François-Thomas-Marie de Baculard d'Arnaud, *Le comte de Comminge, ou Les amans malheureux: Drame* (The Hague, 1764), xxvii–xxviii.

45. Jean-Jacques Lefranc, marquis de Pompignan, *Œuvres de M. le marquis de Pompignan: Tome Cinquième, contenant la traduction des tragédies d'Eschyle* (Paris, 1770), vol. 5, 75–76.

46. Nicolas Boileau-Despréaux, "L'art poëtique," in *Œuvres diverses du sieur D**** (Paris, 1674), 119. This expression was frequently republished. See, for example, Hardion, *Nouvelle Histoire poëtique*, 54–55.

47. Boileau-Despréaux, "Lettre à M. Perrault, de l'Académie Françoise," in *Œuvres de M. Boileau-Despréaux* (Paris, 1747), vol. 3, 371–72.

48. Voltaire, *Commentaires sur Corneille* [1761], ed. David Williams, in *Les œuvres complètes de Voltaire* (Banbury: Voltaire Foundation, 1973), hereafter *OCV*, vol. 54, 314.

49. Voltaire, *Commentaires*, in *OCV*, vol. 54, 409.

50. Voltaire, *Commentaires*, in *OCV*, vol. 55, 680.

51. Voltaire, *Commentaires*, in *OCV*, vol. 55, 653, 668, 676, 678, 680, and 703.

52. Voltaire, *Commentaires*, in *OCV*, vol. 55, 729, 767, and 781.

53. Voltaire, *Commentaires*, in *OCV*, vol. 55, 818, and 819.

54. Voltaire, *Commentaires*, in *OCV*, vol. 55, 859, 886, and 919.

55. Pierre-Laurent Buirette de Belloy, "Préface," *Gaston et Baïard: Tragédie* (Paris, 1770), 8.

56. Batteux, *Quatre poëtiques*, vol. 1, 318.

57. D'Arnaud, "Préface," in *Fayel: Tragédie* (Yverdon, 1770), 7. Emphasis in the original.

58. Antoine Sabatier de Castres, *Les trois siècles de notre littérature . . .* (Amsterdam, 1773), vol. 1, s.v. "Corneille," 355–56.

59. Racine, "Préface," in *Phèdre*, no page number.

60. Hilaire Bernard de Requeleyne, baron de Longepierre, "Parallèle de Mr Corneille, et de Mr Racine," (1686) in Baillet, *Jugemens*, vol. 5, 443. Emphasis in the original.

61. Abbé Jean-François de Pons, "Dissertation sur le poëme épique: Par Monseiur l'Abbé Depons; Contre la doctrine de Madame Dacier," *Le nouveau Mercure: Janvier 1717* (Paris, 1717), 34.

62. Jean-Baptiste de Boyer, marquis d'Argens, "XI. Lettre. De Monsieur L.M.D.," in Babet Cochois and Jean-Baptiste de Boyer, marquis d'Argens, *Lettres philosophiques et critiques: Par Mademoiselle Co** avec les réponses de Monsieur D'Arg.*** (The Hague, 1744), 113 and 123–26. In a book that appeared the following year, d'Argens again repeatedly praised Racine for the terror and pity that his plays induced. *Pensées diverses et critiques, sur les principaux auteurs François* (Berlin, 1745), 77, 78, 105, 108, and 110.

63. Mallet, *Principes*, vol. 2, 23.

64. P[ierre-] A[ntoine] de La Place, "Discours sur le théâtre anglois," in *Le théâtre anglois* (London [i.e., Paris?], 1746), vol. 1, xcvii–xcviii.

65. Voltaire, *Commentaires*, in *OCV*, vol. 55, 973.

66. WorldCat lists editions from 1709, 1711, 1712, 1717, 1718, 1719, 1720, 1722, 1729, 1730, 1743, 1748, 1749, 1750, 1754, 1765, 1767, 1768, 1770, 1772, 1775, 1777, 1782, 1784, 1785, and 1788. It was also popular during the Revolution, with editions appearing in 1789, 1791, 1792, 1793, 1796, and 1797.

67. Prosper Jolyot de Crébillon, preface to "Atrée et thyeste, tragédie, représentée, pour la première fois, le 14 mars 1707," in *Œuvres complettes de Crébillon: Nouvelle édition, augmentée & ornée de belles gravures* (Paris, 1785), vol. 1, 97.

68. D'Argens, *Pensées diverses*, 238.

69. Jean-Bernard Le Blanc, *Lettres d'un françois* (The Hague, 1745), vol. 3, 86–87.

70. Gabriel-Henri Gaillard, *Poëtique françoise, à l'usage des dames . . .* (Paris, 1749), vol. 2, 397.

71. *Bibliothèque impartiale, pour les mois de juillet et août, MDCCL: Tome II; Première partie* (Leiden, 1750), 60 and 61.

72. "Suite des Observations sur la Collection complette des Œuvres de Mr. De Voltaire," in *Journal encyclopédique . . . Du 1. décembre 1756* (Liège, 1756), vol. 8, part 2, 108.

73. "Lettre VI. Mort de M. de Crébillon," in *L'Année littéraire: Année M.DCC. LXII . . .* (Amsterdam, 1762), vol. 7, 133–34.

74. "Ode sur la mort de M. de Crébillon," in *Œuvres de Crébillon, nouvelle édition, corrigée, revûe, & augmentée de la vie de l'auteur* (Paris, 1775), vol. 1, 40.

75. Claude Henri de Fusée, Abbé de Voisenon, "Discours de réception à l'académie françoise, prononcé le samedi 22 janvier 1763, par M. l'Abbé de Voisenon, nommé à la place de M. Joliot de Crébillon," in *Œuvres complettes de l'abbé de Voisenon, de l'Académie Françoise* (Paris, 1781), vol. 3, 469–70.

76. Paul-Hippolyte de Beauvilliers, duc de Saint-Aignan, "Réponse de M. le Duc de Saint-Aignan, au discours de M. l'Abbé de Voisenon," in Voisenon, *Œuvres*, vol. 3, 483. Emphasis in the original.

77. Pierre-Laurent Buirette de Belloy, "Préface: Observations historiques," in *Gabrielle de Vergy: Tragédie* (Paris, 1770), 7; and Michel de Cubières-Palmézeaux, "Lettre à une femme sensible," in *La manie des drames sombres, comédie en trois actes, en vers . . .* (Paris, 1777), 2–3.

78. Nicolas Bricaire de la Dixmerie, *Les deux âges du goût et du génie français sous Louis XIV. et sous Louis XV . . .* (Amsterdam, 1770), 29.

79. Jean-Antoine Rigoley de Juvigny, *Discours sur le progrès des lettres en France . . .* (Paris, 1772), 141–43; and *De la décadence des lettres et des mœurs, depuis les Grecs et les Romains jusqu'à nos jours* (Paris, 1787), 336. On Rigoley's hostility to the *philosophes*, see Darrin M. McMahon, "The Counter-Enlightenment and the Low-Life of Literature in Pre-Revolutionary France," *Past and Present* 159 (May 1998): 102 and 102n.

80. Jean Le Rond d'Alembert, "Éloge de Crébillon," in *Histoire des membres de l'Académie Françoise, morts depuis 1700 jusqu'en 1771 . . .* (Paris, 1787), vol. 1, 479–80. Emphasis in the original. For additional valorizations of Crébillon's ability to instill terror, see [De Castres], *Trois siècles*, vol. 1, s.v. "Crébillon," 239; and *Almanach musical, pour l'année mil-sept-cent-quatre-vingt-deux* (Paris, 1782), 225.

81. Michel Guyot de Merville, *Œuvres de théâtre . . .* (Paris, 1742), xii.

82. D'Arnaud, "Préface," in *Fayel: Tragédie*, 8. Emphasis in the original.

83. Clément, *De la tragédie*, 215–16.

84. Voltaire, "Éloge de M. de Crébillon," (1762) in Moland, *Œuvres complètes*, vol. 24, 346–47.

85. Voltaire, "Éloge," 350.

86. Voltaire, "Éloge," 358.

87. "Lettres sur Œdipe" [1719], in *Théâtre complet de Mr. de Voltaire* (Geneva, 1768), vol. 1, 102.

88. Voltaire, "Dissertation sur les principales tragédies," 601 and 603.

89. Voltaire to Marie Anne Dangeville, December 12, 1730, in *Electronic Enlightenment* (database published by the Bodleian Library, Oxford University).

90. Voltaire to Frederick the Great, March 17, 1749, in *OCV*, vol. 95, letter D3893, 18.

91. Voltaire, *Œuvres complètes de Voltaire* ([Kehl], 1785), vol. 64, 50.

92. Frederick II, King of Prussia, *Œuvres du philosophe de Sans-Souci* (n.p., 1750), 293.

93. Frederick II, *Éloge de M. Voltaire . . .* (Berlin, [1778]), 23.

94. Gabriel-Henri Gaillard, *Parallèle des quatre Électres de Sophocle, d'Euripide, de M. de Crébillon, & de M. de Voltaire* (The Hague, 1750), 30. Clément offered a similar assessment of *Zaïre*: "Voltaire understood . . . that a jealous and furious lover, stabbing his mistress because he believes her a liar and unfaithful and stabbing himself when he

recognizes that she is innocent, must agitate and lacerate the soul with all the arrows of pity and terror." Clément, *De la tragédie*, 174.

95. Gaillard, *Parallèle*, 39.

96. Louis Petit de Bachaumont, *Mémoires secrets pour servir à l'histoire de la république des lettres en France* . . . (London [i.e., Amsterdam?], 1781), vol. 15, 173–74.

97. Charles Palissot de Montenoy, "Éloge de M. de Voltaire," *Œuvres complètes de M. Palissot* (Liège, 1779), vol. 7, 90.

98. *Almanach des muses, ou Choix des poësies fugitives de 1767* ([Paris], 1767), 158.

99. D'Arnaud, "Préface," in *Fayel: Tragédie*, 20–21. Emphasis in the original.

100. *L'Année littéraire: Année M.DCC.LXXV* . . . (Amsterdam, 1775), vol. 2, 10–11.

101. Voltaire, "Discours sur la tragédie à Mylord Bolingbroke [1731]," in Moland, *Œuvres complètes*, vol. 2, 318.

102. D'Argens, "XI. Lettre. De Monsieur L.M.D.," in *Lettres philosophiques*, 122–23.

103. Belloy, "Préface," *Gabrielle de Vergy*, 8.

104. *Journal encyclopédique ou universel: 15 juin 1782; Tome IV; Partie III*, 486–87.

105. Rigoley de Juvigny, *Décadence des lettres*, 423–24. Emphasis in the original.

106. La Place, "Discours," lxxiii, lxxix, and xcvii–xcviii.

107. D'Arnaud, *Comte de Comminge*, xxxiv and 5–6. Emphasis in the original.

108. *Almanach des muses* (1771), 191.

109. *L'année littéraire: Année M.DCC.LXXVI* . . . (Paris, 1776), vol. 6, 157–58.

110. Jean-François Marmontel, *Éléments de littérature* (s.l., 1787), vol. 5, 367–68.

111. Margaret-M. Moffat, " 'Le siège de Calais' et l'opinion publique en 1765," *Revue d'histoire littéraire de la France* 39, no. 3 (1932): 339–54.

112. *L'année littéraire: Année M.DCC.LXV* . . . (Amsterdam, 1765), vol. 8, 309–10.

113. *Journal des beaux-arts et des sciences . . . Tome Second: Mai, 1770* (Paris, 1770), 304 and 307–8.

114. *L'année littéraire: Année M.DCC.LXXIX* . . . (Paris, 1779), vol. 3, 152.

115. Belloy, "Préface," 6.

116. Sabatier de Cavaillon, "Réflexions sur les vraisemblances théatrales," in *Œuvres diverses* . . . (Avignon, 1779), vol. 2, 248–49.

117. *Correspondance secrète, politique & littéraire, ou Mémoires pour servir à l'histoire des cours, des sociétés & de la littérature en France, depuis la mort de Louis XV* (London [i.e., Paris?], 1787), vol. 7, 173.

118. *Bibliographie parisienne, ou Catalogue des ouvrages de sciences, de littérature, & de tout ce qui concerne les beaux arts, tels que la musique, la gravure, &c. imprimés ou vendus à Paris* . . . (Paris, 1770), 94–95.

119. *Journal des beaux-arts et des sciences . . . Juin, 1768* (Paris, 1768), 546.

120. *L'année littéraire: Année M.DCC.LXXVII* . . . (Paris, 1777), vol. 3, 91, 97, 98, 99, and 100.

121. *Journal politique, ou Gazette des gazettes: Supplément pour les journaux politiques; Des mois de juillet, août & septembre 1772* (Bouillon, [1772]), 85–86.

122. *Histoire de la république des lettres et arts en France: Année 1779* (Amsterdam, 1780), 37.

123. *Mercure de France* . . . *Fevrier: 1735* (Paris, 1735), 344 (Richer); *L'esprit des journaux, françois et étrangers*, November 1782, 380 (Chamfort); *Pot-pourri*, vol. 3, no. 13 (1782), 9–10 (Rochefort).

124. *Mémoires* . . . *à Trévoux* . . . *Juillet première partie 1736* (Paris, 1736), 1755 (Maffei); Joseph de Laporte, *Anecdotes dramatiques* . . . (Paris, 1775), vol. 3, s.v. "Gomez, (Magdeleine-Angélique Poisson de)," 213 (Gomez); *Journal des sçavants, pour l'année M.DCC.LVIII: Janvier* (Paris, 1758), 463–64 (Colardeau); *Journal des sçavans, pour l'année M.DCC.LXIV: Juin* (Paris, 1764), 330 (La Harpe); *L'Année littéraire: Année M.DCC. LXVIII* . . . (Amsterdam, 1768), vol. 7, 227 (Saurin); and *L'Année littéraire: Année M.DCC. LXXXII* (Paris, 1782), vol. 8, 149 (Fallet).

CHAPTER FIVE

1. According to the classicist D. A. Russell, "European literary criticism owes most, among Greek writers, to Aristotle. Its next biggest creditor it knows as Longinus." D[onald] A[ndrew] Russell, *"Longinus" on the Sublime* (Oxford: Clarendon Press, 1964), ix.

2. Nicolas Boileau-Despréaux, "Traité du sublime ou du merveilleux dans le discours," in *Œuvres diverses du sieur D*** avec le traité du sublime, ou Du merveilleux dans le discours traduit du grec de Longin* (Paris, 1674), 5.

3. Boileau-Despréaux, "Traité," 7.

4. Boileau-Despréaux, "Traité," 19. In the original Longinus used the word *deinos*.

5. Boileau-Despréaux, "Traité," 28. In the original Longinus used the word *phoberos*.

6. WorldCat lists publication dates of 1674, 1675, 1677, 1678, 1680, 1682, 1683, 1685, 1686, 1688, 1689, 1692, 1694, 1695, 1697, 1700, 1701, 1702, 1703, 1707, 1708, 1710, 1713, 1714, 1716, 1717, 1718, 1722, 1724, 1729, 1735, 1736, 1740, 1741, 1743, 1746, 1747, 1749, 1757, 1758, 1764, 1766, 1767, 1768, 1769, and 1772.

7. Burke, who did not read Greek, would have read an anonymous translation of Boileau "which set Boileau's French alongside the Greek and English versions" and "remained the key edition during Burke's education." C[ressida] Ryan, "Burke's Classical Heritage: Playing Games with Longinus," in *The Science of Sensibility: Reading Burke's Philosophical Enquiry*, ed. Koen Vermeir and Michael Funk Deckard (Dordrecht: Springer, 2012), 228.

8. Edmund Burke, *Recherches philosophiques sur l'origine des idées que nous avons du beau et du sublime* . . . (London [i.e., Paris?], 1765), vol. 1, 109–10. Cf. Burke, *A Philosophical Enquiry into the Origin of Our Ideas of the Sublime and the Beautiful* (London, 1759), 83–84.

9. Burke, *Recherches*, vol. 1, 78. Cf. the English original: "Whatever is fitted in any sort to excite the ideas of pain and danger; that is to say, whatever is in any sort terrible, or is conversant about terrible objects, or operates in a manner analogous to terror, is a source of the *sublime*; that is, it is productive of the strongest emotion which the mind is capable of feeling." *Philosophical Enquiry* (1759), 58–59. Note that the original does not contain the word "horrible," which Des François interpolated (as *épouvantable*) into his translation.

10. For the distinction between pleasure and contentment see Burke, *Recherches*, vol. 1, 65–73. Cf. the English original, in which Burke uses the term "delight" rather than "contentment," *Philosophical Enquiry* (1759), 47–54.

11. Burke, *Recherches*, vol. 1, 123–24. Cf. Burke, *Philosophical Enquiry*, 96–97.

12. Burke, *Recherches*, vol. 1, 126–27. Cf. Burke, *Philosophical Enquiry*, 99–100.

13. Burke, *Recherches*, vol. 2, 134–37. Emphasis in the original. Cf. Burke, *Philosophical Enquiry*, 272–75.

14. Burke, *Recherches*, vol. 1, 141–43. Cf. Burke, *Philosophical Enquiry*, 110–12.

15. Burke, *Recherches*, vol. 1, 143–45. Cf. Job 39:19–24. Cf. Burke, *Philosophical Enquiry*, 112–13.

16. Burke, *Recherches*, vol. 1, 147–49. Cf. Burke, *Philosophical Enquiry*, 115–16.

17. Burke, *Recherches*, vol. 1, 149–50. Cf. Burke, *Philosophical Enquiry*, 116–17.

18. Burke, *Recherches*, vol. 1, 150–53. Cf. Burke, *Philosophical Enquiry*, 117–20.

19. Burke, *Recherches*, vol. 1, 153, 155–56. Cf. Pss. 139:14 and 114:7. Cf. Burke, *Philosophical Enquiry*, 120, 121–22.

20. Burke, *Recherches*, vol. 1, 154. Cf. Burke, *Philosophical Enquiry*, 120–21.

21. Burke, *Recherches*, vol. 1, 157–59. Cf. Burke, *Philosophical Enquiry*, 122–24.

22. Burke, *Recherches*, vol. 1, 190–93. Emphasis in the original. Cf. Burke, *Philosophical Enquiry*, 150–53.

23. Burke, *Recherches*, vol. 2, 112–13. Cf. Burke, *Philosophical Enquiry*, 254–55.

24. On the eighteenth-century distinction between "gross" and "fine" parts of the body see Aris Sarafianos, "Pain, Labor, and the Sublime: Medical Gymnastics and Burke's Aesthetics," *Representations* 91 (Summer 2005): 75.

25. Burke, *Recherches*, vol. 2, 115–16. Cf. Burke, *Philosophical Enquiry*, 256–57.

26. *Journal encyclopédique, par une société de gens de lettres, dédié à Son Alt. Ser. & Emin. Jean-Théodore, duc de Bavière, cardinal, évêque & prince de Liège, de Freysing & Ratisbonne, &c: Du 1. Juillet 1757; Tome V; Première partie* (Liège, 1757), 3–5.

27. *Journal encyclopédique*, 10–13.

28. *Journal encyclopédique*, 17–18. Emphasis in the original.

29. As Thomas Munck has observed, historians seeking to study the transmission of ideas should take into account the impact of book-review journals and not restrict their analysis to books alone. Munck, "Eighteenth-Century Review Journals and the Internationalization of the European Book Market," *International History Review* 32 (September 2010): 415–35.

30. I have adopted the phrase from Darrin McMahon, *Enemies of the Enlightenment: The French Counter-Enlightenment and the Making of Modernity* (New York: Oxford University Press, 2001). On Fréron and Voltaire's hatred of him, see McMahon, *Enemies*, 24.

31. "Lettre IX: Recherches philosophiques," in *L'Année littéraire: Année M.DCC. LXII; Par M. Fréron . . .* (Amsterdam, 1765), vol. 1, 211–12.

32. "Lettre IX," 209.

33. *Gazette littéraire de l'Europe: Tome quatrième; Comprenant les mois de décembre 1764, janvier & février 1765* (Paris, 1765), 207–8.

34. *Le journal des sçavans, pour l'année M.DCC.LXVII* (Paris, 1767), May, 331 and 333–34.

35. Denis Diderot, *Salons*, ed. Jean Seznec and Jean Adhémar (Oxford: Clarendon Press, 1975), 2nd ed., vol. 1, 64. For the images, see *Salons*, vol. 1, no. 6 (Medea) and no. 10 (Carthusians). The *Medea* is in the Charlottenburg Palace, Berlin. The *Carthusians* is in the Église St. Bernard de la Chapelle, Paris.

36. Diderot, *Salons*, vol. 1, 121. For the image see *Salons*, vol. 1, no. 51. The original is in the Musée de Rouen.

37. Diderot, *Salons*, vol. 1, 131–32. For the image see *Salons*, vol. 1, no. 73. The original is at the Hermitage, Saint Petersburg.

38. Diderot, *Salons*, vol. 1, 125. The painting is not reproduced in Seznec and Adhémar, and I have not been able to find the original.

39. Diderot, *Salons*, vol. 1, 212. The painting is not reproduced in Seznec and Adhémar, and I have not been able to find the original.

40. Diderot, *Salons*, vol. 2, 92–93. The painting is not reproduced in Seznec and Adhémar, and I have not been able to find the original.

41. Diderot, *Salons*, vol. 2, 97. The painting is not reproduced in Seznec and Adhémar, and I have not been able to find the original.

42. Diderot, *Salons*, vol. 2, 97–98. For the image see *Salons*, vol. 2, no. 22. The original is in the Église Saint-Louis at Versailles.

43. Diderot, *Salons*, vol. 2, 100–104. The painting is not reproduced in Seznec and Adhémar, and I have not been able to find the original.

44. On Diderot's use of Burke, see Gita May, "Diderot and Burke: A Study in Aesthetic Affinity," *PMLA* 75 (December 1960): 527–39.

45. Diderot, *Salons*, vol. 3, 158.

46. Diderot, *Salons*, vol. 3, 160.

47. Diderot, *Salons*, vol. 3, 162.

48. Diderot, *Salons*, vol. 3, 165. Cf. Burke, *Recherches*, vol. 1, 124–26.

49. Diderot, *Salons*, vol. 3, 165. Cf. Burke, *Recherches*, vol. 1, 127.

50. Diderot, *Salons*, vol. 3, 166. Cf. Burke, *Recherches*, vol. 1, 192–93.

51. Diderot, *Salons*, vol. 3, 165. Cf. Burke, *Recherches*, vol. 1, 143–45.

52. Claude-Adrien Helvétius, *De l'esprit* (Paris, 1758), 248–49.

53. Robert Darnton ranks *De l'homme* twenty-eighth on his list of "forbidden best-sellers." Darnton, *The Forbidden Best-Sellers of Pre-Revolutionary France* (New York: Norton, 1996), 64.

54. Helvétius, *De l'homme*, vol. 2, 343. Reiterating his view that the sublime positively *required* terror, Helvétius wrote, "In image the sublime therefore always supposes the feeling of an incipient terror, and cannot be the product of another sentiment." *De l'homme*, vol. 2, 346.

55. Helvétius, *De l'homme*, vol. 2, 344.

56. Burke, *Recherches*, vol. 1, 153.

57. Helvétius, *De l'homme*, vol. 2, 344–45. *The Fall of the Giants* is in the Palazzo del Te in Mantua. Image accessed via Artstor and provided by SCALA, Florence/Art Resource, NY. *The Toilet of Venus* is in the Prado, Madrid. Image accessed via Artstor and provided by Erich Lessing Culture and Fine Arts Archives/Art Resource, NY.

58. Helvétius, *De l'homme*, vol. 2, 346–47, 349, 351–52, and 352–53.

59. Helvétius, *De l'homme*, vol. 2, 345–46.

60. Helvétius, *De l'homme*, vol. 2, 346n and 355.

61. Frederika MacDonald, *Jean-Jacques Rousseau: A New Criticism* (London, 1906), vol. 1, 41.

62. Pliny the Elder, *Traduction des xxxiv, xxxv et xxxviᵉ livres de Pline l'Ancien avec des notes, par Etienne Falconet* (Amsterdam 1772; reprint: The Hague, 1773), 281–82.

63. Étienne Falconet, "Quelques idées sur le beau dans l'art, occasionnées par un passage de Pline," in *Œuvres d'Étienne Falconet, statuaire . . .* (Lausanne, 1781), vol. 5, 50.

64. [Marie-Jeanne de Chatillon, trans.], *Les Saisons: Poëme traduit de l'Anglois de Thomson* (Paris, 1769), 262 and 266–67. Cf. James Thomson, *The Seasons* (London, 1730), 191 and 196–97.

65. WorldCat lists editions from 1769, 1771, 1773, 1775, 1777, 1779, 1780, 1782, 1783, and 1788.

66. Antoine de Cournand, *Les styles: Poème en quatre chants* (Paris, 1781), 147–48.

67. Alexandre Frédéric Jacques de Masson, marquis de Pezay, *Les soirées helvé-tiennes, alsaciennes, et fran-comtoises* (Amsterdam, 1771), 18.

68. "Lettre V," *L'Année littéraire: Année M.DCC.LXX; Par M. Fréron . . .* (Paris, 1770), vol. 8, 113.

69. *L'esprit des journaux*, March 1786, 111. The review was of Marc-Théodore Bourrit, *Nouvelle description des glacières, vallées de glace et glaciers qui forment la grande chaîne des Alpes, de Savoye, de Suisse et d'Italie* (Geneva, 1783–85), 3 vols.

70. Horace Bénédict de Saussure, *Voyages dans les alpes, précédés d'un essai sur l'histoire naturelle des environs de Genève* (Geneva, 1786), vol. 2, 29–30.

71. Thomas Whately, *L'art de former les jardins modernes, ou L'art des jardins anglois* (Paris, 1771), 82. Cf. Thomas Whately, *Observations on Modern Gardening, Illustrated by Descriptions* (London, 1770), 62.

72. Whately, *L'art de former les jardins modernes*, 139. Cf. Whateley, *Observations*, 106. A positive review of the French translation of Whately's book, including a quotation from the passage about terror and the sublime, appeared in Abbé François Rozier, *Introduction aux observations sur la physique, sur l'histoire naturelle et sur les arts . . .* (Paris, 1777), vol. 1, 259. Rozier was a botanist and agronomist.

73. Jacques-Pierre Brissot de Warville, *Mémoires (1754–1793)*, ed. Claude Perroud (Paris: Picard et fils, 1911), vol. 1, 71.

CHAPTER SIX

1. Julien Offray de La Mettrie, *Histoire naturelle de l'ame . . .* (Oxford [i.e., Paris], 1747), 109. The same quotation appears in La Mettrie's commentary on the work of the renowned Dutch physician Herman Boerhaave, *Institutions de médecine de Mr. Herman Boerhaave, seconde édition, avec un commentaire par M. de la Mettrie, Docteur en Médecine* (Paris, 1747), vol. 5, 107–8.

2. Friedrich Hoffmann, *La médecine raisonnée . . .* (Paris, 1742), vol. 4, 157–58. By "spirits" Hoffmann was referring to the substance that since the time of Plato had been reputed to inhere in the blood and organs of the human body. Divided into "natural,"

"vital," and "animal," these spirits were crucial to the health of the organism. Whether they were liquid, particulate, or immaterial was a matter of long-standing debate, but their concentration, speed, and location were important factors in health and illness. On the spirits see Sidney Ochs, *A History of Nerve Functions: From Animal Spirits to Molecular Mechanisms* (Cambridge: Cambridge University Press, 2004), 25–29.

3. Hoffmann, *Médecine raisonnée*, vol. 4, 158. Cf. Marcello Malpighi, *De viscerum structura exercitatio anatomica . . .* (Bologna, 1666), 164–65.

4. Hoffmann, *Médecine raisonnée*, vol. 4, 158–59. Möbius listed "terror" as one of the causes of paralysis. Gottfried Möbius, "Synopsis paraliseos," in *Synopses epitomes institutionum Medicinae . . .* (Padua, 1667), 14.

5. Hoffmann, *Médecine raisonnée*, vol. 4, 159–60.

6. Hoffmann, *Médecine raisonnée*, vol. 4, 161–62. Cf. Carl Rayger, "LXX. Mensium obstructio ex terrore," in *Observationum Medicinalium Centuria . . .* (Frankfurt, 1691), 130–31.

7. Hoffmann, *Médecine raisonnée*, vol. 4, 165–67. Cf. Rayger, "XCVI. Ex terrore mira symptomata," in *Observationum*, 171.

8. François Planque, *Bibliothèque choisie de medicine* (Paris, 1748–66), vol. 9, s.v., "Passion," 214. Emphasis in the original.

9. Robert James, *Dictionnaire universel de médecine, de chirurgie, de chymie, de botanique, d'anatomie, de pharmacie, d'histoire naturelle, &c. . . .* (Paris, 1747), vol. 3, s.v., "Epilepsia," 1363. Cf. James, *A Medicinal Dictionary; Including Physic, Surgery, Anatomy, Chymistry, and Botany, in all their Branches Relative to Medicine . . .* (London, 1745), vol. 3, s.v. "Epilepsia," no page number.

10. James, *Dictionnaire universel*, vol. 3, s.v. "Diaeta," 1069. Cf. James, *Medicinal Dictionary*, vol. 3, s.v. "Diaeta," no page number.

11. Isaac Bellet, *Lettres sur le pouvoir de l'imagination des femmes enceintes* (Paris, 1745), 201.

12. Bellet, *Lettres*, 215. Bellet shared Hoffmann's opinion that terror could lead to sudden death. *Lettres*, 195–96.

13. François Chicoyneau, *Traité des causes, des accidens, et de la cure de la peste . . .* (Paris, 1744), 75. In this respect Chicoyneau seconded the opinion of Étienne-François Geoffroy, who had previously written that "everyone knows what effect terror produces, and how it is suited to augment the violence of the plague." Geoffroy, *Traité de la matière médicale . . .* (Paris, 1743), vol. 6, 120.

14. François de Paule Combalusier, *Pneumato-pathologie . . .* (Paris, 1754), vol. 2, 140.

15. Joseph Lieutaud, *Précis de médecine pratique . . .* (Paris, 1761), 2nd ed., 37.

16. Lieutaud, *Précis*, 271.

17. Lieutaud, *Précis*, 195. Lieutaud's claim was plagiarized by Philippe Fermin, who wrote, "Great terror, excessive sorrow, and adversity often cause memory loss and make one stupid." Fermin, *Instructions importantes au peuple, sur l'oeconomie animale . . .* (The Hague, 1767), 98.

18. Anton von Störck, *Observations nouvelles sur l'usage de la cigüe . . .* (Vienna, 1762), 263.

19. Mazars dc Cazelles, "Sur une Catalepsie occasionnée par la terreur," *Journal de médecine, chirurgie, pharmacie, &c.* (February 1762): 131–32.

20. Toussaint Bordenave, *Essai sur la physiologie* (Paris, 1764), 67.

21. Jean Ferapie Dufieu, *Dictionnaire raisonné d'anatomie et de physiologie* (Paris, 1766), vol. 2, 322.

22. Antoine Petit, *Premier rapport, en faveur de l'inoculation* . . . (Paris, 1766), 23.

23. François Boissier de Sauvages de Lacroix, *Nosologie methodique* . . . (Lyon, 1772), vol. 7, 409 (memory loss) and 242 (convulsions); and vol. 2, 420 (lassitude), 609 (hallucinations), 615 ("hysterical vertigo"), 152 (fainting), and 49 ("suffocating nightmares").

24. Francis Home, *Principes de médecine* . . . (Paris, 1772), 23–4. Cf. Home, *Principia medicinae* (Edinburgh, 1758), 16.

25. Home, *Principes*, 88 (fever) and 411 (paralysis and impotence). Cf. Home, *Principia*, 63 (fever) and 219 (paralysis and impotence).

26. Robert Whytt, *Des maladies nerveuses hypocondriaques et hysteriques* . . . (Paris, 1777), vol. 1, 288–89. Cf. Whytt, *Observations on the Nature, Causes, and Cure of those Disorders which have been Commonly Called Nervous, Hypochondriac, or Hysteric* . . . (Edinburgh, 1765), 212 and 212n.

27. Whytt, *Maladies nerveuses*, vol. 1, 290. Cf. Whytt, *Observations*, 213.

28. Jean-Baptiste Pressavin, *Nouveau traité des vapeurs, ou Traité des maladies des nerfs* . . . (Lyon, 1770), 20; *Nouveaux mémoires de l'Académie Royale des Sciences et Belles-Lettres: Année MDCCLXXIV* . . . (Berlin, 1776), 402; Georg Zimmermann, *Traité de l'expérience en général, et en particulier dans l'art de guérir* . . . (Paris, 1774), vol. 3, 225 (cf. Zimmermann, *Von der Erfahrung in der Arzneykunst* [Zurich, 1764], vol. 4, 434–35); Jean-Gaspard d'Ailhaud, *Traité de la vraie cause des maladies, et manière la plus sûre de les guérir par le moyen d'un seul remède* (Carpentras, 1776), 75; Daniel de La Roche, *Analyse des fonctions du système nerveux* . . . (Geneva, 1778), vol. 1, 9–10; Joseph Raulin the Elder, *Traité de la conservation des enfans* . . . (Paris, 1779), vol. 2, 551–52; and Michel du Tennetar, *Éléments de séméiotique* . . . (Bouillon, 1777), s.v. "Mort," 347.

29. Danilo Samoilovich, *Mémoire sur l'inoculation de la peste* . . . (Strasbourg, 1782), 6.

30. *Dictionnaire universel des sciences morale, économique, politique et diplomatique* . . . (London, 1783), vol. 30, s.v. "Sens interne," 551.

31. Félix Vicq-d'Azyr, *Encyclopédie méthodique: Médicine* (Paris, 1787), s.v. "Affectations de l'âme," vol. 1, 260.

32. William Cullen, *Élémens de médecine-pratique* . . . (Paris, 1787), vol. 2, 344–45. Cf. Cullen, *First Lines of the Practice of Physic* (Edinburgh, 1777), vol. 3, 331.

33. Aulus Cornelius Celsus, *Traduction des ouvrages d'Aurélius-Cornélius Celse, sur la médecine* (Paris, 1753), vol. 1, book 3, chapter 18, 269. Cf. *De medicina* (Cambridge, MA: Harvard University Press, 1935), vol. 1, 302.

34. Planque, *Bibliothèque choisie*, vol. 9, 215. Planque gave the following citation: "*Rolfincius, comment. in lib. I, act. aph. I.*" This appears to be a reference to Werner Rolfinck, *Commentarius in Hippocratis primum libri aphorismum* (Jena, 1662), but I have been unable to locate the story in that work.

35. "Fin de l'extrait du tome XXV de la Bibliothèque choisie de médecine, par M. Planque," *Gazette salutaire* . . . Du jeudi 17 octobre 1771, no. 42, no page number.

36. Home, *Principes*, 327. Cf. Home, *Principia*, 235.

37. Cullen, *Élémens*, vol. 2, 487. Cf. Cullen, *First Lines*, vol. 4, 154.

38. William Falconer, *A Dissertation on the Influence of the Passions upon Disorders of the Body* (London, 1788), 82–83.

39. Falconer, *De l'influence des passions, sur les maladies du corps humain* (Paris, 1788), 113–15.

40. According to WorldCat, the *Précis* was published in 1759, 1760, 1761, 1762, 1765, 1766, 1768, 1769, 1770, 1774, 1775, 1776, 1777, 1781, 1787, and 1789.

41. Lieutaud, *Précis*, 447.

42. Jan Baptista van Helmont, *Opera omnia* . . . (Frankfurt, 1682), 764. Elsewhere in this work Van Helmont wrote that "the terror of submersion stops rabies." *Opera*, 831.

43. Nima Bassiri writes that by the middle of the eighteenth century "the entire brain . . . came to assume the very name that had already been used to define the white matter: *sensorium commune*, the undifferentiated site of the convergence and unification of the nerves." "The Brain and the Unconscious Soul in Eighteenth-Century Nervous Physiology: Robert Whytt's *Sensorium Commune*," *Journal of the History of Ideas* 74 (July 2013): 438.

44. Vicq-d'Azyr, *Encyclopédie méthodique: Médecine*, vol. 1, s.v. "Affectations de l'âme," 260.

45. Vicq-d'Azyr, *Encyclopédie méthodique: Médecine*, vol. 1, s.v. "Affectations de l'âme," 260.

46. François Valleriola, *Francisci Valleriolae doctoris medici observationvn medicinalivm libri sex* . . . (Lyon, 1573), 78–79.

47. Valleriola, *Observationvn medicinalivm libri sex*, 83.

48. Hoffmann, *Médecine raisonnée*, vol. 4, 167–69.

49. Robert James, *Dictionnaire universel*, vol. 5, s.v. "Pyretos," 962. Cf. James, *Medicinal Dictionary*, vol. 3, s.v. "Pyretos," no page number.

50. Planque, *Bibliothèque choisie*, vol. 9, s.v. "Passion," 215.

51. "Fin de l'extrait."

52. Boissier de Sauvages de Lacroix, *Nosologie*, vol. 2, 278 and 278–79n.

53. Mazars de Cazelles, "Sur une Catalepsie," 133.

54. Joseph Aignan Sigaud de la Fond, *Dictionnaire des merveilles de la nature* (Paris, 1781), vol. 2, s.v. "Terreur," 371–72. In fact, Schenck did report that case, but he gave credit to Valleriola. Johannes Schenck von Grafenberg, *Observationes medicae de capite humano* (Basel, 1584), obs. 181, no page number.

55. IJsbrand van Diemerbroeck, *Anatome corporis humani* . . . (Drunen, 1672), book 8, chapter 1 ("De Nervis in genere"), 745.

56. Mazars de Cazelles, "Sur une Catalepsie, 133.

57. Sigaud de la Fond, *Dictionnaire*, vol. 2, s.v. "Terreur," 371–72.

58. La Mettrie, *Histoire naturelle*, 109; and Boerhaave, *Institutions*, vol. 5, 107–8.

59. Boissier de Sauvages de Lacroix, *Nosologie*, vol. 2, 278 and 278–79n.

60. Philip Salmuth, *Philippi Salmuthi archiatri Anhaltini observationum medicarum centuriae tres posthumae* . . . (Brunswick, 1648), 32.

61. Vicq-d'Azyr, *Encyclopédie méthodique: Médecine*, vol. 1, s.v. "Affectations de l'âme," 260.

62. Wilhelm Fabricius Hildanus, *Gvilhelmi Fabricii Hildani* . . . *Opera quae extant Omnia* . . . (Frankfurt an der Oder, 1646), 993.

63. Falconer, *Influence des passions*, 75–76. Cf. Falconer, *Influence of the Passions*, 47. Van Swieten did write that gout could be cured "by powerful terror" (*terrore valido*), but he did not cite Hildanus. Gerard van Swieten, *Commentaria in Hermanni Boerhaave Aphorismos de cognoscendis et curandis morbis* (Leiden, 1742), vol. 4, §1262, 291.

64. Falconer, *Influence des passions*, 76. Cf. Falconer, *Influence of the Passions*, 47.

65. Falconer, *Influence des passions*, 75n.

66. Van Swieten, *Commentaria*, vol. 4, §1262, 291.

67. La Mettrie, *Histoire naturelle*, 109; and Boerhaave, *Institutions*, vol. 5, 107–8.

68. Abraham Kaau-Boerhaave, *Impetum faciens dictum Hippocrati . . .* (Leiden, 1745), 356–57.

69. The French-language edition of Zimmermann's *Von der Erfahrung in der Arzneykunst* [On Experience in the Medical Art] roughly translated Kaau-Boerhaave's account from Latin, recalling the "event that will always do honor to the sagacity of the famous Boerhaave." Zimmermann added a detail that was absent from Kaau-Boerhaave's telling of the story: "The weakest one among [the children], excessively struck by the terrible operation to which he was going to be subjected, fell dead on the spot," though "all the others were happily cured." The report of this casualty reinforced the idea, also common among early modern doctors, that although terror was sometimes salutary, it was also dangerous and potentially fatal. Zimmermann, *Traité de l'expérience*, vol. 3, 226–28. Cf. Zimmermann, *Von der Erfahrung*, vol. 4, 446–48.

70. *Nouveau dictionnaire universel et raisonné de médecine, de chirurgie, et de l'art vétérinaire . . .* (Paris, 1772), vol. 6, s.v. "Terreur panique," 239.

71. Cullen, *Eléments*, vol. 2, 357. Cf. Cullen, *First Lines*, vol. 3, 217.

72. According to the Académie Française dictionary of 1762, a *charlatan* was chiefly a "vendor of drugs, of orvietan, and who sells in public places, in theaters, on stages." The definition added that this was "ordinarily a term of contempt" but did not indicate that this was always the case. Consulted on the *Dictionnaires d'autrefois* database, generated by the Analyse et traitement informatique de la langue française (ATILF) research unit at the Centre national de la recherche scientifique (CNRS) and the University of Chicago. http://artflsrv02.uchicago.edu/cgi-bin/dicos/pubdico1look.pl?strippedhw=charlatan, accessed May 4, 2016. Colin Jones reports that enemies of a popular tooth-puller in eighteenth-century Paris called him a charlatan, but the tooth-puller used this word to describe himself. Colin Jones, "Pulling Teeth in Eighteenth-Century Paris," *Past and Present* 166 (February 2000): 100, 102, and 119.

73. *L'esprit des journaux, françois et étrangers . . . Novembre, 1778: Tome XI.*, 29–30.

74. Thomas Bartholin, *Thomae Bartholini Historiarum anatomicarum rariorum centuria III & IV . . .* (The Hague, 1657), 58.

75. Valleriola, *Observationvn medicinalivm libri sex*, 82.

76. Hoffmann, *Médecine raisonnée*, vol. 4, 169.

77. Whytt, *Maladies nerveuses*, vol. 1, 52. Cf. Whytt, *Observations*, 31.

78. Planque, *Bibliothèque choisie*, vol. 9, s.v. "Passion," 216.

79. Lieutaud, *Précis*, 57.

80. Vicq-d'Azyr, *Encyclopédie méthodique: Médecine*, vol. 1, s.v. "Affectations de l'âme," 260.

81. *Nouveau dictionnaire*, vol. 6, s.v. "Terreur panique," 239.

82. Cullen, *Élémens*, vol. 2, 399. Cf. Cullen, *First Lines*, vol. 3, 288.

83. Cullen, *Elémens*, vol. 2, 31. Cf. Cullen, *First Lines*, vol. 2, 178.

84. Hoffmann, *Médecine raisonnée*, vol. 4, 168.

85. Hoffmann, *Médecine raisonnée*, vol. 4, 168. This claim was repeated in Planque, *Bibliothèque choisie*, vol. 9, 215; and "Fin de l'extrait," *Gazette salutaire . . . 17 octobre 1771*, no. 42, no page number. It was based on Pechlin, who also reported (in a chapter called "Terror morborum Remedium," or "Terror a Remedy for Illnesses") that terror could cure "many fevers," rabies, arthritis, gout, various hemorrhages, hiccups, and hernia carnosa (a fleshy growth surrounding the testes). Johann Nicolas Pechlin, *Observationum physico-medicarum libri tres . . .* (Hamburg, 1691), 451–53.

86. Lieutaud, *Précis*, 57.

87. Vicq-d'Azyr, *Encyclopédie méthodique: Médecine*, vol. 1, s.v. "Affectations de l'âme," 260.

88. Hoffmann, *Médecine raisonnée*, vol. 4, 167. Cf. Planque, who closely followed Hoffmann's wording: "Despite an infinity of examples of the bad effect [sic] of terror, we learn from other observations that it has cured many illnesses." Planque, *Bibliothèque choisie*, vol. 9, 215.

89. Albrecht von Haller, *Élémens de physiologie . . .* (Paris, 1749), 95. Other French editions of this work were published in 1752, 1761, and 1769.

90. Zimmermann, *Traité de l'expérience*, vol. 3, 225. Cf. Zimmermann, *Von der Erfahrung*, vol. 4, 443–44.

91. Jean-Paul Marat, *De l'homme, ou Des principes et des loix de l'influence de l'âme sur le corps, et du corps sur l'âme* (Amsterdam, 1775), vol. 2, 54–55.

92. Antoine de Baecque, *The Body Politic: Corporeal Metaphor in Revolutionary France, 1770–1800*, trans. Charlotte Mandell (Stanford, CA: Stanford University Press, 1997).

93. On the riots see Laura Rodríguez, "The Spanish Riots of 1766," *Past and Present* 59 (May 1973): 117–46.

94. *Mercure historique et politique . . . pour le mois de juillet 1766* (The Hague, 1766), 20.

95. Cullen, *Eléments*, vol. 2, 399–400. Cf. Cullen, *First Lines*, vol. 3, 289.

96. Leonard Stocke, *Dissertatio medica inauguralis de terrore ejusque effectis in corpus humanum . . .* (Utrecht, 1733), 36.

97. Reinhart Koselleck, "Crisis," trans. Michaela W. Richter, *Journal of the History of Ideas* 67 (April 2006): 357–400.

98. De Baecque, *Body Politic*.

99. It is worth recalling here that for Burke it was "the power . . . to harm" that distinguished the sublime bull from the docile ox. Edmund Burke, *Recherches philosophiques sur l'origine des idées que nous avons du beau & du sublime . . .* (London [i.e., Paris?], 1765), vol. 1, 143. Cf. Burke, *A Philosophical Enquiry into the Origin of Our Ideas of the Sublime and the Beautiful* (London, 1759), 112–13.

100. Clifford Geertz memorably wrote of the "inherent sacredness of sovereign power." "Centers, Kings, and Charisma: Reflections on the Symbolics of Power," in *Local Knowledge: Further Essays in Interpretive Anthropology* (New York: Basic Books, 1983), 123.

CHAPTER SEVEN

1. On the emergence of nationalism in the long eighteenth century, see David A. Bell, *The Cult of the Nation in France: Inventing Nationalism, 1680–1800* (Cambridge, MA: Harvard University Press, 2001).

2. *Reimpression [sic] de l'ancien Moniteur, seule histoire authentique et inaltérée de la Révolution française depuis la réunion des Etats-Généraux* . . . (Paris, 1847–54), vol. 2, no. 78 (October 26–28, 1789), 89–90.

3. Jérôme Mavidal et al., eds., *Archives parlementaires de 1787 à 1860, première série (1787–1799)* (Paris: 1867–2005), vol. 11, 655–56.

4. *Archives parlementaires*, vol. 11, 665 and 674.

5. *Archives parlementaires*, vol. 84, 333.

6. Not to be confused with the Parisian *comité des recherches*. On the latter see Barry M. Shapiro, *Revolutionary Justice in Paris, 1789–1790* (Cambridge: Cambridge University Press, 1993), especially 14–25.

7. *Archives parlementaires*, vol. 12, 161. For Augeard's account of his arrest and detention see *Mémoires secrets de J. M. Augeard, secrétaire des commandements de la reine Marie-Antoinette (1760 à 1800)* . . . (Paris, 1866), 206–30.

8. *Archives parlementaires*, vol. 12, 161. Cf. *L'ancien Moniteur*, vol. 3, no. 31 (January 31, 1790), 248.

9. *Archives parlementaires*, vol. 18, 167.

10. *Archives parlementaires*, vol. 20, 594.

11. *L'ancien Moniteur*, vol. 6, no. 326 (November 22, 1790), 435.

12. Louis-Sébastien Mercier, *Tableau de Paris* (Amsterdam, 1789), vol. 9, 136. Mercier would later serve as a moderate deputy in the Convention, where he opposed the execution of the king and the proscription of the Girondins. He was imprisoned during the Terror.

13. *Archives parlementaires*, vol. 17, 665. On Brevet's politics, see Édouard Bougler, *Mouvement provincial en 1789: Biographie des députés de l'Anjou depuis l'Assemblée Constituante jusqu'en 1815* (Paris, 1865), vol. 1, 252–72.

14. *Archives parlementaires*, vol. 22, 345.

15. See Donald M. G. Sutherland, *The French Revolution and Empire: The Quest for a Civic Order* (Malden, MA: Blackwell, 2003), 100–103.

16. *Archives parlementaires*, vol. 20, 156.

17. *Archives parlementaires*, vol. 23, 541.

18. *Archives parlementaires*, vol. 21, 281.

19. *Archives parlementaires*, vol. 21, 289.

20. On Vieillard's political affiliation, see Timothy Tackett, *Becoming a Revolutionary: The Deputies of the French National Assembly and the Emergence of a Revolutionary Culture (1789–1790)* (Princeton, NJ: Princeton University Press, 1996), 203n.

21. *Archives parlementaires*, vol. 21, 150–52.

22. *Archives parlementaires*, vol. 26, 322.

23. *Archives parlementaires*, vol. 26, 619–20. For Prugnon's opinion on the inviolability of the king, see *Gazette des cours de l'Europe: Le royaliste, ami de l'humanité*, no. 82, July 18, 1791, 362.

24. *Archives parlementaires,* vol. 26, 683–84. On Mercier-Terrefort's execution, see Louis Marie Prudhomme, *Dictionnaire des individus envoyés à la mort judiciairement, révolutionnairement et contre-révolutionnairement pendant la révolution, particulière- ment sous le règne de la convention nationale* (Paris, 1796), vol. 2, 166.

25. *Archives parlementaires,* vol. 26, 711. For Riffard de Saint-Martin's opinion on the king's fate, see *Archives parlementaires,* vol. 57, 307–11. Cf. François-Jérôme Riffard de Saint-Martin, *Opinion de F. J. Riffard-St-Martin, député du département de l'Ardèche, dans l'affaire du ci-devant roi* (n.p., n.d.).

26. *Archives parlementaires,* vol. 26, 721. On Tuaut's politics, see Tackett, *Becoming a Revolutionary,* 203n.

27. *Archives parlementaires,* vol 34, 425.

28. *Archives parlementaires,* vol. 37, 125. Cf. *L'ancien Moniteur,* vol.11, no. 8 (January 7, 1792), 63.

29. *Archives parlementaires,* vol. 40, 695.

30. *Archives parlementaires,* vol. 46, 356. On Demée's *feuillantiste* politics, see Timothy Tackett, *The Coming of the Terror in the French Revolution* (Cambridge, MA: Harvard University Press, 2015), 151 and 175.

31. *Archives parlementaires,* vol. 48, 702.

32. *Archives parlementaires,* vol. 40, 662. On Tardiveau's conservatism, see C. J. Mitchell, *The French Legislative Assembly of 1791* (Leiden and New York: Brill, 1988), 318; and Mitchell, "Divisions within the Legislative Assembly of 1791," *French Historical Studies* 13 (Spring 1984): 359n.

33. *Archives parlementaires,* vol. 49, 672. On Dupont-Grandjardin's political leanings, see Mitchell, *French Legislative Assembly,* 308. On his execution, see Paul Piolin, *L'église du Mans durant la Révolution* (Le Mans, 1869), vol. 3, 3.

34. *Archives parlementaires,* vol. 42, 252–53. Cf. *Journal de l'Assemblée nationale, ou Journal logographique . . . ,* vol. 16, 427–28.

35. *Archives parlementaires,* vol. 36, 46.

36. *Archives parlementaires,* vol. 36, 61. Cf. Jeremy Bentham, *Panoptique* (Paris, 1791), 5.

37. *Archives parlementaires,* vol. 36, 63. Cf. Bentham, *Panoptique,* 14. In the English original Bentham wrote that the first purpose of his panopticon was "*Example,* or the preventing others by the terror of the example from the commission of similar offenses." He added, "This is the main end of all punishment, and consequently of the particular mode here in question." *Panopticon: or, The Inspection-House* (Dublin, 1791), 347–48.

38. *L'ancien Moniteur,* vol.13, no. 241 (August 28, 1792), 544. Cf. Armand Carrel and Albert Laponneraye, eds., *Œuvres de Maximilien Robespierre* (New York: Lenox Hill, 1970), vol. 2, 9.

39. *Archives parlementaires,* vol. 49, 266. Cf. *L'ancien Moniteur,* vol.13, no. 249 (September 5, 1792), 612. In November Garat, replacing Danton as Minister of Justice, referred to the September Massacres indulgently as "the terrible movement that the people of Paris had to initiate to break the new shackles that had been prepared with such dexterity." *L'ancien Moniteur,* vol.14, no. 318 (November 13, 1792), 458. Again, "terrible" implied "just."

40. *L'ancien Moniteur,* vol.13, no. 250 (September 6, 1792), 614.

41. *Archives parlementaires*, vol. 52, 71. Cf. *L'ancien Moniteur*, vol.14, no. 266 (September 22, 1792), 7.

42. *Archives parlementaires*, vol. 52, 82. Cf. *L'ancien Moniteur*, vol.14, no. 267 (September 23, 1792), 13.

43. *Archives parlementaires*, vol. 60, 63. Cf. *L'ancien Moniteur*, vol.15, no. 71 (March 12, 1793), 682.

44. *Archives parlementaires*, vol. 61, 279. Cf. *L'ancien Moniteur*, vol.16, no. 97 (April 7, 1793), 57.

45. *Archives parlementaires*, vol. 61, 342. Cf. *L'ancien Moniteur*, vol.16, no. 98 (April 8, 1793), 71.

46. *Archives parlementaires*, vol. 53, 607. Cf. *L'ancien Moniteur*, vol.14, no. 333 (November 28, 1792), 583.

47. *Archives parlementaires*, vol. 54, 77. Cf. *L'ancien Moniteur*, vol.14, no. 340 (December 5, 1792), 648.

48. *Archives parlementaires*, vol. 54, 159.

49. *Archives parlementaires*, vol. 54, 127. Cf. Louis François Jauffret, *Histoire impartiale du procès de Louis XVI, ci-devant Roi des Français . . .* (Paris, 1793), vol. 3, 161.

50. *Archives parlementaires*, vol. 54, 210. Cf. Jauffret, *Histoire impartielle*, vol. 3, 102.

51. *Archives parlementaires*, vol. 54, 172.

52. *Archives parlementaires*, vol. 56, 464.

53. *Archives parlementaires*, vol. 56, 560.

54. *Archives parlementaires*, vol. 56, 498.

55. *Archives parlementaires*, vol. 57, 254.

56. *Archives parlementaires*, vol. 56, 309.

57. *Archives parlementaires*, vol. 57, 314.

58. *Archives parlementaires*, vol. 57, 403.

59. *L'ancien Moniteur*, vol. 15 (January 20, 1793), 199. The version of Sergent's speech in the *Archives parlementaires* contains the sentence, "The head of a king only falls with a crash." But the clause is not followed by, "and his execution inspires salutary terror." *Archives parlementaires*, vol. 57, 364.

60. *Archives parlementaires*, vol. 57, 382.

61. *Archives parlementaires*, vol. 57, 367. Cf. *L'ancien Moniteur*, vol.15, no. 20 (January 20, 1793), 201.

62. *Archives parlementaires*, vol. 57, 394. Cf. Thomas-François-Ambroise Jouenne-Longchamp, *Opinion de Jouenne-Longchamp, député du Calvados, sur le jugement du Louis Capet* ([Paris, 1793]).

63. *Archives parlementaires*, vol. 57, 354. Cf. *L'ancien Moniteur*, vol.15, no. 20 (January 20, 1793), 191.

64. *Archives parlementaires*, vol. 57, 406.

65. *Archives parlementaires*, vol. 57, 175.

66. *Archives parlementaires*, vol. 57, 239.

67. *Archives parlementaires*, vol. 57, 403. Cf. Philippe Charles François Séguin, *Opinion de P. C. F. Seguin, député du Doubs, sur le jugement de Louis XVI* ([Paris, 1793]), 3.

68. *Archives parlementaires*, vol. 59, 319.

69. *Archives parlementaires*, vol. 58, 431.

70. *Archives parlementaires*, vol. 59, 316.

71. *Archives parlementaires*, vol. 12, 308.

72. *Archives parlementaires*, vol. 27, 122.

73. *Archives parlementaires*, vol. 34, 481.

74. *Archives parlementaires*, vol. 67, 283.

75. *Archives parlementaires*, vol. 68, 636.

76. *Archives parlementaires*, vol. 68, 709.

77. *Archives parlementaires*, vol. 68, 711.

78. *Archives parlementaires*, vol. 69, 5–6.

79. *Archives parlementaires*, vol. 69, 410.

80. *Archives parlementaires*, vol. 72, 181.

81. Dan Edelstein, *The Terror of Natural Right: Republicanism, the Cult of Nature, and the French Revolution* (Chicago: University of Chicago Press, 2009).

82. *Archives parlementaires*, vol. 22, 538. Cf. *L'ancien Moniteur*, vol. 7, no. 30 (January 30, 1791), 255.

83. "The Declaration of Pillnitz, 27 August, 1791," in *A Documentary History of the French Revolution*, ed. John Hall Stewart (New York: Macmillan, 1951), 223–24.

84. *Archives parlementaires*, vol. 36, 405.

85. *Archives parlementaires*, vol. 42, 738. Cf. *Archives parlementaires*, vol. 47, 442.

86. *Archives parlementaires*, vol. 44, 5.

87. *Archives parlementaires*, vol. 53, 26.

88. *Archives parlementaires*, vol. 55, 378.

89. *Archives parlementaires*, vol. 56, 571.

90. *Archives parlementaires*, vol. 58, 502.

91. *Archives parlementaires*, vol. 59, 528.

92. *Archives parlementaires*, vol. 60, 58.

93. *Archives parlementaires*, vol. 69, 226.

94. *Archives parlementaires*, vol. 69, 358.

95. *Archives parlementaires*, vol. 72, 358.

96. *Archives parlementaires*, vol. 60, 537.

97. *Archives parlementaires*, vol. 60, 614.

98. *Archives parlementaires*, vol. 65, 545.

99. *Archives parlementaires*, vol. 72, 364.

100. *Archives parlementaires*, vol. 69, 316.

101. *Archives parlementaires*, vol. 69, 558.

102. *Archives parlementaires*, vol. 70, 13.

103. *Archives parlementaires*, vol. 72, 471–72.

104. *Archives parlementaires*, vol. 60, 730.

105. George Armstrong Kelly, *Victims, Authority, and Terror: The Parallel Deaths of d'Orléans, Custine, Bailly, and Malesherbes* (Chapel Hill: University of North Carolina Press, 1982), 128.

106. Kelly, *Victims*, 129.

107. *Archives parlementaires*, vol. 67, 658.

108. *Archives parlementaires*, vol. 64, 667.

109. *Archives parlementaires*, vol. 53, 307.

110. *Archives parlementaires*, vol. 66, 724.

111. *Archives parlementaires*, vol. 72, 277–78.

112. *Archives parlementaires*, vol. 69, 169.

113. *Archives parlementaires*, vol. 74, 187.

114. *Archives parlementaires*, vol. 57, 172.

115. *Archives parlementaires*, vol. 65, 501.

116. *Archives parlementaires*, vol. 70, 548.

117. *Archives parlementaires*, vol. 60, 522.

118. *Archives parlementaires*, vol. 47, 163. Cf. *L'ancien Moniteur* 13, no. 213 (July 31, 1792): 280.

119. *Archives parlementaires*, vol. 47, 412.

120. *Archives parlementaires*, vol. 23, 543.

121. *Archives parlementaires*, vol. 43, 561.

122. *Archives parlementaires*, vol. 57, 400.

123. *Archives parlementaires*, vol. 57, 365.

124. *L'ancien Moniteur*, vol.15, no. 60 (March 1, 1793), 584. Cf. *Archives parlementaires*, vol. 59, 335–36.

125. *Archives parlementaires*, vol. 42, 510.

126. *Archives parlementaires*, vol. 8, 109–10. Cf. *L'ancien Moniteur*, vol. 1, no. 7 (June 10–15, 1789), 71.

127. See chapter 3.

128. For different versions of Mirabeau's words, see *Archives parlementaires*, vol. 8, 146 and 146n.

129. The revolutionaries' own feelings of fear or terror have been an important focus in two recent works by experts on the Revolution. See, in particular, Marisa Linton, *Choosing Terror: Virtue, Friendship, and Authenticity in the French Revolution* (Oxford: Oxford University Press, 2013); and Tackett, *Coming of the Terror*.

CHAPTER EIGHT

1. The Year II of the republican calendar began on September 21, 1793. This chapter will focus on sources from September 5 until the fall of Robespierre on 9 Thermidor (July 27, 1794). Therefore some sources will technically be from the Year I, but I will follow the convention of using the terms "the Terror" (when conceived of as a period) and "the Year II" synonymously.

2. Undated, received by the Convention on January 19 (30 Nivôse). Jérôme Mavidal et al., eds., *Archives parlementaires de 1787 à 1860, première série (1787–1799)* (Paris, 1867–2005), vol. 83, 462.

3. *Archives parlementaires*, vol. 86, 702.

4. Undated, received by the Convention on April 22 (3 Floréal). *Archives parlementaires*, vol. 89, 173.

5. *Archives parlementaires*, vol. 82, 99. Cf. Collot's speech of April 18 (29 Germinal), which advised the Convention against making peace with the "tyrants" precisely "at the moment . . . when punishment and terror have cut down and restrained their partisans and emissaries everywhere." *Archives parlementaires*, vol. 89, 32.

6. The report that recalled this speech and the festival was written on January 9 (20 Nivôse) by the General Council of the Commune of Belley and sent to the Convention. *Archives parlementaires*, vol. 84, 370.

7. Undated, received by the Convention on May 2 (13 Floréal). *Archives parlementaires*, vol. 89, 545.

8. *Archives parlementaires*, vol. 76, 338–39.

9. *Archives parlementaires*, vol. 76, 461. This order is reprinted in *Archives parlementaires*, vol. 77, 244.

10. *Archives parlementaires*, vol. 81, 79.

11. *Archives parlementaires*, vol. 88, 177; vol. 89, 96 and 518; and vol. 92, 365.

12. *Archives parlementaires*, vol. 76, 7. Undated, received by the Convention on October 4 (13 Vendémiaire).

13. *Archives parlementaires*, vol. 83, 230.

14. *Archives parlementaires*, vol. 89, 539.

15. *Archives parlementaires*, vol. 73, 419.

16. *Archives parlementaires*, vol. 77, 355.

17. *Archives parlementaires*, vol. 79, 456.

18. *Archives parlementaires*, vol. 83, 697.

19. *Archives parlementaires*, vol. 87, 550.

20. *Archives parlementaires*, vol. 91, 78.

21. Charles William Ferdinand, the duke of Brunswick-Wolfenbüttel, was the husband of Princess Augusta, who in turn was a sister of King George III. Evidently he was rumored to be in French hands.

22. *Archives parlementaires*, vol. 80, 563.

23. For additional statements linking terror and vengeance, see *Archives parlementaires*, vol. 80, 588; vol. 82, 647; and vol. 87, 618.

24. *Archives parlementaires*, vol. 79, 374.

25. *Archives parlementaires*, vol. 86, 728. On saltpeter drives, see Mary Ashburn Miller, *A Natural History of Revolution: Violence and Nature in the French Revolutionary Imagination, 1789–1794* (Ithaca, NY: Cornell University Press, 2011), 94–103.

26. *Archives parlementaires*, vol. 78, 350; vol. 80, 92 and 218; vol. 85, 153, 484, and 636; vol. 87, 371; vol. 88, 171 and 679; vol. 90, 101 and 628; vol. 91, 118; vol. 92, 58; and vol. 93, 64 and 84.

27. *Archives parlementaires*, vol. 80, 218.

28. Undated, read by Deputy Charles Millard to the Convention on February 8 (20 Pluviôse). *Archives parlementaires*, vol. 84, 458.

29. *Archives parlementaires*, vol. 86, 371.

30. *Archives parlementaires*, vol. 74, 524–25; vol. 76, 579–80; vol. 77, 32–33; vol. 78, 76–77; vol. 84, 568; vol. 85, 493; vol. 87, 68, 323, and 618; vol. 88, 551; vol. 89, 275, 318, and 439; vol. 90, 192; vol. 91, 126, 183–84, and 330; and vol. 93, 63 and 209.

31. *Archives parlementaires*, vol. 73, 419.

32. *Archives parlementaires*, vol. 87, 323. An abbreviated version of the address appears in *Archives parlementaires*, vol. 89, 17.

33. *Archives parlementaires*, vol. 89, 197.

34. *Archives parlementaires*, vol. 76, 405.

35. Undated address, received by the Convention on July 19 (1 Thermidor). *Archives parlementaires*, vol. 93, 307.

36. Undated address, received by the Convention on April 21 (23 Germinal). *Archives parlementaires*, vol. 88, 467.

37. *Archives parlementaires*, vol. 89, 546; and vol. 90, 431. Cf. the remarks of deputy Jacques Léonard Laplanche, who had been sent *en mission* to the Loiret and Cher departments and was under scrutiny for his commitment to the Revolution. On October 19 (28 Vendémiaire) he proclaimed, "I have made terror everywhere the order of the day," and he insisted that "it is only the toads of the swamp that croak against me." *Archives parlementaires*, vol. 77, 30. Cf. *Reimpression [sic] de l'ancien Moniteur, seule histoire authentique et inaltérée de la Révolution française depuis la réunion des Etats-Généraux* . . . (Paris, 1847–54), vol. 18, no. 30 (October 21, 1793), 167.

38. *Archives parlementaires*, vol. 73, 419.

39. *Archives parlementaires*, vol. 78, 22. Cf. *L'ancien Moniteur*, vol.18, no. 39 (October 30, 1793), 291.

40. *Archives parlementaires*, vol. 79, 157. Cf. *L'ancien Moniteur*, vol.18, no. 55 (November 15, 1793), 420–21.

41. *Archives parlementaires*, vol. 87, 427.

42. Other revolutionary groups called for terror against "monsters." See *Archives parlementaires*, vol. 87, 468; vol. 88, 273; vol. 88, 313; vol. 89, 173; and vol. 91, 265.

43. Undated, received by the Convention on January 30 (11 Pluviôse). *Archives parlementaires*, vol. 84, 74.

44. *Archives parlementaires*, vol. 85, 272.

45. *Archives parlementaires*, vol. 89, 439. For other endorsements of volcanic terror, see *Archives parlementaires*, vol. 89, 232–33, and vol. 90, 563.

46. *Archives parlementaires*, vol. 82, 185.

47. *Archives parlementaires*, vol. 86, 300.

48. *Archives parlementaires*, vol. 86, 672. For additional descriptions of the Mountain as a force capable of spreading terror in the form of thunderbolts see *Archives parlementaires*, vol. 87, 423–24, and vol. 90, 231.

49. For an excellent discussion of the revolutionary sublime, see Miller, *Natural History*, especially 117–23.

50. *Archives parlementaires*, vol. 79, 674.

51. *Archives parlementaires*, vol. 83, 668.

52. *Archives parlementaires*, vol. 88, 632.

53. Undated, received by the Convention on March 22 (2 Germinal). *Archives parlementaires*, vol. 87, 63–64.

54. *Archives parlementaires*, vol. 80, 588.

55. *Archives parlementaires*, vol. 81, 396.

56. Undated, received by the Convention on April 10 (21 Germinal). *Archives parlementaires*, vol. 88, 389.

57. In 607 cases the expression was "sainte Montagne" (the capitalization varied, and in some cases a hyphen was inserted between the two words), and in 280 cases the expression was "Montagne sainte" (with variations in capitalization). For a full list of

the references, see Ronald Schechter, "The Holy Mountain and the French Revolution," *Religion(s) and the Enlightenment*, ed. David Allen Harvey, special issue, *Historical Reflections/Réflexions historiques* 40 (Summer 2014): 78–107.

58. *Archives parlementaires*, vol. 62, 673.

59. *Archives parlementaires*, vol. 77, 363.

60. *Archives parlementaires*, vol. 86, 281n.

61. *Archives parlementaires*, vol. 89, 45.

62. *Archives parlementaires*, vol. 76, 579; vol. 77, 9; vol. 79, 387, 440–41, and 502; vol. 81, 611; vol. 83, 306; vol. 85, 242–43, 326, and 636; vol. 86, 322 and 366; vol. 87, 286 and 523; vol. 89, 27, 192, 263, 366, and 546; and vol. 92, 288, 349, and 350.

63. *Archives parlementaires*, vol. 85, 484; vol. 87, 393; vol. 89, 521; and vol. 90, 174.

64. Exod. 20:18.

65. *Archives parlementaires*, vol. 76, 436.

66. *Archives parlementaires*, vol. 79, 393.

67. *Archives parlementaires*, vol. 84, 105.

68. *Archives parlementaires*, vol. 93, 176.

69. *Archives parlementaires*, vol. 86, 409.

70. Undated, received by the Convention on May 19 (30 Floréal). *Archives parlementaires*, vol. 90, 468.

71. *Archives parlementaires*, vol. 75, 441; vol. 80, 194; and vol. 92, 414.

72. *Archives parlementaires*, vol. 76, 106.

73. *Archives parlementaires*, vol. 87, 690.

74. *Archives parlementaires*, vol. 82, 556.

75. *Archives parlementaires*, vol. 81, 116–17.

76. *Archives parlementaires*, vol. 88, 429–30.

77. For more on the role of the shades in revolutionary language and spirituality, see Ronald Schechter, "Terror, Vengeance and Martyrdom in the French Revolution: The Case of the Shades," in *Terrorism and Martyrdom: Pre-Modern to Contemporary Perspectives*, ed. Dominic Janes and Alex Houen (Oxford: Oxford University Press, 2014), 152–78.

78. *Archives parlementaires*, vol. 73, 420.

79. *Archives parlementaires*, vol. 80, 191.

80. *Archives parlementaires*, vol. 81, 9.

81. *Archives parlementaires*, vol. 82, 121; vol. 83, 210; vol. 83, 528; vol. 84, 473; and vol. 93, 207; and Jacques-Louis David, *Rapport sur la fête héroïque pour les honneurs au Panthéon à décerner aux jeunes Barra et Viala . . . du 23 messidor, an 2 de la république . . .* [Paris, 1794], 7.

82. *Archives parlementaires*, vol. 90, 140.

83. Undated, received by the Convention on June 18 (30 Prairial). *Archives parlementaires*, vol. 91, 728–29.

84. *Archives parlementaires*, vol. 91, 172 and 287.

85. *Archives parlementaires*, vol. 91, 594.

86. For other expressions of gratitude for the "terror" of the Law of 18 Floréal, see *Archives parlementaires*, vol. 91, 329; vol. 92, 166; and vol. 93, 42 and 460.

87. *Archives parlementaires*, vol. 90, 136.

88. *Archives parlementaires*, vol. 90, 139.

89. *Archives parlementaires*, vol. 91, 228.

90. *Archives parlementaires*, vol. 91, 724.

91. *Archives parlementaires*, vol. 93, 41.

92. Undated, received by the Convention on July 3 (15 Messidor). *Archives parlementaires*, vol. 92, 349.

93. It would be monotonous to describe all the instances in the *Archives parlementaires* in which people are described as "the terror" of aristocrats, tyrants, the wicked, etc. For descriptions of the Convention (or "the Mountain") as a terror, see *Archives parlementaires*, vol. 79, 290; vol. 80, 92 and 219; vol. 83, 374; vol. 84, 106; vol. 85, 499; vol. 86, 571; vol. 87, 21, 22, 27, 336–37, and 620; vol. 88, 17 and 479; vol. 89, 189–90 and 469; vol. 90, 319; vol. 91, 204, 292, 372, and 517; and vol. 92, 117. For similar descriptions of government institutions (such as the army, the National Guard, the Committee of Public Safety, and the Committee of General Security), see *Archives parlementaires*, vol. 81, 392; vol. 83, 625; vol. 86, 276; vol. 87, 512; and vol. 90, 420. For the designation of Jacobin Clubs as "terrors," see *Archives parlementaires*, vol. 87, 298 and 409; vol. 88, 555; vol. 89, 438; vol. 91, 46; and vol. 92, 51. Parisian *sections* bestowed this name upon themselves, as indicated in *Archives parlementaires*, vol. 75, 116; vol. 90, 130; and vol. 91, 512. For claims that specific individuals were terrors of the nation's enemies, see *Archives parlementaires*, vol. 74, 653; vol. 75, 376; vol. 79, 573; vol. 81, 178 and 307; vol. 82, 528; vol. 84, 31; vol. 85, 538; vol. 86, 63, 380, 586 and 671; vol. 88, 159 and 416; vol. 89, 189 and 385; vol. 90, 236; vol. 91, 664–65 and 685; and vol. 92, 22.

94. *Archives parlementaires*, vol. 73, 687. Cf. *L'ancien Moniteur*, vol. 17, no. 255 (September 12, 1793), 628.

95. *Archives parlementaires*, vol. 74, 45.

96. *Archives parlementaires*, vol. 76, 544–45.

97. *Archives parlementaires*, vol. 75, 90 (D'Aoust); vol. 76, 671, and vol. 80, 119 (Jourdan); vol. 78, 527 (Delatre); vol. 83, 563 (Michaud) and 679 (Lacombe-Saint-Michel); vol. 88, 650 (Bonnet); vol. 90, 463 (Dumerbion); and vol. 93, 372 (Jourdan/Namur).

98. *Archives parlementaires*, vol. 74, 365.

99. *Archives parlementaires*, vol. 74, 265.

100. *Archives parlementaires*, vol. 76, 499; vol. 77, 451; and vol. 84, 413.

101. *Archives parlementaires*, vol. 74, 546.

102. *Archives parlementaires*, vol. 88, 610–11.

103. *Archives parlementaires*, vol. 90, 103.

104. *Archives parlementaires*, vol. 93, 537.

105. On December 14 (24 Frimaire) Deputy Garnier de Saintes wrote to the Convention to announce the liberation of Le Mans from counterrevolutionary "brigands." He was pleased to report that "terror so greatly pursued these sanguinary dévots that within twenty-four hours they had fled as far as Laval." *Archives parlementaires*, vol. 81, 518. The honor of delivering encouraging reports such as this one most frequently belonged to Bertrand Barère, who spoke on behalf of the Committee of Public Safety. Barère explained French victories in Alsace, Ostende and Namur in terms of the enemy's feelings of terror. *Archives parlementaires*, vol. 83, 561 (Alsace); vol. 92, 391 (Ostende); and vol. 93, 371 (Namur).

106. *Archives parlementaires*, vol. 75, 41–42; vol. 85, 634; and vol. 93, 382.

107. Undated, received by the Convention on October 26 (5 Brumaire). *Archives parlementaires*, vol. 77, 559. Many other examples could be cited of revolutionaries

pronouncing or writing some form of the verb *trembler* in close proximity to the word *terreur*. See *Archives parlementaires*, vol. 76, 88; vol. 78, 647; vol. 79, 635; vol. 81, 597; vol. 86, 284; vol. 88, 109; and vol. 91, 136.

108. Undated, received by the Convention on April 7 (18 Germinal). *Archives parlementaires*, vol. 88, 250. For other examples, see *Archives parlementaires*, vol. 78, 673; and vol. 90, 196.

109. *Archives parlementaires*, vol. 88, 107. As Lynn Hunt has shown, revolutionaries highly valued transparency as a guarantor of republican virtue. Here we see the desire for transparency extended to enemies of the Republic, whose hostility could be "recognized by the pallor of their brows." *Politics, Culture, and Class in the French Revolution* (Berkeley and Los Angeles: University of California Press, 1984), 44. For the Rousseauian sources of the revolutionary desire for transparency, see Jean Starobinski, *Jean-Jacques Rousseau: La transparence et l'obstacle, suivi de sept essais sur Rousseau* (Paris: Gallimard, 1970). Other sources in the *Archives parlementaires* point to a tendency to focus on pallor as a sign of terror. *Archives parlementaires*, vol. 86, 691; vol. 87, 295–96; and vol. 89, 294.

110. Excerpt from the minutes of the Popular Society of Parthenay, December 22 (2 Nivôse). *Archives parlementaires*, vol. 87, 239.

111. *Archives parlementaires*, vol. 86, 271.

112. *Archives parlementaires*, vol. 89, 302. Similarly, in a letter reporting on a local festival of the Supreme Being, the Popular Society of Neuville (Pas-de-Calais) recalled, "You said that victories are the order of the day in our armies, and terror in [those of the] enemy," adding, "[These] motives are very consoling for the French nation." Undated, received by the Convention on July 26 (8 Thermidor). *Archives parlementaires*, vol. 93, 526.

113. *Archives parlementaires*, vol. 76, 437.

114. Undated, received by the Convention on November 4 (14 Brumaire). *Archives parlementaires*, vol. 78, 244.

115. *Archives parlementaires*, vol. 80, 121.

116. *Archives parlementaires*, vol. 81, 457. There were other instances of revolutionaries referring to the enemy's terror and revolutionaries' courage in the same sentence. See *Archives parlementaires*, vol. 83, 668; and vol. 92, 11.

117. Undated, received by the Convention on November 21 (1 Frimaire). *Archives parlementaires*, vol. 79, 565.

118. *Archives parlementaires*, vol. 83, 423.

119. *Archives parlementaires*, vol. 86, 145.

120. *Archives parlementaires*, vol. 85, 181; vol. 88, 635; and vol. 93, 127 and 470.

121. *Archives parlementaires*, vol. 86, 696.

122. *Archives parlementaires*, vol. 88, 552.

123. *Archives parlementaires*, vol. 79, 532. Similarly, on April 15 (25 Germinal) the military prosecutor and officers of security police for the Army of the West wrote to the Convention in support of military tribunals "composed of honest patriots who . . . are the terror of the perverse and the shield of innocence." *Archives parlementaires*, vol. 90, 368.

124. *Archives parlementaires*, vol. 93, 500. Cf. the petition on behalf of Jean-François Rosoy, a concierge of the Compiègne prison who had been arrested when two prisoners

escaped: "The laws . . . are the safeguard of the innocent, and the terror of the guilty."
However, it denied that Rosoy was guilty of violating any law. Undated, read aloud at the
Convention on May 8. *Archives parlementaires*, vol. 90, 153. Cf. also the letter of June 27
(9 Messidor) from the administrators of the district of Tarbes (Hautes-Pyrénées) in praise
of the decree on revolutionary government, "which is the terror of Tyranny and the safeguard of liberty." *Archives parlementaires*, vol. 93, 278.

125. Undated, received by the Convention on February 26 (8 Ventôse). *Archives parlementaires*, vol. 85, 493. The perceived need for "protection" is also apparent in a letter
that the officers, sub-officers, and gendarmes of the Thirty-fourth Division of the Army of
the North wrote on February 15 (27 Pluviôse) to notify the Convention of the collection
they had taken for the repair of French vessels, "so that the Republic one and indivisible
may inform all the tyrants of the world, by land and by sea, that it can at any time carry
terror, benevolence and protection." *Archives parlementaires*, vol. 86, 622. It is similarly
evident in an address of April 7 (18 Germinal) from the Popular Society of Beaurepaire to
the Convention denouncing the Dantonists and praising "justice, that *tutelary divinity
of empires*, protectress of good citizens and the terror of the wicked." *Archives parlementaires*, vol. 88, 630. Emphasis in the original.

126. *Archives parlementaires*, vol. 85, 551.

127. Undated, received by the Convention on July 21 (3 Thermidor). *Archives parlementaires*, vol. 93, 391.

128. *Archives parlementaires*, vol. 91, 482.

129. *Archives parlementaires*, vol. 79, 481.

130. *Archives parlementaires*, vol. 85, 520.

131. *Archives parlementaires*, vol. 89, 278.

132. William Reddy, *The Navigation of Feeling: A Framework for the History of
Emotions* (Cambridge: Cambridge University Press, 2001), esp. 96–107.

CONCLUSION

1. For an overview of the historiography of the Terror (to 1998), see Hugh Gough, *The
Terror in the French Revolution* (New York: St. Martin's Press, 1998), 1–9. See also Antoine de Baecque, "Apprivoiser une histoire déchaînée: dix ans de travaux historiques sur
la Terreur (1992–2002)," *Annales: Histoire, Sciences Sociales* 57 (July 2002): 851–65. For a
review of more recent literature, see Jack Censer, "Historians Revisit the Terror—Again,"
Journal of Social History 48 (Winter: 2014): 383–403.

2. Abbé Augustin Barruel, *Mémoires pour servir à l'histoire du Jacobinisme* (London,
1797–98), 4 vols.; and Joseph Marie, comte de Maistre, *Considérations sur la France*
(London [i.e., Basel], 1797). On Barruel, see Amos Hofman, "Opinion, Illusion and the
Illusion of Opinion: Barruel's Theory of Conspiracy," *Eighteenth-Century Studies* 27 (Au-
tumn 1993): 27–60; and Darrin M. McMahon, *Enemies of the Enlightenment: The French
Counter-Enlightenment and the Making of Modernity* (New York: Oxford University
Press, 2001), 112–14 and passim. On Maistre, see the provocative essay by Isaiah Berlin,
"Joseph de Maistre and the Origins of Fascism," in *The Crooked Timber of Humanity:
Chapters in the History of Ideas*, ed. Henry Hardy (New York: Vintage, 1992), 91–174.

3. Hippolyte Taine, *Les origines de la France contemporaine* (Paris, 1876–85), 3 vols.; and Augustin Cochin, *Les sociétés de pensée et la démocratie: Études d'histoire révolutionnaire* (Paris: Plon, 1921).

4. François Furet, *Interpreting the French Revolution*, trans. Elborg Forster (Cambridge, New York, and Paris: Cambridge University Press and Éditions de la Maison des sciences de l'homme, 1981).

5. Keith Michael Baker, *Inventing the French Revolution* (Cambridge: Cambridge University Press, 1990), 305.

6. Simon Schama, *Citizens: A Chronicle of the French Revolution* (New York: Knopf, 1989).

7. Patrice Gueniffey, *La politique de la Terreur: Essai sur la violence révolutionnaire, 1789–1794* (Paris: Fayard, 2000).

8. Dan Edelstein, *The Terror of Natural Right* (Chicago: University of Chicago Press, 2009).

9. Jonathan Israel, *Revolutionary Ideas: An Intellectual History of the French Revolution from the Rights of Man to Robespierre* (Oxford and Princeton, NJ: Princeton University Press, 2014), esp. 503–44. Israel's emphasis on Rousseau echoes the analysis of Jacob Talmon, *The Origins of Totalitarian Democracy* (London: Secker & Warburg, 1952).

10. Alphonse Aulard, *Histoire politique de la Révolution française: Origines et développement de la démocratie et de la république (1789–1804)* (Paris: Libraire Armand Colin, 1901), 355, 357, and 359.

11. Augustin Cochin, *La crise de l'histoire révolutionnaire: Taine et M. Aulard* (Paris: Librairie Ancienne Honoré Champion, 1909), 2nd ed., 33–42.

12. Albert Mathiez, *La Révolution française* (Paris: Librairie Armand Colin, 1922–24), 436–37.

13. Mathiez, *Révolution française*, 495–507. Cf. Mathiez, "Études sur la Terreur: Les citra et les ultra," *Annales historiques de la Révolution française* 18 (November–December 1926): 513–35.

14. Georges Lefebvre, *The French Revolution from 1793 to 1799*, trans. John Hall Stewart and James Friguglietti (New York: Columbia University Press, 1964), 91.

15. Lefebvre, *The French Revolution from 1793 to 1799*, 119 and 120. Cf. Donald Greer, *The Incidence of the Terror during the French Revolution: A Statistical Interpretation* (Cambridge, MA: Harvard University Press, 1935). Greer also saw the Terror as a response to counterrevolution: "It is the right and duty of governments to put down revolts and to punish treason and espionage; and unless we are to become hopelessly entangled in the hypothetics of history, we must agree that repression was a necessity in 1793 and 1794." At the same time, Greer did not believe "that the terrorists were moved solely by the logic of political circumstances" and saw "mob pressure" as "often decisive." *Incidence of the Terror*, 124–25.

16. Albert Soboul, *Précis d'histoire de la Révolution française* (Paris, Éditions Sociales, 1962), 283; and *La Iᵉ République* (Paris: Calman-Lévy, 1968), 80–81.

17. Michel Vovelle, "L'historiographie de la Révolution française à la veille du bicentenaire," *Annales historiques de la Révolution française* 272 (April–June 1988): 117.

18. Jean-Clément Martin, *Violence et révolution: Essai sur la naissance d'un mythe national* (Paris: Éditions du Seuil, 2006). The circumstantial view of the Terror extends beyond the Sorbonne. See, for example, David Andress, *The Terror: The Merciless War for Freedom in Revolutionary France* (New York: Farrar, Straus & Giroux, 2006); and Peter McPhee, *The French Revolution, 1789–1799* (Oxford and New York: Oxford University Press, 2002), 131–52.

19. As far as I can tell, Jan Plamper coined this term. "Emotional Turn? Feelings in Russian History and Culture. Introduction," *Slavic Review* 69 (Summer 2009): 229. The "affective turn" is an only slightly older formulation. Patricia Ticineto Clough and Jean O'Malley Halley, eds., *The Affective Turn: Theorizing the Social* (Durham, NC: Duke University Press, 2007).

20. Sophia Rosenfeld, "Thinking about Feeling, 1789–1799," *French Historical Studies* 32 (Fall 2009): 697–706. Rosenfeld notes that Burke, Michelet, and Lefebvre all took emotion into account in their diverse interpretations, but the recent rediscovery of emotions in the Revolution began with Timothy Tackett, *Becoming a Revolutionary: The Deputies of the French National Assembly and the Emergence of a Revolutionary Culture (1789–1790)* (Princeton, NJ: Princeton University Press, 1996). Rosenfeld, "Thinking about Feeling," 698–99. Rosenfeld largely welcomes this development. By contrast, Rebecca Spang objects to historical accounts that psychologize revolutionary actors, because this in her view typically leads to pathologizing. Spang, "Paradigms and Paranoia: How Modern Is the French Revolution?" *American Historical Review* 108 (February 2003): 127–28.

21. Sophie Wahnich, "De l'économie émotive de la Terreur," *Annales E.S.C.* 57 (2002): 889–913. Cf. Jacques Guilhaumou, *La mort de Marat, 1793* (Brussels: Éditions Complexe, 1989).

22. Arno Mayer, *The Furies: Violence and Terror in the French and Russian Revolutions* (Princeton, NJ: Princeton University Press, 2000), ix. Mayer returns regularly to the theme of revolutionary violence as the product of fear. For the French case in particular see, for example, *The Furies*, 36, 104, 101, 119, 177, and 184.

23. Patrice Higonnet, "Terror, Trauma, and the 'Young Marx' Explanation of Jacobin Politics," *Past and Present* 191 (May 2006): 162.

24. Marisa Linton, *Choosing Terror: Virtue, Friendship, and Authenticity in the French Revolution* (Oxford and New York: Oxford University Press, 2013), 229.

25. Timothy Tackett, *The Coming of the Terror in the French Revolution* (Cambridge, MA: Harvard University Press, 2015), 7.

26. David Andress, "Living the Revolutionary Melodrama: Robespierre's Sensibility and the Construction of Political Commitment in the French Revolution," *Representations* 114 (Spring 2011): 122.

27. Ronald Schechter, "The Terror of Their Enemies: Reflections on a Trope in Eighteenth-Century Historiography," *Historical Reflections/Réflexions historiques* 36 (Spring 2010): 56–62; and "Conceptions of Terror in Eighteenth-Century Europe," in *Facing Fear: The History of an Emotion in Global Perspective*, ed. Michael Laffan and Max Weiss (Princeton, NJ: Princeton University Press, 2012), 40–43.

28. Schechter, "Conceptions of Terror," 45–48.

29. Schechter, "Conceptions of Terror," 49.

30. Immanuel Kant, "Über das Gefühl des Schönen und Erhabenen" [1764], in *Vorkritische Schriften bis 1768*, ed. Wilhelm Weischedel (Wiesbaden: Insel-Verlag, 1960), 827–29 and 868–71.

31. Peter McPhee, *The French Revolution, 1789–1799* (Oxford and New York: Oxford University Press, 2002), 131–52.

32. Peter R. Campbell, Thomas E. Kaiser, and Marisa Linton, eds., *Conspiracy in the French Revolution* (Manchester: Manchester University Press, 2007).

33. Spang, "Paradigms and Paranoia," 128. Spang's remarks refer to the argument of Timothy Tackett, "Conspiracy Obsession in a Time of Revolution: French Elites and the Origins of the Terror, 1789–1792," *American Historical Review* 105 (June 2000): 691–713.

34. Lindsay A. H. Parker, "Veiled Emotions: Rosalie Jullien and the Politics of Feeling in the French Revolution," *Journal of Historical Biography* 13 (Spring 2013): 208–30.

35. On the concept of "emotives," see William Reddy, *The Navigation of Feeling: A Framework for the History of Emotions* (Cambridge: Cambridge University Press, 2001), 96–107. On my modification of this concept, see the introduction.

36. For a thought-provoking discussion of emotional energy in the French Revolution, see Lynn Hunt, *Writing History in the Global Era* (New York: Norton, 2014), 140–43. Hunt attributes the "explosion of new energies" in the Revolution to expanding and competing claims on behalf of the self and society, respectively. This is plausible, though not in contradiction with my account of emotional energy during the Terror.

37. For an explanation of why the sansculottes did not rally to Robespierre on 9–10 Thermidor, see Colin Jones, "The Overthrow of Maximilien Robespierre and the 'Indifference' of the People," *American Historical Review* 119 (June 2014): 689–713.

38. Clifford Geertz, "Thick Description: Toward an Interpretive Theory of Culture," in *The Interpretation of Cultures: Selected Essays* (New York: Basic Books, 1973), 3–30.

39. Jérôme Mavidal et al., eds., *Archives parlementaires de 1787 à 1860, première série (1787–1799)*, (Paris, 1867–2005), vol. 93, 633.

40. *Archives parlementaires*, vol. 84, 333.

41. By coming to signify a period, "terror" fulfilled one of Reinhart Koselleck's prerequisites for a "fundamental concept" (*Grundbegriff*): temporalization (*Verzeitlichung*). Reinhart Koselleck, "Einleitung," in *Geschichtliche Grundbegriffe: Historisches Lexikon zur politisch-sozialen Sprache in Deutschland*, ed. Otto Brunner, Werner Konze, and Reinhart Koselleck (Stuttgart: Ernst Klett Verlag, 1972), vol. 1, xvi.

42. *Archives parlementaires*, vol. 94, 30.

43. *Archives parlementaires*, vol. 94, 86.

44. *Archives parlementaires*, vol. 94, 127.

45. *Archives parlementaires*, vol. 94, 381.

46. *Archives parlementaires*, vol. 94, 370.

47. *Archives parlementaires*, vol. 94, 370.

48. *Archives parlementaires*, vol. 95, 297. Emphasis in the original.

49. *Archives parlementaires*, vol. 95, 490.

50. In one speech on August 28 (11 Fructidor), Tallien denounced Robespierre's "system of terror" four times. *Archives parlementaires*, vol. 96, 57–58. He repeated the expression in a speech of August 30 (13 Fructidor) and again when addressing the Convention on September 8 (22 Fructidor). *Archives parlementaires*, vol. 96, 104 and 368.

51. *Archives parlementaires*, vol. 96, 58.

52. *Archives parlementaires*, vol. 99, 78.

53. *Archives parlementaires*, vol. 99, 105.

54. *Archives parlementaires*, vol. 99, 372.

55. *Archives parlementaires*, vol. 100, 459.

56. *Archives parlementaires*, vol. 100, 197.

57. Carl L. Becker, with a foreword by Johnson Kent Wright, *The Heavenly City of the Eighteenth-Century Philosophers* (New Haven, CT: Yale University Press, 2003), 1–31.

58. For examples of "transvaluation," or *Umwerthung* (then spelled with an "h"), see "Zur Genealogie der Moral," in *Nietzsche's Werke*, ed. Ernst Holzer and Otto Crusius (Leipzig, 1899), vol. 7, 313 and 315. See also Nietzsche's "Jenseits von Gut und Böse," in *Werke*, vol. 7, 71 and 138.

59. As Foucault put it, Nietzsche's genealogy "retrieves an indispensable restraint: it must record the singularity of events outside of any monotonous finality." Michel Foucault, "Nietzsche, Genealogy, History," in Paul Rabinow, *The Foucault Reader* (New York: Pantheon, 1984), 76.

60. Maurice Halbwachs, *On Collective Memory*, ed., trans., and with an introduction by Lewis A. Coser (Chicago: University of Chicago Press, 1992), 60.

BIBLIOGRAPHY

PRIMARY SOURCES

Journals

Almanach des muses
Almanach musical
L'année littéraire
Bibliographie parisienne
Bibliothèque impartiale
L'esprit des journaux, françois et étrangers
Gazette des cours de l'Europe
Gazette littéraire de l'Europe
Gazette salutaire
Histoire des ouvrages des savans
Histoire de la république des lettres et arts en France
Journal de l'Assemblée nationale, ou Journal logographique
Journal de médecine, chirurgie, pharmacie, &c.
Journal des beaux-arts et des sciences
Journal des sçavants
Journal encyclopédique
Journal politique
Mémoires pour l'histoire des sciences & des beaux arts
Mercure de France
Mercure historique et politique
Nouveaux mémoires de l'Académie Royale des Sciences et Belles-Lettres
Le nouveau Mercure
Pot-pourri

Books

Accarias de Sérionne, Jacques. *L'ordre moral, ou Le développement des principales loix de la nature.* . . . 2 vols. Augsburg, 1780.

Aguesseau, Henri-François d'. *Œuvres de M. le Chancelier d'Aguesseau.* 13 vols. Paris, 1787.

Ailhaud, Jean-Gaspard d'. *Traité de la vraie cause des maladies, et manière la plus sûre de les guérir par le moyen d'un seul remède.* Carpentras, 1776.

Alègre, Angélique d'. *Sermons nouveaux.* . . . Avignon, 1778.

Alembert, Jean Le Rond d'. *Histoire des membres de l'Académie Françoise, morts depuis 1700 jusqu'en 1771.* . . . 6 vols. Paris, 1787.

―――. *Mélanges de littérature, d'histoire, et de philosophie. Nouvelle édition, revue, corrigée & augmentée très-considérablement par l'Auteur.* 5 vols. Amsterdam, 1772.

Anecdotes échappées à l'Observateur anglois et aux Mémoires secrets, en forme de correspondance; pour servir de suite à ces deux ouvrages. 2 vols. London [i.e., Paris?], 1788.

Archives parlementaires de 1787 à 1860, première série (1787–1799). Edited by M. J. Mavidal et al. 101 vols. Paris, 1867–2005.

Arcq, Philippe-Auguste de Sainte-Foy, chevalier d'. *Histoire du commerce et de la navigation des peuples anciens et modernes.* Amsterdam, 1758.

―――. *Mes loisirs.* Paris, [1756].

―――. *La noblesse militaire, opposée à La noblesse commerçante, ou Le patriote françois.* Amsterdam, 1756.

Argens, Jean-Baptiste de Boyer, marquis d'. *Pensées diverses et critiques, sur les principaux auteurs François.* Berlin, 1745.

Aristotle. *Aristotle's Theory of Poetry and Fine Art with a Critical Text and Translation of the Poetics.* Translated and edited by S[amuel] H[enry] Butcher. London: MacMillan, 1923.

Arleville, Bridel. *Le petit rhétoricien françois.* . . . London, 1791.

Arnaud, François-Thomas-Marie de Baculard d'. *Le comte de Comminge, ou Les amans malheureux, drame.* Paris, 1768.

―――. *Fayel: Tragédie.* Yverdon, 1770.

Arnauld, Antoine. *De la fréquente communion.* Paris, 1643.

Arrest du Parlement . . . du trois mars mil sept cent soixante-quatre. . . . Paris, 1764.

Arrêt de la Cour de Parlement, qui ordonne qu'un imprimé . . . intitulé: Mémoire justificatif, pour trois hommes condamnés à la roue . . . seront [sic] lacérés [sic] & brûlés [sic]. . . . Paris, 1786.

L'Attaignant, Gabriel Charles de, Abbé. *Poesies.* London [i.e., Paris?], 1756–57.

Augeard, Jacques-Mathieu. *Mémoires secrets de J. M. Augeard, secrétaire des commandements de la reine Marie-Antoinette (1760 à 1800).* . . . Paris, 1866.

Augustine. *The Confessions of Saint Augustine.* Edited by John Gibb and William Montgomery. Cambridge: Cambridge University Press, 1908.

―――. *S. Aurelius Augustinus episcopus Hipponensis: De catechizandis rudibus, De fide rerum quæ non videntur, De utilitate credendi.* . . . Edited by C. Marriott. Oxford: J. Parker, 1869.

―――. *Sermones.* In *Opera omnia: Patrologiae cursus completus . . . , Series Latina.* Vol. 38. Edited by J.-P. Migne. Paris: Migne, 1861.

Bachaumont, Louis Petit de. *Mémoires secrets pour servir à l'histoire de la république des lettres en France. . . .* 36 vols. London [i.e., Amsterdam?], 1781–89.

Baillet, Adrien. *Jugements des savants sur les principaux ouvrages des auteurs.* 8 vols. Paris, 1722–30.

Barral, Pierre. *Manuel des souverains.* Paris, 1754.

Barruel, Abbé. *Mémoires pour servir à l'histoire du Jacobinisme.* 4 vols. London, 1797–98.

Bartholin, Thomas. *Thomae Bartholini Historiarum anatomicarum rariorum centuria III & IV. . . .* The Hague, 1657.

Batteux, Charles. *Cours de belles lettres distribué par exercices.* 4 vols. Paris, 1750.

Beccaria, Cesare, marchese di. *Dei delitti e delle pene.* Haarlem and Paris, 1766.

———. *Traité des délits et des peines, traduit de l'italien, d'après la troisieme édition revue, corrigée & augmentée par l'auteur. . . .* Philadelphia [i.e., Paris], 1766.

Bellet, Isaac. *Lettres sur le pouvoir de l'imagination des femmes enceintes.* Paris, 1745.

Belloy, Pierre-Laurent Buirette de. *Gabrielle de Vergy: Tragédie.* Paris, 1770.

———. *Gaston et Baïard: Tragédie.* Paris, 1770.

Belloni, Girolamo. *Dissertation sur le commerce.* The Hague, 1755.

Bentham, Jeremy. *Panopticon, or The Inspection-House.* Dublin, 1791.

———. *Panoptique.* Paris, 1791.

Bérault-Bercastel, Antoine-Henri de. *Histoire de l'Église.* 21 vols. Paris, 1778–90.

La Bibliotheque des prédicateurs. . . . 4 vols. Lyon, 1731.

Bodin, Jean. *Six livres de la république.* Paris, 1576.

Boerhaave, Herman. *Institutions de médecine de Mr. Herman Boerhaave, seconde édition, avec un commentaire par M. de la Mettrie, Docteur en Médecine.* 6 vols. Paris, 1742–47.

Boileau-Despréaux, Nicolas. *Œuvres de M. Boileau-Despréaux.* 5 vols. Paris, 1747.

———. *Œuvres diverses du sieur D***.* Paris, 1674.

Boissier de la Croix de Sauvages, François. *Nosologie methodique. . . .* 10 vols. Lyon, 1772.

Bordenave, Toussaint. *Essai sur la physiologie.* Paris, 1764.

Bornier, Philippe. *Conferences des nouvelles ordonnances de Louis XIV. . . .* 2 vols. Paris, 1694.

Boulainvilliers, Henri, comte de. *Etat de la France. . . .* 8 vols. London, 1727–28.

Bossuet, Jacques-Bénigne. *Elévations à Dieu sur tous les mystères de la religion chrétienne.* 1727. Reprint, Paris: Vrin, 1962.

———. *Politique tirée des propres paroles de l'Ecriture-Sainte. . . .* Brussels, 1710.

———. *Recueïl des oraisons funèbres.* Paris, 1699.

Bougeant, Guillaume Hyacinthe. *Exposition de la doctrine chrétienne par demandes et par réponses.* Paris, 1741.

Bouhours, Dominique. *The Art of Criticism, or the Method of Making a Right Judgment upon Subjects of Wit and Learning.* London, 1705.

———. *Pensées ingénieuses des anciens et des modernes.* Paris, 1698.

Bourdaloue, Louis. *Sermons. . . .* 2 vols. Lyon, 1770.

Bricaire de La Dixmerie, Nicolas. *Les deux âges du goût et du génie français sous Louis XIV et sous Louis XV. . . .* Amsterdam, 1770.

———. *La Sibyle gauloise.* London [i.e., Paris], 1775.

Brissot de Warville, Jacques-Pierre. *Bibliothèque philosophique du législateur, du politique, du jurisconsulte.* . . . 10 vols. Berlin and Paris, 1782.

———. *Mémoires (1754–1793).* 2 vols. Edited by Claude Perroud. Paris: Picard & fils, 1911.

Brumoy, Pierre. *Le théâtre des grecs.* 6 vols. Amsterdam, 1732.

Burke, Edmund. *A Philosophical Enquiry into the Origin of Our Ideas of the Sublime and the Beautiful.* London, 1759.

———. *Recherches philosophiques sur l'origine des idées que nous avons du beau & du sublime.* . . . 2 vols. London [i.e., Paris?], 1765.

Cambacérès, Étienne Hubert de. *Sermons.* . . . Paris, 1781.

Caracciolli, Louis-Antoine de. *Dialogue entre le siècle de Louis XIV et le siècle de Louis XV.* The Hague, 1751.

Carnandet, Jean Baptiste, ed. *Le trésor des pièces rares et curieuses de la Champagne et de la Brie: Documents pour servir à l'histoire de la Champagne.* Chaumont, 1863–66.

Castilhon, Jean-Louis. *Considérations sur les causes physiques et morales de la diversité du génie, des mœurs, et du gouvernement des nations.* . . . Bouillon, 1770.

———. *Discours qui a remporté le prix, par le jugement de l'Académie des Jeux Floraux, en l'année M.DCC.LVI.* . . . [Toulouse], 1756.

———. *Discours sur l'origine de l'inegalité parmi les hommes. Pour servir de réponse au discours que M. Rousseau, citoyen de Géneve, a publié sur le même sujet.* Amsterdam, 1756.

Celsus, Aulus Cornelius. *De medicina.* 3 vols. Cambridge, MA: Harvard University Press, 1935–38.

———. *Traduction des ouvrages d'Aurélius-Cornélius Celse, sur la médecine.* 2 vols. Paris, 1753.

Châlons, Vincent-Claude de. *Règles de la poesie Françoise.* . . . Paris, 1716.

Changeux, Pierre-Jacques. *Traité des extrêmes, ou Éléments de la science de la réalité.* 2 vols. Amsterdam, 1767.

[Chaudon, Louis Mayeul]. *Nouveau dictionnaire historique.* 6 vols. Paris, 1772.

Cheminais de Montaigu, Timoléon. *Sermons du Père Cheminais, de la Compagnie de Jésus.* 5 vols. Paris, 1764.

Chicoyneau, François. *Traité des causes, des accidens, et de la cure de la peste.* . . . Paris, 1744.

Ciceri, Paul-César de. *Sermons et panegyriques.* Avignon, 1761.

Clément, Denis-Xavier. *Sermons de M. L'Abbé Clément. Mystères.* 8 vols. Paris, 1771.

———. *Sermons pour l'Avent.* Paris, 1770.

Clément, Jean Marie Bernard. *De la tragédie, pour servir de suite aux lettres à Voltaire.* Amsterdam, 1784.

Cochois, Babet, and Jean-Baptiste de Boyer, marquis d'Argens. *Lettres philosophiques et critiques: Par Mademoiselle Co** avec les réponses de Monsieur D'Arg.***.* The Hague, 1744.

Collection universelle des mémoires particuliers relatifs à l'histoire de France. 65 vols. London [i.e., Paris?], 1785–90.

Combalusier, François de Paule. *Pneumato-pathologie.* . . . 2 vols. Paris, 1754.

Commynes, Philippe de. *Mémoires.* London [i.e., Paris], 1747.

Condorcet, Jean-Antoine-Nicolas de Caritat, marquis de. *Recueil de pièces sur l'état des protestans en France.* London [i.e., Paris?], 1781.

Considérations sur l'influence des mœurs, dans l'état militaire des nations: Par l'auteur d'Azémor. London, 1788.

Copel, Jean François. *Sermons du R. Père Élisée, Carme Déchaussé, Prédicateur du Roi.* 4 vols. Paris, 1785.

[Couchot], *Le Praticien des juges et consuls, ou Traité de commerce de terre et de mer.* Paris, 1742.

Cournand, Antoine de. *Les styles: Poème en quatre chants.* Paris, 1781.

Court de Gébelin, Antoine. *Les toulousaines, ou Lettres historiques et apologétiques en faveur de la religion reformée.* Edinburgh [i.e., Toulouse?], 1763.

Coxe, William. *Travels into Poland, Russia, Sweden, and Denmark. . . .* 2 vols. Dublin, 1784.

———. *Voyage en Pologne, Russie, Suède, Dannemarc, &c. . . .* 4 vols. Geneva, 1786.

Coyer, Gabriel-François. *Œuvres de M. l'Abbe Coyer.* 2 vols. London [i.e., Paris?], 1765.

Crébillon, Prosper Jolyot de. *Œuvres complettes. . . .* 3 vols. Paris, 1785.

———. *Œuvres de Crébillon, nouvelle édition, corrigée, revûe, & augmentée de la vie de l'auteur.* 3 vols. Paris, 1775.

Cubières-Palmézeaux, Michel de. *La manie des drames sombres, comédie en trois actes, en vers. . . .* Paris, 1777.

Cullen, William. *Élémens de médecine-pratique. . . .* 2 vols. Paris, 1785–87.

———. *First Lines of the Practice of Physic.* 4 vols. Edinburgh, 1784.

Daniel, Gabriel. *Histoire de France, depuis l'établissement de la monarchie françoise dans les Gaules.* 10 vols. Amsterdam, 1720.

David, Jacques-Louis. *Rapport sur la fête héroïque pour les honneurs au Panthéon à décerner aux jeunes Barra et Viala . . . du 23 messidor, an 2 de la république. . . .* [Paris, 1794.]

Démeunier, Jean-Nicolas. *L'esprit des usages et des coutumes des différens peuples. . . .* 3 vols. London [i.e., Paris?], 1776.

Deshoulières, Antoinette. *Œuvres choisies.* 2 vols. London [i.e., Paris], 1780.

Le dictionnaire de l'Académie françoise. 2 vols. Paris, 1694. http://artfl-project.uchicago .edu.proxy.wm.edu/content/dictionnaires-dautrefois.

Dictionnaire universel des sciences morale, économique, politique et diplomatique. . . . 30 vols. London, 1777–83.

Diderot, Denis. *Salons.* Edited by Jean Seznec and Jean Adhémar. 2nd ed. 3 vols. Oxford: Clarendon Press, 1975.

Diderot, Denis, and Jean Le Rond d'Alembert, eds. *Encyclopédie, ou Dictionnaire raisonné des sciences, des arts et des métiers.* 17 vols. Paris, 1751–72.

Diemerbroeck, IJsbrand van. *Anatome corporis humani. . . .* Geneva, 1679.

Domat, Jean. *Les loix civiles dans leur ordre naturel.* 5 vols. Paris, 1695.

———. *Les lois civiles dans leur ordre naturel.* 2 vols. The Hague, 1703.

Dreux du Radier, M. *Tablettes historiques et anecdotes des rois de France, depuis Pharamond jusqu'à Louis xiv.* 3 vols. London, 1766.

Dubos, Jean-Baptiste. *Réflexions critiques sur la poésie et la peinture.* Paris, 1740.

Du Buat, Louis-Gabriel. *Les maximes du gouvernement monarchique, pour servir de suite aux Éléments de la politique.* London [i.e., Paris?], 1778.

Duclos, Charles. *Essais sur les ponts et chaussées: La voirie et les corvées.* Amsterdam, 1759.

Dufieu, Jean Ferapie. *Dictionnaire raisonné d'anatomie et de physiologie.* 2 vols. Paris, 1766.

Dupaty, Charles-Marguerite-Jean-Baptiste Mercier. *Mémoire justificatif pour trois hommes condamnés à la roue.* Paris, 1786.

Du Rousseaud de la Combe, Guy. *Traité des matières criminelles, suivant l'ordonnance du mois d'août 1670, & les Edits, Déclarations du Roi, Arrêts & Réglemens intervenus jusqu'à présent.* Paris, 1762.

Durosoy, Barnabé Farmian. *Annales de la ville de Toulouse. . . .* 4 vols. Paris, 1771–76.

Les edicts et ordonnances des roys de France depuis l'an 1226. iusques à present. . . . Lyon, 1571.

Les efforts de la liberté & du patriotisme contre le despotisme. 4 vols. London, 1772–73.

Encyclopédie méthodique. Grammaire et littérature. . . . 3 vols. Paris, 1782–86.

Eon de Beaumont, Charles Geneviève Louis Auguste André Timothée d'. *Mémoires pour servir à l'histoire générale des finances.* London [i.e., Paris], 1758.

Espeisses, Antoine d'. *Œuvres de M. Antoine d'Espeisses, advocat et jurisconsulte de Montpellier.* 4 vols. Lyon, 1685.

Falconer, William. *A Dissertation on the Influence of the Passions upon Disorders of the Body.* London, 1788.

———. *De l'influence des passions, sur les maladies du corps humain.* Paris, 1788.

Falconet, Étienne. *Œuvres d'Étienne Falconet, statuaire. . . .* 6 vols. Lausanne, 1781.

Fénelon, François de Salignac de La Mothe. *Dialogues sur l'éloquence en général, et sur celle de la chaire en particulier. . . .* Amsterdam, 1718.

———. *Œuvres spirituelles.* 2 vols. Antwerp, 1718.

Fermin, Philippe. *Instructions importantes au peuple, sur l'œconomie animale. . . .* The Hague, 1767.

Ferrière, Claude de. *Corps et compilation de tous les commentateurs anciens et modernes sur la coutume de Paris. . . .* 3 vols. Paris, 1692.

Ferrière, Claude-Joseph de. *Dictionnaire de droit et de pratique. . . .* 2 vols. Toulouse, 1779.

Feuquière, Antoine de Pas, marquis de. *Mémoires de M. le Marquis de Feuquière. . . . Nouvelle éd.* 4 vols. London [i.e., Paris?], 1736.

Fléchier, Esprit. *Œuvres completes. . . .* 10 vols. Nîmes, 1782.

———. *Panegyriques et autres sermons.* 3 vols. Paris, 1741.

Formule de cérémonies et prières pour le sacre de Sa Majesté Louis XVI, qui se fera dans l'Église Métropolitaine de Reims, le Dimanche de la Trinité, 11 juin 1775. Paris, 1775.

Frederick II, king of Prussia. *Éloge de M. Voltaire. . . .* Berlin, [1778].

———. *Œuvres du philosophe de Sans-Souci.* N.p., 1750.

———. *Les raisons d'établir ou d'abroger les loix.* Utrecht, 1751.

Frey de Neuville, Charles. *Sermons du Père Charles Frey de Neuville. . . .* 8 vols. Paris, 1776.

Furetière, Antoine. *Dictionnaire universel.* The Hague, 1690.

Gaillard, Gabriel-Henri. *Histoire de Charlemagne*. 2 vols. Paris, 1782.

———. *Parallèle des quatre Électres de Sophocle, d'Euripide, de M. de Crébillon, & de M. de Voltaire*. The Hague, 1750.

———. *Poëtique françoise, à l'usage des dames*. . . . 2 vols. Paris, 1749.

Gaullyer, Denis. *Règles de poëtique, tirées d'Aristote, d'Horace, de Despreaux, et d'autres célèbres auteurs*. Paris, 1728.

Gazaignes, Jean Antoine. *Manuel des pélerins de Port-Royal des Champs*. N.p., 1767.

Geoffroy, Étienne-François. *Traité de la matière médicale*. . . . 7 vols. Paris, 1743.

Le grand vocabulaire françois. 30 vols. Paris, 1773.

Guibert, Jacques Antoine Hippolyte, comte de. *Éloge du Maréchal de Catinat*. Edinburgh [i.e., Paris?], 1775.

———. *Éloge du roi de Prusse: Par l'auteur de l'Essai général de tactique*. London [i.e., Paris?], 1787.

———. *Essai général de tactique, précédé d'un discours sur l'état actuel de la politique & de la science militaire en Europe*. 2 vols. London [i.e., Liège], 1773.

Guyon, Jeanne-Marie Bouvier de La Motte. *Lettres chrétiennes et spirituelles sur divers sujets*. . . . 5 vols. Cologne, 1717–18.

[Guyot, Joseph Nicolas]. *Répertoire universel et raisonné de jurisprudence civil, criminelle, canonique et bénéficiale*. . . . 64 vols. Paris, 1776–83.

Guyot de Merville, Michel. *Œuvres de théâtre*. . . . Paris, 1742.

Haller, Albrecht von. *Élémens de physiologie*. . . . Paris, 1749.

Hardion, Jacques. *Nouvelle Histoire poëtique*. . . . Paris, 1751.

Helmont, Jan Baptista van. *Opera omnia*. . . . Frankfurt, 1682.

Helvétius, Claude-Adrien. *De l'esprit*. Paris, 1758.

———. *De l'homme, de ses facultés intellectuelles, et de son éducation*. 2 vols. London [i.e., Paris?], 1773.

Hénault, Charles Jean François. *Nouvel abrégé chronologique de l'histoire de France*. 3 vols. Paris, 1768.

Herder, Johann Gottfried von. *Auch eine Philosophie der Geschichte zur Bildung der Menschheit*. [Riga], 1774.

Hildanus, Wilhelm Fabricius. *Gvilhelmi Fabricii Hildani . . . Opera quae extant Omnia*. . . . Frankfurt an der Oder, 1646.

Histoire de Robert François Damiens, contenant les particularités de son parricide et de son supplice. Amsterdam, 1757.

Histoire universelle, depuis le commencement du monde jusqu'à présent. 42 vols. Amsterdam and Leipzig, 1742–80.

Hoffmann, Friedrich. *La médecine raisonnée*. . . . 9 vols. Paris, 1742–51.

Holbach, Paul Henri Thiry, baron d'. *La contagion sacrée, ou Histoire naturelle de la superstition*. 2 vols. London [i.e., Amsterdam?], 1768.

———. *Système de la nature, ou Des loix du monde physique & du monde moral*. London [i.e., Amsterdam], 1770.

Home, Francis. *Principes de médecine*. . . . Paris, 1772.

———. *Principia medicinae*. Edinburgh, 1758.

Huet, Pierre-Daniel. *Mémoires sur le commerce des Hollandois, dans tous les états et empires du monde*. Amsterdam, 1717.

Irailh, Augustin Simon. *Histoire de la réunion de la Bretagne à la France.* 2 vols. Paris, 1764.

James, Robert. *Dictionnaire universel de médecine, de chirurgie, de chymie, de botanique, d'anatomie, de pharmacie, d'histoire naturelle. . . .* 6 vols. Paris, 1746–48.

———. *A Medicinal Dictionary: Including Physic, Surgery, Anatomy, Chymistry, and Botany, in all their Branches Relative to Medicine. . . .* 3 vols. London, 1743–45.

Jaubert, Pierre. *Éloges historiques et moraux de St. Denis, de Ste Geneviève, et de St. Louis, patrons de la France.* Paris, 1786.

———. *Eloge de la roture dedié aux roturiers.* London [i.e., Paris?], 1766.

Jauffret, Louis François. *Histoire impartiale du procès de Louis XVI, ci-devant Roi des Français. . . .* 8 vols. Paris, 1792–93.

Jouenne-Longchamp, Thomas-François-Ambroise. *Opinion de Jouenne-Longchamp, député du Calvados, sur le jugement du Louis Capet.* [Paris, 1793.]

Jousse, Daniel. *Commentaire sur l'édit du mois d'avril 1695: Concernant la juridiction ecclésiastique. . . .* Paris, 1764.

Justinian. *Institutiones.* Edited by Paul Krueger. Berlin, 1905.

Kaau-Boerhaave, Abraham. *Impetum faciens dictum Hippocrati. . . .* Leiden, 1745.

La Mettrie, Julien Offray de. *Histoire naturelle de l'ame. . . .* Oxford [i.e., Paris], 1747.

Lamy, Bernard. *La rhétorique, ou L'art de parler.* Amsterdam, 1737.

La Place, Pierre Antoine de. *Le théâtre anglois.* 8 vols. London [i.e., Paris?], 1746–49.

La Porte, Joseph de. *Anecdotes dramatiques. . . .* 3 vols. Paris, 1775.

La Roche, Daniel de. *Analyse des fonctions du système nerveux. . . .* 2 vols. Geneva, 1778.

Laureau, Pierre. *Éloge de Frédéric II, Roi de Prusse, Électeur de Brandebourg.* Paris, 1787.

———. *Histoire de France avant Clovis.* Paris, 1789.

Le Blanc, Jean-Bernard. *Lettres d'un françois.* 3 vols. The Hague, 1745.

Le Franc de Pompignan, Jean-Jacques. *Œuvres de M. le marquis de Pompignan.* 5 vols. Paris, 1770.

Leibniz, Gottfried Wilhelm, Freiherr von. *Essais de Théodicée.* Paris: Aubier, 1962.

Le Jeune, *Clovis, poeme héroi-comique, avec des remarques historiques et critiques.* 3 vols. The Hague, 1763.

Lenglet-Dufresnoy, Nicolas. *Tablettes chronologiques de l'histoire universelle, sacrée et profane, ecclésiastique et civile, depuis la Création du Monde jusqu'à l'an 1775. . . .* 2 vols. Paris, 1778.

Léonard, Frédéric. *Recueil des traitéz de paix. . . .* Paris, 1693.

Lévesque de Pouilly, Louis-Jean. *Théorie des sentimens agréables.* Geneva, 1747.

Lieutaud, Joseph. *Précis de médecine pratique. . . .* Paris, 1761.

Linguet, Simon-Nicolas-Henri. *Considérations politiques et philosophiques, sur les affaires présentes du nord et particulièrement sur celles de Pologne.* London, 1778.

Lockman, John. *A New History of England.* Dublin, 1741.

Longinus. *"Longinus" on the Sublime.* Translated and edited by D[onald] A[ndrew] Russell. Oxford: Clarendon Press, 1964.

Louis XVI, king of France. *Déclaration du roi, relative à l'ordonnance criminelle.* Versailles, 1788.

Mably, Gabriel Bonnot de. *De la législation, ou Principes des loix.* Amsterdam, 1777.

_____. *Observations sur l'histoire de France.* 4 vols. Kehl, 1788.

———. *Œuvres completes.* 13 vols. London, 1789–90.

Maistre, Joseph Marie, comte de. *Considérations sur la France.* London [i.e., Basel], 1797.

Mallet, Edme-François. *Principes pour la lecture des poëtes.* 2 vols. Paris, 1745.

Mallet, Paul Henri. *Histoire de Dannemarc.* 6 vols. Geneva, 1763.

Malpighi, Marcello. *De viscerum structura exercitatio.* . . . Bologna, 1666.

Malvin de Montazet, Antoine de. *Instruction pastorale de Monseigneur l'Archevêque de Lyon, sur les sources de l'incrédulité & les fondemens de la Religion.* Paris and Lyon, 1776.

Marat, Jean-Paul. *De l'homme, ou Des principes et des loix de l'influence de l'âme sur le corps, et du corps sur l'âme.* 3 vols. Amsterdam, 1775–76.

Marchands merciers. Au roi. N.p., [1758?].

Marmontel, Jean-François. *Éléments de littérature.* 6 vols. N.p., 1787.

———. *Poétique françoise.* 2 vols. Paris, 1763.

Massillon, Jean-Baptiste. *Conférences et discours synodaux sur les principaux devoirs des ecclésiastiques, avec un recueil de mandemens sur différens sujets.* 2 vols. Paris, 1761.

Maugré, abbé de. *Le militaire chrétien, ou Extraits des sermons de M. l'abbé de Maugré, prieur de Chablis, ci-devant curé de Givet.* Vienne and Paris, 1779.

Mauriceau, François. *Observations sur la grossesse et l'accouchement des femmes, et sur leurs maladies, & celles des enfans nouveau-nez.* Paris, 1694.

Mercier, Louis-Sébastien. *L'an deux mille quatre cent quarante: Rêve s'il en fût jamais.* London [i.e., Paris?], 1771.

———. *Tableau de Paris.* 12 vols. Paris, 1789.

[Metra, Louis-François]. *Correspondance secrète, politique & littéraire, ou Mémoires pour servir à l'histoire des cours, des sociétés & de la littérature en France.* . . . 18 vols. London [i.e., Paris?], 1787–90.

Millot, Abbé Claude François Xavier. *Élémens de l'histoire de France, depuis Clovis jusqu'à Louis XV.* 3 vols. Paris, 1773.

[Mirabeau, Honoré Gabriel de Riqueti, comte de]. *Essai sur le despotisme.* London [i.e., Paris], 1776.

———. *L'ami des hommes, ou Traité de la population.* Avignon, 1756.

———. *Errotika Biblion.* Rome [i.e., Paris?], 1783.

———. *Réponse à l'essai sur les ponts et chaussées: La voierie et les corvées.* Avignon, 1761.

Möbius, Gottfried. *Synopses epitomes institutionum medicinae.* . . . Padua, 1667.

Mongin, Edme. *Œuvres de Messire Edme Mongin, évêque et seigneur de Bazas.* . . . Paris, 1745.

Montesquieu, Charles-Louis de Secondat, baron de. *De l'esprit des loix.* . . . Geneva, 1748.

Montpensier, Mademoiselle de. *Mémoires de mademoiselle de Montpensier.* 7 vols. London [i.e., Paris], 1746.

Mulot, François-Valentin. *Essais de Sermons prêchés à l'Hôtel-Dieu de Paris.* Paris, 1781.

Muyart de Vouglans, Pierre-François. *Réfutation des principes hasardés dans le Traité des délits et peines.* Lausanne, 1767.

Nouveau dictionnaire universel et raisonné de médecine, de chirurgie, et de l'art vétéri-naire. . . . 6 vols. Paris, 1772.

Nouveaux mémoires des missions de la Compagnie de Jésus dans le Levant. 9 vols. Paris, 1745.

L'Office de la nuit et des laudes, imprimé par l'ordre de Monseigneur l'Archevêque. Paris, 1745.

Ordines coronationis Franciae: Texts and Ordines for the Coronation of Frankish and French Kings and Queens in the Middle Ages. 2 vols. Edited by Richard A. Jackson. Philadelphia: University of Pennsylvania Press, 2000.

Pacaud, Pierre. *Discours de piété sur les plus importans objets de la religion.* . . . 3 vols. Liège, 1762.

Palissot de Montenoy, Charles. *Œuvres complètes.* . . . 7 vols. Liège, 1779.

Pallu, Martin. *Sermons du père Pallu, de la Compagnie de Jésus: Avent.* Paris, 1759.

Pechlin, Johann Nicolas. *Observationum physico-medicarum libri tres.* . . . Hamburg, 1691.

Petit, Antoine. *Premier rapport, en faveur de l'inoculation.* . . . Paris, 1766.

Petitpied, Nicolas. *Obedientiæ credulæ vana religio.* . . . 2 vols. N.p., 1708.

Pezay, Alexandre Frédéric Jacques de Masson, marquis de. *Les soirées helvétiennes, alsaciennes, et fran-comtoises.* Amsterdam, 1771.

Philipon de la Madelaine, Louis. *Discours sur la nécessité et les moyens de supprimer les peines capitales.* N.p., 1770.

Piron, Alexis. *Œuvres complettes.* 7 vols. Paris, 1776.

Pitaval, Gayot de. *Causes célèbres et intéressantes, Avec les jugemens qui les ont déci-dées.* 22 vols. The Hague, 1750.

———. *Continuation des causes célèbres et intéressantes.* . . . 4 vols. Amsterdam and Liège, 1775.

Planque, François. *Bibliothèque choisie de médecine.* 27 vols. Paris, 1748–66.

Pliny the Elder. *Traduction des xxxiv, xxxv et xxxvie livres de Pline l'Ancien.* . . . Trans-lated and edited by Etienne Falconet. The Hague, 1773.

Le point d'appui entre Thérèse et Frédéric. Frankfurt, 1758.

Poulain de Nogent, Mlle. *Nouvelle histoire abrégée de l'Abbaye de Port-Royal.* . . . 4 vols. Paris, 1786.

Poulle, Nicolas-Louis. *Sermons.* . . . 2 vols. Paris, 1778.

Pressavin, Jean-Baptiste. *Nouveau traité des vapeurs, ou Traité des maladies des nerfs.* . . . Lyon, 1770.

Prévost, Claude-Joseph. *De la manière de poursuivre les crimes dans les différens tribu-naux du royaume avec les loix criminelles.* . . . 2 vols. Paris, 1739.

Procez Verbal de l'Assemblée générale dv clergé de France . . . és années 1665 & 1666. Paris, 1666.

Pufendorf, Samuel, Freiherr von. *De officio hominis & civis, juxta legem naturalem libri duo.* 2 vols. Cambridge, 1682.

———. *Le droit de la nature et des gens.* . . . 3 vols. London [i.e., Paris], 1740.

Racine, Bonaventure. *Abrégé de l'histoire ecclésiastique, contenant les événemens con-sidérables de chaque siècle.* . . . 13 vols. Cologne, 1767.

Racine, Louis. *Remarques sur les tragédies de Jean Racine.* . . . 3 vols. Amsterdam, 1752.

Racine, Jean. *Œuvres de Racine.* . . . 2 vols. Lyon, 1781.

———. *Phèdre et Hippolyte: Tragédie.* Paris, 1677.

Raulin, Joseph, the Elder. *Traité de la conservation des enfans.* . . . 2 vols. Paris, 1779.

Rayger, Carl. *Observationum Medicinalium Centuria.* . . . Frankfurt, 1691.

Raynal, [Guillaume-Thomas-François], Abbé. *Histoire du parlement d'Angleterre.* London [i.e., Paris?], 1748.

———. *Histoire philosophique et politique, des établissemens & du commerce des Européens dans les deux Indes.* 6 vols. Amsterdam, 1772.

Récit des principales circonstances de la maladie de feu Monseigneur le Dauphin. Paris, 1766.

Recueil des actes, titres et mémoires concernant les affaires du clergé de France. . . . Paris and Avignon, 1771.

Recueil des édits, déclarations, arrests, et autres pièces concernant les duels & rencontres. Paris, 1699.

Recueil des oraisons funèbres de Louis XIV. . . . The Hague and Nancy, 1716.

Recueil des pièces d'éloquence et de poësie qui ont remporté les prix donnés par l'Académie Françoise en l'année MDCCXXIX. . . . Paris, 1730.

Recveil de harangves faites av roy, avx reynes, la reyne de svede, et avtres personnes de qualité, auec plusieurs lettres, odes & sonnets, sur toutes sortes de sujets. Paris, 1668.

Remontrance du parlement de Dauphiné, concernant la lettre de cachet. Grenoble, 1788.

Remontrances du Parlement au Roi, du 4 août 1756. N.p., [1756].

Rigoley de Juvigny, Jean-Antoine. *De la décadence des lettres et des mœurs, depuis les Grecs et les Romains jusqu'à nos jours.* Paris, 1787.

———. *Discours sur le progrès des lettres en France.* . . . Paris, 1772.

Robespierre, Maximilien. *Œuvres de Maximilien Robespierre.* 3 vols. Edited by Armand Carrel and Albert Laponneraye. New York: Lenox Hill, 1970.

Robin, abbé. *Nouveau voyage dans l'Amérique septentrionale, en l'année 1781; et campagne de l'armée de M. le comte de Rochambeau.* Philadelphia [i.e., Paris?], 1782.

Rolfinck, Werner. *Commentarius in Hippocratis primum libri aphorismum.* Jena, 1662.

Rousseau, Jean-Jacques. *Œuvres choisies de J. J. Rousseau de Geneve.* . . . 7 vols. London [Paris?], [1785?].

———. *Du contral social.* . . . Amsterdam, 1762.

Roustan, Antoine Jacques. *Réponse aux difficultez d'un théiste.* . . . London, 1771.

Rozier, François. *Introduction aux observations sur la physique, sur l'histoire naturelle et sur les arts.* . . . 23 vols. Paris, 1777–93.

Sabatier de Castres, Antoine. *Les trois siècles de notre littérature.* . . . 3 vols. Amsterdam, 1773.

Sabatier de Cavaillon. *Œuvres diverses.* . . . 2 vols. Avignon, 1779.

Sacy, Claude-Louis-Michel de. *L'honneur françois, ou Histoire des vertus et des exploits de notre nation, depuis l'établissement de la monarchie jusqu'à nos jours.* 8 vols. Paris, 1772.

Saint-Pierre, Charles Irénée Castel de. *Abrégé du projet de paix perpétuelle.* . . . Rotterdam, 1729.

Saint-Simon, Louis de Rouvroy, duc de. *Mémoires de Monsieur le Duc de S. Simon.* . . .
    3 vols. London [i.e. Paris?], 1789.
*La Sainte Bible contenant l'Ancien et le Nouveau Testament, traduite en françois sur la
    Vulgate.* 23 vols. Translated by Isaac-Louis Le Maistre de Sacy. Paris, 1742.
Salmuth, Philip. *Philippi Salmuthi archiatri Anhaltini observationum medicarum cen-
    turiae tres posthumae.* . . . Brunswick, 1648.
Samoilovich, Danilo. *Mémoire sur l'inoculation de la peste.* . . . Strasbourg, 1782.
Sartoris, Jean-Pierre. *Elémens de la procédure criminelle.* 2 vols. Amsterdam, 1773.
Saussure, Horace-Bénédict de. *Voyages dans les alpes, précédés d'un essai sur l'histoire
    naturelle des environs de Genève.* 4 vols. Geneva, 1786.
Savary des Brûlons, Jacques. *Dictionnaire universel de commerce.* 4 vols. Paris, 1750.
[Scot, Alexander]. *Nouveau recueil, ou Mélange littéraire, historique, dramatique et
    poétique.* London, 1785.
Schenck von Grafenberg, Johannes. *Observationes medicae de capite humano.* Basel,
    1584.
Séguin, Philippe Charles François. *Opinion de P. C. F. Seguin, député du Doubs, sur le
    jugement de Louis XVI.* [Paris, 1793.]
*Sermons des plus célèbres prédicateurs de ce tems, pour le Caresme, & quelques autres
    tems de l'année.* 3 vols. Brussels, 1740.
Serpillon, François. *Code criminel, ou Commentaire sur l'Ordonnance de 1670.* . . . 2 vols.
    Lyon, 1767.
Servin, Antoine-Nicolas. *De la législation criminelle.* . . . Basel, 1782.
Sigaud de la Fond, Joseph Aignan. *Dictionnaire des merveilles de la nature.* 2 vols. Paris,
    1781.
Soanen, Jean. *Sermons sur différents sujets prêchés devant le Roi, par le Père Soanen,
    Prêtre de l'Oratoire.* Lyon, 1769.
Stewart, John Hall, ed. *A Documentary History of the French Revolution.* New York:
    Macmillan, 1951.
Stocke, Leonard. *Dissertatio medica inauguralis de terrore ejusque effectis in corpus
    humanum.* . . . Utrecht, 1733.
Störck, Anton von. *Observations nouvelles sur l'usage de la cigüe.* . . . Vienna, 1762.
Swieten, Gerard van. *Commentaria in Hermanni Boerhaave Aphorismos de cognoscen-
    dis et curandis morbis.* 5 vols. Paris, 1773.
Swift, Jonathan. *Voyages du capitaine Lemuel Gulliver, en divers pays éloignez.* 2 vols.
    The Hague, 1730.
Tennetar, Michel du. *Éléments de séméiotique.* . . . Bouillon, 1777.
Terrasson, Jean. *Dissertation critique sur l'Iliade d'Homère.* . . . 2 vols. Paris, 1715.
Thomson, James. *Les Saisons: Poëme traduit de l'Anglois de Thomson.* Paris, 1769.
———. *The Seasons.* London, 1730.
Torné, Pierre-Anastase. *Sermons prêchés devant le roi, pendant le Carême de 1764.* Paris,
    1765.
Torsellini, Orazio. *Abrégé de l'histoire universelle.* . . . 4 vols. Paris, 1757.
Tourreil, Jacques de. *Œuvres de Mr de Tourreil.* . . . 2 vols. Paris, 1721.
Valleriola, François. *Francisci Valleriolae doctoris medici observationvn medicinalivm
    libri sex.* . . . Lyon, 1573.

Velly, Paul François, Claude Villaret, and Jean-Jacques Garnier. *Histoire de France, depuis l'établissement de la monarchie jusqu'au regne de Louis XIV*. 15 vols. Paris, 1755–86.

Vicq-d'Azyr, Félix. *Encyclopédie méthodique: Médicine*. 13 vols. Paris, 1787–1830.

Villette, Charles-Michel. *Discours au Roi*. N.p., [1781?].

Voisenon, Claude Henri de Fusée de. *Œuvres complettes*. 5 vols. Paris, 1781.

Voltaire, François-Marie Arouet de. *La Henriade, divers autres poèmes*. [Geneva], 1775.

———. *Histoire de Charles XII, roi de Suede*. London, 1756.

———. *Histoire d'Elizabeth Canning, et de Jean Calas. . . .* London, 1762.

———. *Histoire de la guerre de mil sept cent quarante & un*. London, 1756.

———. *Œuvres complètes de Voltaire*. 52 vols. Edited by Louis Moland. Paris, 1877–85.

———. *Les œuvres complètes de Voltaire/The Complete Works of Voltaire*. 143 vols. Edited by Theodore Besterman. Geneva: Institut et Musée Voltaire, 1968–.

———. *Œuvres complettes de Voltaire*. 70 vols. Kehl, 1785–89.

———. *Siècle de Louis XIV*. Geneva, 1769.

———. *Théâtre complet de Mr. de Voltaire*. 5 vols. Geneva, 1768.

———. *Traité de la tolérance, à l'occasion de la mort de Jean Calas*. N.p., 1763.

Wandelaincourt, Antoine-Hubert. *Cours de littérature. . . .* Bouillon, 1776.

Whately, Thomas. *L'art de former les jardins modernes, ou L'art des jardins anglois*. Paris, 1771.

———. *Observations on Modern Gardening, Illustrated by Descriptions*. London, 1770.

Whytt, Robert. *Des maladies nerveuses hypocondriaques et hysteriques. . . .* 2 vols. Paris, 1777.

———. *Observations on the Nature, Causes, and Cure of those Disorders which have been Commonly Called Nervous, Hypochondriac, or Hysteric. . . .* Edinburgh, 1765.

Zimmermann, Georg. *Traité de l'expérience en général, et en particulier dans l'art de guérir. . . .* 3 vols. Paris, 1774.

———. *Von der Erfahrung in der Arzneykunst*. 2 vols. Zürich, 1764.

SECONDARY SOURCES

Andress, David. "Living the Revolutionary Melodrama: Robespierre's Sensibility and the Construction of Political Commitment in the French Revolution." *Representations* 114 (Spring 2011): 103–28.

———. *The Terror: The Merciless War for Freedom in Revolutionary France*. New York: Farrar, Straus & Giroux, 2006.

Aulard, Alphonse. *Histoire politique de la révolution française. . . .* Paris: Libraire Armand Colin, 1901.

Austin, J[ohn] L[angshaw]. *How to Do Things with Words*. Cambridge, MA: Harvard University Press, 1962.

Baecque, Antoine de. "Apprivoiser une histoire déchaînée: Dix ans de travaux historiques sur la Terreur (1992–2002)." *Annales. Histoire, Sciences Sociales* 57 (July 2002): 851–65.

———. *The Body Politic: Corporeal Metaphor in Revolutionary France, 1770–1800*. Translated by Charlotte Mandell. Stanford, CA: Stanford University Press, 1997.

Baker, Keith Michael. *Inventing the French Revolution*. Cambridge: Cambridge University Press, 1990.

Bassiri, Nima. "The Brain and the Unconscious Soul in Eighteenth-Century Nervous Physiology: Robert Whytt's *Sensorium Commune*." *Journal of the History of Ideas* 74 (July 2013): 425–48.

Becker, Carl L. *The Heavenly City of the Eighteenth-Century Philosophers*. With a foreword by Johnson Kent Wright. New Haven, CT: Yale University Press, 2003.

Bell, David A. *The Cult of the Nation in France: Inventing Nationalism, 1680–1800*. Cambridge, MA: Harvard University Press, 2001.

———. *The First Total War: Napoleon's Europe and the Birth of Warfare as We Know It*. New York: Houghton Mifflin, 2007.

Berengier, Théophile. *Notice sur Mgr. Jean-Baptiste de Surian, éveque de Vence, 1727–1754*. Marseille, 1894.

Berlin, Isaiah. "Joseph de Maistre and the Origins of Fascism." In *The Crooked Timber of Humanity: Chapters in the History of Ideas*, edited by Henry Hardy, 91–174. New York: Vintage, 1992.

Bibles imprimées du xve au xviiie siècle conservées à Paris. Edited by Martine Delaveau and Denise Hillard. Paris: Bibliothèque Nationale de France, 2002.

Bougler, Édouard. *Biographie des députés de l'Anjou depuis l'Assemblée Constituante jusqu'en 1815*. 2 vols. Paris, 1865.

Bryner, Cyril. "The Issue of Capital Punishment in the Reign of Elizabeth Petrovna." *Russian Review* 49 (October 1990): 389–416.

Burke, Peter. *The Fabrication of Louis XIV*. New Haven, CT: Yale University Press, 1992.

Burrows, Simon. "French Banned Books in International Perspective, 1770–1789." In *Experiencing the French Revolution*, edited by David Andress, 19–45. Oxford: Voltaire Foundation, 2013.

Caradonna, Jeremy. *The Enlightenment in Practice: Academic Prize Contests and Intellectual Culture in France, 1670–1794*. Ithaca, NY: Cornell University Press, 2012.

Censer, Jack. "Historians Revisit the Terror—Again." *Journal of Social History* 48 (Winter 2014): 383–403.

Chartier, Roger. *The Cultural Origins of the French Revolution*. Translated by Lydia G. Cochrane. Durham, NC: Duke University Press, 1991.

Cobb, Richard. *The People's Armies: The Armées Révolutionnaires, Instrument of the Terror in the Departments, April 1793 to Floréal Year II*. Translated by Marianne Elliott. New Haven, CT: Yale University Press, 1987.

Cochin, Augustin. *La crise de l'histoire révolutionnaire: Taine et M. Aulard*. Second edition. Paris: Librairie Ancienne Honoré Champion, 1909.

———. *Les sociétés de pensée et la démocratie: Études d'histoire révolutionnaire*. Paris: Plon, 1921.

Darnton, Robert. *The Forbidden Best-Sellers of Pre-Revolutionary France*. New York: Norton, 1995.

———. *The Great Cat Massacre and Other Episodes in French Cultural History*. New York: Vintage, 1984.

———. "Policing Writers in Paris Circa 1750." *Representations* 5 (Winter 1984): 1–31.

Dictionnaire de spiritualité: Ascétique et mystique; Doctrine et histoire. Paris: Beauchesne, 1935–95.

Diggins, John P. "Arthur O. Lovejoy and the Challenge of Intellectual History." *Journal of the History of Ideas* 67 (January 2006): 181–208.

Edelstein, Dan. "Enlightenment Rights Talk." *Journal of Modern History* 86 (September 2014): 530–65.

———. *The Terror of Natural Right: Republicanism, the Cult of Nature, and the French Revolution.* Chicago: University of Chicago Press, 2009.

Fabre, A[ntonin]. *La jeunesse de Fléchier.* 2 vols. Paris, 1882.

Foucault, Michel. *Discipline and Punish: The Birth of the Prison.* Translated by Alan Sheridan. New York: Vintage, 1995.

———. "Nietzsche, Genealogy, History." In *The Foucault Reader*, edited by Paul Rabinow, 76–100. New York: Pantheon, 1984.

Furet, François. *Interpreting the French Revolution.* Translated by Elborg Forster. Cambridge and New York: Cambridge University Press, and Paris: Éditions de la Maison des sciences de l'homme, 1981.

Geertz, Clifford. "Centers, Kings, and Charisma: Reflections on the Symbolics of Power." In *Local Knowledge: Further Essays in Interpretive Anthropology*, 121–46. New York: Basic Books, 1983.

———. "Thick Description: Toward an Interpretive Theory of Culture." In *The Interpretation of Cultures: Selected Essays*, 3–30. New York: Basic Books, 1973.

Geschichtliche Grundbegriffe: Historisches Lexikon zur politisch-sozialen Sprache in Deutschland. 8 vols. Edited by Otto Brunner, Werner Konze, and Reinhart Koselleck. Stuttgart: Ernst Klett Verlag, 1972–97.

Glendon, Mary Ann. *Rights Talk: The Impoverishment of Political Discourse.* New York: Free Press, 1991.

Gordon, Peter E. "Contextualism and Criticism in the History of Ideas." In *Rethinking Modern European Intellectual History*, edited by Darrin M. McMahon and Samuel Moyn, 32–55. Oxford and New York: Oxford University Press, 2014.

Gough, Hugh. *The Terror in the French Revolution.* New York: St. Martin's Press, 1998.

Greer, Donald. *The Incidence of the Terror during the French Revolution: A Statistical Interpretation.* Cambridge, MA: Harvard University Press, 1935.

Gueniffey, Patrice. *La Politique de la Terreur: Essai sur la violence révolutionnaire, 1789–1794.* Paris: Fayard, 2000.

Guilhaumou, Jacques. "La formation d'un mot d'ordre: 'Plaçons la terreur à l'ordre du jour' (13 juillet 1793–5 septembre 1793)." In *La rhétorique du discours, objet d'histoire (XVIIIᵉ–XXᵉ siècles)*, edited by Bertrand Conein and Jacques Guilhaumou, 149–96. Lille: Presses universitaires de Lille, 1981.

———. *La mort de Marat, 1793.* Brussels: Éditions Complexe, 1989.

———. "*La terreur à l'ordre du jour*: Un parcours en révolution (1793–1794)," *Révolution Française.net, Mots*, January 6, 2007. http://revolution-francaise.net/2007/01/06/94 -la-terreur-a-lordre-du-jour-un-parcours-en-revolution-juillet-1793-mars-1794.

Halbwachs, Maurice. *On Collective Memory.* Edited, translated, and with an introduction by Lewis A. Coser. Chicago: University of Chicago Press, 1992.

Hesbert, René-Jean. *Saint Augustin Maître de Bossuet*. Paris: Nouvelles éditions latines, 1980.

Heuvel, Gerd van den. "Terreur, terroriste, terrorisme." In *Handbuch politisch-sozialer Grundbegriffe in Frankreich, 1680–1820*, edited by Rolf Reichardt et al, vol. 3, 89–132. Munich: Oldenbourg, 1985.

Higonnet, Patrice. "Terror, Trauma, and the 'Young Marx' Explanation of Jacobin Politics." *Past and Present* 191 (May 2006): 121–64.

Hofman, Amos. "Opinion, Illusion and the Illusion of Opinion: Barruel's Theory of Conspiracy." *Eighteenth-Century Studies* 27 (Autumn 1993): 27–60.

Horkheimer, Max, and Theodor W. Adorno. *Dialektik der Aufklärung*. Frankfurt: Fischer, 1969. First published 1944.

Hunt, Lynn. *Writing History in the Global Era*. New York: Norton, 2014.

Israel, Jonathan. *Revolutionary Ideas: An Intellectual History of the French Revolution from the Rights of Man to Robespierre*. Princeton, NJ: Princeton University Press, 2014.

Jones, Colin. "The Overthrow of Maximilien Robespierre and the 'Indifference' of the People." *American Historical Review* 119 (June 2014): 689–713.

———. "Pulling Teeth in Eighteenth-Century Paris." *Past and Present* 166 (February 2000): 100–145.

Jourdan, Annie. "Les discours de la terreur à l'époque révolutionnaire (1776–1798): Étude comparative sur une notion ambiguë." *French Historical Studies* 36 (Winter 2013): 52–81.

Kelly, George Armstrong. "Conceptual Sources of the Terror." *Eighteenth-Century Studies* 14 (Autumn 1980): 18–36.

———. *Victims, Authority, and Terror: The Parallel Deaths of d'Orléans, Custine, Bailly, and Malesherbes*. Chapel Hill: University of North Carolina Press, 1982.

Kettering, Sharon. *French Society: 1589–1715*. Harlow and New York: Longman, 2001.

Kley, Dale Van. *The Religious Origins of the French Revolution: From Calvin to the Civil Constitution, 1560–1791*. New Haven, CT: Yale University Press, 1996.

Koselleck, Reinhart. "Crisis." Translated by Michaela W. Richter. *Journal of the History of Ideas* 67 (April 2006): 357–400.

Lefebvre, Georges. *The French Revolution from 1793 to 1799*. Translated by John Hall Stewart and James Friguglietti. New York: Columbia University Press, 1964.

Linton, Marisa. *Choosing Terror: Virtue, Friendship, and Authenticity in the French Revolution*. Oxford: Oxford University Press, 2013.

Lovejoy, Arthur O. *The Great Chain of Being*. Cambridge, MA: Harvard University Press, 1936.

MacDonald, Frederika. *Jean-Jacques Rousseau: A New Criticism*. 2 vols. London, 1906.

McMahon, Darrin M. "The Counter-Enlightenment and the Low-Life of Literature in Pre-Revolutionary France." *Past and Present* 159 (May 1998): 77–112.

———. *Enemies of the Enlightenment: The French Counter-Enlightenment and the Making of Modernity*. New York: Oxford University Press, 2001.

———. "The Return of the History of Ideas?" In *Rethinking Modern European Intellectual History*, edited by Darrin M. McMahon and Samuel Moyn, 13–31. New York: Oxford University Press, 2014.

McPhee, Peter. *The French Revolution, 1789–1799*. New York: Oxford University Press, 2002.

Malou, Jean-Baptiste. *La lecture de la Sainte Bible en langue vulgaire. . . .* 2 vols. Louvain, 1846.

Martin, Jean-Clément. *Nouvelle histoire de la Révolution française*. Paris: Perrin, 2012.

———. *Violence et révolution: Essai sur la naissance d'un mythe national*. Paris: Seuil, 2006.

Mathiez, Albert. "Études sur la Terreur: Les citra et les ultra." *Annales historiques de la Révolution française* 18 (November–December 1926): 513–35.

———. *La Révolution Française*. Paris: Librairie Armand Colin, 1922–24.

May, Gita. "Diderot and Burke: A Study in Aesthetic Affinity." *PMLA* 75 (December 1960): 527–39.

Mayer, Arno. *The Furies: Violence and Terror in the French and Russian Revolutions*. Princeton, NJ: Princeton University Press, 2000.

Medlin, Dorothy. "André Morellet, Translator of Liberal Thought." *Studies on Voltaire and the Eighteenth Century* 174 (1978): 189–201.

Miller, Mary Ashburn. *A Natural History of Revolution: Violence and Nature in the French Revolutionary Imagination, 1789–1794*. Ithaca, NY: Cornell University Press, 2011.

Mitchell, C. J. "Divisions within the Legislative Assembly of 1791." *French Historical Studies* 13 (Spring 1984): 356–89.

———. *The French Legislative Assembly of 1791*. Leiden and New York: Brill, 1988.

Moffat, Margaret-M. " 'Le Siège de Calais' et l'opinion publique en 1765." *Revue d'Histoire littéraire de la France* 39, no. 3 (1932): 339–54.

Munck, Thomas. "Eighteenth-Century Review Journals and the Internationalization of the European Book Market." *International History Review* 32 (September 2010): 415–35.

Nietzsche, Friedrich. *Nietzsche's Werke*. Edited by Ernst Holzer and Otto Crusius. 15 vols. Leipzig, 1899.

———. *On the Genealogy of Morals and Ecce Homo*. Translated, edited, and with commentary by Walter Kaufmann. New York: Random House, 1967.

Ochs, Sidney. *A History of Nerve Functions: From Animal Spirits to Molecular Mechanisms*. Cambridge: Cambridge University Press, 2004.

Ozouf, Mona. "War and Terror in French Revolutionary Discourse (1792–1794)." *Journal of Modern History* 56 (December 1984): 579–97.

Parker, Lindsay A. H. "Veiled Emotions: Rosalie Jullien and the Politics of Feeling in the French Revolution." *Journal of Historical Biography* 13 (Spring 2013): 208–30.

Pasta, Renato. "*Dei delitti e delle pene* et sa fortune italienne." In *Beccaria et la culture juridique des lumières*, edited by Michel Porret, 119–48. Geneva: Droz, 1997.

Piolin, Paul. *L'église du Mans durant la Révolution*. 10 vols. Le Mans, 1851–71.

Plamper, Jan. "Emotional Turn? Feelings in Russian History and Culture: Introduction." *Slavic Review* 69 (Summer 2009): 229–37.

Pocock, J. G. A. "Political Languages and Their Implications." In *Politics, Language and Time: Essays on Political Thought and History*, 3–41. Chicago: University of Chicago Press, 1971.

Reddy, William. "Historical Research on the Self and Emotions." *Emotion Review* 1 (October 2009): 302–15.

———. *The Navigation of Feeling: A Framework for the History of Emotions.* Cambridge: Cambridge University Press, 2001.

Richter, Melvin. *The History of Political and Social Concepts: A Critical Introduction.* New York: Oxford University Press, 1995.

Rodríguez, Laura. "The Spanish Riots of 1766." *Past and Present* 59 (May 1973): 117–46.

Rosenfeld, Sophia. "Thinking about Feeling, 1789–1799." *French Historical Studies* 32 (Fall 2009): 697–706.

Rosenwein, Barbara H. "Problems and Methods in the History of Emotions." *Passions in Context: Journal of the History and Philosophy of the Emotions* 1 (2010): 1–32. www .passionsincontext.de/uploads/media/01_Rosenwein.pdf.

———. "Worrying about Emotions in History." *American Historical Review* 107 (June 2002): 821–45.

Ryan, C[ressida]. "Burke's Classical Heritage: Playing Games with Longinus." In *The Science of Sensibility: Reading Burke's Philosophical Enquiry*, edited by Koen Vermeir and Michael Funk Deckard, 225–45. Dordrecht: Springer, 2012.

Sarafianos, Aris. "Pain, Labor, and the Sublime: Medical Gymnastics and Burke's Aesthetics." *Representations* 91 (Summer 2005): 58–83.

Saussure, Ferdinand de. *Course in General Linguistics.* Translated by Roy Harris. LaSalle, IL: Open Court, 1983.

Sauvy, Anne. "Lecture et diffusion de la Bible en France." In *Le siècle des Lumières et la Bible*, edited by Yvon Belaval and Dominique Bourel, 25–46. Paris: Beauchesne, 1986.

Schama, Simon. *Citizens: A Chronicle of the French Revolution.* New York: Knopf, 1989.

Schechter, Ronald. "Conceptions of Terror in Eighteenth-Century Europe." In *Facing Fear: The History of an Emotion in Global Perspective*, edited by Michael Laffan and Max Weiss, 31–53. Princeton, NJ: Princeton University Press, 2012.

———. "The Holy Mountain and the French Revolution." In *Religion(s) and the Enlightenment*, edited by David Allen Harvey. Special issue of *Historical Reflections/ Réflexions Historiques* 40 (Summer 2014): 78–107.

———. "Terror, Vengeance and Martyrdom in the French Revolution: The Case of the Shades," in *Terrorism and Martyrdom: Pre-Modern to Contemporary Perspectives*, edited by Dominic Janes and Alex Houen, 152–78. Oxford: Oxford University Press, 2014.

———. "The Terror of Their Enemies: Reflections on a Trope in Eighteenth-Century Historiography." *Historical Reflections/Réflexions historiques* 36 (Spring 2010): 53–75.

Schechter, Ronald, ed. *The French Revolution: The Essential Readings.* Oxford: Blackwell, 2001.

Shapiro, Barry M. *Revolutionary Justice in Paris, 1789–1790.* Cambridge: Cambridge University Press, 1993.

Showalter, English, Jr. "Writing off the Stage: Women Authors and Eighteenth-Century Theater." *Yale French Studies* 75 (1988): 95–111.

Skinner, Quentin. "Meaning and Understanding in the History of Ideas." *History and Theory* 8, no. 1 (1969): 3–53.

Soboul, Albert. *Précis d'histoire de la Révolution Française.* Paris: Éditions Sociales, 1962.

————. *La I^e République*. Paris: Calman-Lévy, 1968.

Spang, Rebecca. "Paradigms and Paranoia: How Modern Is the French Revolution?" *American Historical Review* 108 (February 2003): 119–47.

Starobinski, Jean. *Jean-Jacques Rousseau: La transparence et l'obstacle, suivi de sept essais sur Rousseau*. Paris: Gallimard, 1970.

Stearns, Peter N. with Carol Z. Stearns. "Emotionology: Clarifying the History of Emotions and Emotional Standards." *The American Historical Review* 90 (October 1985): 813–36.

Stuurman, Siep. "Literary Feminism in Seventeenth-Century Southern France: The Case of Antoinette de Salvan de Saliez." *Journal of Modern History* 71 (March 1999): 1–27.

Sutherland, Donald M. G. *The French Revolution and Empire: The Quest for a Civic Order*. Malden, MA: Blackwell, 2003.

Tackett, Timothy. *Becoming a Revolutionary: The Deputies of the French National Assembly and the Emergence of a Revolutionary Culture (1789–1790)*. Princeton, NJ: Princeton University Press, 1996.

————. *The Coming of the Terror in the French Revolution*. Cambridge, MA: Harvard University Press, 2015.

————. "Conspiracy Obsession in a Time of Revolution: French Elites and the Origins of the Terror, 1789–1792." *American Historical Review* 105 (June 2000): 691–713.

Taine, Hippolyte. *Les origines de la France contemporaine*. 3 vols. Paris, 1876–85.

Talmon, Jacob. *The Origins of Totalitarian Democracy*. London: Secker & Warburg, 1952.

Vovelle, Michel. "L'historiographie de la Révolution Française à la veille du bicentenaire." *Annales historiques de la Révolution française* no. 272 (April–June 1988): 113–26.

Wahnich, Sophie. "De l'économie émotive de la Terreur." *Annales E.S.C.* 57 (July–August 2002): 889–913.

————. *La liberté ou la mort: Essai sur la terreur et le terrorisme*. Paris: La Fabrique, 2003.

Watts, George B. "Thomas Jefferson, the 'Encyclopédie' and the 'Encyclopédie méthodique.'" *French Review* 38 (January 1965): 318–25.

Wickberg, Daniel. "In the Environment of Ideas: Arthur Lovejoy and the History of Ideas as a Form of Cultural History." *Modern Intellectual History* 11 (August 2014): 439–64.

Wright, Johnson Kent. *A Classical Republican in Eighteenth-Century France: The Political Thought of Mably*. Stanford, CA: Stanford University Press, 1997.

INDEX